AA

BEST

AY · WHERE TO EAT · WHERE TO STAY

VA£UE

· WHERE TO EAT · WHERE TO STAY · WHERE TO E

BRITAIN

EAT · WHERE TO STAY · WHERE TO EAT

Editor: Julia Hynard
Gazetteer compiled by: Julia Cady, Daphne Jolley, Ruth Baldwin in cooperation with the Accommodation Inspectorate of the Automobile Association
Features by Myrrhine Raikes
Art Editor: Glyn Barlow
Illustrations: KAG Design Ltd

Phototypset and printed by Blackmore Press, Shaftesbury, Dorset.
Colour supplement produced by: J.B. Shears Ltd, Basingstoke, Hampshire.

Published by the Automobile Association, Fanum House, Basingstoke, Hampshire RG21 2EA

ISBN 0 86145 637 8
AA Reference 51046

CONTENTS

PREFACE

'Never mind how many stars it's got . . . is it the kind of place *you* yourself would like to stay at or eat in? And most important of all, if you were putting your hand in your own pocket would you feel you'd had value for money?'

That's the brief we gave our team of hotel and food inspectors — and this is the book that they have written. To be honest, I think they had some doubts at first. After all, their training and experience is in how to assess establishments against the demanding criteria of the AA's appointment scheme — should it have one, two, three stars or whatever.

But let's remember that our inspectors are people like you and I who have our favourite places to stay and eat and they do know good value when they experience it.

Please write to me if you disagree with their judgement.

PETER TYER
Director, Publishing, AA

PS: If you know of any places which ought to be in this book but are not, I'd like to hear from you.

ABOUT THE BOOK

All the entries in this book have been selected by the AA's Hotel and Restaurant Inspectors as representing good value for money. Using their combined experience, knowledge and judgement, they have spent months in researching and evaluating all kinds of establishments for the guide.

By no means all the places they recommend fall into a budget category: among the entries listed you will find some quite luxurious establishments suitable for a special celebration. Whether the places they looked at fell into a luxury or a budget rating, the question they always asked themselves was: 'Do I feel that I have had value for money?'

Among the hundreds of establishments listed you will find hotels, country manors, exclusive French restaurants, pubs with outstanding bar food or a superb atmosphere, guesthouses and farmhouses for a peaceful family holiday, bistros and wine-bars for informal eating out, and many a traditional village inn with comfortable overnight accommodation.

In short, however much or little you want to spend, and whatever the occasion, you should be assured of finding somewhere to suit you among our recommendations.

All the entries are organised alphabetically under the appropriate town or village name, and are also plotted on the location atlas at the end of the book. If the establishments are already classified by the AA, we print the classification symbols before the name of the establishment. Some of the more informal restaurants, for example, pubs with bar food, wine-bars, and bistros are not classified by the AA and are not listed in any of our other publications, and these entries therefore carry no symbol.

HOW WE CLASSIFY

The star classification of hotels by the AA, in addition to providing an indication of the type of hotel, may be regarded as a universally accepted standard from the simplest to the most luxurious hotel. The majority of hotels are classified with black stars, a method which was introduced by the AA in 1912 and is still used.

★ Hotels and inns generally of small scale with good facilities and furnishings. Adequate bath and lavatory arrangements. Meals are provided for residents but their availability to non-residents may be limited.

★★ Hotels offering a higher standard of accommodation and some bedrooms containing a private bath/shower room with lavatory.

★★★ Well-appointed hotels with more spacious accommodation with the majority of bedrooms containing a private bath/shower room with lavatory. Fuller meal facilities are provided.

★★★★ Exceptionally well-appointed hotels offering a high standard of comfort and service with all bedrooms providing a private bath/shower room with lavatory.

★★★★★ Luxury hotel offering the highest international standards.

♣ This symbol is used to denote an AA Country House Hotel where a relaxed, informal atmosphere and a personal welcome prevail. However, some of the facilities may differ from those found in urban hotels of the same classification. These hotels are often secluded and, though not always rurally situated, are quiet. Hotels attracting frequent conferences or functions are not normally granted this symbol.

RED STAR HOTELS

Red stars indicate those hotels that AA Inspectors consider to be of outstanding merit within their classification. In each of them it is hoped that you will find a warm welcome and a high standard of hospitality. Red stars are awarded only after a great deal of consideration, and a change of management or ownership is likely to result in the award being carefully reviewed. In the whole of Great Britain there are only 76 Red Star hotels. They are shown in this book by the word RED after the star classification.

MERIT AWARDS

The black star awards for hotels are based on an objective assessment by the AA Inspectors, in accordance with a carefully laid down set of criteria. In many cases, however, there are particular aspects of a hotel that are very good and better than that implied by the star classification awarded. In order to highlight these more subjective assessments a system of merit awards was introduced. Three symbols are used and a hotel may qualify for any or all of them:

H Indicates that hospitality, friendliness and service are well above the average for hotels similarly classified.

B Bedrooms at these hotels will be significantly better than those to be expected within the star classification.

L Exceptionally good lounges, bars and public areas will be found here.

RESTAURANTS

Restaurants are awarded 'crossed knives and forks' to denote their physical amenities, but they must all, of course, have a high standard of cuisine, prompt and courteous service and a pleasant atmosphere. Value for money is always a consideration, but those restaurants selected to be in this guide offer really top value.

× Modest but good restaurant.

×× Restaurant offering a higher standard of comfort than above.

××× Well-appointed restaurant.

×××× Exceptionally well-appointed restaurant.

××××× Luxury restaurant.

NB Some restaurants do have accommodation available, but it must not be assumed to be of a standard suitable for hotel appointment.

ROSETTES

These subjective awards are given to both hotels and restaurants and are an indication that the food and service can be specially recommended.

❀ Food here is of a higher standard than is expected for its classification.

❀❀ Excellent food and service irrespective of classification.

❀❀❀ Outstanding food and service irrespective of classification.

GUESTHOUSES

The term 'guesthouse' can lead to some confusion, particularly when many include the word 'hotel' in their name. For our purposes we include small and private hotels in this category when they lack some of the requirements for our star classification system. This is not to say that they are inferior to hotels, just that they are different, and many offer a very high standard of accommodation. It is not unusual to be offered en suite bathrooms, for instance, or to find a colour television in your room. It is true that some guesthouses will only offer a set meal in the evening, but many provide a varied and interesting menu and a standard of service which one would expect of a good restaurant.

FARMHOUSES

Farmhouse accommodation has a special quality and is particularly noted for being inexpensive and cosy, with a high standard of good home cooking. They are often on working farms and some farmers are happy to allow visitors to look around the farm or help to feed the animals. Others will run the guest accommodation as a separate concern and visitors are discouraged from wandering beyond the house and garden.

INNS

The idea of a traditional inn conjures up visions of a cosy bar, convivial atmosphere, good beer and wholesome pub food. Obviously the character will vary from place to place and some of the inns which we list are in fact small licensed hotels. All of them must, of course, meet our basic requirements. They must be clean, comfortable, well-maintained and with facilities adequate for their bedrooms (which usually number between three and fifteen). Breakfast must be served and there should also be at least light meals available during licensing hours.

PRICE BANDING

The price band indicates the price of overnight accommodation and breakfast for a single room or person.

Price band A	£15 or less
Price band B	£16–£30
Price band C	£31–£50
Price band D	more than £50

MEAL PRICES

Table d'hôte (td) and à la carte (alc) prices are given where applicable. À la carte prices are based on an average figure for three courses without wine.

CREDIT CARDS

1 Access
2 American Express
3 Barclaycard/Visa
4 Carte Blanche
5 Diners

ABBERLEY Hereford & Worcester Map 7 SO76

❀ ★★★ ♣♣ L **Elms Hotel** ✆ Great Witley (029921) 666 Tx 337105	Twelve acres of gardens and grounds lend an air of tranquillity and seclusion to this magnificent Queen Anne house. Every aspect of a stay here reflects the luxurious atmosphere of an English country house: period furnishings, open fires, comfortable chairs and fresh flowers are features of the public rooms, while bedrooms are thoughtfully provided with extras such as sherry, fruit and books. All 27 bedrooms have CTV, telephones and private facilities. The grounds offer tennis, croquet and putting, and there is a fine herb garden which, together with the hotel's own kitchen garden, supplies the chef with fresh produce. The hotel staff, under the management of Miss Rita Mooney, are all welcoming and helpful, and service is friendly but professional, not least in the elegant Brooke Room Restaurant. Here both set-price meals and à la carte are available. The Elms also serves bar lunches. Children are accepted (there are three family bedrooms), but dogs are not.	Price band D Lunch td £11 Dinner td £18 or alc £19.50 Last dinner 9pm Credit cards 1 2 3 4 5 Parking on premises
★★ **Manor Arms** ✆ Great Witley (029921) 507	Here a village inn has been successfully refurbished and reorganised into a very popular little hotel. The ten bedrooms are small but have many extras that help to ensure a comfortable stay, and all rooms have private facilities. The restaurant, also very popular, offers a choice of three or four-course meals, and the menu is changed every few weeks to make the most of fresh foods in season.	Price band B Lunch td £9 Dinner td £12.50 Last dinner 9.30pm Credit cards 1 2 3 5 Parking on premises

ABERDEEN Grampian *Aberdeenshire* Map 15 NJ90

GH Cedars Private Hotel ✆ (0224) 583225	The enthusiam and dedication of the proprietors is always evident in the running of this faultlessly decorated and meticulously maintained private hotel. The modern bedrooms (some of which have private baths or showers) are equipped with tea/coffee-making facilities and colour television and are all thoughtfully arranged, although they vary in size. Guests can relax in a comfortable lounge (where there is also a small snooker table for their diversion), and the beautiful ceiling of the dining room is a typically attractive feature.	Price band B B&b only Credit card 2 Parking on premises
★★★ L **New Marcliffe** 51–3 Queens Rd ✆ (0224) 321371	The conversion of two granite buildings has produced a small, elegant hotel where the attractive, period-style Royal Lounge — its selection of comfortable chairs and daily papers creating a club-like atmosphere — offers a relaxing haven from the bustle of the city. The theme is carried through in the lounge-bar, and small restaurant looks down from a higher level. Bedrooms vary in size and range from the tastefully furnished upstairs to the more functional on the ground floor, but all are well-equipped.	Price band B/C Lunch alc £6.50 Dinner td fr £14 & alc Last dinner 10pm Credit cards 1 2 3 5 Parking on premises
× **Poldino's** 7 Little Belmont St ✆ (0224) 647777	Home cooking, generous portions and competitive prices help to ensure the success of this lively trattoria/pizzeria, set in a quiet back street near the	Lunch td £4.70 & alc Dinner alc £11

city centre. Most of the pasta dishes (available as either starter or main course) are home-made, as are all the pizzas. More substantial entrées such as chicken, veal and steak, are correspondingly more expensive, but the portions can be enormous — as was the case with our Inspector's veal escalopes — and vegetables and potatoes are included in their prices. Vegetarian meals are available. Service is enthusiastic, enabling customers to either hurry or linger as they wish. There is no bar, but a full drinks service is provided at the tables. The house wine is acceptable, and the espresso coffee good. All in all, Poldino's is jolly good value for those with a hearty appetite.

Last dinner 10.45pm
Credit cards [1] [2] [3] [5]
No parking on premises
Closed Xmas Day & New Year's Day
Closed Sun

ABERDOUR Fife Map 11 NT18

★★ L
Woodside Hotel
✆ (0383) 860328

A recently modernised hotel in the centre of this popular Fife village. The Woodside will appeal to both tourists and business people. Its 21 comfortable bedrooms all have private facilities, telephones and CTV and, while compact, they are attractively decorated and have solid fitted furniture. Downstairs there is a modern foyer/lounge and a lounge-bar, a popular meeting place lent character by its decor, which uses woodwork from HMS *Orontes*. The restaurant, which is split into three areas to add atmosphere and intimacy, serves interesting and well-prepared food.

Price band C
Lunch/dinner £12.50 & alc
Last dinner 9.45pm
Credit cards [1] [2] [3] [4] [5]
Parking on premises

ABERDOVEY Gwynedd Map 6 SN69

★ **Maybank**
✆ (065472) 500

Good food, comfortable accommodation and friendly, hospitable service are all to be found at Mr and Mrs Hughes' little hotel, which overlooks Aberdovey's beautiful harbour. Two of the six bedrooms have a private bathroom and all the rest have showers. One family bedroom is available, and all rooms can be equipped with TV on request. Mrs Hughes has a good reputation locally for her excellent cooking: she provides bar lunches as well as dinner, and a selection of wines is available to complement her meals.

Price band B
Bar lunch fr £1
Dinner td £10.50
Last dinner 9.30pm
Credit card [3]
No parking on premises
Closed Jan

★★ L
Penhelig Arms
✆ (065472) 215
Tx 338751

Proprietress Mrs Breeze personally supervises the running of this small, comfortable hotel which enjoys a lovely setting between the hillside and the Dovey estuary. The 11 bedrooms, though on the small side, are generally well-equipped, and all have private bath or shower and CTV. The comfortable first-floor lounge is complemented by two attractive bars, and meals of a high standard are served in the cosy restaurant. Vegetarians can be catered for. The hotel does not accept dogs, or children under 10.

Price band B
Bar lunch fr £2
Dinner td fr £7 & alc
Last dinner 9pm
Credit cards [1] [2] [3] [5]
Parking on premises
Closed Xmas

ABERFELDY Tayside *Perthshire* Map 14 NN84

GH **Caber Feidh**
56 Dunkeld St
✆ (0887) 20342

An attractive Scottish stone house of 1885 has been converted and modernised to form this pleasant and well-appointed little guesthouse. The six bedrooms (including two family rooms) are on the small side, but are attractively decorated, with homely touches such as continental quilts, tissues and pot-pourri. The lounge and dining room are attractively decorated and furnished, and there is a colour television. For dinner, residents can choose either a set-price menu or à la carte, which offers steaks, burgers and Italian dishes.

Price band A
Dinner alc £7
Last dinner 9pm
Limited parking on premises

ABERGAVENNY Gwent Map 3 SO21

★★ B
Llanwenarth Arms
Brecon Rd (W of Abergavenny on A40)
✆ (0873) 810550

This 16th-century inn on the old coaching route to South Wales stands on the bank of the River Usk between Abergavenny and Crickhowell. Now modernised and extended, it offers today's travellers comfortable accommodation and good food. The 18 well-equipped bedrooms, all with bathrooms, CTV and telephone, and most with river views, are in an annexe adjacent to the main building. The inn itself — formerly called Pantrhiwgoch — has a cheerful bar, where a wide selection of bar meals and a range of real ales are served, and a restaurant where imaginative, freshly prepared meals (including vegetarian dishes) can be eaten for moderate prices. There is a second bar in the restaurant, and a well-balanced wine list is available. The hotel does not admit dogs.

Price band C
Bar lunches £4
Lunch alc £8
Dinner alc £11
Last dinner 10pm
Credit cards [1] [2] [3] [5]
Parking on premises

ABERSOCH Gwynedd Map 6 SH32

★★ H **Neigwl**
Lon Sarn Bach
✆ (075881) 2363

This small, family-run hotel, close to beaches and shops, is a useful and pleasant stop-over point for the boating enthusiast. Six of its eight bedrooms, one of which is a family room, have a private shower or bath. Special facilities are provided for children; dogs, however, are not accepted. The proprietors, the Heponstall family, take particular care to ensure that the visitor has a comfortable stay. A complimentary aperitif is offered before dinner, at which the menu is imaginative and the food freshly prepared.

Price band B
Lunch td £7
Dinner td £11
Last dinner 10pm
Credit cards [1] [2] [3] [5]
Parking on premises

ABERYSTWYTH Dyfed Map 6 SN58

★★ B
Court Royale Hotel
Eastgate
✆ (0970) 611722

Recently refurbished to provide accommodation of a high standard, this friendly little hotel is in the heart of the town, yet not far from the beach. Telephones and CTV are provided in all 10 bedrooms and all (including three family rooms) have en suite bath or shower. The busy dining room serves good grills and other dishes, including vegetarian food, and bar meals are also available. The hotel offers off-season bargain breaks and a special Christmas programme.

Price band B
Lunch td £4.95
Dinner alc £9
Last dinner 10pm
Credit cards [1] [2] [3]
Limited parking on premises

ACHNASHEEN Highland *Ross & Cromarty* Map 14 NH15

★★ 🌳 HL **Ledgowan Lodge** ✆ (044588) 252	Proprietor Graham Millard has done much to ensure a friendly, relaxed atmosphere in this converted shooting lodge, and it is a tribute to his untiring efforts on his guests' behalf that many of them return year after year. The house, warm and welcoming, retains much of its original charm and character. Open fires burn when necessary in the two comfortable lounges and there is a well-stocked bar. Over half the 17 bedrooms have private bathrooms, and all are comfortably and practically furnished. There are four family bedrooms.	Price band B Lunch fr £5.50 Dinner td fr £13.50 Last dinner 9pm Credit cards [1] [2] [3] [4] [5] Parking on premises Closed mid Oct–Easter

ADLINGTON Lancashire Map 7 SD61

★★ **Gladmar** Railway Rd ✆ (0257) 480398	This small, family-run hotel offers travellers a convenient and peaceful place to stay. Close to both the M61 and A6 roads, it is also only a few minutes drive from the attractive park and moorland of Ribington and the Anglecarte reservoirs. Nearer at hand are two golf courses and a leisure centre. The Gladmar stands in its own grounds, and the interior is well-furnished throughout. Of the 13 well-equipped bedrooms (including one family room), 10 have private showers and 11 have CTV. The small, pleasant dining room serves good honest English fare and vegetarians can be catered for. The Gladmar does not accept coach parties, or dogs.	Price band B Lunch td fr £3.50 Dinner td fr £7.80 Last dinner 8.30pm Credit cards [1] [3] Parking on premises Closed Xmas Day & New Year's Day

ALDBOURNE Wiltshire Map 4 SU27

×× **Raffles** The Green ✆ Marlborough (0672) 40700	An attractive Wiltshire village not far from the M4 motorway is the setting for this well-appointed cottage-style restaurant. An interesting menu includes courses such as crab fritters with lobster sauce, salmon mousse, or risotto primavera, while for main course one might be offered fresh local trout, breast of duck, or fresh brill. Vegetables and desserts are both good. The restaurant has live music on Fridays.	Lunch/dinner alc £10.85 Last dinner 11pm Credit cards [1] [2] [3] [5] Limited parking Closed Sun, Mon & Sat lunch

ALKMONTON Derbyshire Map 7 SK13

FH **Dairy House** (7 miles S of Ashbourne) ✆ Great Cabley (033523) 359	This fine old red-brick farmhouse, parts of which date back to the 16th century, stands on an 82-acre dairy farm amid pleasant countryside. All six bedrooms are well-furnished and extremely comfortable, with modern bathroom and toilet facilities. Lounge and dining room are typical of the charm and character of the house, featuring exposed beams, a large inglenook fireplace and some antique furnishings and bric-à-brac. Alton Towers, the Peak National Park and several stately homes are within easy reach of the farm.	Price band A Dinner td fr £6 Last dinner 8pm Parking on premises

ALDWARK Derbyshire Map 8 SK25

FH **Lydgate** ✆ Carsington (062985) 250	Situated in a tiny hamlet, high up in the Peak District, this 300-acre traditional dairy, beef and sheep farm provides an excellent base from which to tour the many attractions of the area. The peaceful 17th-century stone farmhouse has three large and comfortable bedrooms, one of which is a family room. These are furnished with antiques and attractive bric-à-brac, as are the lovely large reception rooms. Dogs are not accepted.	Price band A Dinner, b&b £14.50–£16 Last dinner 7pm Parking on premises

ALLENDALE Northumberland Map 12 NY85

FH **Bishopfield** (1m W of village on Whitfield Rd) ✆ (043483) 248	This elegant 18th-century stone farmhouse standing in 200 acres is run by the Fairless family, who are the third generation to live here. The house and outbuildings have been tastefully converted by them to give eight bedrooms. All have en suite bathroom or shower and are furnished and equipped to a surprisingly high standard, with CTV and telephone in each one. Other facilities at Bishopfield include a games room with a full-size snooker table, a library, a drying room, and outdoor sports such as clay pigeon shooting, canoeing and salmon or trout fishing. Kathy Fairless ensures that her guests are well-fed: dinner menus feature home-made soups, fresh vegetables and specialities such as lamb bred on the farm, or home-baked ham (enjoyed by our Inspector). The dining room table seats 18, and candlelight sometimes adds to the dinner-party atmosphere. Bishopfield is licensed, and offers a good selection of wines.	Price band B Dinner, b&b £25 Last dinner 7.30pm Parking on premises

ALNMOUTH Northumberland Map 12 NU21

GH **Marine House Private Hotel** 1 Marine Rd ✆ Alnwick (0665) 830349	Especially suitable for familes, this large ivy-clad house (formerly a granary) on the seafront offers a friendly welcome and courteous service. Several of the eight cheerfully decorated bedrooms have en suite showers, and four are family rooms. A bonus for guests with children is the games room in the cellar, while the first-floor residents' lounge is inviting and comfortable, with suberb views over the links and the sea beyond. Also on the first floor is a small cocktail bar. Traditional home-cooked three-course dinners are served, and there is a good-value wine list. Packed lunches are also available. Dogs are admitted at the proprietor's discretion.	Price band A Dinner, b&b £19–£22.50 Last dinner 6.30pm Parking on premises Closed Dec–Jan

ALSTON Cumbria Map 12 NY74

★★RED 👥 **Lovelady Shield Country House Hotel** (2½m E of Alston, off A689) ✆ (0498) 81203	This secluded country house stands in two acres of attractive and sheltered gardens amid the wild scenery of the High Pennines. Inside, the welcome is warm and hospitable. Log fires burn in the comfortable drawing room, where guests can enjoy afternoon tea after a day spent exploring the surrounding fells or playing tennis or croquet in the hotel grounds. Later, one can relax over a drink in the cocktail bar before an excellent five-course dinner. Food is interesting, fresh	Price band B Dinner td £15 Last dinner 8.30pm Credit cards [2] [5] Parking on premises Closed mid Dec–

and of a very high standard, with menus changed daily and a choice of several dishes. First courses might include port and rabbit terrine with honey and mint sauce, or melon with thin slices of smoked Herdwick ham, while to follow there might be boned saddle of lamb stuffed with spinach, mushrooms and calves' liver, or chicken cooked with shallots, wine, cream and prawns. Lovelady Shield has 12 bedrooms some with lovely views and all with private facilities, CTV, electric blankets and hairdriers. The hotel accepts dogs by prior arrangement only.

mid March
Closed lunch, except Sun

ALTON Hampshire Map 4 SU73

★★ The Grange
17 London Rd
Holybourne
✆ (0420) 86565

Friendly proprietors Mr and Mrs Levene personally supervise the running of this small but well-equipped hotel. There are 15 bedrooms, six of them in an adjoining house. All have en suite facilities, CTV and telephones, and although the rooms are plainly furnished and decorated they are comfortable and many have pleasant views over the garden. There is one family room, and one ground-floor room suitable for the disabled. Public rooms have a homely atmosphere, with a log fire in the foyer/lounge in winter. There are plans to extend both this room and the bar. Our Inspector especially recommends The Grange for its high standard of English home-cooking. Top-quality fresh ingredients, including local produce, are used, and in addition to the enterprising à la carte menu, both bar meals and a fixed-price menu are available. Recreational facilities at The Grange include an outdoor swimming pool, putting and croquet.

Price band C
Lunch £7.95 or alc £11.50
Dinner £7.95 or alc £14
Last dinner 9pm
Credit cards [1] [2] [3] [4] [5]
Parking on premises
Closed Xmas & New Year

ALYTH Tayside *Perthshire* Map 15 NO24

★★ ♣
Lands of Loyal Hotel
(Off B952, N of town)
✆ (08283) 3151

Built in 1850 by Captain Ogilvy of Waterloo fame, this imposing house stands in eight acres of ground overlooking the town of Alyth, the Strathmore Valley and the Sidlaw Hills. A sweeping staircase, massive marble fireplace and lofty glass-domed ceiling lend grandeur to the oak-panelled lounge/hall, while the dining room has an elaborate ceiling of moulded plasterwork. The 10 bedrooms vary, some have traditional furnishings, including one with a four-poster bed, while others are modern in style; most have en suite facilities. For dinner, guests can choose between table d'hôte and à la carte menus, and vegetarians can be catered for. Service, both in the pleasant dining room and elsewhere, is cheerful and willing.

Price band B
Lunch td £6.50 or alc £10.50
Dinner td £10.50 or alc £13.50
Last dinner 9pm
Credit cards [1] [2] [3]
Parking on premises

Inn Losset
Losset Rd
✆ (08283) 2393

Dating from 1730 but recently modernised and converted, the Losset Inn maintains its tradition of offering warmth and hospitality to travellers. Low, beamed ceilings and stone fireplaces help to retain the character of the building, which stands in a narrow street in the centre of this small linen-manufacturing town. Bedrooms are small and modern but tasteful in their décor, and all have en suite facilities. Duvets and

Price band A
Lunch td fr £2.65
Dinner td fr £3
Last dinner 9pm
No parking on premises

CTV are standard in all rooms. Meals at the Losset Inn are simple but enjoyable, with good value for money.

AMBLESIDE Cumbria — Map 7 NY30

GH **Grey Friar Lodge**
Brathay
(1m West of Ambleside off A593)
✆ (05394) 33158

This delightful country house of Lakeland stone stands in its own gardens in a peaceful spot at the foot of Loughrigg Fell. The entire house is comfortably and attractively furnished, and proprietors Mr and Mrs Sutton are attentive and friendly. There are eight bedrooms, five of which have private facilities and all CTV. There is one family room, though children under 12 are not accepted. Food is a highlight of most guests' stay here: a hearty breakfast begins the day, while the five-course dinner menu is most imaginative and might include unusual but delicious dishes such as mushroom and coriander soup, pork with fresh pineapple and yogurt sauce, and whisky and orange pancakes. Fresh vegetables in season are cooked with flair; the choice might include red cabbage with orange or carrots with hazelnuts and honey. Guests are requested not to smoke in the dining room.

Price band B inc dinner
Last dinner 7.30pm
Parking on premises
Closed Nov–Feb

★★ HBL
Kirkstone Foot
Kirkstone Pass Rd
✆ (05394) 32232

Proprietors Simon and Jane Bateman have converted this beautifully situated 17th-century manor house into a smart and comfortable 15-bedroom hotel. Furnishings and décor are of a high standard throughout. All bedrooms have en suite facilities, CTV, radios and telephones, and three of them have king-size beds. The elegant lounge has a good selection of books, magazines, daily papers and board games. There is an open fire on chilly days, while in warmer weather afternoon tea and morning coffee are served on the verandah. The well-stocked bar offers a good selection of malt whiskies. Mrs Bateman ensures that the five-course dinner is a highlight of the day: everything is home-made from fresh produce in season, and there is a good and reasonably priced wine list. Special diets can be catered for by prior arrangement. For those who prefer to look after themselves, there are several self-contained apartments and cottages in the hotel's secluded two-acre grounds. Kirkstone Foot does not accept dogs, or children under five.

Price band B
Dinner td £13.50
Last dinner 8pm
Credit cards [1] [2] [3] [5]
Parking on premises
Closed Dec–mid Feb
Closed lunch

GH **Rydal Lodge**
(2m NW of Ambleside on A590)
✆ (05394) 33208

This small, friendly, family-run hotel, surrounded by attractive riverside gardens, is five minutes' walk away from Rydal Water. The main lounge, a spacious and comfortable room on the first floor, overlooks the garden and stream. Books and games are provided for guests, and there is also a snug little TV lounge with an open fire. The eight bedrooms, including one family room, are neat and comfortable. Meals are served in an attractive dining room, again overlooking the garden. Proprietors Mr and Mrs Haughan pride themselves on their home-cooked English food. Quality fresh ingredients are used, and the sweets are especially tempting. Dinner should be ordered by 6pm. Children and dogs accepted.

Price band A
Dinner, b&b £19.85–£21
Last dinner 7pm
Credit cards [1] [3] [5]
Parking on premises
Closed Jan

Sheila's Cottage The Slack ✆ (0966) 33079	Despite being hidden down a little lane, Sheila's Cottage is always busy, confirming our Inspector's view of its quality and value. The old cottage has been tastefully converted into a cosy little restaurant open for morning coffee, lunch and afternoon tea. The menu is really unusual with many Swiss specialities such as 'Swiss ham special' — slices of ham on biscotte bread, covered with mushroom and sour cream sauce, topped with Swiss roelette cheese and served with salad. Desserts such as Austrian souhertorte and luscious banana flan are irresistable. Wine is available by the glass.	Lunch alc £6 Last meal 5.30pm Parking nearby Closed Jan Closed Sun

ANSTRUTHER Fife Map 12 NO50

❀ ×× **The Cellar** 24 East Green ✆ (0333) 310378	Predictably, this little restaurant — handily situated for visitors to the Scottish Fisheries Museum — specialises (though not exclusively) in seafood. Its cuisine has earned an excellent reputation, for it makes use of first-quality fresh fish and light, modern-style sauces, notable examples being West Coast scallops with Chablis sauce and pastry-wrapped salmon accompanied by a shrimp sauce. Some meat (possibly lamb or beef) is always featured on the menu, and this is equally good. The general ambience of the picturesque little fishing village is reflected in the open fires, stone walls and beamed ceiling of the restaurant, and the warm, friendly atmosphere is complemented by pleasant service.	Lunch alc £8 Dinner td fr £15 Last dinner 9.30pm Credit cards [1] [2] [3] No parking on premises Closed 3 days Xmas, New Year's Day, 1 wk May Closed Sun

APPLEBY-IN-WESTMORLAND Cumbria Map 12 NY62

★★ **Royal Oak Inn** Bargate ✆ (0930) 51463	This village inn is full of charm and character, with oak beams and roaring open fires throughout. Bedrooms are not large, but they have recently been completely transformed — delightfully furnished (with interesting antiques in some cases) and decorated in coordinating colour schemes. There is a cosy little lounge upstairs, while the ground floor comprises public bar, lounge-bar and a restaurant offering an extensive yet reasonably priced selection of dishes. Prawns St Jacques or port and stilton pâté, for example, can be followed by such main courses as seafood mornay, cheddar chicken or local steaks, and a vegetarian option is always available. The tempting array of sweets is home-made, like everything else on the menu.	Price band A Dinner, b&b £23.50 Last dinner 9pm Credit cards [1] [2] [3] Parking on premises

APPLETON-LE-MOORS North Yorkshire Map 8 SE78

★★ HL **Dweldapilton Hall** ✆ Lastingham (07515) 227	An air of gracious living is sustained at this comfortable period house on the edge of a delightful moorland village. The attractively furnished lounge has a welcoming log fire in colder months, and the 12 bedrooms, all with bath or shower en suite, are pleasant and equipped with CTV. There are two family rooms. Dinner and lunch are served in an elegant dining room, where the food is good and the service friendly and attentive. At lunch-time, meals	Price band B Lunch td £6.50 Dinner td fr £11.50 or alc £15.50 Last dinner 8pm Credit cards [1] [3] Parking on

are also served in the small snug bar. Dweldapilton Hall stands in attractively landscaped grounds and is a relaxing and peaceful place to stay for anyone keen to explore the beautiful North York Moors. The hotel offers a special programme at Christmas.

premises
Closed Jan–Feb

ARDELVE Highland *Ross & Cromerty* Map 14 NG82

❀ ★ HL
Loch Duich Hotel
✆ Dornie (059 985) 213

Close to historic Eileau Donan Castle, this pleasant little roadside hotel is an ideal base for exploring the Western Highlands and Skye. It is especially worth visiting for its food: proprietors Mr and Mrs Stenson serve the kind of meals that visitors to the Highlands frequently expect, but rarely find. The fixed-price dinner menu is changed daily, and includes some choice descriptions, such as 'A good plate of minestrone soup — hooching with garlic and parmesan'. The food, though, is far from frivolous, and uses the best of local produce in dishes like roast haunch of venison with myrtle, rowan and juniper. Mr Stenson has carefully chosen an interesting list of wines to suit most palates. The Loch Duich has 18 modest but charming bedrooms, including one family room.

Price band B
Dinner td £12
Last dinner 9pm
Credit cards [1] [3]
Parking on premises
Closed Nov–Mar
Closed lunch

ARMITAGE Staffordshire Map 7 SK01

×× **Old Farmhouse**
✆ (0543) 490353

Consistently high standards of British cooking at reasonable prices attract diners to this timber-framed Elizabethan farmhouse. Menus — three courses at lunch and four at dinner — are priced according to the main course chosen, which might be local pigeon, one of several fish dishes, or steak, kidney and mushroom pie. Vegetarian dishes are available, and children's portions from the main menu. First courses might include baby haddock smokies, hot filled vol-au-vents or various salads, while the choice of sweets includes a special gâteau made without flour. The wine list will provide something to everyone's taste and is very reasonably priced. Tea or coffee is served in the lounge. Service is attentive and pleasant.

Lunch td fr £5.25
Dinner td fr £9.75
Last dinner 9.30pm
Credit cards [1] [2] [3] [5]
Parking on premises
Closed Mon, & Sun dinner

ARUNDEL West Sussex Map 4 TQ00

★ ♣♣ **Burpham Country Hotel**
Old Down, Burpham
(3m NE of Arundel off A27)
✆ (0903) 882160

The peaceful village of Burpham, overlooking the South Downs and just three miles from Arundel, is the setting for this delightful country house. The hotel has a relaxing, friendly atmosphere, and a warm welcome is extended by proprietors Mr and Mrs Potter. There are eight spacious and comfortable bedrooms, all tastefully decorated and well-equipped, each with CTV. Good, honest home cooking is the mainstay of the charming restaurant, where the menu lists mainly English dishes. Vegetarian meals are also available. Reservations are preferred for a full lunch, but bar lunches are served. The hotel does not accept children or dogs.

Price band B
Lunch td £6.95
Dinner fr £9
Last dinner 8pm
Credit card [1]
Parking on premises

Inn **Swan Hotel**
High St
✆ (0903) 882314

Situated close to Arundel Castle and the River Arun, this Georgian-style inn has recently been upgraded to provide comfortable, modern accommodation. There are 11 bedrooms, eight with bathroom and three with shower en suite, and all with CTV and tea/coffee-making equipment. There is a spacious, open-plan lounge-bar, and a pleasant restaurant whose comprehensive menu features sound English and French-style cooking using good basic ingredients. The hotel has a friendly, informal atmosphere, and the staff are willing and helpful.

Price band B/C
Lunch alc £8.50
Dinner td £8.50 or alc £10
Last dinner 9.30pm
Credit cards [1] [2] [3] [4] [5]
No parking on premises

ASHBURTON Devon Map 3 SX77

GH **Gages Mill**
Buckfastleigh Rd
✆ (0364) 52391

Surrounded by beautiful open countryside, this 16th-century former wool mill stands in an acre of lawned gardens. It is an ideal base from which to visit the many places of interest on Dartmoor, situated as it is on the edge of the National Park, and, being ½ mile from the A38, it is a good point from which to tour South Devon including its coastline. The building has been restored with care to retain its original character and now provides eight spacious and attractive bedrooms, four with private facilities. There is one family bedroom, and children over five years of age are welcome, though dogs are not allowed. The public areas have a welcoming atmosphere and guests may enjoy a drink in either of the two lounges. Friendly proprietors Bett and Brian Cox offer good home-cooked meals and encourage guests to come and go as they please.

Price band A
Dinner td £6.50
Last dinner 7pm
Parking on premises
Closed mid Nov–mid Mar

ASHFORD Middlesex London

×× **Terrazza**
45 Church Rd
✆ (07842) 244887

An extensive à la carte menu features authentic Italian and other Continental dishes at this charming trattoria-style restaurant in the town centre. Diners may also choose their first course from a beautifully presented trolley of antipasti (hors-d'oeuvres), while other trolleys display fresh fish or a range of tempting sweets (including tiramisu, recommended by our Inspector). Vegetarian dishes are available and children's portions of main courses. Impeccable service is provided by a large team of staff headed by the restaurant manager. Tasteful furnishings and air-conditioning help make the Terrazza a comfortable and pleasant place to eat.

Lunch/dinner td £12.75 or alc £25
Last dinner 10pm
Credit cards [1] [2] [3] [5]
No parking on premises
Closed Sun, Bank Hols, Sat lunch

ASHINGTON West Sussex Map 4 TQ11

★★ H
Mill House
Mill Ln
(off A24)
✆ (0903) 892426

Here, on the southern edge of the village a small 18th-century mill house has been skilfully extended and converted into a delightfully welcoming small hotel. Many original features have been retained, including beams and inglenook fireplaces, and the antique furnishings are in keeping. A homely atmosphere prevails in the spacious, split-level lounge, which has plenty of comfortable armchairs, a writing desk, conveniently placed tables and several friendly house

Price band B/C
Lunch td £7.50
Dinner td £8.50 or alc £11
Last dinner 9.30pm
Credit cards [1] [2] [3] [4] [5]

cats as well. There is also a small bar, and the candlelit dining room, very popular in the evening, offers reliable cooking using top-quality ingredients and plenty of local produce. Meals may be chosen from à la carte or fixed-price menus, and portions are usually very generous. A good selection of moderately priced wines is available. Lunch is served to residents only. The Mill House has 11 prettily decorated bedrooms, most with facilities en suite and all with CTV and telephones.

Parking on premises

ASHWELL Hertfordshire Map 4 TL23

Inn **THREE TUNS**
6 High St
✆ (046274) 2387

A delightful country inn in an historic village, the Three Tuns combines the charms of a village pub and a simple hotel. Real ale is available in the public bar, where pub games such as darts and pool can be played. The lounge-bar and little dining room offer good, home-made food, including game in season. There are seven bedrooms, four of them in a skilfully renovated Victorian terrace a short distance away. All have washbasins and two have bath or shower en suite. One is a family room. All the bedrooms have attractive furnishings, some of them antique, and fresh flowers are often provided, giving a homely touch. Facilities in all the rooms include CTV, tea/coffee-making equipment and clock/radio.

Price band B
Lunch/dinner alc £5
Last dinner 10.30pm
Credit cards [1] [2] [5]
Parking on premises

ATHERSTONE Warwickshire Map 4 SP39

GH **Chapel House**
✆ (0827) 718949

The style and elegance of a bygone age are recaptured in this lovingly restored 18th-century house, where guests are greeted with a warm welcome and given attentive service for the duration of their stay. Bedrooms are cosy, compact and spotlessly clean, several of them overlooking the quaint walled garden and swimming pool. There is a comfortable lounge and an elegantly appointed dining room where meals are served at a manificent antique table. During the week, these meals are selected from a set menu of satisfying proportions, but on Friday and Saturday evenings the dining room becomes an à la carte restaurant with a fast-growing reputation for quality dishes based on game and other fresh local produce, popular with visitors and residents alike.

Price band B
Dinner td fr £7.50 or alc £15.50
Last dinner 7pm
Credit cards [1] [3] [5]
Parking on premises
Closed Xmas

AUCHENCAIRN Dumfries & Galloway *Kirkcudbrightshire* Map 11 NX75

★★★ ♣♣ HL
Balcary Bay
✆ (055664) 217

This historic whitewashed building, once used by smugglers, enjoys a lovely secluded setting, its lawns extending to the shore of the Solway Firth. Present owners, the Lamb family, have recently undertaken improvements to bedrooms and public areas alike. Of 10 bedrooms, eight have en suite facilities, and two have four-poster beds. TV is available in rooms on request. The hall/lounge has an attractive beamed ceiling and there are two bars, one with a balcony overlooking the bay, and the other a vaulted cellar bar. Snooker is among the leisure facilities available to

Price band B
Lunch alc £10
Dinner td £11 or alc £13
Last dinner 9pm
Credit cards [1] [3]
Parking on premises
Closed Dec–Feb

guests. Cuisine is straightforward, using fresh local produce as much as possible, and the wine list is limited but reasonably priced.

AUDLEY Staffordshire Map 7 SJ75

FH **Domvilles**
(From M6 junct 16 take Barthomley signs, in village turn L at White Lion Inn)
☎ Stoke-on-Trent (0782) 720378

The large, brick farmhouse sits on a hilltop above junction 16 of the M6 (the noise of which is effectively masked by double glazing), with extensive views over farmland towards the Cheshire Plain. Visitors will be impressed by orderly farmyard and outbuildings where they will be permitted to view the milking and other activities. An aviary of tropical birds is an additional point of interest. Recent improvements to the house have added an attractive lounge and a bedroom (which houses a splendid brass bed). Home-produced dinners featuring traditional roasts and casseroles are available if ordered in advance, while traditional farm breakfasts amply fulfil one's expectations. This is an excellent centre from which to tour the industrial features and heritage of the Potteries or Cheshire.

Price band A
Dinner td £5
Last dinner 7pm
Parking on premises

AYLESBURY Buckinghamshire Map 4 SP81

× **Pebbles**
Pebble Ln
☎ (0296) 86622

Low ceilings and wooden beams characterise this cosy, cottage-style restaurant, tucked away in a narrow cobbled street off the town centre. Young proprietors Susan and David Cavalier bring flair and imagination to the cooking here. The short, select menu offers freshly prepared dishes with a French influence, making use of good basic materials. Vegetarian dishes are available. Sweets are especially interesting, and the menu is complemented by a short wine list of mostly popular, inexpensive wines. The atmosphere is relaxing and informal, and the service very good.

Lunch td £10.25 or alc £20
Dinner td fr £18 or alc £25
Last dinner 10pm
Credit cards 1 2 3 5
No parking on premises
Closed Mon

Seatons
Market Sq
☎ (0296) 27582

In the restfully lit Dickensian-style interior of this centrally situated restaurant, pre-dinner drinks may be enjoyed at the bar. A small but interesting dinner menu is offered, including several vegetarian dishes. A selection of fresh vegtables accompanies the main course. Our inspector enjoyed well-flavoured prawn and tuna vol-au-vents in light puff pastry, followed by a richly sauced beef bourguignon. At lunch-time an imaginative range of generous open sandwiches and salads are served with a choice of home-made dressing. Try for example, spinach and lentil pâté, or chicken, orange and toasted almonds, both available in either sandwich or salad form. Booking is essential on Friday and Saturday evenings.

Lunch fr £2.25
Dinner alc £8
Last dinner 10pm
Credit cards 1 3
Parking nearby
Closed Sun, Mon dinner, Bank Hols

BAGSHOT Surrey Map 4 SU96

×× **Sultan's Pleasure**
13 London Rd
(Bagshot Bypass)
☎ (0276) 75114

Traditional Turkish food, all home-made and cooked to order, is the speciality at this well-established, family-run Turkish restaurant. Many of the delicious main courses consist of meat or fish marinated and cooked kebab-style over a charcoal fire, while starters include authentic Turkish dishes such as dolma

Dinner alc £13.50
Last dinner 10.30pm
Parking on premises

	(stuffed vine leaves), çaçik (cucumber and yogurt, served with pitta bread) or tarama (red caviar purée). Typical Turkish desserts served include baklava, sambali and lokma, and some Turkish wines are listed. Vegetarians are catered for, and English food is available for the less adventurous. The restaurant is full of character and charm, and its low ceilings, candlelit tables and dim lights all help to create a warm, intimate atmosphere.	Closed 1st 2 wks Aug Closed lunch, Sun, & Mon dinner

BAKEWELL Derbyshire Map 8 SK26

★★ 🌲 B L **Croft Country House Hotel** ✆ Great Longstone (062987) 278	Four acres of gardens and grounds surround this charming Victorian country house, which is an ideal base for a holiday or weekend in the Peak District National Park. The eight prettily-furnished bedrooms lead off an attractive galleried landing above the spacious main hall. Five of the rooms have en suite bath or shower, and all have CTV. Two have been specially adapted to accommodate wheelchairs, and the hotel also has a lift, making it especially suitable for disabled guests. Public rooms are comfortably and tastefully furnished, with many good-quality period pieces in keeping with the character of the house. The atmosphere is peaceful and relaxed, and the service informal and friendly, with proprietors Clive and Rosemary Sheridan very much involved. The value-for-money table d'hôte menu offers a small but imaginative choice of good wholesome dishes, with the emphasis on fresh seasonal produce. Special diets can be catered for, and packed lunches are available on request.	Price band B/C Dinner td £10.95 Last dinner 8pm Credit cards [1] [3] Parking on premises Closed Xmas, mid Jan–mid Feb
❀ × **Fischer's** Woodhouse, Bath St ✆ (062981) 2687	When Max and Susan Fischer took over this little restaurant several years ago, it was a fairly ordinary eating house, serving teas, roasts and fish and chips to Bakewell's many tourists. Using the skills they had acquired in restaurants throughout Europe, the Fischers have gradually turned their restaurant into something rather special. The fish dishes are particularly worth a mention, being imaginative and unusual. Max loves cooking fish and regards it as an enjoyable challenge to serve delicious meals, using the freshest of seafood, in a restaurant so far from the coast. Main dishes might include sea bass with tomato and ginger sauce, paupiettes of salmon and Dover sole with lobster and wild rice. The menu changes monthly, and there is an occasional special set menu.	Lunch td fr £8.25 Dinner alc £20 Last dinner 9.30pm Credit cards [1] [2] [3] [5] Limited parking on premises Closed Xmas & New Year, last wk Jul, 1st wk Aug Closed Mon, Sat lunch, Sun dinner
★★ H **Milford House** Mill St ✆ (062981) 2130	Good old-fashioned hospitality is the hallmark of this hotel, which has been owned by the Hunt family for over 30 years. Guests are made to feel welcome and comfortable and, despite being near the centre of Bakewell, the beautifully maintained Georgian house has a tranquil atmosphere. The 11 bedrooms (now all with private facilities), while not luxurious, are quite adequate, and CTV is available on request. Food at Milford house is traditional English home cooking,	Price band B Dinner td fr £8.60 Last dinner 7.30pm Parking on premises Closed Jan–Feb Restricted

using the best of fresh local produce. Apart from the friendly dining room, public areas include a comfortable lounge with CTV, and a bar. The hotel also has an attractive garden. Milford House does not accept dogs or children under 10.

service Nov, Dec & Mar (weekends only)
Closed lunch (except Sun) but bar snacks available

BALSALL COMMON West Midlands Map 4 SP27

★★ H **Haigs Hotel**
273 Kenilworth Rd
✆ Berkswell (0676) 33004

Close to Birmingham Airport and the National Exhibition Centre, this small, family-run hotel is ideal for the business traveller. The 14 bedrooms (11 with shower en suite) are simple but adequate, and all are equipped with CTV. Proprietors Mr and Mrs Cooper have recently made improvements to the bar and restaurant, and have appointed a chef who has continued to raise the standard of the food. Tomato and prawn sorbet, terrine of pork and chicken livers with Oxford sauce, and paupiettes of sole stuffed with tomato and crab are among many interesting dishes listed on the à la carte menu. Vegetarian meals are available. Nothing seems to be too much trouble for the Coopers and their staff, and many guests return repeatedly for the warm welcome and friendly, relaxing atmosphere to be found here. Haigs does not accept children under four, or dogs.

Price band B
Lunch td £6.80
Dinner td £8.85 or alc £12
Last dinner 9pm
Credit cards [1] [2] [3] [5]
Parking on premises
Closed 24 Dec–3 Jan & 1 wk Aug

BANAVIE Highland *Inverness-shire* Map 14 NN17

★★ **Moorings**
✆ (03977) 550

This modern, low-rise building, standing in its own grounds on the banks of the Caledonian Canal, offers accommodation in compact, smartly-decorated and well-fitted bedrooms; an annexe contains three rooms with en suite private facilities. The downstairs lounge and dining room, furnished in Jacobean style, are spacious and comfortable, with patio doors leading into the garden. The standard of meals served, coupled with the attention of a helpful proprietor and friendly staff, are rapidly earning popularity for the hotel.

Price band B/C
Lunch td £5.50 or alc £12.50
Dinner td £13.80 or alc £16
Last dinner 9pm
Credit cards [1] [3] [5]
Parking on premises
Closed 25 Dec–5 Jan

BANGOR Gwynedd Map 6 SH57

★★ **Ty Uchaf**
(2m E of Bangor off A55)
(0248) 352219

Converted with painstaking care from an old farmhouse, this comfortable hotel is well-appointed in all respects. Telephones, CTV and clock-radios are provided in the nine bedrooms, all of which have en suite facilities. Downstairs there is a congenial lounge-bar, kept cosy by a wood-burning stove, and with attractive alcoves to sit in. The foyer/lounge is tastefully decorated and has a stone inglenook fireplace and comfortable seating. Meals at Ty Uchef are always well-cooked and imaginative. A good choice of bar meals is available, either in the bar or in one part of the dining room. Vegetarian dishes are available. Service at the hotel is friendly and helpful. Noise can sometimes be a problem here, since Ty

Price band B
Lunch td fr £5
Dinner td fr £7.50 or alc £10
Last dinner 8.30pm
Credit cards [1] [3]
Parking on premises

Uchaf is situated near a railway line, but double glazing has done much to counteract this. The hotel does not accept dogs, or children under 10.

BARKSTON Lincolnshire Map 8 SK94

×× **Barkston House**
✆ Lovedon (0400) 50555

This lovely old Georgian farmhouse has been converted into a small restaurant with two beautifully decorated and appointed bedrooms. Though it stands at the centre of the village, it is set well back from the road behind huge cedar trees, providing an oasis of calm and quietness. The menu offers a small but well-balanced selection of English dishes in the light, modern style, such as poached sole with watercress sauce and herbed lamb cutlets, accompanied by a good range of fresh vegetables. Desserts include both the traditional treats like treacle and apple tarts and modern tempters such as ginger ice-cream.

Lunch alc £8.40
Dinner alc £12.95
Last dinner 9.15pm
Credit cards [1] [2] [3] [5]
Parking on premises
Closed 25–31 Dec
Closed Sat lunch, Sun & Mon dinner

BARMOUTH Gwynedd Map 6 SH61

Inn **Crown Hotel**
Church St
✆ (0341) 280326

Completely refurbished by present owners Rob and Jayne Potter, the Crown offers a pleasant place to stay in this popular part of Wales with its lovely beaches and mountain scenery. All nine bedrooms have showers, CTV and tea/coffee-making equipment, and two also have en suite toilets. The bar downstairs incorporates an attractive dining area where a good selection of bar meals is served. Many are quite substantial dishes, with a choice of steaks and some vegetarian food. Breakfast is also served here.

Price band A/B
Lunch td fr £3.80
Dinner td fr £4
Last dinner 10pm
Credit cards [1] [3]
Parking on street frontage

BARNSLEY South Yorkshire Map 8 SE30

×× **Brooklands**
Barnsley Rd
(Few 100 yards W of M1 junct 37)
✆ (0226) 299571

This very popular restaurant, conviently sited for those travelling on the M1, offers excellent value for money in the generous portions it serves. Guests choose from a selection of English, French, German and Italian dishes, and there are freshly-prepared 'specials' each day. Meals are complemented by an extensive wine list and by caring service, for the well-being of the customer comes first here. A menu here once said, 'Beneath the portals 'tis no sin to ask for more and it shall be freely given'. Motel accommodation is also available if required.

Lunch td fr £5.50
Dinner alc £10.50
Last dinner 9.30pm
Credit cards [1] [2] [3] [4] [5]
Parking on premises
Closed 25–26 Dec

The price band indicates the price of bed and breakfast for a single person or room. Price band A = £15 or less; price band B = £16–£30; price band C = £31–£50; price band D = more than £50.

BARRY South Glamorgan Map 3 ST16

★★ **Aberthaw House** 28 Porthkerry Rd ✆ (0446) 737314	Modern, comfortable accommodation is to be found at this small family-run hotel. Five of the ten bedrooms have en suite bath or shower, and there is one family room and one room with a four-poster bed. All have CTV. Food here is home-cooked, using fresh produce where possible. The small table d'hôte menu is supplemented by an extensive à la carte selection.	Price band B Bar lunch fr £4 Dinner td fr £9 or alc £15 Last dinner 9.30pm Credit cards 1 3 5 Parking on premises Closed Xmas & New Year

BASSENTHWAITE Cumbria Map 11 NY23

★★ HL **Overwater Hall Hotel** Ireby (2m N of Bassenthwaite) ✆ Bassenthwaite Lake (059681) 566	Unspoilt Lakeland countryside surrounds this attractive 18th-century mansion, which stands in the heart of John Peel country close to the little-known lake of Overwater. The hotel is set in its own extensive gardens and woodland grounds, and offers magnificent views. Public rooms, elegantly furnished in keeping with the style of the house, include a comfortable drawing room, a hall/lounge and a cocktail lounge. There is also a snooker room and a sun terrace. The pleasant dining room offers a good-value fixed-price five-course dinner, with a choice of main courses such as gourjons of sole, roast duckling, trout and chicken, and traditional first courses such as pâté maison or prawn cocktail. Light lunches are also served to residents, and packed lunches are available. Food is attractively presented, and there is a reasonably priced wine list representing most of the main growing areas. The hotel's 13 well-appointed bedrooms include four family rooms and three with four-poster beds. All rooms have CTV, radios and telephones, and nine have their own bath or shower en suite. Most bedrooms have fine countryside views.	Price band B Dinner td £12.50 Last dinner 8.30pm Credit cards 1 3 Parking on premises Closed 24 Dec–19 Feb

BATH Avon Map 3 ST76

Woods 9–13 Alfred St ✆ (0225) 314812	A wide choice of food with a distinctly French theme is served at this large, informal restaurant. Three fixed-price set menus are supplemented by an à la carte selection, and special dishes of the day are advertised on the blackboard. A vegetarian choice is always available. Service here is friendly and attentive, and the L-shaped restaurant is attractively decorated and furnished with pine tables and comfortable, tubular-steel chairs. On the walls is a large collection of old prints, mainly with a horse-racing theme. Woods has a separate, spacious bar, at the entrance, for pre-dinner drinks.	Lunch/dinner td fr £9.95 or alc £11 Last dinner 10.15pm Credit card 3 Parking nearby Closed Mon

BATTLE East Sussex Map 5 TQ71

FH **Little Hemingfold Farmhouse**
Telham
(2½m SE of Battle off A210)
☎ (04246) 4338

A large, secluded period farmhouse set in 26 acres of woodland and fields, Little Hemingfold offers handsomely appointed accommodation and excellent cooking, much of it using home-produced food. All of the 12 bedrooms have bathrooms en suite, CTV, radios, electric blankets and tea/coffee-making equipment. Most of the bedrooms are on the ground floor, with doors to the garden, and are grouped around an attractive courtyard. The two comfortable sitting rooms have log fires, interesting antiques and curios and plenty of books. Two large polished Victorian tables accommodate guests in the dining room, where Ann Benton's superb four-course dinner is served. There is a choice of five or six starters such as home-made soup, smoked trout or home-grown asparagus in season. The set main course of the day might be fresh salmon or duckling, beef Wellington, or local plaice. An alternative can be chosen if it is ordered in advance. Sweets, using home-grown soft fruit in season and fresh home-produced cream, can be chosen from four or five dishes of the day. Cheese and biscuits, coffee and a glass of wine are included in the price. Vegetables are mostly home-grown and all bread is home-baked. Jersey cows, sheep, pigs and hens are all kept on the farm and there is a two-acre fishing lake, which also provides swimming for the brave. In addition there is a grass tennis court. Children under 12 are not accepted.

Dinner, b&b fr £25
Last dinner 7.15pm
Credit cards [1] [2] [3]
Parking on premises

RED ★★★

Netherfield Place
Netherfield
(3m NW of Battle on B2096)
☎ (04246) 4455
Tx 95284

The 30 acres of parkland that surround this gracious country house include a well-tended one-acre walled kitchen garden, which supplies the kitchen with fresh fruit, vegetables and herbs. Proprietor/chef Michael Collier uses this fresh produce to advantage in his imaginative and excellent cooking. The set 'executive lunch' is especially good value, with menus at £10.95 and £12.50 including half a bottle of house wine. Main courses range from simple grilled lamb cutlets to chicken garnished with asparagus and prawns, served with a lobster sauce. Coffee is included, and comes with petits fours. A full à la carte menu is also available at lunch and dinner, and there is an extensive wine list. Vegetarians can be catered for. Meals are served in a beautifully appointed panelled dining room, and other public rooms are equally attractive, including a drawing room, a cocktail bar and a small sitting room. The 12 luxuriously furnished bedrooms are spacious and very comfortable. All have bathrooms en suite, CTV and telephones, and are provided with quality toiletries, flowers and fruit. Hospitality at Netherfield Place is relaxed and friendly, and caring personal service is provided by the proprietors and their team of young staff. No dogs, please.

Price band C
Dinner td £15 or alc £18
Lunch td fr £10.95 or alc £18
Last dinner 9.45pm
Credit cards [1] [2] [3] [5]
Parking on premises

BEACONSFIELD Buckinghamshire Map 4 SU99

★★★ Santella
43 Aylesbury End
✆ (04946) 6806

Established eight years ago in Beaconsfield, this smart Italian restaurant has built up a reputation for authentic Italian food, competent service and a stylish atmosphere. Décor is fresh and attractive, especially in the bar at the front, where bowls of fresh crudités are served with pre-dinner drinks while orders are taken. The comprehensive à la carte menu is supplemented by special dishes of the day, and there is also a very reasonably priced business lunch menu. Pasta is all home-made, and vegetarian dishes are available. The Italian staff provide professional and efficient service and still find time to be jovial and friendly.

Lunch td £10.25 & alc
Dinner alc £12.50
Last dinner 11pm
Credit cards [1] [2] [3] [5]
No parking on premises
Closed Sun

★★ White Hart Osprey Hotel
Aylesbury End
(On A40 at junct with B474)
✆ (04946) 71211

Though now one of a group of hotels, the White Hart retains all the character and individuality of an old town-centre coaching inn. Bedrooms are all well-equipped: 28 are in a modern annexe, reached by a covered walkway. These are all spacious and have private bathrooms, while the five older rooms in the main hotel have more character but tend to be smaller and lack en suite facilities. All bedrooms have CTV and telephones, and five are set aside for non-smokers. Public rooms are open-plan, and include GK's Restaurant with its cheerful, rustic décor. American-style food is served with a 34-item salad bar. Chinese food is also a speciality, and vegetarians are catered for.

Price band B/C
Lunch td fr £8
Dinner td fr £10
Last dinner 10pm
Credit cards [1] [2] [3] [5]
Parking on premises

BEAMINSTER Dorset Map 3 ST40

× The Bridge House
Prout Bridge
✆ (0308) 862200

This pleasant restaurant (which also has three bedrooms to let) occupies an attractive period house with a secluded garden. Fresh local produce is used wherever possible in the range of imaginative and well-cooked dishes on offer, and house wines are good. Meals are served in an attractive beamed dining-room, where no smoking is permitted, and there is also a lounge, with bar off, for aperitifs. Breakfasts, too, are good for those accommodated in the letting rooms.

Lunch td fr £2.50 or alc £6.50
Dinner td £11.50 or alc £15
Last dinner 9pm
Parking on premises
Lunch Mon–Sat by arrangement
Closed Sun dinner

BEARSTED Kent Map 5 TQ85

×× Suefflé
The Green
✆ Maidstone (0622) 37065

Part of a charming English country scene, this appealing cottage overlooks a pretty village green with a cricket pitch. The interior is an attractive beamed restaurant, decorated and furnished in delicate pastel shades. Meals feature French-style cooking: at lunch-time choice is limited, but the set-price menu is good value, whereas in the evening the menu is more extensive, offering a well-balanced choice which includes fish dishes of the day. There is a varied wine list, and service is pleasant and efficient.

Lunch td £9.95
Dinner alc £22
Last dinner 10pm
Credit cards [1] [2] [3] [4] [5]
Parking on premises
Closed Sun, Sat lunch & Mon dinner

BEATTOCK Dumfries & Galloway *Dumfriesshire* Map 11 NT00

★★★ HL
Auchen Castle Hotel
(1m N of Beattock, SP from A74)
✆ (06833) 407

The Younger family (of brewery fame) built this sandstone mansion in the mid 19th century, and, despite the distant hum of traffic on the A74, it retains much of the feel of a period country house. Set in south-west Scotland's lovely border country, the hotel has 50 acres of magnificent gardens and grounds, including its own trout loch. Recent years have seen a steady programme of improvements inside the house, and the bedrooms are undergoing much-needed refurbishment. There are 25 in all, and although all have private facilities, telephone and CTV, the ones in the main building are preferable to the 10 annexe rooms. Public rooms are comfortable and opulent, and mainly traditional in style. Imaginative use of local produce is a feature of the cuisine here; guests will be offered generous helpings of dishes such as casserole of pheasant and partridge with okra and ginger, or sea trout with cucumber sauce, as well as vegetarian dishes. The cheerful, informal atmosphere of the dining room is particularly enjoyable, and the Beckh family are genial hosts with a genuine interest in each of their guests — to the extent that our Inspector sometimes has difficulty retaining his anonymity.

Price band B
Bar lunch £1.85
Last dinner 9pm
Credit cards [1] [2] [3] [4] [5]
Parking on premises
Closed Xmas & New Year

BEAULIEU Hampshire Map 4 SU30

★★★
Montagu Arms
✆ Brockenhurst (0590) 612324
Tx 47276

This popular, well-managed hotel, creeper-clad and Tudor in style, has all the attractions of a traditional English inn — right down to the rose garden. Standards of comfort and service are high, and the restaurant offers good, imaginative cooking with an excellent choice of dishes, and a good carving trolley of traditional roasts. The menu is predominantly à la carte, and includes vegetarian dishes, and there are also fixed-price gourmet dinners. Fresh, high-quality ingredients are always used, including organically grown fruit and vegetables and hormone-free meat. The lounge, beautifully panelled, with a wood-block floor, and with log fires in winter, has a homely, old-world atmosphere. It is sometimes let for small conferences. The 26 individually furnished bedrooms are especially attractive, and are equipped to a very high standard. All have bathrooms with both bath and shower, and telephones and CTV are standard in all rooms, as are many little extras such as bathrobes. There are six four-poster rooms and four family rooms.

Price band C
Lunch td £13.75 or alc £20
Dinner td £16.50 or alc £20
Last dinner 9.30pm
Credit cards [1] [2] [3] [5]
Parking on premises

BEAUMARIS Gwynedd Map 6 SH67

★★ **Bishopsgate House**
54 Castle St
✆ Menai Bridge (0248) 810302

Do not be put off by the rather bland exterior of this pleasant and comfortable hotel, situated only 100 yards from Edward I's Beaumaris Castle. The Rawlinsons, proprietors here for a number of years, are always making improvements to the accommodation, and nothing seems to be too much

Price band B
Lunch td fr £5.75
Dinner td fr £8.95
Last dinner 9pm

trouble for them or their staff. The beamed bedrooms are comfortably furnished and have fabrics tastefully chosen to suit the character of the well-proportioned Georgian building. All 10 rooms have private facilities and CTV. Public rooms comprise a warm, chintzy lounge, a congenial bar and a dining room with an equally pleasant atmosphere. The hotel does not take children under five.

Credit cards [1] [3]
Parking on premises
Closed Xmas

BEDFORD Bedfordshire Map 4 TL04

★★★ H
Woodlands Manor
Green Ln, Clapham
(2m N of Bedford on A6)
✆ (0234) 63281

Peace and tranquillity, just a few miles from the centre of Bedford, are to be found at this Victorian manor house, set in 3½ acres of grounds. Our Inspector especially commends the hotel's team of dedicated and friendly staff, who overlook no detail in their eagerness to please guests. Evening room service includes a hot water bottle in winter, and a fresh flower accompanies every tray. Pre-dinner drinks are served in the comfort of the sumptuous lounge, and bedrooms are equally tasteful. All 21 rooms have en suite facilities and many extras including telephones; the three rooms in the cottage annexe (reached by a heated path) are especially spacious. Classic dishes, both traditional and modern, are featured on the extensive à la carte dinner menu, and there is also a set menu at £13.50 for four courses including a refreshing home-made sorbet. Woodlands Manor does not accept dogs, or children under seven.

Price band C
Lunch td fr £9.25 or alc £20
Dinner td £13.50 or alc £20
Last dinner 9.45pm
Credit cards [1] [2] [3]
Parking on premises

BEERCROCOMBE Somerset Map 3 ST32

FH **Frog Street Farm**
✆ Taunton (0823) 480430

Tranquil countryside surrounds this idyllic spot in the heart of Somerset, equidistant from the north and south coasts. Frog Street Farm dates back to the 15th century, and the house, though tastefully restored and modernised, retains historic features such as inglenook fireplaces, exposed timber beams and fine Jacobean panelling. The secluded garden has a heated swimming pool for summer use, and a trout stream runs through adjacent meadows. Guests here can be sure of a warm welcome from Mrs Cole, who takes charge of preparing the excellent evening meal. Home produce from the 160-acre farm is supplemented by raw materials in season such as salmon from the River Severn or pheasants from the local shoot. Dinner is available to residents only, and must be ordered by 4pm. The farmhouse has three bedrooms available, one a family room, two with facilities en suite. All are decorated and furnished to a high standard, as are the attractive lounge (with CTV), dining room and reading room. Dogs are not accepted here, nor children under 11.

Price band A
Dinner td £10
Last dinner 7.30pm
Parking on premises
Closed Xmas & New Year

FH **Whittles Farm**
(1m from Beercrocombe)
✆ Taunton (0823) 480301

Superior accommodation and good food are to be found at this 16th-century farmhouse which, though in a secluded setting, is within an easy drive of many places of interest. The house is decorated and furnished to a high standard, and retains many

Price band A/B
Dinner, b&b £23–£24.50
Last dinner 7pm
Parking on

original features. Three of the four en suite, attractive bedrooms have CTV and tea/coffee-making facilities. Downstairs, the two elegant lounges have log fires and comfortable seating. Drinks are served in one (Whittles Farm is licensed), while the other serves as a quiet room. The dining room is spacious, with a table shared by up to six guests. Home produce is used in Mrs Mitchem's carefully prepared meals (available to resident only; please order dinner by 11.30am), and she is always on hand to ensure a relaxing and enjoyable stay. Whittles Farm does not accept children under 12, or dogs.

premises
Closed 1 Dec–15 Jan

BEESTON Nottinghamshire Map 8 SK53

×× **Les Artistes Gourmands**
61 Wollarton Rd
Nottingham
(0602) 228288

So popular is this comfortable little restaurant that it is advisable to book in advance, even for a mid-week meal. Light-coloured walls hung with watercolours of French scenery and châteaux (which may be purchased) provide a fitting background to the enjoyment of traditional French dishes prepared in the light, modern style and attractively presented. Very good use is made of fresh fish and other seafood, not only simply cooked, but also in various mousses, terrines and soups; poultry and game also figure prominently on the menu, often casseroled.

Lunch td fr £7.30
Dinner td fr £10.90
Last dinner 9.30pm
Credit cards [1] [2] [3]
Parking limited
Closed 1 wk Jan
Closed Sat lunch & Sun dinner

BELPER Derbyshire Map 8 SK34

×× **Remy's Restaurant Français**
84 Bridge St
(077382) 2246

An old Derbyshire textile town on the edge of the Peak District seems an unlikely setting for a French restaurant, but this very pleasant example, with its welcoming, intimate atmosphere, was founded almost ten years ago by Remy Bopp, and although he has moved on, the type of cuisine and the style of the restaurant that he created still prevails. French food prepared in the light modern style is enhanced by sauces of a traditional richness, and a well-balanced wine list gives sufficient choice to complement any meal selection. Vegetarian dishes are also available.

Lunch td fr £5.95
Dinner td fr £10.95
Last dinner 9.30pm
Credit cards [2] [3] [5]
No parking on premises
Closed 1 wk Jan, 2 wks Aug
Closed Mon & Sat lunch, Sun dinner

BETWS-Y-COED Gwynedd Map 6 SH75

★★ H **Ty Gwyn**
(06902) 383

Open fires, beamed ceilings and antique furniture all help to recall the days when this friendly little hotel beside the River Conwy was a stopping place for travellers on the important North Wales coaching route (now the A5). Bedrooms are a delight, with tasteful colour schemes and interesting bric-à-brac to add a homely touch. Eight of the 12 rooms (including a family room) have shower or bath en suite, and there are three four-poster beds. Public rooms are just as agreeable and welcoming, and include a cosy TV lounge as well as a cottage-style lounge-bar and a

Price band A/B
Lunch/dinner td £6.95 or alc
Last dinner 9.30pm
Credit cards [1] [3]
Parking on premises

dining room full of interesting curios. Our Inspector found meals here enjoyable and well-cooked. Fresh local produce is used whenever possible, and vegetarian dishes are always available. The dining room menu is supplemented by a wide range of inexpensive bar meals. Children and dogs are welcome.

BIDDENDEN Kent Map 5 TQ83

Three Chimneys
(On A262, 1m W of Biddenden)
✆ (0580) 291472

Imaginative home-cooked food can be eaten either pub-style or in the dining room at this delightful free house. Dishes of the day, listed on blackboards, might include leek and ham mornay or pork and celery with cider sauce, preceded by hot crab or a home-made terrine and followed by a home-made sweet such as date and walnut pudding or Bakewell tart with fresh Jersey cream. Vegetables are fresh and delicious. The bars offer a good range of real draught beers, and the large public bar has a selection of traditional pub games. Rush matting, wooden panelling and old settles complete the homely, village pub atmosphere, and service is suitably friendly and cheerful. Some of the rooms are candlelit at night, and one has a fire in the winter. Tables can be booked in advance.

Lunch/dinner alc fr £7
Last dinner 10pm
Parking on premises
Closed Sun lunch

×× **Ye Maydes Restaurant**
High St
✆ (0580) 291306

This fine half-timbered medieval building has historic connections with Flemish weavers and with legendary Siamese twins the Biddenden Maids, who are depicted on the village sign. The restaurant retains a period atmosphere: aperitifs can be enjoyed by the log fire that burns in the bar's inglenook fireplace, and the dining room is divided by leaded-light windows. Tables are well-spaced and look attractive, and oil paintings displayed for sale on the walls provide added interest. Proprietor Mrs Sheila Daniels and her team of young staff produce English and French-style dishes, using good local produce as much as possible. The à la carte menu, which changes monthly, offers a balanced and varied choice including vegetarian dishes, and the splendid selection of home-made puddings was particularly commended by our Inspector. Service is warm and friendly, the tone being set by Mrs Daniels' jovial style. A good choice of wines is always available.

Lunch td £7.30 or alc £15.25
Dinner alc £15.25
Last dinner 9.30pm
Credit cards [1] [2]
No parking on premises
Closed 1st wk Feb, 1st 2wks Sep, 1st wk Nov, Bank Hols
Closed Sun & Mon

BIDFORD-ON-AVON Warwickshire Map 4 SP15

FH **Bidford Grange**
(1m E of Bidford-on-Avon, off A439)
✆ Stratford-upon-Avon (0789) 773376

This beautiful Cotswold stone farmhouse on the banks of the Avon offers comfort and facilities that are well above average. Bedrooms, all three of them with private bathrooms and CTV, are especially luxurious. One has a whirlpool bath, while another has a splendid four-poster bed, and all have deep, comfortable armchairs or sofas. There is one family bedroom, but children under seven are not accepted, and neither are dogs. Bidford Grange's outstanding

Continued on page 37.

Price band B
Dinner td £10.95
Last dinner 8.30pm
Credit card [2]
Parking on premises

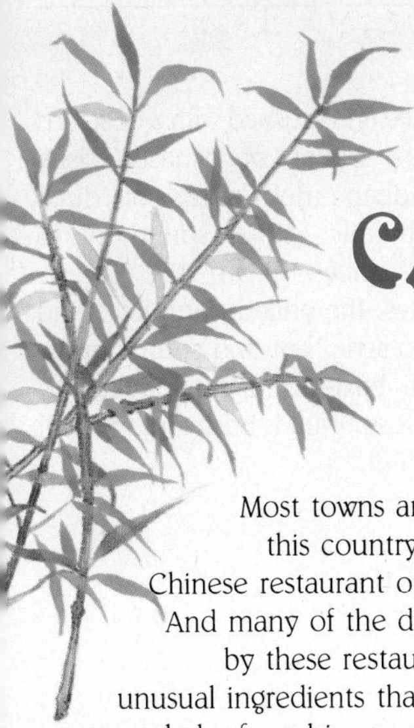

Birmingham's Chinese Community and Restaurants

Most towns and villages in this country now have a Chinese restaurant or 'take-away'. And many of the dishes created by these restaurants require unusual ingredients that can usually only be found in specialist oriental supermarkets and shops. In major cities where there are large numbers of Chinese restaurants this sometimes results in an area which has so many specialist Chinese shops that it becomes a veritable 'China town'.

London, Liverpool and Manchester have had their respective 'China towns' for some time, but now Birmingham also has such an area, used regularly by a staggering 15,000 Midlands' Chinese for shopping, meeting friends and obtaining staff. To cater for the specific needs of this growing community increasing numbers of specialist supermarkets, bakeries, beansprout growers, travel agents, bookshops, hairdressers and a casino have sprung up. There is even a school to maintain the cultural connections with China.

Although it is often said by food writers and restaurant critics that a Chinese restaurant can best be judged by the number of Chinese that actually eat there, this is not, in reality, the case. The Chinese go to particular restaurants for companionship — to meet friends, conduct business or to find staff. They choose restaurants that will allow them to sit for a considerable period of time chatting, drinking a great deal of tea and consuming, perhaps, just a little food. Once the restaurant that they use is recommended to Westerners and becomes crowded at lunch and dinner time, the restaurant proprietor usually becomes less keen for the Chinese custom. This means that the Chinese are forced to move on to another restaurant and when the critics discover their new meeting place the whole process starts all over again.

Many of the most exciting dishes served in a Chinese restaurant have really unusual ingredients, so to taste new flavours and textures it is necessary to be fairly adventurous when making a selection from the menu. For example, chicken and duck are shown in many combinations — but do try their feet. This may sound far-fetched but after an intricate cooking process they really do end up with a lovely flavour. In addition you can dumbfound your disbelieving friends with the details of your meal afterwards. 'Assorted meats' is a term often seen on the menu of a Chinese restaurant that usually refers to types of offal not easily — and perhaps not wisely — translated into English.

Most of the AA's Inspectors really enjoy Chinese food and Birmingham's thriving Chinese quarter, in and around 'the markets' area, does have some excellent Chinese restaurants, some of which have adjoining supermarkets to encourage diners to DIY at home. Although it would be difficult to single out any one establishment as the very best, we have come up with a shortlist of 10 Chinese restaurants in Birmingham that are all highly recommended by our Inspectors.

Chung Ying

16-18 Wrottesley St
This was one of the first Chinese restaurants to maintain such a consistently high standard that in 1984 it was awarded an AA rosette. Although the décor is rather plain and the waiters a little serious, the food served here really is Cantonese cooking at its very best. Casserole dishes are particularly interesting and full of flavour. Try the unusual stewed eel and roast belly pork, chicken and liver or the duck and goose webs.

In this restaurant diners can discover the delights of the 'daily special' menu (rather than the widespread businessmens' lunch menu). Although they may have to ask for this, and also for a translation, it will be well worth the trouble to sample the day's market best.

Dynasty

93-103 Hurst St
With its modern pastel décor and large branches of pink cherry blossom, this is one of the Chinese restaurants that particularly appeals to the English. The food served here is predominantly Cantonese but Peking and Szechuan cuisines are also represented. Try Peking duckling — succulent pieces of duckling with a crispy golden skin rolled up in a thin pancake and brushed with a delicious combination of sauces, or Dynasty crispy duckling — deep fried slices of duck marinated with garlic, ginger, spring onions and selected spices. From the spicier Szechuan dishes, the grilled dumplings and prawns 'Peking style' hot and sour soup or king prawn in birdsnest are all delicious. Service in this restaurant is brisk and the staff extremely helpful.

Forbidden City

36 Hurst St
Quite possibly the most attractive Chinese restaurant in Birmingham, and certainly the one with the most authentic atmosphere. Forbidden City has a huge dining room, all on one floor, cleverly divided into sections with trellis work and ornate, decorated screens, to ensure diners' privacy.

The menu is almost wholly Cantonese and contains some of the most exotic and unusual ingredients to be found in any of Birmingham's Chinese restaurants.

Szechuan and Peking dishes are also to be found on the menu along with the usual recommendation for set meals to assist the unsure. In addition there is a special section of 'Gourmet Menus' created by Chef Tai Chiu which offer some quite outstanding dishes.

The many Chinese families that eat in Forbidden City provide the necessary atmosphere to ensure that a visit to this restaurant by Westerners is a tremendous experience. Children seem to be especially welcome.

Happy Gathering

54-56 Pershore St

This is probably the oldest of Birmingham's Chinese restaurants and should not be confused with another restaurant (also recommended) of the same name in Station Street.

Although at first glance Happy Gathering may look a little worn around the edges, don't be deceived, the warm and friendly atmosphere generated in its four dining rooms ensures that it is still one of the most popular places to dine. It is particularly favoured by large parties who can often take over one whole dining room.

The menu shows particular strength in its range of soups, and the set meals, including groups of vegetarian dishes, also give a wide range of choice.

Henrys

27 St Pauls Square

Henrys is located in the corner of a fine old church square in an area where many of the buildings and warehouses are being restored. This Chinese eating house is a fairly new venture and is a sister restaurant to Henry Wongs of Harborne.

The opulent and comfortable décor and furnishings have been designed to appeal to Westerners and there is also the advantage of ample parking close by. While the menu offers all the old favourites and currently popular items such as yuk-shung (shredded meats and crispy lettuce leaves for diners to make their own parcels) and 'sizzling' dishes, there are also some interesting combinations such as stuffed crispy chicken wings and various meats served with a powerful satay sauce.

Service is brisk and friendly and the staff ready to offer assistance to anyone struggling with a choice of dishes or the use of chopsticks.

Henry Wong

283 High St, Harborne
This restaurant is well out of the city centre and because it is in a village setting with so little competition nearby it does get very busy — so booking is advisable. The building was formerly a bank, but the sedate atmosphere that may once have prevailed has been well and truly dispelled.

This restaurant is run by the same family as Henrys in the town centre and has a very similar menu. This combines the really sound Cantonese dishes, so popular with the British, with a few novel touches such as sweet fruit sauces and spicier Szechuan-inspired ones.

Ho Tung

308 Bull Ring Centre
This restaurant may be difficult to find as its main ground floor entrance is off the Smallbrook Queensway (it can also be approached entirely undercover at the first floor level of the Bull Ring Centre), but it is well worth the effort once you get there.

Ho Tung is a restaurant which has a really good atmosphere perfected by the attentive and bustling staff. The menu takes some studying, but all the classic Cantonese dishes are there. A feature of this restaurant is the cabaret that takes place at weekends.

House of Mr Chan

167 Bromsgrove St
This restaurant has the reputation of teaching its diners how to enjoy Chinese food and does much to dispel the mysticism that surrounds the choosing of dishes. All this is done by a humorous, but extremely informative booklet entitled 'The Thoughts of Chairman Chan'. The introduction is followed by the menu which lists special items under 'Chairman's Choice' with Szechuan and Peking dishes highlighted, and even a favourite prawn dish from the island of Macao. Dim sum, soups and vegetable dishes follow and there is a final section which details the wide variety of sauces available (including chilli and black bean, ginger and spring onion, and oyster sauces) together with the meats and seafood that they accompany best.

Loon Fung

37-41 Pershore St
At the time of our Inspector's visit this restaurant had only recently opened. It is prominently placed and has a bright red oriental-style canopy front that looks both attractive and inviting.

The interior of the restaurant is equally attractive but more quietly decorated and has a comfortable bar and lounge area. Here the diner can indulge in standard Cantonese dishes or try some of the more exotic fare such as duck webs. Set menus priced at £8 a head are available for parties of two or more, and the range of dishes increases with the size of the group.

Oriental Corner

82 Hurst St
Quite an unobtrusive entrance from Hurst Street leads into this attractive restaurant. The dining room has a partitioned area set aside for non-smokers. All the usual favourites will be found on the Cantonese menu and the helpful staff ensure that diners get the very best from the wide choice of dishes.

recreational facilities include coarse fishing, croquet, a grass tennis court, a swimming pool, a sauna and a golf driving range. A beautiful dining room, with a large antique table, is the setting for the four-course dinner. Mrs Muscott is a Cordon Bleu cook, and makes a point of using fresh local produce with skill and imagination. Breakfasts will satisfy even the heartiest appetite, and are served in the conservatory where guests can watch the visiting wildlife outside.

BIRMINGHAM West Midlands Map 7 SP08

×× **Chung Yin**
16-8 Wrottesley St
✆ 021-622 5669

See Birmingham's Chinese restaurants feature page 33.

Lunch td £7
Dinner td £10
Last dinner 11.45pm
Credit cards [1] [2] [3] [5]
Parking on premises

×× **Dynasty**
93–103 Hurst St
✆ 021-622 5306

See Birmingham's Chinese restaurants feature page 33.

Lunch td £5.95 or alc £7
Dinner td £7.50 or alc £7.50
Last dinner 11pm
Credit cards [1] [2] [3] [5]
Parking on premises

×× **Forbidden City**
36 Hurst St
✆ 021-622 2454

See Birmingham's Chinese restaurants feature page 33.

Lunch alc £5
Dinner alc £10
Last dinner 11.45pm
Credit cards [1] [2] [3] [5]
Parking nearby

× **Giovanni's**
27 Poplar Rd,
Kings Heath
✆ 021-443 2391

For a reasonably priced Italian meal, cheerfully served in convivial surroundings, you cannot do better than Giovanni's. Gay yellow and black awnings make the trattoria-style restaurant easy to find, but you would be well-advised to reserve a table, for it has a large regular clientele. At lunch-time there is a set meal plus daily 'specials', and the main menu offers not only a good selection of pasta dishes but also some interesting variations on the use of veal. The wine list has a choice of 16 Italian wines, all at realistic prices.

Lunch td fr £5.90
Dinner alc fr £10.70
Last dinner 10.30pm
Credit cards [1] [3] [5]
No parking on premises
Closed 24 Dec for 2 wks, 19 Jul for 3 wks

À la carte prices are based on an average for three courses without wine.

Happy Gathering 54–6 Pershore St ✆ 021-622 2324	See Birmingham's Chinese restaurants feature page 33.	Lunch td £2.20 Dinner td £8.50 Last dinner 11pm Credit cards [1] [2] [3] [5] Parking nearby Closed Sun
×× **Henry's** 27 St Pauls Sq ✆ 021-200 1136	See Birmingham's Chinese restaurants feature page 33.	Lunch alc £7 Dinner alc £9 Last dinner 11pm Credit cards [1] [2] [3] [5] No parking on premises Closed Sun
× **Henry Wong** 283 High St Harbourne ✆ 021-427 9799	See Birmingham's Chinese restaurants feature page 33.	Lunch/dinner td £8.50 Last dinner 11pm Credit cards [1] [2] [3] [5] Parking nearby Closed Sun
Home of Mr Chan 167 Bromsgrove St ✆ 021-622 1725	See Birmingham's Chinese restaurants feature page 33.	Dinner td £15 Last dinner 11.30pm Credit cards [1] [2] [3] [5] Parking nearby Closed Xmas
Ho Tung 308 Bull Ring Centre ✆ 021-643 0033	See Birmingham's Chinese restaurants feature page 33.	Lunch td £3 Dinner td £4.50–£12 Last dinner 5am Credit cards [1] [2] [3] [5] Parking on premises
Loon Fung 37–41 Pershore St ✆ 021-622 7395	See Birmingham's Chinese restaurants feature page 33.	Lunch £5 Dinner £5–£7 Last dinner 11.45pm Credit cards [1] [2] [3] [5] Parking on premises
Oriental Corner 82 Hurst St ✆ 021-622 5850	See Birmingham's Chinese restaurants feature page 33.	Lunch/dinner td £22.50 Last dinner mdnt Credit cards [1] [2] [3] [5] Parking on premises

× **Le Provençal** 1 Albany Rd, Harborne ✆ 021-426 2444	Booking is advisable for dinner at this popular restaurant in the cosmopolitan suburb of Harborne, which has a wide range of different eating houses. Cuisine here is predominantly French, with some native dishes created by Swiss chef René Ernst, who owns and runs the establishment with his English partner Geoff Rhodes, who manages the front-of-house operation in a friendly and welcoming manner. The set lunch menu lists specialities of the day, while in the evening the choice is à la carte, with chef's specials highlighted on the menu. A house speciality, served with main courses, is rösti, a potato and onion pancake.	Lunch td £6.50 Dinner alc £14 Last dinner 10.30pm Credit cards 1 3 5 No parking on premises Closed Sun, & Sat lunch
❀ ×× **Rajdoot** 12–22 Albert St ✆ 021-643 8805	Silk screen prints on the walls, whirling gay-coloured tumbas and the national dress worn by the staff all contribute to the exotic atmosphere of this Indian restaurant. More importantly, however, its consistent standards of cuisine have earned it a reputation as one of the best of its kind in England, leading to its being featured on TV food programmes. A sympathetic use of fresh herbs and spices makes the food here palatable even to those who have previously been dubious about Indian cuisine for none of the dishes is 'hot'. Orders for meals are taken in a cocktail bar overlooking the dining room, and the waiter will gladly advise you on your choice. The à la carte menu features Tandoori dishes, cooked in a clay oven, and a businessman's lunch is also available.	Lunch td fr £5.50 Dinner td fr £9.50 or alc £13 Last dinner 11.30pm Credit cards 1 2 3 4 5 No parking on premises Closed Bank Hols Closed Sat lunch
Waterloo Hotel Waterloo Rd, Smethwick ✆ 021-558 0198	Our Inspector recommends the popular basement restaurant of this large Victorian public house for its traditional lunch-time grills. An old-fashioned black-leaded, coke-fired range is used to cook each customer's chosen cut of fresh meat, supplied by a local butcher who is permanently on call. Vegetables tend to be overcooked by modern standards, but this does not seem to deter customers. A remarkable array of Victorian wall tiles forms a conversation piece, and the busy little bar in the centre serves a range of Midland beers and other usual drinks.	Lunch alc £8 Last lunch 2pm Credit cards 1 2 3 5 Parking nearby Closed dinner (except Thu), Sat & Sun

BLANDFORD FORUM Dorset Map 3 ST80

❀ ×× **La Belle Alliance** Portman Lodge, Whitecliff Mill St ✆ (0258) 52842	Unobtrusive good taste and a relaxed atmosphere are features of this restaurant in a spacious Victorian house not far from the town centre. A welcoming aperitif and tasty savouries are offered in the elegant lounge. Patron/chef Philip Davison produces an interesting choice of dishes using top-quality materials. Menus might include a terrine of smoked salmon and prawns; breast of chicken with basil and grapes; and, to follow, raspberry and kiwi fruit syllabub. Sorbets are usually served between courses, and the sweets display particular flair. Sunday lunches are popular here, and traditional roasts usually feature on the menu, though vegetarians are also catered for. A well-balanced wine list complements Mr Davison's cooking, and service is attentive but unhurried.	Dinner td £14.50 Last dinner 9.30pm Credit cards 1 2 3 5 Limited parking on premises Closed Mon & Sun dinner

BODENHAM Hereford and Worcester Map 3 SO55

FH **Maund Court**
✆ (056884) 282

Nothing could be more relaxing than to sit in the well-tended English garden of this 15th-century farmhouse, surrounded by beautiful countryside. The grounds contain a heated swimming pool and croquet lawn, and there are miles of walks around the farm itself. Your bedroom will be well-equipped (with colour television on request), and a large traditional breakfast can be served to you there. Dogs are allowed on the farm (though housed in purpose-built kennels in the yard), and a portrait of your pet could be a pleasant souvenir of your stay, as Mrs Edwards takes commissions for oil paintings of animals.

Price band A
B&b only
Closed Dec-Jan

BODINNICK Cornwall Map 2 SX15

× L **Old Ferry Inn**
✆ Polruan (072687) 237

The charm of a traditional English inn, together with modern comforts and good food, is to be found here beside the River Fowey. The hotel's two small bars are frequented by locals and guests alike, and the large, comfortable lounge gives access to a terrace which has restful views over the estuary, dotted with small craft, and across to Fowey. The elegant restaurant offers a three-course table d'hôte dinner menu and the cooking, English and French in style, shows imagination and flair. Seven of the 13 bedrooms have en suite facilities, and nearly all have CTV. There is one family room and one room with a four-poster bed.

Price band B
Dinner td £14 or alc £17
Last dinner 8.30pm
Credit card [3]
Parking on premises
Restricted service Nov–Feb

BO'NESS Central *West Lothian* Map 11 NS98

FH **Kinglass Farm**
Borrowstoun Rd
✆ (0506) 822861

Accommodation here is more in the style of a private hotel than a farmhouse, with attractively decorated public rooms and a restaurant that is open to non-residents as well as residents. Six of the seven bedrooms have washbasins and all have TV, radios and tea/coffee-making facilities. There is a small bar in the corner of the dining room. The tables look smart and appealing, and the food is always freshly prepared. Dinner should be ordered by 6pm.

Price band A
Dinner, b&b £16–£20
Last dinner 6.30pm
Parking on premises

BORELAND Dumfries & Galloway *Dumfriesshire* Map 11 NY19

FH **Gall**
✆ (05766) 229

This 1,066-acre working farm raises some beef cattle but specialises in pedigree sheep. The post-war whitewashed farmhouse, lying close to the quiet village of Boreland, looks out across beautiful rolling hills and pastureland. Stay here for a walking holiday or as a break during a long journey across the border. There are three spacious, well-appointed bedrooms one of which can accommodate a family. Good substantial meals are served and proprietor Mrs Maxwell, assisted by her daughter, is an excellent hostess, happy to share her knowledge of the farm and surrounding countryside.

Price band A
Dinner, b&b £15–£15.50
Last dinner 7pm
Parking on premises
Closed Nov–Mar

BORROWDALE Cumbria Map 11 NY21

GH **Green Bank** ✆ (059684) 215	Set in its own attractive gardens in the heart of Borrowdale Valley, this beautifully situated house commands magnificent views. It makes an ideal centre for fell-walking, climbing, or just relaxing and enjoying the scenery. Guests are greeted with a welcome pot of tea on arrival, and the warm, friendly atmosphere of the place is matched by the comfort of its two well-furnished lounges with their log fires. Each evening interesting menus offer a very good four-course meal, all home-cooked from fresh produce — and the day is rounded off by a bedtime pot of tea with biscuits!	Dinner, b&b £18.50–£24 Last dinner 7pm Parking on premises Closed Dec

BOSCASTLE Cornwall Map 2 SX09

GH **St Christopher's Country House** ✆ (08405) 412	Once part of the manor of Boscastle, St Christopher's was also once the village store. It is now a small, friendly little hotel where Anthony and Pamela Hardy provide hospitality and good food for up to 15 guests. There are eight cottage-style bedrooms, five of which have en suite shower rooms, and one with its own private lounge with CTV. Mrs Hardy takes pride in her home-cooked food, which includes hearty breakfasts. At dinner, a set main course is accompanied by a choice of starter and sweet, and menus are changed daily. Fresh Cornish produce is used, including butter and cream, and sometimes there is smoked fish from Charlestown. A range of wines is also available.	Price band A/B Dinner, b&b £19–£24.50 Last dinner 7pm Parking nearby Closed Nov–Feb

BOSHAM West Sussex Map 4 SU80

×× B **Millstream Hotel** Bosham Ln ✆ (0243) 573234	Close to the quay in the delightful, peaceful village of Bosham stands this attractive and homely hotel. The atmosphere here is informal and relaxing, the staff willing and helpful. There are 29 bedrooms, all with bathrooms en suite, CTV and telephones. Two are family rooms, and one has a four-poster bed. The bedrooms are all tastefully and individually decorated and comfortably furnished, as are the public rooms. The pleasant restaurant offers a varied menu of English and French-style dishes, and cooking is of a high standard. The hotel runs a special Christmas programme.	Price band C Lunch td fr £9.50 Dinner td fr £11.50 Last dinner 9.30pm Credit cards 1 2 3 5 Parking on premises

BOTHWELL Strathclyde *Lanarkshire* Map 11 NS75

★★ **Silvertrees** Silverwells Cres ✆ (0698) 852311	The 90-year-old building, attractively converted, overlooks the River Clyde from its own grounds at the centre of a quiet residential area. Beyond its impressive entrance, a beautiful wooden staircase leads to the bedrooms, and this area also contains a comfortable and attractive lounge-bar. The dining room, smartly set out with booths and banquette seating, is on the lower ground floor, together with another small bar and a sun lounge which looks on to the river.	Price band C Lunch td £7.50 or alc £16.50 Dinner td £9.50 & alc £16.50 Last dinner 8.45pm Credit cards 1 2 3 5 Parking on premises

BOUGHTON MONCHELSEA Kent Map 5 TQ75

★ H **The Tanyard** Wierton Hill ✆ Maidstone (0622) 44705	National winner of the AA's 1986–7 Guesthouse of the Year award, this beautiful 14th-century timbered house offers a warm welcome, comfortable accommodation and good food, all in a peaceful, rural setting in the Weald of Kent. The five bedrooms (all with CTV and bathrooms en suite) are tastefully renovated and well-equipped with thoughtful extras such as toiletries and good-quality towels. The top floor of the house has been converted into a luxurious three-room family suite. The lounge and dining room, where log fires blaze in winter, are cosy and attractively furnished with antiques. Proprietor Mrs Jan Davies is an excellent cook and a most hospitable and caring hostess. She offers a set dinner menu, but will happily prepare alternative dishes if required. An excellent cheeseboard of English farmhouse varieties is usually available to finish your meal. The Tanyard is licensed. No children under six, or dogs, are accepted.	Price band B Dinner td £12 Last dinner 8pm Credit cards [1] [2] [3] [5] Parking on premises Closed Oct–Mar

BOURNEMOUTH Dorset Map 4 SZ09

★★ H **Arlington Hotel** Exeter Park Rd ✆ (0202) 22879	This friendly, family-run hotel has a good central position and overlooks the pleasure gardens. All of the 28 neat bedrooms have en suite facilities, and there are six family rooms. Simple, home-cooked food is the mainstay of the dinner menu, and the wine list includes some half-bottles as well as house wines by the glass or carafe. A good snack-lunch menu is available in the comfortable bar. Dogs are not permitted in the hotel.	Price band B Bar lunch fr £3.50 Dinner td £9.50 Last dinner 7.30pm Credit cards [1] [3] Limited parking on premises Closed Jan
★★★ H **Belvedere Hotel** Bath Rd ✆ (0202) 21080	Personally run by its owners, Mr and Mrs Heller, with the aid of their friendly staff, the Belvedere has comfortable accommodation and good facilities. There is CTV and a telephone in each of the 35 modern bedrooms (including five family rooms), which all have bath or shower en suite. The lounge, which has a large sun balcony, is on the first floor, and there are two bars, one of which is open to non-residents and serves good bar snacks. The restaurant is open for lunch and dinner. The hotel has a lift, and is within a short walk of Bournemouth's main amenities.	Price band B Lunch td fr £5.25 or alc £7.50 Dinner td fr £7.25 or alc £9 Last dinner 8.30pm Credit cards [1] [2] [3] [5] Limited parking on premises
★★ B **Connaught Court Hotel** West Hill Rd, West Cliff ✆ (0202) 21944	Present owners Jan and Annette Murray have transformed this conveniently postioned family hotel, which is five minutes' walk from Bournemouth's principal shops and beaches and many other amenities. Bedrooms (which can be reached by lift) have been refurbished to a high standard, and all 34 have en suite bath or shower, CTV, telephone and radio intercom with baby-listening. Two rooms include specially fitted bathrooms for the disabled. General facilities in the hotel include a games room with table tennis, pool table and video games, a solarium, a fully equipped laundry room, a shop and a	Price band B Dinner td £6.50 Last dinner 7.30pm Credit cards [1] [2] [3] [5] Parking on premises

bookstall. Public rooms include a small lounge and a larger bar giving access to a patio with tables and chairs. Hot and cold lunch-time snacks are available in the bar or outside. The dining room offers traditional lunch on Sundays only, but well-cooked four-course dinners are served every night, with a choice of appetiser, main course (including a cold buffet selection) and sweet. Breakfasts offer an ample choice. The hotel stands in an acre of attractive gardens and has plenty of parking space.

★★★ L
Heathlands Hotel
Grove Rd, East Cliff
✆ (0202) 23336
Tx 8954665
VBSTLXG Ref QUA

A modern hotel with 116 bedrooms, Heathlands stands in its own grounds near the East Cliff. The most up-to-date facilities are to be found here: all rooms have en suite facilities, CTV and telephones, and there is a sauna, a solarium and a gymnasium, as well as a heated outdoor pool. Entertainment includes a weekly discothéque, and the hotel offers a special Christmas programme. Good meals (including vegetarian dishes) are available in the Bracken Restaurant, while the useful Four Seasons Coffee Shop provides snacks and drinks.

Price band C
Lunch td fr £8
Dinner td fr £9
Last dinner 8.30pm
Credit cards 1 2 3 4 5
Parking on premises

GH **Naseby Nye Hotel**
Byron Rd, Boscombe
✆ (0202) 34079

Recommended for its home-cooked food, old-world courtesy and comfortable accommodation, the Naseby Nye is a small hotel of charm and character, standing in well-kept grounds just a minute away from the cliff-top. Some of the 13 bedrooms have sea views, and all are comfortable and well-decorated. Three rooms have private bathrooms, and four are family rooms (though the hotel does not accept children under five). There is one lounge with CTV and another, set aside as a quiet room, for those who wish to read. Both are comfortably furnished and have interesting antiques, pictures and ornaments. Good English fare is served (to residents only) in the attractive dining room by proprietors Mr and Mrs Jenkins, who are always on hand to look after their guests.

Price band A
Dinner, b&b £19
Last dinner 7pm
Parking on premises

★ **New Dorchester Hotel**
64 Lansdowne Rd
✆ (0202) 21271

Here is a comfortable, quiet and friendly little hotel, situated to the north-east of Bournemouth town centre, yet easily accessible and convenient for most amenities. Five of the 10 bedrooms have private bathrooms, and the rest have toilets; two of the rooms are on the ground floor, and all of them have TV. The lounge looks out on to a secluded garden, and there is a small bar. Good home-cooked breakfast and dinner are available in the attractive dining room, and bar snacks are served, to residents only, at lunch-time. Dogs are not allowed in bedrooms, and children under 10 are not accepted.

Price band A/B
Bar lunch £1–£3
Dinner td £7
Last dinner 7pm
Credit cards 1 2 3 4 5
Parking on premises
Closed 24 Dec–2 Jan

★★★ BL
Wessex Hotel
West Cliff Rd
✆ (0202) 21911
Tx 418172 Wessex G

Convenient for both the town centre and the West Cliff, this large Victorian building is equipped with many modern amenities. All 90 of the well-decorated bedrooms have bath or shower en suite, telephones and CTV, and 15 of them are family rooms. Recreational facilities include a heated outdoor swimming pool and a snooker room, and there is also

Price band C
Bar lunch £5
Dinner td fr £11.50
Last dinner 9.30pm
Credit cards 1

a sauna. The main public rooms are an attractive open-plan lounge and an unusual bar where there is a good choice of lunch-time snacks. The dining room offers good set meals, and vegetarian dishes are available. The Wessex can accommodate disabled people, and has a lift.

[2] [3] [5]
Parking on premises

Westover Inn
(In ★★★★Palace Court Hotel)
Westover Rd
✆ (0202) 27681
Tx 418451

Our Inspector has chosen this pleasant restaurant on the first floor of the Palace Court as an ideal eating place to combine with a cinema or theatre visit. Dinner is served from 6.30pm to 10.30pm, so one can eat before or after the performance, and the hotel is close to most of Bournemouth's cinemas and theatres. The à la carte menu is good value and offers an extensive choice, including a good range of pasta dishes that can be eaten either as a starter or as a main course. Fish, steaks and chicken dishes are among the other options, and there are several interesting salads and other vegetarian dishes. The menu is supported by a sound wine list, and good house wine is available by the bottle or glass.

Lunch td £8.50
Dinner td £12.50
Last dinner 10.30pm
Credit cards [1] [2] [3] [5]
Parking on premises (charge)
Closed Sun

GH **Wood Lodge**
10 Manor Rd,
East Cliff
✆ (0202) 290891

Comfortable accommodation and a friendly atmosphere ensure that guests return repeatedly to Wood Lodge. It is in a peaceful location, convenient for both central Bournemouth and the Boscombe/Southbourne area with its shopping centre and beaches. Personally run by Mr and Mrs Grindall, the hotel offers good food and helpful service. Almost all the 15 bedrooms (including five family rooms) have en suite bath or shower, and all have CTV. Public rooms are two pleasant lounges, an unusual small bar and a very attractive dining room (guests are asked to order dinner by 6pm).

Price band A/B
Dinner, b&b £17–£21.50
Last dinner 7pm
Credit cards [1] [3]
Parking on premises
Closed Nov–Mar

BRAMHALL Greater Manchester Map 7 SJ88

× **Belmondo**
Bramhall Centre
✆ 061-439 6290

Situated in a modern shopping precinct at the centre of the village, this colourful little Italian restaurant is reputed to have been one of the first to open in the Cheshire area. Business lunches represent particularly good value and the à la carte menu offers a wide selection of pasta specialities. The wine list is predominantly Italian, though some French and German wines are featured, and service is cheerful and efficient.

Lunch td fr £3.95 or alc £13
Dinner alc £13
Last dinner 10.30pm
Credit cards [1] [2] [3] [5]
No parking on premises
Closed Sun

BRAMPTON Cumbria Map 12 NY56

❀ ★★RED ♣♣
Farlam Hall
(2¾m SE on A689)
✆ Hallbankgate (06976) 234

Originally a farmhouse dating from the 17th century, Farlam Hall was later enlarged and is now a delightful country house hotel. It stands in four acres of the most attractive gardens featuring an ornamental lake with ducks, a stream and a croquet lawn. The 13 bedrooms are individually styled and extremely comfortable, each with private facilities, CTV and many thoughtful extras. One room has a four-poster bed. The traditionally appointed public rooms are inviting, being decorated with pictures, china, bric-à-brac and

Dinner, b&b £55
Last dinner 8pm
Credit cards [1] [2] [3]
Parking on premises
Closed Feb

fresh flowers, and in winter guests may enjoy a drink beside one of the open fires. It would be difficult to find friendlier hosts than the Quinnion family who take every care over their guests' comfort. The kitchens are supervised by Barry, the son of the family, who has earned our rosette for his excellent four-course dinner which includes an especially mouthwatering display of puddings. His cooking is traditional in style but with many individual touches. Children over five years of age are welcome.

BREDWARDINE Hereford & Worcester Map 3 SO34

GH **Bredwardine Hall**
Moccas (09817) 596

A peaceful village beside the River Wye is the setting for this 19th-century manor house. Bredwardine Hall has close connections with famous local diarist the Rev Francis Kilvert (1840–79), who is buried at Bredwardine. The house was used for location filming of the TV series based on Kilvert's diaries. Aside from its literary interest, the house offers very comfortable accommodation. All five individually decorated bedrooms have CTV and tea trolleys, and three have bathrooms en suite. There is one family room. The elegant lounge has large windows overlooking the garden, while the dining room, again with garden views, has a small cocktail bar. Cooking is traditional English, using local produce as much as possible. Bredwardine Hall does not accept dogs, or children under 10.

Price band A
Dinner, b&b £19.50–£23.50
Last dinner 7.30pm
Parking on premises
Closed Dec–Feb

BRENT ELEIGH Suffolk Map 5 TL94

FH **Street Farm**
Lavenham (0787) 247271

Proprietor Mrs Gage extends a warm welcome to guests at this historic farmhouse in a quiet Suffolk village only two miles from the popular and beautiful village of Lavenham, with its magnificent guildhall and church. Street Farm has three tastefully furnished double bedrooms and one single room. The house is full of character, with beams throughout and an inglenook fireplace in the comfortable sitting room. Mrs Gage serves substantial traditional breakfasts and, though dinner is not available, she is able to recommend several small local restaurants and good public houses where guests can enjoy an evening meal. She does not take dogs, or children under 12.

Price band A
B&b only
Parking on premises
Closed Dec–Feb

BRIDGNORTH Shropshire Map 7 SO79

★ **The Croft**
(07462) 67155/6

The Croft, a Grade II listed building, stands among terraced houses and shops in a narrow side street near the historic town hall in Bridgnorth High Town. Recent improvements to this small, family-run hotel have given more rooms en suite facilities and have added a small lounge and new toilets. Friendly proprietors offer a warm welcome, and the fixed-price menu will have a chef's special dish of the day as well as such choices as crunchy pork, honey-glazed lamb, ham stuffed with peaches and whisky steak.

Price band A
Lunch td £4.50
Dinner td fr £7.95
Last dinner 9pm
Credit cards 1 3
No parking on premises

BRIDGWATER Somerset Map 3 ST33

★★★ **The Walnut Tree** North Petherton ✆ (0278) 662255	This former coaching inn on the A38 (near junction 24 of the M5) has been extensively enlarged to provide 20 well-equipped bedrooms, 14 of which are in a modern annexe. All rooms have private bathrooms, CTV and telephones and offer a high level of comfort. There is one family bedroom. Light meals, including lunch, are served in the Cottage Room restaurant, while, for a more formal lunch or dinner, an à la carte menu is available in the Sedgemoor Room. The Walnut Tree has a convivial bar, and recent improvements at the hotel have included the installation of a solarium. Dogs are not accepted.	Price band C Bar meals £2.40–£9 Dinner alc £10 Last dinner 9.45pm Credit cards [1] [2] [3] [5] Parking on premises Closed 25–31 Dec

BRIDPORT Dorset Map 3 SY49

GH **Britmead House Hotel** 154 West Bay Rd (Between Bridport and West Bay) ✆ (0308) 22941	This small, family-run guesthouse is within easy walking distance of the centre of Bridport and also convenient for the beach and West Bay harbour. Bedrooms are comfortable, attractively decorated and well-equipped. Four of the six have bathrooms en suite, and all have CTV, electric blankets and tea/coffee-making equipment. There is one family bedroom, but children must be over five years old. The hotel is licensed, and freshly prepared meals are served by proprietors Mr and Mrs Beckhelling in the cosy dining room, which is open to residents only. Dinner should be ordered by 5pm.	Price band A/B Dinner, b&b £20.75–£25.50 Last dinner 7pm Credit cards [1] [3] Parking on premises Closed Jan
★★ HL **Roundham House** Roundham Gardens, West Bay Rd (Between Bridport and West Bay) ✆ (0308) 22753	Built of mellow local stone at the turn of the century, Roundham House stands in an acre of well-tended gardens in an elevated position between Bridport and the pretty harbour of West Bay. Many rooms in this attractive little country house have views of the sea and the surrounding landscapes. There are eight comfortable bedrooms, all but one with en suite facilities and all with (optional) CTV. Three are family rooms. The hotel restaurant is open to both residents and non-residents for lunch and dinner. Menus change frequently, and are based on good home-cooked dishes using local raw materials which often include vegetables and fruit from the hotel's own garden. Vegetarian cooking is available. Roundham House holds a residential and restaurant licence, and the hall/bar is a good place for a relaxing pre-dinner drink. In fine weather, guests may enjoy the magnificent views from the terrace, which is equipped with tables and chairs. The hotel does not accept dogs.	Price band B Lunch td fr £4.75 or alc £6 Dinner td fr £8.75 or alc £10.50 Last dinner 10pm Credit card [1] Parking on premises

BRIGHTON & HOVE East Sussex Map 4 TQ30

GH **Adelaide Hotel** 51 Regency Sq ✆ (0273) 205286 Tx 877159 BHUTXSG	Shops, seafront and pier are all within easy reach of this well-appointed 11-bedroom hotel. The tastefully decorated bedrooms, two with private bathrooms and the rest with private showers and WCs, are of a good size and well-equipped. CTV, telephones, hairdriers, toiletries and tea/coffee-making equipment are provided in all the rooms, and the accommodation is	Price band B/C Dinner (by negotiation), b&b £34–£46 Credit cards [1] [2] [3] [5] No parking on

well-maintained. The ground-floor lounge, which has a writing-desk and tourist information, is supplemented by a cosy bar in the basement. The dining room is furnished in Regency style, and offers a table d'hôte dinner menu. Dogs are not accepted.

premises
Closed 22 Dec-mid Jan

★★★ B
Courtlands
22 The Drive, Hove
✆ (0273) 731055
Tx 87574

This long-established family hotel has recently been refurbished to provide more comfortable accommodation and modern facilities, but retains the best aspects of traditional hotel-keeping. Services such as early-morning tea, and evening turning-down of beds, which have disappeared from most hotels, continue to flourish here. Public rooms, such as the spacious and elegant Golden Dolphin Bar, are furnished in smart, traditional style. The Dolphin Restaurant is particularly recommended for its value-for-money set menus, but an à la carte selection is also available. Vegetarian meals can be provided. The hotel has 53 bedrooms, nearly all with private bath or shower, plus five more in an annexe in the grounds. All have telephones and CTV as well as extras such as hairdriers. Good recreational facilities are available, including a covered, heated swimming pool, a solarium and spa whirlpool bath, a children's playground and a pool table.

Price band C
Lunch fr £8.50 or alc £13.50
Dinner td fr £11.50 or alc £15
Last dinner 9.30pm
Credit cards [1] [2] [3] [5]
Limited parking on premises

Piero's
30 Spring St
✆ (0273) 29426

Worth seeking out, is this traditionally decorated Italian restaurant established 14 years ago by Piero Tinelli. It is small and the tables are close together, but the atmosphere at lunch-time is lively and good-natured, while there is romantic candlelight in the evenings. The inexpensive lunch menu provides filling wholesome dishes such as meatballs in tomato and herb sauce and profiteroles with almond cream filling. In the evenings a wider choice is offered. Vegetarian meals are available by special request. Piero's is popular with local residents, making booking advisable for both lunch and dinner.

Lunch fr £3.75
Dinner alc £10
Last dinner 10.30pm
Credit cards [1] [2] [3] [5]
Parking nearby
Closed 1 wk end Feb & 3 wks Jul-Aug
Closed Sun & Tue

GH **Twenty One**
21 Charlotte St, Marine Parade
✆ (0273) 686450

Attractive, well-equipped bedrooms (including one with a four-poster bed) make this unassuming terraced house, close to the seafront in Kemptown, an out-of-the-ordinary guesthouse. Direct-dial telephones, CTV, radios and drinks-making equipment are standard in all seven rooms, and several also have private facilities. Rooms are tastefully furnished with coordinated décor and fabrics, and are modern in style with the exception of the four-poster room, which has antique furnishings. Proprietors Mr Fargaharson and Mr Ward are very welcoming, and maintain their guesthouse well. The lounge and dining room are comfortable and elegant. Dinner is available on certain nights only, and should be ordered by noon. No children under 12 are accepted.

Price band B
Dinner, b&b £32–£49
Last dinner 8.30pm
Credit cards [1] [2] [3] [5]
Parking nearby
Closed Xmas

À la carte prices are based on an average for three courses without wine.

★★ B
Whitehaven
34 Wilbury Rd,
Hove
✆ (0273) 778355
Tx 877159
Ref: Whitehaven

Fresh, clean, well-equipped bedrooms and attractive public rooms are to be found at this family-run, modern hotel in a residential area of Hove. The whole establishment has the air of being well-looked after. The 17 bedrooms (including two family rooms and one room with a four-poster bed) are equipped with trouser-presses, radios and hairdriers as well as the more customary facilities such as CTV, tea/coffee-making equipment and telephones. They also have proper writing facilities — certainly a bonus for business travellers. Downstairs is a cosy bar and a no-smoking lounge together with the small, elegant Rolling Clock Restaurant, which offers popular set meals of excellent value, as well as an à la carte selection. Vegetarians can be catered for. The hotel does not accept dogs, or children under eight.

Price band C
Bar lunch £1.50–£6.50
Dinner td fr £10.50 or alc £14
Last dinner 9.30pm
Credit cards [1] [2] [3] [5]
Parking nearby

BRIMFIELD Shropshire Map 7 SO56

❀ × **Poppies**
(Roebuck Inn)
✆ (058472) 230

Our Inspector has been pleased to see this former simple pub dining room blossom in recent years to become a restaurant of repute which has gone on to earn an AA rosette. Cooking here has always shown flair and imagination, but the kitchen has steadily become more adventurous and more skilled, while the dining space has been upgraded and extended to handle increasing business. Recent additions to the menu have been local quails' eggs in a nest of filo pastry with hollandaise sauce, and the same pastry used in interesting vegetarian dishes. Fish and game continue to feature prominently, and farmed guinea fowl and venison appear on the menu when game is out of season. Pigeon continues to be a firm favourite with many customers. A local baker supplies the delicious rolls. The Roebuck Inn remains one of the best places in the area for bar meals. The excellent steak and kidney pie has been joined by a lamb and apricot pie, and proprietor Carole Evans has rediscovered her Scottish grandmother's recipe for a wonderful fruity chutney, which is served with the substantial ploughmans' lunches.

Bar lunch alc £5
Lunch/dinner alc £12
Last dinner 10pm
Parking on premises

BRISTOL Avon Map 3 ST57

Le Château Wine-Bar
Park St
✆ (0272) 268654

Very popular with business people at lunch-time, this bustling wine-bar is in a central shopping area. The décor has a Victorian theme, enhanced by the fine old bar counter and the iron spiral staircase leading to the basement. A comprehensive wine list accompanies the wide range of hot and cold food: hot dishes (some suitable for vegetarians) are advertised on cards at the bar, while cold dishes, including salads, pâtés, cold meats, cheeses and home-made sweets, are displayed buffet-style. The wine-bar is run by jovial proprietor Robert Lewis and his wife Denise. Recorded jazz music completes the lively atmosphere.

Bar lunch alc £1–£3.25
Lunch/dinner alc £5.25
Last dinner 8pm
Credit card [1]
No parking on premises
Closed Sun (for food), & Sat dinner

× **Edwards** 24 Alma Vale Rd, Clifton ✆ (0272) 741533	Omelettes of various kinds — often containing unusual combinations of ingredients such as banana and watercress — are a particular speciality at this simply furnished little bistro. All sorts of other interesting dishes are featured on the blackboard which lists dishes of the day, and the choice (which includes vegetarian food) is extended by a short standard menu as well. Patrons can watch the chefs at work, and service, often by John and Margot Pitchford who own and run the restaurant, is friendly and attentive. Fresh vegetables are always available, and customers love the traditional English puddings such as spotted dick or treacle tart.	Lunch/dinner alc £10.12 Last dinner 10.30pm Credit cards [1] [3] No parking on premises Closed Sun, Mon, & Sat lunch
× **Howard's** 1A Avon Cres ✆ (0272) 262921	This informal, bistro-style restaurant stands at the edge of the River Avon, close to the city's floating harbour, which is rapidly becoming a popular tourist attraction. Howard's has an established reputation, both for a fine standard of imaginative, cosmopolitan cuisine and for good service. Vegetarian dishes such as cheese fondu and cheese and spinach pancakes are also available. On a Saturday evening, live music provides an additional lure, if one were needed.	Dinner alc £13.50 Last dinner 11pm Credit card [1] No parking on premises Closed 1 wk Xmas, 2 wks summer Closed lunch

BRIXHAM Devon Map 3 SX95

★ **Smugglers Haunt** Church St ✆ (08045) 3050	This 400-year-old stone-built inn, full of history and mystique, stands next to Brixham Harbour and not far from shops. Four of its 14 cheerfully decorated bedrooms have a private bathroom, and two are suitable for family occupation. On the ground floor are an attractive bar and restaurant where good fresh 'pub standard' food is served in congenial surroundings. Vegetarian meals are available. The inn is family-run and service is friendly and enthusiastic.	Price band B Lunch alc fr £4 Dinner alc fr £8 Last dinner 9.45pm Credit cards [1] [2] [3] Limited parking on premises
× **The Elizabethan** 8 Middle St ✆ (08045) 3722	Traditional home-cooked dishes are the mainstay of this popular little restaurant near the harbour. Behind the Continental awning is a cosy, bright restaurant with Tudor-style décor. The two and three-course lunches are excellent value, and dinner, while more expensive, offers more imaginative and sophisticated dishes. Quality ingredients and local produce are used with flair in the cooking, and the food is complemented by friendly, attentive service.	Lunch td fr £4.75 Dinner alc £10.12 Last dinner 10pm Credit cards [2] [5] No parking on premises Closed Mon

BROAD MARSTON Hereford and Worcester Map 4 SP14

GH **Broad Marston Manor** ✆ Stratford-upon-Avon (0789) 720252	Broad Marston Manor, a superb 12th-century mansion built from golden Cotswold stone, stands in a peaceful hamlet half-way between Stratford and the Cotswold countryside. It offers a tranquil haven for tourists who do not wish to stay amid the bustle of Stratford, and the first sight of this guesthouse must be more than adequate compensation for the drive through winding	Price band B B&b only Parking on premises Closed Xmas

country lanes. The proprietors offer a warm welcome and delight in explaining to visitors the fascinating history of the place and its connection with Shakespeare. Meals served at an enormous circular table in a dining room with an inglenook fireplace must in themselves recall the glories of a bygone age, and in the spacious, comfortable bedrooms the furnishings include two four-poster beds. A wealth of ancient timbers, exposed beams and valuable antiques make smoking too great a hazard to be acceptable, however, which may deter some potential guests.

BROADSTAIRS Kent Map 5 TR36

The Mad Chef's Bistro
The Harbour
(Opposite Harbour office)
✆ Thanet (0843) 69304

Suitably nautical décor sets the scene for a wide selection of fresh fish and seafood at this cheerful restaurant. Tempting à la carte choices include three types of lobster ('availability subject to winds, gales, strikes etc'); bouillabaisse; crab, cockle and mussel omelette; risottos; fish pie; and a good list of vegetarian dishes, plus a children's menu. There is also a 'quickies' menu and a daily special which, on our Inspector's visit, was a healthy portion of two locally caught plaice served with French fries and salad (£2.75). For the curious, the 'Mad Chef' is Paul Ward, while Josephine Ward masterminds the front of the operation. The fully licensed dining room is simple but cosy, with a roaring log fire in winter.

Lunch/dinner alc £5.50
Last dinner 10pm
Credit cards [1] [2] [3] [5]
No parking on premises
Closed Xmas
Closed Tue lunch in winter

★★ Royal Albion Hotel
Albion St
✆ Thanet (0843) 68071
Tx 965761

Courteous and caring service are part of the traditional style of hospitality which prevails at this family-run hotel overlooking the harbour and the bay. The cosy bar and one of the two lounges have sea views, as do many of the 19 spacious and well-decorated bedrooms. All have private bathrooms, CTV with video channel, and telephones. There are three family bedrooms. Diners may choose between the hotel dining room and its adjacent independent restaurant, Marchesi's, which has been run by the family for a century. Vegetarians can be catered for. Particularly suitable for golfers, the Royal Albion is five minutes away from the golf course, and a hotel bus is available.

Price band C
Lunch td fr £8.25 or alc £14
Dinner td fr £10.50 & alc
Last dinner 9.30pm
Credit cards [1] [2] [3] [5]
Limited parking on premises

BROADWAY Hereford & Worcester Map 4 SP03

★★ ♣♣ H
Collin House Hotel
Collin Ln
✆ (0386) 858354

Set on the outskirts of this most popular of Cotswold villages, Collin House is an attractive 16th-century stone building with a pleasant garden. Popular, yet retaining a tranquil atmosphere, the hotel is personally run by owners Mr and Mrs Mills, who are usually on hand to greet guests and ensure that everything is satisfactory. All but one of the seven individually styled bedrooms have private facilities, two have four-poster beds, and CTV is available in bedrooms on request. There is an open-air swimming pool. Dinner is served in the elegant restaurant, where fresh fish is always available and the menu includes vegetarian dishes, as well as unusual meat specialities such as

Price band C
Bar lunch fr £2.50
Dinner fr £11.50
Last dinner 9pm
Credit cards [1] [3]
Parking on premises
Closed Xmas

wild rabbit in a cider and tarragon sauce or roast kid with a sauce of marjoram and red wine. Fresh local vegetables are much in evidence, and the delicious home-made ice-creams and other sweets make full use of fresh fruits from the nearby Vale of Evesham. Collin House does not accept dogs.

BROCKDISH Norfolk Map 5 TM27

❀ ××
Sheriff House
✆ Hoxne (067975) 316

The aim of Sheriff House's proprietor is to give every party the opportunity of enjoying classic French dishes which have been freshly prepared for them. Ideally, therefore, tables are booked and requirements discussed well in advance so that the freshest of ingredients may be purchased, although a 'speciality' menu does cater for the chance caller. A fine wine list, dominated by excellent clarets and burgundies, offers bottles, magnums and double magnums, while an extensive collection of cognacs dates back as far as 1802.

Lunch/dinner alc fr £7
Last dinner 9.30pm
Credit cards [1] [3]
Parking on premises
Closed Wed

BROCKENHURST Hampshire Map 4 SU20

★★★ L
Carey's Manor
Lyndhurst Rd
✆ (0590) 23551
Tx 47442

King Charles II was an early guest at this historic manor, in the days when it was used as a hunting lodge. Today Carey's Manor is a large and very popular hotel with up-to-the-minute facilities including an excellent leisure centre with indoor, heated swimming pool, solarium, gymnasium, sauna and whirlpool bath. Professionally managed keep-fit programmes are run here, and more sedate pursuits at the hotel include croquet and putting. There is dancing on Fridays and Saturdays. Relaxation is invited in the spacious, very attractive beamed lounge, which has a polished pine floor and a feature fireplace. There is a good, rather small restaurant where both à la carte and fixed-price menus are available. The kitchen uses fresh, quality ingredients, and attentive service is by professionally supervised young staff. Most of the 80 bedrooms are in the modern garden wing, which is linked to the main hotel by a covered walkway. These rooms are modern, spacious and well-equipped. All bedrooms have private bathrooms and are provided with CTV, telephones, hairdriers, trouser-presses and bathrobes. Twenty-two rooms are reserved for non-smokers, and there are four splendid four-poster rooms.

Price band C/D
Lunch td fr £9 or alc £15
Dinner td fr £15 or alc £17
Last dinner 10pm
Credit cards [1] [2] [3] [5]
Parking on premises

×× **Le Poussin**
57–9 Brookley Rd
✆ Lymington (0590) 23063

This top-class restaurant continues to maintain its high standards. Proprietors Alex and Caroline Aitken and their capable staff specialise in producing inventive dishes using the best of local produce in season, including game. Mr Aitken's sauces are especially good. Our Inspector has chosen Le Poussin for inclusion in this guide particularly on account of the excellent value it offers, both in its regularly held gourmet evenings and in its new venture into the bed and breakfast trade. For a very reasonable inclusive price, the gourmet evenings offer a four or five-course

Price band A
Lunch td fr £8.95 and alc
Dinner td (gourmet evenings) fr £15 or alc £21
Last dinner 10.30pm
Credit cards [1] [3]

set menu with a suitable wine to accompany each course. Examples of dishes from a recent gourmet dinner here include ratatouille terrine, pastry puff of mussels in an aromatic turmeric sauce, and guinea fowl with lime sauce. Sometimes these evenings have a special theme, such as a recent 'Evening of Traditional Fayre', when steak, kidney and oyster pudding was the main course. For the bed and breakfast side of their business, the Aitkens let five tastefully furnished rooms, all with bathroom or shower en suite.

Parking nearby
Closed Sun & Mon lunch

BROME Suffolk Map 5 TM17

★★ BL
Oaksmere Hotel
Eye (0379) 870326

Originally a Tudor dower house to Brome Hall, the Oaksmere Hotel stands in 20 acres of parkland on the Suffolk/Norfolk border. Several of its rooms have pleasant views over the gardens, which include some fine examples of topiary. The elegant lounge and fine Victorian conservatory are comfortably furnished, and an illuminated well in the beamed bar is a point of interest. Spacious, individually decorated bedrooms feature period furniture and are equipped to a high standard. The modern menu in the dining room changes every two months and includes such interesting dishes as spiced smoked leg of lamb with old-fashioned fruit butter, and delicious puddings like pancakes filled with hot pear soufflé and served on a raspberry sauce.

Price band C
Lunch td £8.95 or alc £14.50
Dinner alc £14.50
Last dinner 9.30pm
Credit cards [1] [2] [3] [5]
Parking on premises

BROMPTON-BY-SAWDON North Yorkshire Map 8 SE98

× **Brompton Forge**
(Alongside A170 between Scarborough and Pickering)
Scarborough (0723) 85409

This picturesque and very popular restaurant, once the blacksmith's shop, has had the excellence of its cuisine recognised by an AA rosette award for many years, and its fixed-price menus offer particularly good value. Because it is so close to Scarborough, seafood figures prominently among the dishes featured, but choice is wide and you could also enjoy lambs' sweetbreads in a cream and Marsala sauce, Stilton pâté with fennel and tomato salad or mushrooms in garlic butter with smoked bacon — and these are just starters! The food is attractively presented, generously served by attentive staff and complemented by an interesting and well-chosen wine list.

Lunch td fr £8 or alc £15
Dinner td fr £12 or alc £18
Last dinner 9pm
Parking on premises
Closed 2 wks Feb
Closed Mon, Tue, Fri, Sat lunch & Sun dinner

BROMYARD Hereford & Worcester Map 3 SO65

× **The Old Penny**
High St
(0885) 83227

Norman Williams welcomes customers, while his wife June does the cooking, at this popular little restaurant. The welcome is helped along by a posy of fresh flowers on each lace-covered table and by the bowl of crudités offered to diners with their aperitifs. The set-price dinner menu is short but offers good variety; try, for example, grilled mushrooms stuffed with garlic, followed by veal in tarragon sauce with a selection of crunchy fresh vegetables. Puddings are on a separate menu, and include Barbados cream, a delicious blend of yogurt, cream and demerara sugar. Coffee is served with a mouthwatering selection of home-made sweets such as white chocolate fudge or meringues. Wines are

Lunch td fr £5.50
Dinner td £11
Last dinner 9pm
Credit cards [1] [2] [3]
No parking on premises
Closed 2 wks Nov
Closed Mon & Tue

reasonably priced. The Old Penny does traditional roast Sunday lunch, which is very popular, so booking is essential. A short set lunch menu is available from Thursday to Saturday inclusive.

BRUNTINGTHORPE Leicestershire Map 4 SP68

Joiners Arms
✆ Peatling Magna
(053758) 258

Well off the beaten track, at the centre of this quaint Leicestershire village, stands the Joiners Arms, a cosy English pub where you will find some of the best food in the area. The restaurant has become very popular with local people, so it is advisable to book a table in advance, and Sunday lunch is by reservation only. You will be made to feel welcome as soon as you enter the lively, bustling atmosphere, and a meal here is a thoroughly enjoyable experience.

Dinner alc £8
Last dinner 10pm
Parking on premises
Closed lunch except Sun

BUCKLERS HARD Hampshire Map 4 SU40

★★ The Master Builder's House
✆ Brockenhurst
(0590) 63253

This comfortable hotel enjoys a lovely location at the head of Bucklers Hard, a perfectly preserved 18th-century shipbuilding hamlet where the New Forest meets the Beaulieu River. It was formerly the home of master shipbuilder Henry Adams (1713–1805); more about him can be discovered in the village's fascinating maritime museum. Today the original house contains six bedrooms while 17 more are in a modern extension. Most have bathrooms, and all rooms have CTV, radios and telephones. Families are welcome, and cots can be provided. Sweeping views of the Beaulieu River are a feature of the restaurant, where standards of cooking are reliable and food is skilfully prepared. Both à la carte and fixed-price menus are available, and vegetarian meals can be provided. The hotel has good facilities for small conferences.

Price band B
Lunch/dinner td fr £7.95 or alc £12
Last dinner 9.45pm
Credit cards [1] [2] [3] [5]
Parking on premises

BURFORD Oxfordshire Map 4 SP21

GH Corner House Hotel
High St
✆ (099382) 3151

Just off the A40, in Burford's attractive High Street, stands this Cotswold stone house which dates back to the 15th century. The nine bedrooms all have private facilities and CTV, and there are two family rooms. Furnishings include many antiques, which complement the character of the building. Public rooms are a comfortable lounge, a cocktail bar and a licensed restaurant. Meals are mainly grills and traditional English fare, and a reasonably priced wine list is available. Service is by friendly, helpful staff under the guidance of the proprietor Mr Carlton.

Price band B
Lunch alc £5
Dinner alc £7
Last dinner 9pm
No parking on premises
Closed Nov–Feb

★★ The Golden Pheasant
High St
✆ (099382) 3223
Tx 849041

Parts of this attractive old house can be traced back to the 14th and 15th centuries. Now a well-equipped and charming small hotel, the Golden Pheasant has a bustling, beamed restaurant which is open most of the day for meals and refreshments. All 12 bedrooms have private facilities, CTV and telephones as well as welcome extras like radios and hairdriers. Fresh flowers add a homely touch. One of the rooms has a 17th-century four-poster bed. The hotel runs a special Christmas programme.

Price band B/C
Lunch td fr £6.95 or alc £9.50
Dinner td £11.75 or alc £15.75
Last dinner 9.30pm
Credit cards [1] [3]
Parking on premises

BURNHAM MARKET Norfolk Map 9 TF84

× **Fishes**
Market Place
✆ Fakenham (0328) 738588

The freshest of seafood from the nearby fishing ports of north Norfolk, as well as locally reared shellfish and home-smoked fish and meat, are the specialities at this pleasant, informal restaurant. As befits the freshness of all the ingredients, cooking is without any hint of fussiness and is in a light, modern style. The wine list has been carefully chosen to complement seafood, and its prices are modest. Fishes also offers counter sales of fish, meat, pâtés, etc from 10.30am to 12 noon.

Lunch td fr £6.80
Dinner alc £12
Last dinner 9.30pm
Credit cards [1] [2] [3] [5]
No parking on premises
Closed Xmas & 3 wks end Jan
Closed Mon & Sun dinner in winter

BURY ST EDMUNDS Suffolk Map 5 TL86

★★★ HBL
Angel Hotel
Angel Hill
✆ (0284) 3926
Tx 81630 (ANGEL G)

Situated in the centre of this medieval town, the Angel looks across the square to the ruins of St Edmund's Abbey, set in attractive gardens. Travellers have been served here for more than 500 years, and illustrious past clients have included Charles Dickens, after whom one of the rooms is named. Five luxurious four-poster rooms and a large, comfortable suite are among the 39 individually designed bedrooms, which have steadily been upgraded to provide more comfort. All have private bathrooms, CTV and telephones. The public rooms have recently been refurbished to a high standard, and good food is served in both the Regency Restaurant and the Medieval Vaults. The imposing creeper-clad hotel is well-known locally for its literary dinners and musical evenings, and a more recent attraction is the tea-time harp and piano recitals on certain days.

Price band D
Lunch td fr £12 or alc £15
Dinner td fr £12.50 or alc £15
Last dinner 9.45pm
Credit cards [1] [2] [3] [5]
Parking on premises

BYWORTH West Sussex Map 4 SU92

Black Horse Inn
✆ Petworth (0798) 42424

Outwardly an unassuming country pub, this free house has a very pleasant rustic interior where customers can choose from a range of hand-pulled real ales and an even wider selection of food. There are several dining areas, including one upstairs which is not to be missed for its outstanding views. Scrubbed pine tables, bare floorboards, beams, and a large collection of old sepia photographs lend the whole pub something of the atmosphere of a country inn of bygone days. Meals here can be as simple as a ploughman's lunch, or as ambitious as a three-course feast of, perhaps, courgette and prawn au gratin, or fresh mussels in white wine, followed by duck with cherry brandy sauce, with a choice of sweet that includes ice-creams and sorbets of 15 different flavours. Reasonably priced 'chef's daily specials' are advertised on blackboards. The wine list is modest but quite adequate, and includes a choice of house wines that are available by the bottle or by the glass. The Black Horse is understandably popular, and reservations are recommended in the evening.

Lunch/dinner alc £5.65
Last dinner 9.45pm
Credit cards [1] [2] [3] [5]
Parking on premises

CADNAM Hampshire Map 4 SU21

FH **Budd's Farm**
Winsor Rd, Winsor
(2m NE of Cadnam on unclassified rd)
☎ Southampton (0703) 812381

Here, on the edge of the New Forest, a high standard of bed and breakfast accommodation is offered by members of the Dawes family at Budd's Farm and neighbouring Kent's Farm (see below). Budd's Farm, a whitewashed, thatched building with a pretty cottage garden, stands next to its farmyard. There are two letting bedrooms, including one family room. Both have washbasins, and share a pine-panelled bathroom with modern fittings. The bedrooms are comfortably furnished in pine, and have duvets on the beds. Downstairs, both lounge and dining room have wood-burning stoves which keep the house cosy. The lounge has large, relaxing armchairs, CTV, and plenty of books and games. Breakfast is served in the dining room, which is furnished with antique pine. No other meals are served. Budd's Farm does not accept dogs.

Price band A
Parking on premises
Closed Nov–Mar

FH **Kent's Farm**
Winsor Rd, Winsor
☎ Southampton (0703) 813497

A beautiful flower garden surrounds this lovely thatched farmhouse built of rose-pink bricks — an idyllic English rural scene. As at neighbouring Budd's Farm (see above), the interior is not a disappointment: exposed beams, inglenook fireplaces, antique furniture and a homely atmosphere complete the picture. Recently renovated, the farmhouse offers comfortable, tasteful accommodation. Two bedrooms (one of them a family room) each have bath or shower en suite, and are nicely furnished, with duvets and pretty bedlinen. The cosy lounge has a wood-burning stove, comfortable sofas and easy chairs, and CTV. There is also a separate dining room. Mrs Dawes the friendly and very helpful proprietor, cooks breakfasts farmhouse-style on the Aga. No other meals are served. Kent's Farm does not take children under two, or dogs.

Price band A
Parking on premises
Closed Oct–Apr

CALLANDER Central *Perthshire* Map 11 NN60

★ HL **Bridgend House**
Bridgend
☎ (0877) 30130

This small hotel on the road to Glasgow, close to the town centre and River Teith, is owned by affable hosts Bill and Pauline Thomson, who work hard to ensure their guests are comfortable and well-looked after. Meals are home-made and good, and make use of excellent local produce. A bonus in the smartly furnished dining room is the lovely view to the rear of the hotel, across the gardens and towards Ben Ledi. Other public rooms, all tastefully decorated, are two bars and a comfortable beamed lounge, which has leather chairs and an open fire. There are five attractive and well-equipped first-floor bedrooms with bath or shower en suite and CTV, and two further, simpler, rooms on the floor above.

Price band A
Lunch alc £4
Dinner alc £12
Last dinner 9.30pm
Credit cards [1] [2] [3] [5]
Parking on premises

GH **Highland House Hotel**
☎ (0877) 30269

Though it occupies a quiet position in a side street, this quiet little private hotel is not far away from the main road through the popular touring centre of Callander. It offers bedrooms which are clean, well-

Price band A
Dinner, b&b £21.50–£23.25
Last dinner

decorated and furnished in the modern style, together with comfortable and attractive public rooms. Guests can relax in the lounge with its CTV and good selection of reading materials, or congregate to chat in the cosy little bar. The establishment's reputation for warm and friendly service is being successfully maintained by its new proprietors, Mr and Mrs Cooper.

7.30pm
No parking on premises
Closed mid Nov–mid Mar

★ HBL **Lubnaig Hotel**
Leny Feus (off A84)
☏(0877) 30376

Peacefully tucked away off the main road, this 10-bedroom hotel stands in carefully tended gardens surrounded by pine trees. All bedrooms have private facilities, including the four rooms in the annexe, and two family rooms. There are two lounges, one has restful country house-style décor and furnishings and is equipped with CTV, games, books and magazines. The other, the beamed lounge-bar, overlooking the garden, is where guests gather before dinner. The dining room is compact but smartly decorated, and meals are always freshly prepared. At dinner there is always a good selection of starters and sweets, though the choice of main courses is limited. The hotel does not accept children under seven.

Price band B
Dinner td £10
Last dinner 7.30pm
Parking on premises
Closed Nov–Easter

★★★ ♣♣ BL
Roman Camp
☏ (0877) 30003

A peaceful location on the banks of the River Teith, and 20 acres of lovely gardens, help to ensure a relaxing atmosphere at this former hunting lodge, which dates back to 1625. The furnishings and décor are in keeping with the château-style architecture of the turreted building, and everything is planned with comfort in mind. The 14 bedrooms (including two family rooms) have en suite facilities, CTV and telephones, and are all elegantly and individually furnished. Three lounges include a sun lounge and a lovely panelled library, and all overlook the river, where guests are welcome to fish. The restaurant, which features an unusual painted ceiling based on 16th-century Scottish designs, serves excellent food prepared by chef/proprietor Mr Denzler. Menus are short but feature the best of local produce such as beef, venison and lamb.

Price band C
Lunch td fr £9.50
Dinner td fr £17.50
Last dinner 8.45pm
Parking on premises
Closed mid Nov–mid Mar

CANNICH Highland *Inverness-shire* Map 14 NH33

★★ ♣♣ HBL
Cozac Lodge
Glen Cannich
(8m W of Cannich)
☏ (04565) 263

Here, amid rugged Highland scenery, a small hotel of much charm and character has been created out of a former hunting lodge. Tasteful furnishings and superb views are features of public areas and bedrooms alike. Each of the seven bedrooms (including one family room) has its own facilities and is furnished in individual style, with some fine antiques. CTV is provided in all rooms. Fresh floral displays add to the appeal of the comfortable public rooms, which have a friendly, tranquil atmosphere. Food in the well-appointed dining room is varied and imaginative, and service is good. The hotel has its own garden, and fishing is available. Children under eight are not accepted.

Price band B
Lunch td fr £6
Dinner td £14.50
Last dinner 8.30pm
Credit cards [1] [2] [3]
Parking on premises
Closed Nov–Mar (except Xmas and New Year)

CANONBIE Dumfries & Galloway *Dumfriesshire* Map 11 NY37

❀ ★ HBL
Riverside Inn
✆ (05415) 512

A warm welcome, well-equipped bedrooms and excellent food await guests at this 17th-century stone house three miles north of the English border. Proprietors Mr and Mrs Phillips and their small staff have overlooked no detail: bedrooms are even provided with fruit, home-made biscuits and sweets. The six bedrooms (including two in an annexe), all with private facilities and CTV, have a wealth of country charm, and public rooms are in the same vein. Low, beamed ceilings and stone fireplaces are set off by thoughtfully coordinated soft furnishings and well-chosen antiques and bric-à-brac, including framed prints and burnished brassware. Dinner is prepared by Mr Phillips, whose impressive dishes, such as baked mushroom cheesecake, or crispy roast duck with fresh cranberry sauce, have earned the Riverside Inn our rosette. Vegetables are fresh and varied, and local produce is used wherever possible.

Price band C
Bar lunch £5.50
Dinner alc £14.50
Last dinner 8.30pm
Credit cards [1] [3]
Parking on premises
Closed end Feb, 1st wk Nov

CANON PYON Hereford & Worcester Map 3 SO44

GH **Hermitage Manor**
✆ Hereford (0432) 760317

At the heart of rural Herefordshire, yet within easy reach of its busy city, this stone-built manor house offers the ideal location for a peaceful, relaxing holiday. Backed by wooded hills, its setting is breathtaking, with a panoramic view over some four-hundred square miles of countryside. Bedrooms have been refurbished to a high standard, and an air of luxury pervades the elegant lounges and dining room. You may choose to stay on a bed and breakfast basis or to rent one of the self-catering apartments, either way your break should prove as refreshing as the natural spring water that supplies the house.

Price band B
Parking on premises
Closed Jan–Feb

CANTERBURY Kent Map 5 TR15

Cogan House
53 St Peter's St
(Over Joanna Gray's shoe shop)
✆ (0227) 472986

Morning coffee, lunches, teas, theatre suppers, dinners and snacks are all served at this 'English brasserie', which is open from 10.30am to 10.30pm. Cogan House is of medieval origin (first documented in the year 1170), and retains many old features such as carved oak panelling, flagstones and exposed beams which give the restaurant a distinctly historic atmosphere. As to food, one can choose anything from a simple snack to a full meal, safe in the knowledge that only quality, fresh ingredients are used and that cooking is interesting and of a high standard. The more unusual dishes on offer might include duck liver and orange pâté, or a puff-pastry case filled with mushrooms in a creamy sauce, while old favourites such as steak, kidney and mushroom pie, or jacket potatoes with a variety of fillings, are equally good. Look out for the specialities of the day, advertised on blackboards. Service is friendly and efficient. Cogan House holds a restaurant licence.

Lunch/dinner td £7 & alc
Last dinner 10.30pm
Credit cards [1] [3]
Parking nearby
Closed 25–6 Dec & 1 Jan
Closed Mon

GH **Ebury Hotel**
65–7 New Dover Rd
✆ (0227) 68433

Three acres of well-kept grounds surround this gabled Victorian house, yet it is within easy walking distance of the city centre and its historic visitor attractions. The 17 spacious and comfortable bedrooms, including six family rooms, all have private facilities, CTV and tea/coffee-making equipment. There is a large lounge, and a licensed restaurant, open daily for lunch and dinner, which offers home cooking of a high standard. The hotel is family-run, and service is always pleasant and efficient. Children are welcome.

Price band B
Dinner, b&b £19–£29
Dinner td fr £8.50
Last dinner 8.30pm
Credit cards [1] [2] [3]
Parking on premises
Closed 2 wks Jan

★★★
Falstaff Hotel
St Dunstan's St
✆ (0227) 462138

This former coaching inn, dating back to the 14th century, stands just outside the city's ancient Westgate. Convenient for the cathedral and the town centre, it has 25 comfortable bedrooms, most of them not large, but well-appointed and all with CTV, telephones and bath or shower en suite. Two are family rooms, and two have four-poster beds. Public rooms are full of character: the two-section lounge has a fireplace and exposed beams, and both the bars and the beamed and panelled restaurant have an equally warm, cheerful atmosphere. Continental and English cooking of a high standard (including vegetarian dishes) is available in the restaurant, where meals are served by helpful and enthusiastic young staff. The hotel does not accept dogs (except guide dogs).

Price band C
Lunch td £6.75
Dinner td £8.25
Last dinner 9.45pm
Credit cards [1] [2] [3] [5]
Parking on premises

GH **Magnolia House**
36 St Dunstans Ter
(Off London Rd)
✆ (0227) 65121

Quietly situated in a peaceful residential area near the Westgate Towers, this homely guesthouse offers well-maintained accommodation, friendly service and marvellous value for money. The six bedrooms have been tastefully modernised and thoughtfully designed to make the most of the limited space available. Three family rooms are equipped with bunk-beds, and all rooms have washbasins. Furnishings are of good quality and décor bright and attractively coordinated. There is a TV in the small front lounge, and freshly cooked English breakfasts are served in a separate, larger breakfast room furnished in pine. No other meals are available. Magnolia House does not accept dogs.

Price band A
Limited parking on premises

❀ ×× **Restaurant Seventy-Four**
74 Wincheap
✆ (0277) 767411

A tastefully decorated, historic house with a convivial atmosphere provides the backdrop to Ian McAndrew's excellent cuisine at this cosy little restaurant. Cooking and presentation combine artistic flair with a skill in matching top-quality ingredients to achieve a beautiful balance of textures and flavours. Mr McAndrew's style, influenced by the ideas of Nouvelle Cuisine, shows great originality and imagination. The menu might include main courses such as fillet of lamb served with sautéed sliced scallops and scallop mousseline, or roast chicken breasts studded with foie gras and truffle, served with a chicken forcemeat and truffle sauce. Sweets are equally unusual: try the individual walnut tart with home-made orange and Cointreau ice-cream, or a 'dessert of three chocolates':

Lunch td fr £10.50
Dinner td fr £22 or alc £23
Last dinner 9.30pm
Credit cards [1] [2] [3] [5]
Limited parking on premises
Closed 26–30 Dec, 1 wk Easter, 2 wks Sep & Bank Hols
Closed Sun

a dark chocolate marquise, a white chocolate mousse and a milk chocolate ice-cream. Aperitifs (with complimentary appetisers), and coffee, are served in a pleasant lounge.

Il Vaticano Pasta Parlour
35 St Margaret's St
✆ (0227) 65333

You can certainly taste the difference at this small, lively Italian restaurant where all the pasta is freshly made on the premises. Customers choose their own dishes from a reasonably priced range of five types of pasta and nine sauces ranging from well-known bolognese to a more unusual one consisting of seafood in Pernod and cream. Other Italian favourites such as traditional home-made minestrone, Parma ham, lasagne, and cannelloni also appear on the simple menu. Sweets include a good range of Italian ice-creams as well as the day's specialities written on a blackboard. Coffee — of course — is either espresso or cappuccino, and there is a selection of Italian wines that includes red and white house wine. Seating can be a little cramped — the pasta parlour is understandably popular with tourists and locals alike. Tables are simple, but the packaged Grissini and fresh flowers add a nice touch. Service is friendly and attentive.

Lunch/dinner alc £6.40
Last dinner 11pm
Credit cards [1] [3] [5]
Parking nearby

CARDIFF South Glamorgan Map 3 ST17

❀ × **La Chaumière**
Cardiff Rd,
Llandaff
✆ (0222) 555319

Cliff and Kay Morgan, proprietors of this small new restaurant close to the cathedral at Llandaff, are well known to our Inspectors from their days at Mr Midgley's in Usk. Kay's culinary expertise, in the modern French style but tempered by her own distinct originality and flair, is now the driving force behind the menu here at La Chaumière. Her commendable food is admirably complemented by a warm welcome and hospitable attention from her husband. Some fine French wines are included on a small but reasonably priced list. Vegetarian meals are available

Lunch/dinner alc £15
Last dinner 9.30pm
Credit cards [1] [2] [5]
Parking on premises
Closed 1st 2 wks Jan
Closed Mon & Sun dinner

CARRBRIDGE Highland *Inverness-shire* Map 14 NH92

GH Carrmoor
Carr Rd
✆ (047984) 244

Tucked away in a narrow lane just off the main street is this delightful little cottage. Mrs Elizabeth Caldwell is a friendly and welcoming hostess, giving personal attention to the comfort of her guests. The four letting bedrooms are bright, airy and full of character. They include one family room. No charge is made for many extras such as use of hairdriers, drying and ironing facilities, baby-listening or special diets. The comfortable residents' lounge is well-furnished, and has interesting bric-à-brac, a log fire, and a good selection of local literature. Mrs Caldwell serves good breakfasts and dinners in the quaint, low-ceilinged dining room. Dinner is available to residents only, and should be ordered by 5.30pm. Carrmoor is licensed.

Price band A
Dinner, b&b £15
Last dinner 7pm
Parking on premises

CARTMEL Cumbria Map 7 SD37

❀ ××
Uplands Country House Hotel
Haggs Lane
✆ (044854) 248/9

Opened in 1985 by John Tovey, proprietor/chef of the well-known Miller Howe Hotel at Windermere, Uplands has quickly established itself as one of the leading hotels and restaurants in Southern Lakeland. It is run by Tom and Diana Peter, who worked for 12 years at Miller Howe, and is very much in the same style. As one would expect, the welcome is warm and the food superb — Tom Peter was one of John Tovey's head cooks. Four-course dinners are excellent value, offering a range of inventive combinations of flavours, from tomato, apple and celery soup to wood pigeon with pear purée and lemon thyme sauce. A lighter, three-course lunch is available, and menus are changed daily. Uplands has only four bedrooms, but all are prettily decorated and well-equipped, with private facilities, telephones, TV, hairdriers, clocks and books. Public rooms are bright and fresh, tasteful in their décor of pink, grey and blue with coordinated furnishings. Impressionist prints complement the fine views from the comfortable lounge. Uplands does not accept children under 12.

Lunch td £9.50
Dinner td £16
Last dinner 8pm
Credit cards [1] [2]
Parking on premises
Closed 2 Jan–25 Feb

CATLOWDY Cumbria Map 12 NY47

FH **Bessiestown Farm**
✆ Nicholforest (022877) 219

Mr and Mrs Sissons offer ideal family holiday accommodation in a happy, friendly atmosphere here on their busy working farm. The seven bedrooms are individually decorated and attractively furnished, and all of them have private bath or shower. Two are family rooms. Downstairs, the large, quiet lounge has its own small bar, and there is also a snug TV lounge. Mr Sissons provides excellent home-cooked dinner and breakfast in the pleasant dining room. Guests are asked to order dinner by 4pm. Leisure facilities are good: there is a heated indoor swimming pool (summer only), a games room and a children's play area, and horse-riding is also available.

Price band A
Last dinner 7pm
Parking on premises

CHADDESLEY CORBETT Hereford & Worcester Map 7 SO87

★★★ BL
Brockencote Hall
✆ (056283) 876
Tx 333431 BROHAL

This elegant country residence, rather in the style of a French château, stands in 70 acres of landscaped parkland. Young proprietors Mr and Mrs Petitjean have worked hard here to create stylish accommodation and a relaxed, friendly atmosphere. The nine bedrooms all have en suite facilities, and the public rooms are warm and welcoming. A bright, smart conservatory leads through to the dining room, where the cuisine shows influences from both sides of the Channel. Herbs and fruit are used interestingly to complement the flavours of many dishes. The set lunch menu is becoming increasingly popular.

Price band C/D
Lunch td fr £10.50 or alc £13
Dinner alc £15
Last dinner 9.30pm
Credit cards [1] [2] [3] [5]
Parking on premises
Closed end Dec–mid Jan

CHAGFORD Devon Map 3 SX78

★★★ HL
Mill End Hotel
Sandy Park
(2m N of Chagford on A382)
✆ (06473) 2282

This former water mill on the River Teign is set in beautiful countryside and makes an ideal base for fishing, golf, riding or exploring Dartmoor. Proprietors Mr and Mrs Craddock and their staff take a personal interest in the well-being of their guests, and pride themselves particularly on their food. The dinner menu is changed daily, and dishes are freshly prepared from good raw materials, using no short cuts. The hotel has a table licence, and there is a small bar. Most of the 17 bedrooms (including two family rooms) have private bathrooms, and all have CTV and telephones, and are generally of a high standard. Well-behaved dogs are welcome, but are not allowed in public rooms.

Price band B
Lunch/dinner td £15
Last dinner 9pm
Credit cards 1 2 3 5
Parking on premises
Closed 18–28 Dec

CHANNEL ISLANDS Map 16
GUERNSEY FERMAIN BAY

★★ **La Favorita**
✆ Guernsey (0481) 35666

This 48-bedroom holiday hotel is a converted country house, attractively sited in a quiet location overlooking a wooded valley which leads to Fermain Bay. A modern wing has been added to extend the accommodation, all of which is comfortable and well-equipped. Most of the bedrooms, which include six family rooms, have private facilities, and all have CTV and telephones, and the hotel can accommodate disabled persons. Public rooms are well-appointed and comfortable, with open fires in the lounges in winter, and there is a smart bar which offers a selection of light meals. Vegetarians can be catered for. The hotel permits dogs at an additional charge.

Price band B
Bar lunch alc £4.50
Dinner td £8 or alc £12
Last dinner 9.30pm
Credit cards 1 2 3 4 5
Parking on premises
Closed end Oct–mid April

ST MARTIN

★★★ **Green Acres**
Les Hubits
✆ Guernsey (0481) 35711

A quiet inland area in the parish of St Martin is the setting for this attractive hotel, which stands in its own gardens and has a heated outdoor swimming pool and a solarium. Holidaymakers are ensured comfortable accommodation: all 48 bedrooms have en suite facilities, CTV and telephones, and are attractively furnished. Three are family rooms. The lounges are well-appointed and comfortable, and there is a pleasant bar, where light lunches are available. There is also a full meals service in the air-conditioned restaurant. Service at Green Acres is friendly and helpful, and, in our Inspector's opinion, the hotel offers good value for money. It is open all year, and offers a special Christmas programme. Dogs are not accepted at the hotel.

Price band B
Lunch td £5.50
Dinner td £7 or alc £11
Last dinner 8.30pm
Credit cards 1 3
Parking on premises

ST PETER PORT

★★★ **La Collinette**
St Jacques
✆ Guernsey (0481) 710331

Within easy reach of the island's main town, La Collinette offers either full hotel accommodation, or self-catering holidays in a number of modern bungalows in the grounds. The hotel's 27 bedrooms have been refurbished to a high standard, and all are equipped with CTV, telephones and private facilities. The pleasant, split-level restaurant offers either a

Price band A/B
Lunch td £5
Dinner td £7
Last dinner 8.30pm
Credit cards 1 2 3 5

fixed-price menu with some choice of dishes, or a well-planned à la carte selection: both represent good value for money, and restaurant staff are friendly and attentive. Other public rooms include an attractive bar and a comfortable lounge. La Collinette has a heated outdoor swimming pool, a solarium and a sauna. Dogs are accepted, and children are welcome.

Parking on premises

❀ ★★★ **La Frégate Hotel**
Les Côtils
✆ Guernsey (0481) 24624

This converted 17th-century manor house enjoys an elevated position in scented, terraced gardens in a quiet corner of St Peter Port. The 13 nicely refurbished bedrooms all have bathrooms en suite, and telephones, and most have a comfortable seating area for breakfast, which is normally served in rooms. A staircase with a fine timbered ceiling leads to a small lounge and spacious, well-appointed lounge-bar. The attractive restaurant not only serves excellent food but also offers wonderful views, through picture windows, over the harbour and out towards the offshore islands. The restaurant is understandably popular, and booking is essential. A comprehensive à la carte menu of interesting, well-cooked dishes is supplemented by a short list of daily specialities. The seafood is particularly recommended by our Inspector, but everything on the menu is freshly prepared from good raw materials. Vegetarians can be catered for. Service throughout the hotel is pleasant and competent. La Frégate does not accept dogs, or children under 14.

Price band B/C
Lunch td fr £7.50 or alc £14
Dinner td £11.50 or alc £18
Last dinner 9.30pm
Credit cards [1] [2] [3] [4] [5]
Parking on premises

××× **Le Nautique**
Quay Steps
✆ Guernsey (0481) 21714

Fine views of the harbour and its elegant yachts are a bonus at this converted waterside warehouse, now a very popular restaurant. The interior, beamed and with stone walls, is comfortably furnished, and the décor is suitably nautical. There is a small but well-stocked bar, where diners can enjoy an aperitif while choosing from the comprehensive à la carte menu. Food is skilfully cooked and attractively presented; fresh local fish and shellfish are the specialities, and the vegetables are crisp and fresh. Service is friendly and efficient. Children under five are not admitted.

Lunch/Dinner alc £14
Last dinner 10pm
Credit cards [1] [2] [3] [5]
No parking on premises
Closed 1st 2 wks Jan
Closed Sun

★★★★
St Pierre Park
Rohais
✆ Guernsey (0481) 28282
Tx 4191146

Guernsey's newest hotel is a resort in itself. The large and luxurious St Pierre Park stands in 40 acres of grounds and has it own nine-hole golf course, three tennis courts, a heated indoor pool and a shopping arcade. Every amenity is provided, from a beauty salon to a gymnasium, and the parkland includes a lake and a small bird sanctuary. There are three restaurants: the Brasserie (by the pool), the La Fontaine hotel dining room and the elegant Victor Hugo Restaurant. Entertainment includes regular dinner dances and cabaret or a discothèque every night. The hotel has 125 well-equipped modern bedrooms, all with balconies, private bathrooms, CTV, baby listening and telephones. In addition there are several private suites. Public rooms, including the bars, are spacious and comfortable. Offering good conference facilities, the St Pierre Park is as popular with business people as it is with holidaymakers. Dogs are not accepted.

Price band C
Lunch td £6.50 & alc
Dinner £10
Last dinner 10pm
Credit cards [1] [2] [3] [5]
Parking on premises

CHANNEL ISLANDS Map 16

JERSEY CORBIÈRE

××× **Sea Crest**
Restaurant
Petit Port
(On B44, N of Corbière Point and lighthouse)
✆ Jersey (0534) 46353/6

This popular hotel restaurant is near the spectacular rugged coastline of Corbière in the island's south-western corner. Our Inspector found the three-course fixed-price lunch menu here particularly good value for money; dishes are interesting and a reasonable choice is offered. For a more special lunch or dinner there is also an à la carte menu, including some good fish dishes and freshly cooked pasta specialities. Sweets from the trolley are mouthwatering; our Inspector particularly enjoyed the Italian trifle called 'Pick-me-up'. On Sundays a traditional roast lunch is served. Vegetarian meals are available. Service is competent and professional, by smartly uniformed staff under the proprietor's supervision. The restaurant is bright and well-appointed, and there is a comfortable lounge-bar with fine views of the bay.

Lunch td £7.50 or alc £15
Dinner alc £17.50
Last dinner 10pm
Credit cards [1] [2] [3] [4]
Parking on premises
Closed Mon (Nov–Mar only), & Sun dinner

GOREY

Jersey Pottery Restaurant
✆ Jersey (0534) 51119

The showrooms and attractive gardens of the Jersey Pottery are a popular tourist attraction. An excellent restaurant forms part of the complex. It includes both an indoor cafeteria and a delightful vine-hung patio restaurant where the tempting menu specialises in deliciously fresh seafood salads. Portions are generous and food is beautifully presented. A limited range of hot dishes includes soup, grilled lobster, lasagne, pizza and coquilles fruits de mer. Vegetarian meals are available. Delicious sweets are set out on a table buffet-style. Wines chosen especially with seafood in mind form the basis of a well-balanced list. Meals are served all day but, since the restaurant is so popular, booking is necessary around lunch-time. Service is courteous and friendly, under the capable direction of restaurant manager Franco Frezza.

Lunch alc £12
Last meal 5.30pm
Credit cards [1] [2] [3] [5]
Parking on premises
Closed dinner, Sat & Sun

ST BRELADE'S BAY

★★★★
Hotel L'Horizon
✆ Jersey (0534) 43101
Tx 4192281

One of Jersey's best-known hotels, the Hotel L'Horizon enjoys a fine location right alongside the wide sandy beach of St Brelade's Bay. Excellent amenities here include an indoor swimming pool, a sauna, a solarium, a beauty salon and a smart hotel shop. There is dancing most nights in season. The hotel has been modernised and extended in recent years, and public rooms have been refurbished to a high standard. Bedroom accommodation — comprising 104 rooms, all with bathrooms, CTV and telephones — is currently being upgraded, and the completed rooms are very comfortable and well-equipped. There are two restaurants: the pleasant hotel restaurant, and the luxurious Star Grill, popular with tourists and locals alike, especially for the good fish dishes on its comprehensive menu. Vegetarians can be catered for. The wine list is extensive, and includes one Jersey wine. The Hotel L'Horizon does not accept dogs.

Price band C
Lunch alc £8
Dinner td £15 & alc
Last dinner 9.45pm
Credit cards [1] [2] [3] [4] [5]
Parking on premises

ST HELIER

× **La Buca**
The Parade
Jersey (0534) 34283

This busy Italian restaurant is within easy reach of St Helier's shopping centre and is popular with both business people and visitors, so booking is advisable. A warm welcome is offered by proprietors Giuseppe Calvani and Vincenzo Savarese and their cheerful staff, who are always happy to discuss or explain the Italian dishes on the menu. The food is well-prepared and appetising. Our Inspector particularly recommends the seafood dishes, which often feature on the blackboard lists of specialities. There is a choice between fixed-price meals or à la carte, and the wine list, consisting mainly of Italian wines, is short but well-chosen. All in all, La Buca can be confidently recommended for an enjoyable, informal meal.

Lunch td fr £4.95 & alc
Dinner td fr £9.35 & alc
Last dinner 11.30pm
Credit cards 1 2 3 4 5
No parking on premises
Closed Wed

★★★ L
Hotel Savoy
Rouge Bouillon
Jersey (0534) 27521

A Victorian mansion has been converted to produce this very pleasant holiday hotel, and its comfortable, traditionally furnished public rooms are particularly well-appointed. The 61 bedrooms, conservative in style but well-maintained, are equipped with a wide range of facilities and all have en suite bath or shower. Elsewhere in the hotel a small laundrette is provided for guests' use. English, French and Italian dishes appear on the menu of the restaurant, and dances take place there regularly during the season. There is also an outdoor swimming pool at the rear of the building.

Price band B
Lunch td £4.75 or alc £7
Dinner td £7 or alc £10
Last dinner 8.30pm
Credit card 1
Parking on premises
Closed Nov–Mar

ST SAVIOUR

★★★★ RED
Longueville Manor
(On A3, 1½m E of St Helier)
Jersey (0534) 25501
Tx 4192306

Our Inspector's choice for the Channel Isles must include this distinguished hotel, run by three generations of the Lewis family since 1948. Guests are made very comfortable here under the care and attention of Malcolm Lewis and manager Simon Dufty. Parts of the handsome building date back to the 13th century, and the whole has been very tastefully refurbished to provide 35 excellent bedrooms, each in its own individual style. All the rooms have every comfort, from private bathrooms, CTV and telephones to stylish furnishing and many thoughful extras such as flowers, fruit and books. Two suites are available, and there is an 18th-century four-poster room. Public rooms, like the bedrooms, feature many antique pieces and have a homely, restful atmosphere. Longueville's gardens and parkland include not only an attractive heated outdoor pool but also vegetable, fruit and herb gardens which supply the kitchen. Noted for its excellent cuisine, modern and imaginative in style, the restaurant also has magnificent carved oak panelling. Longueville Manor does not take children under seven.

Price band C
Lunch td £13.50 or alc £24
Dinner td £16.50 or alc £24
Last dinner 9.30pm
Credit cards 1 2 3 5
Parking on premises

× **O'Fado**
The Esplanade
Jersey (0534) 71920

Named after a traditional Portuguese love song, this small bright restaurant, situated within easy reach of the waterfront and town centre, is adorned with pictures of well-known Portuguese singers. Not surprisingly, therefore, it specialises in Portuguese

Lunch/dinner alc £12.50
Last dinner 10.30pm
Credit cards 1

cuisine, with the emphasis on good fresh fish, though the à la carte menu offers a range of meat dishes. Guests intending to sample the fish are usually invited to make their choice from the catch of the day. Our Inspector enjoyed a dish of baby hake, lightly fried and served whole, curled round with its tail in its mouth. A dessert worth trying is Molotov, a delicious concoction of eggs and caramel. Accompany your meal with a Portuguese wine from the selection offered and appreciate the friendly attentive service.

[2] [3] [5]
Parking nearby
Closed Sun

CHAPELTOWN South Yorkshire Map 8 SK39

★★★ **Staindrop Lodge**
Lane End
✆ Sheffield (0742) 846727

Formerly the home of a leading local industrialist, this Victorian building in a quiet Sheffield suburb has been pleasingly converted into an up-to-date hotel. Many original interior features have been retained, giving interesting and attractive public rooms, and furnishings and décor are suitably stylish. All 13 bedrooms have private facilities, CTV and telephones. Modern, international-style food, with a good wine list, is the mainstay of the attractive restaurant, which overlooks the gardens. Proprietors Mr and Mrs Bailey can be counted on to give guests a friendly welcome and attentive hospitality during their stay. Staindrop Lodge does not accept dogs.

Price band C
Lunch td fr £7 or alc £14
Dinner td fr £11.50 or alc £14
Last dinner 9.30pm
Credit cards [1] [2] [3]
Parking on premises
Closed Xmas

CHARMOUTH Dorset Map 3 SY39

★★ B
White House Hotel
2 Hillside,
The Street
✆ (0297) 60411

Here a most attractive Georgian house has been converted into a six-bedroom hotel. The interior retains many fine original features such as elegant Georgian carpentry, and public rooms include a peaceful lounge and a dining room which contains a convivial little bar. Good lunch-time snacks are served on the sunny patio in fine weather. (Non-residents should book for lunch out of season.) Mrs Balfour's menus feature interesting, well-prepared dishes and are supported by a good wine list. The better wines are particularly good value. All the bedrooms at the White House are comfortably furnished and have private bathrooms, CTV and telephones. Children under the age of four are not accepted.

Price band B
Lunch td fr £7 & alc
Dinner td fr £11.50 & alc
Last dinner 9.15pm
Credit cards [1] [3]
Parking on premises

CHELMSFORD Essex Map 5 TL70

GH **Boswell House Hotel**
118–20 Springfield Rd
✆ (0245) 287587

Within walking distance of the town centre, this tastefully renovated Victorian house offers comfortable and well-equipped accommodation. The 13 bedrooms (including two family rooms) are mostly spacious, and furnished in old stripped pine, with soft furnishing in pretty, coordinating fabrics. All bedrooms have private facilities, and nine have CTV. There is a cosy lounge-bar downstairs, where guests can enjoy a pre-dinner drink. Dinner is served in the attractive licensed restaurant. The young proprietors of Boswell House are enthusiastic and helpful, and extend a warm welcome.

Price band B
Dinner, b&b £28–£36
Last dinner 8.30pm
Credit cards [1] [2] [3] [5]
Parking on premised
Closed 10 days Xmas

CHEPSTOW Gwent Map 3 ST59

★★ First Hurdle Hotel
9–10 Upper Church St
✆ (02912) 2189

This converted terraced cottage in the centre of town is particularly recommended for its Edwardian-style restaurant, 'Beechers'. Lunches are good but simple, with a choice of salad platters and English fare, whereas more sophisticated French cuisine is featured on the à la carte dinner menu, with specialities such as porc Pierre, foie originale and rognons Meaux. Proprietor Virginia Bonner-Davies, who also has a keen interest in wines, does the cooking. The First Hurdle has 10 attractive bedrooms, several of them with private facilities and all with CTV.

Price band A/B
Lunch £2–£5 or alc £10
Dinner alc £10
Last dinner 9.30pm
Credit cards [1] [2] [3]
Parking nearby

★★★ St Pierre Hotel, Golf & Country Club
(Off A48 on Newport Road from Chepstow – M4 junct 22)
✆ (02912) 5261

Set in a 400-acre park with its own well-known golf course, this beautiful 14th-century manor, complete with Norman church, has been sympathetically adapted as an hotel with a new, purpose-built accommodation block. The elegantly appointed restaurant, which has views across the courses to the magnificent Severn Bridge, offers both table d'hôte and à la carte menus, while the coffee shop serves more economical meals throughout the day. The hotel's facilities include a gymnasium, an indoor swimming pool, tennis courts, badminton, bowling, table tennis and croquet. For relaxation a sauna, solarium and jacuzzi are available.

Price band D
Lunch td £8.50 or alc £18
Dinner td £12.50 or alc £18
Last dinner 10pm
Credit cards [1] [2] [3] [4] [5]
Parking on premises

CHESTER Cheshire Map 7 SJ46

×× Pippa's of Chester
58 Watergate St
✆ (0244) 313721

Close to Chester's famous Rows, this bright city-centre restaurant has a distinctly French flavour to both its décor and its cuisine. Polished wooden floors, fresh white paintwork and plenty of pot plants all add to the atmosphere, and a pianist plays most evenings. Food is expertly cooked, presentation attractive, and service freindly and helpful. The dinner menu offers a choice between an extensive à la carte selection and a more modest table d'hôte meal, while there is a 'lunch-time special' each day and also a businessmen's lunch. Specialities usually available include chicken breast filled with prawns and crabmeat with a lobster sauce, or scallops wrapped in Parma ham with a barbecue sauce. A good wine list is available, and vegetarian dishes can be provided.

Lunch td fr £5.50 or alc £16
Dinner td fr £13.95 or alc £16
Last dinner 10pm
Credit cards [1] [2] [3]

CHESTERFIELD Derbyshire Map 8 SK37

Roosters
177 Chatsworth Rd
✆ (0246) 32724

There is something for everyone, children included, at this American-style family restaurant just outside the town centre. There is a range of burgers, of course, large or small, and in several variations including chilli burgers and burgers with melted cheese and bacon. Other dishes include steaks, chicken, lasagne, curry and home-made steak and kidney pie, all in generous helpings. Suitably transatlantic side dishes include hash browns or Boston-style beans, while for dessert one might choose knickerbocker glory, chocolate fudge cake or a pancake. There is a special children's menu as well, and children's parties are catered for.

Lunch/dinner alc fr £4.50
Last dinner 12 mdnt
Parking nearby
Closed Mon lunch

Roosters is licensed, and offers a range of cocktails as well as a limited selection of wines, beers and spirits. Décor is basic and modern, with formica-topped tables and brick walls decorated with posters and mirrors.

CHIDDINGFOLD Surrey Map 4 SU93

★★ Crown Inn
The Green
✆ Wormley
(042879) 2255/6

This old inn overlooking the village green dates back as far as 1285, and retains much of the character and charm of a bygone age. Mr and Mrs Bosch have run a successful restaurant operation here for some time, but the bedrooms are a relatively new venture. Four are in the original part of the inn and four in new wing. All are well-appointed, and have private facilities and CTV. The Crown has a choice of restaurants. The more formal Elizabethan Restaurant, which has wood-panelled walls and an ornately carved ceiling, offers a large and varied à la carte selection as well as a more modestly priced table d'hôte menu. Imaginative cooking and high-quality food is a feature of both menus, and the wine list is extensive. The more relaxed Woodfyre Restaurant offers a set-price three-course meal, with the added novelty that main courses are cooked over the open wood fire. Vegetarians can be catered for.

Price band B
Lunch/dinner (Elizabethan Restaurant) td £12 or alc £20
Lunch/dinner (Woodfyre Restaurant) td £7.95
Last dinner 9.30pm
Credit cards [1] [2] [3] [5]
Limited parking on premises
Closed Mon lunch

CHIDEOCK Dorset Map 3 SY49

GH **Betchworth House Hotel**
✆ (0297) 89478

A warm welcome is assured at this charming 17th-century house, situated in the mainly thatched village of Chideock, not far from the beautiful Dorset coast. The house, which is furnished to a high standard in the traditional style, has an old fashioned cottage garden. Its six attractively decorated bedrooms include one family room and three have an en suite shower. Guests can sit beside an open fire in the cosy subtly-lit lounge and enjoy a drink at the well-stocked bar in the dining room before a meal. Owner Mrs Scott offers varied set menus, all home-cooked, using fresh produce and local clotted cream. Children over seven years old are welcome; dogs are not accepted.

Price band A
Dinner td £8
Last dinner 7.30pm
Parking on premises

CHILGROVE West Sussex Map 4 SU81

❀ ××
White Horse Inn
✆ (024359) 219

For many years this small, intimate restaurant with its friendly, informal atmosphere has maintained a high standard of excellence. It produces its own style of English and French cuisine, and a choice of vegetarian meals. Its menus are changed frequently to take full advantage of seasonal produce. It is reputed to have the best wine list in Britain, containing some 600 different wines, and the proprietor is always ready to advise any guest who needs assistance in making a choice.

Lunch td £17.90
Dinner td £18.35
Last dinner 9.30pm
Credit cards [1] [2] [3] [4] [5]
Parking on premises
Closed Feb
Closed Sun & Mon

CHIPPING CAMPDEN Gloucestershire Map 4 SP13

×× **King's Arms** The Square ✆ Evesham (0386) 840256	The King's Arms, a hotel built of the mellow local stone, is located in the centre of the town. One of its greatest attractions is the charming 'Old World' bar, where quality snacks are available, and the same high standard of cuisine is maintained in the restaurant. A pleasant, relaxed atmosphere prevails throughout the hotel, and this, coupled with attentive service, is a significant factor in making one's stay here an enjoyable one.	Bar lunch fr £1.25 Dinner td £15.34 Last dinner 9pm Credit cards [1] [3] Parking nearby

CHRISTCHURCH Dorset Map 4 SZ19

★★★ **Avonmouth Hotel** Mudeford (2m E of Christchurch off B3059) ✆ (0202) 483434	Sweeping views over Christchurch Harbour are a feature of the public rooms and many of the bedrooms at this pleasant family hotel. The 41 comfortable bedrooms include 14 in an annexe, three of which are family rooms. Private bathrooms and CTV are standard in all rooms. Leisure facilities include an outdoor heated swimming pool, a garden and a games room. Children are welcome. The restaurant offers a traditional table d'hôte dinner menu, with some choice, and at lunch-time an extensive cold buffet is supplemented by some interesting hot dishes. Service is friendly and efficient.	Price band C Lunch td £4.50 Dinner alc £9.95 Last dinner 9pm Credit cards [1] [2] [4] [5] Parking on premises
★★★ **Waterford Lodge Hotel** 87 Bure Ln, Friars Cliff, Mudeford (2m E of Christchurch off B3059) ✆ Highcliffe (04252) 72948	This warm and friendly hotel is just a stroll from Mudeford's popular harbour and the nearby beaches of Avon and Friars Cliff, and is within easy driving distance of historic Christchurch and, inland, the New Forest. The very comfortable public rooms include a main lounge which has patio doors to the garden, and a second, quiet lounge, as well as a recently extended lounge-bar. Garden views through large picture windows are a feature of the dining room. The 21 bedrooms are all furnished and equipped to the same high standard, and have bathrooms, CTV, radio and telephones. Leisure facilities at Waterford Lodge include a putting green and a snooker table. The hotel is run by resident proprietors, the Badley family who, with their friendly staff, ensure guests of good service and generally excellent value.	Price band C Lunch td £5.75 or alc £12 Dinner td fr £8.50 or alc £12 Last dinner 8.30pm Credit cards [1] [2] [3] [5] Parking on premises

CHURCH STRETTON Shropshire Map 7 SO49

FH **Rectory Farm** Woolstaston (1½m off A49 at Leebotwood) ✆ Leebotwood (06945) 306	This beautiful half-timbered farmhouse, dating from about 1620, stands on the slopes of the Long Mynd. The house is full of character, and exudes that well-cared for feeling that typifies the best farmhouse accommodation. The three comfortable bedrooms all have private bathrooms; warm colours and polished antique furniture give the house a homely air. Breakfast is the only meal served — it will be of the hearty farmhouse type, using home-produced milk, while other produce comes from neighbouring farms. For evening meals, the proprietor, Mrs Davies, will be happy to recommend several inns and hotels within a few miles. Rectory Farm does not accept children under 12 or dogs.	Price band A Parking on premises Closed Nov–Feb

CLANFIELD Oxfordshire Map 4 SP20

❀ ××× **Plough at Clanfield**
✆ (036781) 222
Tx 449848

This harmonious Elizabethan manor house of Cotswold stone offers comfortable, well-equipped rooms and exquisite food. Chef/patron Paul Bernard produces some unusual and carefully prepared dishes which are served in a well-appointed and charming restaurant, where diners can choose between two fixed-price menus. Service is professional yet not too formal, and some good-quality wines are on offer. There is also an elegant bar-lounge, stylishly furnished in keeping with the house's period atmosphere. The four bedrooms all have en suite facilities, CTV, telephones and hairdriers, and, while of varying size, all the rooms are very attractively furnished.

Lunch td £9.95–£20.95
Dinner td £16.95–£20.95
Last dinner 9.30pm
Credit cards [1] [2] [3] [5]
Parking on premises

CLAYGATE Surrey Map 4 TQ16

×× **Les Alouettes**
✆ Esher (0372) 64882

Also featuring for the first time in our *Hotels and Restaurants* guide this year, Les Alouettes is a 'must' for inclusion here — even though it is in an area that has an abundance of restaurants. Recently refurbished, the restaurant provides pleasant surroundings in which to savour the skilled and imaginative cooking of Liam Stewart, the Irish chef, who trained in France. Top-quality seasonal produce is the basis of his fixed-price lunch and dinner menus, which are supplemented by chef's special dishes each day. Impeccable service by a team of French waiters sets off a meal here. Booking is necessary for both lunch and dinner.

Lunch td £12.75–£16.25
Dinner td £19.50
Last dinner 9.30pm
Credit cards [1] [2] [3] [5]
Closed 25 Dec–2 Jan
Closed Sun, & Sat lunch

CLEOBURY MORTIMER Shropshire Map 7 SO67

★★ **Redfern Hotel**
✆ (0299) 270395
Tx 335176

This former pub in a quiet market town offers a warm, friendly atmosphere and comfortable, well-equipped accommodation. A purpose-built, cottage-style annexe houses six of the 11 bedrooms. Private facilities, CTV, radio and telephones are standard in all the rooms, and there are two rooms suitable for families. The English Kitchen Restaurant, decorated with a fascinating collection of domestic bygones, serves traditional English home cooking. It is open for dinner each evening, when table d'hôte and á la carte menus are available. Traditional lunches are served on Sundays. Bar lunches are available during the rest of the week; in addition to the pleasant, cosy bar there is a comfortable lounge area.

Price band B
Lunch alc £5
Dinner alc £10.25
Last dinner 9.30pm
Credit cards [1] [2] [3] [5]
Parking on premises

CLUN Shropshire Map 7 SO38

× **The Old Post Office**
9 The Square
✆ (05884) 687

The freshest of local produce is the basis of the imaginative but simple country cooking at this attractively converted shop in the village square. The menu might include baked field mushrooms with fresh marjoram, or wild rabbit pie. There are vegetarian dishes to tempt even the most determined carnivore: bean cassoulet or a vegetable soufflé, perhaps. British, French and Italian provincial cooking have all contributed ideas to the enticing menus. Food is complemented by a selection of very modestly priced

Lunch alc £9
Dinner td fr £13
Last dinner 9.30pm
No parking on premises
Closed Feb
Closed Sun & Mon, & Tue lunch (Nov–

wines — another aspect of the excellent value for money to be found here. Furnishings are simple but effective and unusual — they even include the original Post Office safe. In addition to the restaurant side of their business, the proprietors also let three very comfortable bedrooms.

Mar)
Closed Sun & Mon dinner (Feb)

COCKERMOUTH Cumbria Map 11 NY13

GH **Low Hall**
Brandlingill
(3m S of Cockermouth on unclassified rd off A5086)
☎ (0900) 826654

This 17th-century house has been charmingly converted into a six-bedroom guesthouse offering comfortable accommodation that is full of character. Bedrooms, which have lovely views, are prettily decorated and four have private facilities. The lounge and beamed dining room have stone fireplaces with open fires in winter. Meals, cooked by proprietor Mrs Edwards, include a full farmhouse breakfast ('Continental platter' or pancakes as an alternative) and a rather special four-course dinner (which must be ordered by 5.30pm). Unusual dishes at dinner might include chilled raspberry and redcurrent soup, followed by turkey in a sauce of yogurt and apricots or, for vegetarians, a creamy leek croustade. Desserts are most tempting, and Low Hall is licensed. Value for money here is excellent, especially the bargain breaks or special house-party weekends. Low Hall does not accept dogs, or children under 10.

Price band A/B
Dinner, b&b £21.50–£25
Last dinner 7.30pm
Credit cards [1] [3]
Parking on premises

COLL (Island of) Strathclyde *Argyllshire* Map 13 NM25

GH **Tigh-na-Mara**
Arinagour
☎ (08793) 354

This modern, purpose-built, licensed guesthouse lives up to its name, which means 'house by the sea'. Its setting is superb, and it has marvellous views towards Mull and the Treshnish Isles. Located on the edge of the small village of Arinagour, it is convenient for the pier from which the ferry sails to Oban, on the mainland. Tigh-na-Mara offers unusually good recreational facilities including cycle and boat hire, sea-angling trips, and putting or croquet on the lawn. The eight bedrooms include two family rooms and a no-smoking room. All rooms have washbasins and tea/coffee-making facilities, and two have TV. The house is tastefully decorated and neatly furnished throughout. Accommodation is comfortable and the atmosphere relaxed and friendly. Good, wholesome Scottish cooking is provided in the small dining room; please order dinner by 6pm.

Dinner, b&b £18–£19
Last dinner 8pm
Parking on premises
Closed Dec 1–Jan 14

COLNE Lancashire Map 7 SD84

FH **Higher Wanless Farm**
Red Ln
☎ (0282) 865301

Shire horses and sheep are bred on this interesting 25-acre farm, in a peaceful setting overlooking the Leeds and Liverpool Canal. The charming farmhouse is run by Mrs Mitson, who welcomes all her guests like friends and is always on hand to ensure they are well-looked after. The two spacious and attractive bedrooms are both suitable for families. Both have washbasins and tea/coffee-making equipment, and one has CTV. Downstairs, the lounge and dining room are

Price band A
Dinner, b&b £18.50–£21
Last dinner 7.30pm
Parking on premises
Closed Dec

full of character, with exposed beams, and there is an open fire in the lounge in winter. Food is good, and always home-cooked; guests requiring dinner are asked to give adequate notice. Dogs are not accepted.

COLONSAY (Island of) Strathclyde *Argyllshire* Map 10 NR39

★ HBL **Isle of Colonsay Hotel**
Scalasaig
✆ (09512) 316

Accommodation is limited on this beautiful, unspoilt Hebridean island, so booking well in advance is recommended at this welcoming hotel. Overlooking the little harbour at Scalasaig, the accommodation has been considerably improved in recent years, but the hotel retains all its traditional hospitality and warmth. The popular bar, focal point of the island's social activity, has a relaxed, friendly atmosphere, and the 11 bedrooms are cheery and comfortable. Eight have private facilities, and two are family rooms. CTV is available in rooms on request. The hotel has a good reputation for its carefully prepared set dinners, which make good use of local produce including vegetables from the hotel's own garden.

Price band B
Dinner td fr £11.75
Last dinner 7.30pm
Credit cards [1] [2] [3] [5]
Parking on premises
Closed lunch

COLYFORD Devon Map 3 SY29

GH **Swallows Eaves Hotel**
✆ (0297) 53184

Devon, Dorset and Somerset are all within touring range of this comfortable little hotel, and the surrounding countryside has plenty to offer by way of leisure activities — particularly to birdwatchers and golfers. The hotel has six bedrooms, all of a very high standard, and some with suberb views. All rooms have en suite facilities, CTV and tea-making equipment and are well-furnished and attractively decorated. Pre-dinner drinks are served in the cosy lounge, and excellent home-cooked dinners (residents only) in the elegant licensed dining room. The hospitable proprietors, Mr and Mrs Beck, are always on hand to ensure their guests enjoy a comfortable stay. Dogs are not accepted.

Price band B
Dinner, b&b £24–£29
Last dinner 8pm
Parking on premises

CONNEL Strathclyde *Argyllshire* Map 10 NM93

★★ **Falls of Lora Hotel**
✆ (063171) 483

This 30-bedroom hotel overlooking beautiful Loch Etive has been steadily upgraded in recent years and now offers a good range of accommodation. At one end of the scale are four modest family rooms with bunk beds, while at the other is a modern luxury room with a 7ft round bed and a jacuzzi bathroom en suite, or another room with a four-poster bed and king-size round bath. Most rooms have private bathrooms and radio/intercom, and CTV is available in rooms. Recent refurbishment has included the cocktail bar, which has also been extended to offer bistro-style meals. Good food (including vegetarian dishes) is available at a reasonable price here or in the restaurant and, after dinner, guests can relax in front of an open fire in the comfortable lounge, or sample one of the enormous range of whiskies available in the bar.

Price band B
Dinner td £11.25
Last dinner 9.30pm
Credit cards [1] [2] [3] [5]
Parking on premises
Closed Xmas & New Year

CONSTANTINE BAY Cornwall Map 2 SW87

★★★ HL
Treglos Hotel
✆ Padstow (0841) 520727
Tx 45795

It is well worth arriving in time for afternoon tea, served with home-made cakes and scones, at this welcoming country house hotel overlooking Constantine Bay and Trevose Golf Course. Five spacious yet cosy lounges are comfortably furnished, and warmed by log fires on chilly days. In the restaurant, guests have a choice between an extensive à la carte menu and a more modest, but well-balanced, table d'hôte list. Fresh local seafood is a speciality, and vegetables come from the hotel's own kitchen garden. A good range of home-made sweets is available, served with Cornish cream. Bar lunches are served from 12 noon to 2.30pm. The 44 bedrooms, all with bathrooms, CTV, radio and telephones, and some with balconies, include 12 family rooms. Children of all ages are welcomed, but those under three are not admitted to the restaurant. However, alternative arrangements for meals, including nursery tea, can be made. Private suites with sitting room are available, and the hotel has a number of self-catering flats to let, with full use of the hotel's amenities. These include an attractive heated indoor pool and jacuzzi, which open onto the gardens, and a croquet lawn. Treglos is particularly commended by our Inspector for the high standard of service and personal attention by proprietors Mr and Mrs Barlow and their friendly staff.

Price band C
Lunch td £7.25 or alc £14.95
Dinner td £11.95 or alc £14.95
Last dinner 9.30pm
Parking on premises
Closed 9 Nov–9 Mar

CORBRIDGE Northumberland Map 12 NY96

×× **Ramblers Country House Restaurant**
Farnley
(On A695 Stocksfield Rd ½m SE of Corbridge)
✆ (043471) 2424

Interesting food with a strong German influence is served at this tastefully converted 19th-century house run by Heinrich and Jennifer Herrmann. The atmosphere is pleasant and service friendly in the two elegant dining rooms, which are furnished in keeping with the style of the house. The à la carte menu offers first courses such as a salad of fennel, mango and cashew nuts; spiced herring fillet; spinach soufflé topped with smoked mussels; or one of a range of home-made soups, while the substantial main courses might include a casserole of venison with black cherries, or turkey breast spiced with ginger and served with peach slices. Sweets from the trolley are generally rich and creamy, but lighter fruit desserts and cheese are offered as alternatives. A three-course table d'hôte menu is also available, and chef/proprietor Heini Herrmann is happy to cook plain dishes or vegetarian meals for customers who prefer them. The wine list is well-balanced, and includes some very good-value wines. Coffee (if you wish, Viennese coffee, served with whipped cream and grated chocolate) is served in an attractive coffee lounge which has a log fire in winter. There is also a cheerful modern bar.

Dinner alc £13.50
Last dinner 10pm
Credit cards [1] [2] [3] [5]
Parking on premises
Closed Sun & Mon
Closed lunch

★ Riverside Hotel
Main St
✆ (043471) 2942

Children and pets are welcome at this small, friendly hotel in Hadrian's Wall country. Resident proprietors Harry and Judy Fawcett and their staff offer comfortable accommodation, good food and courteous personal service. The short table d'hôte dinner menu offers an interesting choice for each course, always using good-quality produce, and everything is freshly prepared. Home-made soups and pâtés are usually among the first courses, with steak or trout, perhaps, to follow, and a range of home-made puddings such as pineapple Romanoff or blackberry and apple pie, or a selection of local cheeses. The hotel has 11 bedrooms, some with private facilities, and including two family rooms. Most bedrooms are quite spacious, and are individually furnished, sometimes with striking antique pieces. The bright, comfortable lounge, which gives lovely views of the countryside behind the house, is supplemented by a small cocktail bar.

Price band B
Dinner td £8.50
Last dinner 8pm
Parking on premises
Closed Xmas–Feb

CORSHAM Wiltshire Map 3 ST86

×× **Copperfields**
High St
✆ (0249) 713982

A good selection of well-presented dishes is available at this first-floor restaurant in the town centre. Food is expertly prepared under the supervision of chef-proprietor Mr Allen, whose well-balanced menus include such dishes as Stilton pâté, crab and mushroom cocotte, guinea fowl, or steak, kidney and smoked oyster pie. Good home-made soups might include fish bisque. Vegetarian dishes can be provided. Desserts are home-made and all very good. Fresh flowers on the tables help create a welcoming, pleasant atmosphere.

Dinner td £9.95 or alc £14
Last dinner 9.30pm
Credit cards [1] [3] [5]
Parking on premises
Closed Tue & Sat
Closed lunch

CORWEN Clwyd Map 6 SJ04

GH **Corwen Court Private Hotel**
London Rd
✆ (0490) 2854

When the Bucklands acquired Corwen's disused police station and adjoining magistrates' court in 1984, they set about converting the premises into a guesthouse with a difference. A comfortable lounge and dining room, furnished in warm colours, have been created out of the former court and the police station's waiting room. The 10 bedrooms, most with private facilities, are individually and tastefully furnished — even the single rooms that were once the cells! Mrs Buckland's fine home cooking is certainly a marked improvement on the former inmates' diet. Please order dinner by 6pm.

Price band A
Dinner, b&b £15
Last dinner 8pm
Parking nearby

COVENTRY West Midlands Map 4 SP37

GH **Hearsall Lodge Hotel**
I Broad Ln
✆ (0203) 74543

Situated on the outskirts of the city centre yet within easy reach of its amenities, Hearsall Lodge offers accommodation in bedrooms equipped with CTV and tea/coffee-making equipment, though none have en suite bathroom facilities. You can relax in the friendly atmosphere of the large, comfortable lounge or in a small bar, and the smooth running of the guesthouse is a tribute to the professional experience of the proprietors, who have been head chef and housekeeper in larger establishments.

Price band A/B
Dinner, b&b £21-£28
Last dinner 7.30pm
Parking on premises

GH **Trinity House Hotel**
28 Lower Holyhead Rd
✆ (0203) 555654

Our Inspector has chosen this small hotel near the town centre not only for its accomodation, but also for its popular, mainly vegetarian restaurant, called Herbs. Substantial vegetarian meals are served here, and fish and chicken dishes are also available. Menus change monthly to make use of fresh produce in season. A typical meal might be parsnip timbale (mousse) served with Dijon vinaigrette and yogurt muffins, followed by pine-nut and asparagus loaf with fresh mango and apricot sauce and, to finish, marbled cheesecake. Side salads and jacket potatoes are also available. Orders are taken in the small cocktail bar. Booking is advisable, since the restaurant is popular and seats only about 40 diners. The hotel has seven comfortable bedrooms, all with washbasins, and including one family room. Children under five are not accepted, however, and neither are dogs.

Price band A
Dinner alc £8
Last dinner 9.30pm
Limited parking on premises
Closed 10 days Xmas
Closed lunch, & Sun dinner

COWDENBEATH Fife Map 11 NT19

GH **Glenbank House**
36 Foulford Rd
✆ (0383) 515466

This solid, stone-built house, standing on a rise above the main road, provides accommodation in five neat, bright bedrooms, all equipped with tea/coffee-making facilities. A spacious ground-floor residents' lounge offers comfortable seating, together with a good selection of magazines, and the nearby dining room is smartly appointed. The genuinely friendly personalities of the house's owners do much to ensure a pleasant stay for their guests.

Price band A
Dinner, b&b £15–£17
Last dinner 9.30pm
Parking on premises

CRACKINGTON HAVEN Cornwall Map 2 SX19

FH **Manor Farm**
✆ St Gennys (08403) 304

A secluded position one mile from the sea, and a history that can be traced back to Domesday, are two of the attractions of this tastefully restored Cornish manor, which stands in lovely gardens with fine rural views. Bedrooms are comfortable and well-decorated, and two of the four have bathrooms en suite. The beamed lounge is kept cosy in winter by a wood-burning stove, and there is also a games room with a full-size snooker table. Produce from the farms and garden features in Mrs Knight's cooking; guests share one large table in the character dining room. Dinner is served to residents only, and should be ordered by 5pm. Smoking is not permitted in the house, and Manor Farm does not accept dogs, or children under 14.

Price band A
Dinner td £7
Last dinner 7pm
Parking on premises

CRANBORNE Dorset Map 4 SU01

×× **La Fosse**
London House, The Square
✆ (07254) 604

Good and imaginative cooking by chef/proprietor Mr La Fosse makes this attractive restaurant (which also has four letting bedrooms) well worth a visit. Mr and Mrs La Fosse have settled here after 25 years' experience in the restaurant business, and offer a friendly welcome and proficient service. Fresh fish and game in season are the specialities, and our Inspector found the set menus to be remarkable value. For lunch there is a choice of three set menus, whereas for dinner

Lunch td fr £4.95
Dinner td fr £7.95
Last dinner 10pm
Credit cards [1] [3]
Parking nearby

there are two, and an à la carte menu is also available. The cuisine is supported by a good wine list, and glasses of house wine are generous.

Closed Sun, & Mon & Sat lunch

CREWKERNE Somerset Map 3 ST40

★★ The Old Parsonage
Barn St
✆ (0460) 73516

Partly dating back to the 15th century, this small hotel, which has its own garden, offers 10 pleasant and comfortable bedrooms. All have private bath or shower, CTV and telephone; six of the rooms, including two family rooms, are in an annexe. Extras such as fresh fruit are provided in bedrooms, and the friendly, attentive proprietors and their staff make every effort to ensure their guests enjoy a comfortable stay. Lounge accommodation is limited to the bar, but this is pleasant and comfortable. Fresh, well-prepared dishes are the basis of lunch and dinner menus in the attractive restaurant, and vegetarian meals can be provided.

Price band B
Lunch/dinner £7–£12
Last dinner 9.30pm
Credit cards [1] [2] [3] [5]
Parking on premises

CRICCIETH Gwynedd Map 6 SH43

★ Abereistedd Hotel
West Parade
✆ (076671) 2710

This unpretentious holiday hotel, right on Criccieth's seafront, is a friendly, family-run establishment offering home cooking in agreeable surroundings. The 14 bedrooms, while modestly furnished, are clean and bright; five have showers en suite and two are family rooms. Guests have a choice of lounges: there is a TV lounge on the first floor, or a small bar downstairs. Proprietors Mr and Mrs Moffatt, who seem to really enjoy looking after their guests, concentrate on cooking fresh food, so although the dinner menu is limited in choice, the quality is excellent. Bar lunches are also available. Children under three years old are not accepted at the hotel.

Price band A
Lunch td fr £2.30
Dinner td fr £6.50
Last dinner 7.30pm
Parking on premises
Closed 2 Jan–4 Mar

CRIEFF Tayside *Perthshire* Map 11 NN82

★ Keppoch House
Perth Rd
✆ (0764) 4341

Owners Colin and Helaine Dale and their staff go out of their way to look after their guests at this busy little hotel set in its own grounds overlooking the Vale of Strathearn and the Ochil Hills. The six bedrooms (four with private shower) include two family rooms and two no-smoking rooms. All have good-quality furnishings and fresh, coordinated décor. CTV and tea/coffee-making equipment are provided in each room. Public rooms, though not large, are tastefully modern. In the restaurant, a choice of Scottish and Continental dishes is available, and lunches and suppers are also served in the bar. Keppoch House does not accept dogs.

Price band B
Bar lunch fr £2
Dinner td £4.50
Last dinner 9.30pm
Credit cards [2] [3]
Parking on premises
Closed Jan

CRINAN Strathclyde *Argyllshire* Map 10 NR79

❀ ★★★ L
Crinan Hotel
✆ (054683) 261

The scenery (especially at sunset) is really magnificent around this popular holiday hotel at the western end of the Crinan Canal. Apart from suberb views, the Crinan Hotel is also known for its seafood — absolutely fresh, and expertly cooked in simple yet interesting ways. There is a choice of two restaurants,

Price band C
Bar lunch alc £6
Dinner td fr £20
Last dinner 9pm
Credit cards [1] [3]

and dining in either is likely to be a memorable experience. Bar lunches are also available. The hotel's 22 bedrooms (including one family room) are cheery and well-furnished, and all have private facilities and telephones. The bar and lounge are relaxing and have a convivial atmosphere.

Parking on premises
Closed Nov–mid Mar

CROMARTY Highland *Ross & Cromarty* Map 14 NH76

❀ × **Le Chardon**
Church St
✆ (03817) 471

Robyn and Mena Aitchison created something of a culinary oasis when they opened their charming little restaurant in a quiet corner of this interesting conservation village, a former seaport on the Black Isle. The kitchen is Robyn's domain; his reputation for imaginative modern and traditional Scottish dishes is growing rapidly. A typical dinner here might be sautéed sweetbread, courgette and rosemary soup, almond pheasant, and, for sweet, a delicious kiwi fruit and Chartreuse mousse. Coffee will probably be served with home-made fudge. Value for money is excellent, and food always expertly cooked.

Lunch td £9
Dinner td £15.50
Last dinner 9.30pm
Credit cards 1 2 3
Parking nearby
Closed Mon
Lunch by arrangement

CROOK Cumbria Map 7 SD49

FH **Greenbank Farmhouse**
(SP from B5284 Kendal-Bowness rd)
✆ Staveley (0539) 821216

This comfortable, peacefully located farmhouse has five letting bedrooms, but it is for the excellent dinners that our Inspector particularly recommends it. Cooking is all done by Mrs Scales, the proprietor, and dinner is available to non-residents as well as guests staying in the farmhouse. The stylishly presented five-course menu offers a good choice. Starters include hot spiced grapefruit with rum, lemon sole with a white wine sauce, egg mornay and prawn cocktail, and are followed by soup with fresh cream and warm rolls, fruit juice, or lemon sorbet. Main courses are traditional: steaks, roast beef, duckling or Dover sole, for example, all served with fresh vegetables. Home-made sweets are chosen from a sumptuous sweet trolley, with cheese and biscuits to finish. All this is served in a charming, licensed restaurant which has a friendly, warm atmosphere and a roaring log fire in winter. For residents there is a sun lounge and a TV lounge with tea-making facilities. Greenbank Farmhouse does not take children under 12.

Price band A
Dinner td fr £10
Last dinner 7pm
Credit card 3
Parking on premises
Closed Dec

CROSSGATES Powys Map 3 SO06

GH **Guidfa House**
✆ Penybont (059787) 241

Situated near a major route junction, yet convenient for exploring the wild uplands of mid Wales, Guidfa House is run by the hospitable Stevens family. Good home cooking is served here, and the premises are licensed. Meals are served to non-residents by prior arrangement. The comfortable accommodation includes seven bedrooms, among them three family rooms and three rooms with en suite facilities. All have tea/coffee-making facilities. Rooms are furnished in traditional style, and the whole house has an agreeable, homely atmosphere.

Price band A
Dinner, b&b £20.50–£23
Last dinner by arrangement
Parking on premises

CUPAR Fife Map 11 NO31

❀× **Ostlers Close**
25 Bonnygate
☎ (0334) 55574

Tucked away in a little lane off the town's busy main street, this attractive cottage-style restaurant is deservedly popular. A friendly welcome is extended to guests by Amanda Graham, whose husband James supervises the preparation of a tempting selection of dishes based largely on fresh fish, game and local produce. The standard of cuisine is exceptionally good, and the menu features such delights as scallops in fennel with garlic butter and breast of wild duck with juniper and blackcurrant sauce. Though the proprietor himself describes his food as French/Swiss, both cooking and presentation are in the modern, light style. The wine list, though not extensive, has been carefully chosen and provides a good selection of clarets and burgundies.

Lunch alc £8
Dinner alc £16
Last dinner 9pm
Credit cards [1] [3]
No parking on premises
Closed Sun, & Mon lunch

CWMDUAD Dyfed Map 2 SN33

GH **Neuadd Wen**
(On A484 mid-way between Carmarthen and Newcastle Emlyn)
☎ Cynwyl Elfed (0267) 87438

This charming rural guesthouse is set in a small village in a beautiful wooded valley, and is within easy reach of many places of interest in west Wales including the south and west coasts. Six comfortable bedrooms are available, two of them family rooms. Good, honest cooking is provided — not only dinner (which is excellent value) but also snacks and teas, which are available to non-residents as well, during the day. Recreational facilities offered include fishing, and children are welcome.

Price band A
Dinner, b&b £12.50–£14.50
Last dinner 11pm
Parking on premises

DARLINGTON Co Durham Map 8 NZ21

×× **Bishop's House**
38 Coniscliffe Rd
☎ (0325) 286666

Built round a small, attractive courtyard, this elegant town-centre restaurant offers good fixed-price menus featuring a range of imaginative dishes. Starters include home-made soups and pâtés as well as unusual dishes such as home-cured salmon and turbot with dill and limes, while main courses range from a plain grilled steak to venison, marinaded and baked in puff pastry, and served with a truffle and madeira sauce. Other inventive combinations might include brill with Stilton, or pork with leeks, cashew nuts and stir-fried eggs. Vegetables are fresh and interesting, and sweets unusual and delicious — possibly including a hot creamed chestnut pancake with coffee and rum sauce, or iced mango parfait. The wine list is extensive. The restaurant is comfortable and intimate, and the décor is enhanced by paintings that are all the work of the proprietors, Mr and Mrs Lee. Well-presented light snacks are served in a recently opened modern bistro to the front of the courtyard.

Lunch td fr £6.50
Dinner td fr £12.50
Last dinner 9.30pm
Credit cards [1] [2] [3]
No parking on premises
Closed Sun & Sat lunch

DARTINGTON Devon Map 3 SX76

INN **Cott**
☎ Totness (0803) 863777

This delightful long, low thatched inn first gained its licence in 1320 and still offers hospitality and commendable food as well as a good choice of draught beers, wines and spirits. Beamed ceilings, flagstone floors and log fires in winter help create a welcoming

Price band B
Lunch alc fr £5
Dinner alc £12
Last dinner 9.30pm

atmosphere, and the management and staff provide friendly service. At lunch-times, a variety of traditional fare is served in the bar, buffet-style. Fresh salmon and crab, home-cured ham and roast beef might be among the offerings on the cold table, while hot dishes might include poachers' pie or fresh monkfish in a garlic and cream sauce. To finish, there are home-made sweets such as real treacle tart, raspberry pavlova or lemon Jamaica. The restaurant menu for dinner offers interesting dishes such as turbot in a sauce made from herbs and Devon cider, or medaillons of beef in Kümmel. First courses might include fresh scallop and salmon mayonnaise. Vegetables are fresh, and again there is a good range of sweets. Six comfortable cottage-style bedrooms are available, all with washbasins. The inn does not accept dogs, or children under eight.

Credit cards [1] [2] [3] [5]
Parking on premises

DARTMOUTH Devon Map 3 SX85

❀ **Bistro 33**
33 Lower St
✆ (08043) 2882

The chef/proprietor of this small restaurant near the harbour is Richard Cranfield, formerly of the well-known Carved Angel (see below). Though this typical, simply appointed bistro is quite different from his former place of work, his expertise in the modern style of cooking is very evident here, and the emphasis is firmly on high quality and attractive presentation. The short menu is supplemented by daily specials, advertised on a blackboard. It might include, as a first course, 'a trio of tartlets': small flaky-pastry tarts containing salmon soufflé, chicken purée and quails' eggs with hollandaise sauce. Main courses are simpler but of a high standard, and sweets are attractive and delicious. The atmosphere is friendly and service is attentive.

Dinner td £14.75
Last dinner 10pm
Parking nearby
Closed last wk Jan & 1st wk Feb
Closed lunch

❀ ×× **The Carved Angel**
2 South Embankment
✆ (08043) 2465

Neatly perched on the River Dart's quayside in a fine tile-hung and balconied building, this established restaurant continues to attract praise on account of Joyce Molyneux's delightful cooking. Many dishes have a distinct Mediterranean feel, such as the brochettes of beef with spiced aubergines and haricot beans, or the provençal fish soup. Salmon with samphire and champagne, and lobster and parsley noodles with shellfish sauce, are among the more unusual specialities. Vegetarians can be catered for. A sound wine list is available, and service is carried out with care. Diners can see what is going on in the open-plan kitchen, and the restaurant is bright and modern in its décor and furnishings. There is no bar, but drinks are served at tables.

Lunch td £15 or alc £20
Dinner td fr £22
Last dinner 9.30pm
No parking on premises
Closed Xmas & Jan
Closed Mon, & Sun dinner

DEDHAM Essex Map 5 TM03

GH **Dedham Hall**
✆ Colchester (0206) 323027

Six acres of well-kept grounds surround this lovely timber-framed house in the heart of Constable country. Seven elegant bedrooms (six with private bath or shower) offer comfortable and well-appointed accommodation, with CTV and tea/coffee-making

Price band B
Dinner, b&b £28.50–£38.50
Last dinner 7.30pm

equipment. The lounges have a pleasant, relaxing atmosphere. Proprietors Mr and Mrs Slingo provide good home cooking, and hold a restaurant and residential licence. Please order dinner by noon if required — and don't bring your dog!

Parking on premises
Closed Nov–Mar
Closed Wed dinner

DENTON Greater Manchester Map 7 SJ99

★★★ **Old Rectory**
Meadow Ln,
Houghton Green
✆ 061-336 7516
Tx 668615

This family-run hotel, set in a peaceful tree-lined cul de sac only a short walk from the Tame Valley Country Park, is something of a haven in the hurly-burly of the Greater Manchester conurbation. The 26 bedrooms are very well-equipped: CTV, radio/alarm, telephone, trouser-press and refrigerator are standard in each, and all the rooms have en suite bathrooms with showers and bidets as well as baths. Proprietor Mr Challenor-Chadwick is justly proud of his restaurant, Chadwick's Place. Well-balanced menus include main courses as homely as braised oxtail or leg of mutton Victorian-style, and as unusual as 'tripe à la mode de Denton', Sauerbraten or matelote of eel. Fish, fresh from Manchester Market nearby, is hand-picked by Mr Challenor-Chadwick himself. First courses are chosen from a wide range which might include taramasalata, barbecued chicken wings, fish soup or rollmop herring. Vegetarians can be catered for. Pipes and cigars may not be smoked in the restaurant, and 'cigarette smokers should inhale only'! The hotel does not accept dogs, or children under five.

Price band B/C
Lunch alc £8.50
Dinner alc £11
Last dinner 10pm
Credit card [1]
Parking on premises
Closed 25 Dec–1 Jan
Restaurant closed Sun, Sat lunch & Bank Hols

DERBY Derbyshire Map 8 SK33

Ben Bowers
13–5 Chapel St
✆ (0332) 367688

Opened in 1987, the popular, cottage-style restaurant — a sister establishment to its namesake in Nottingham — is situated above the Blessington Carriage pub. It is within easy reach of the city centre, with parking at a multi-storey car park immediately opposite. À la carte and table d'hôte menus offer an extensive choice of dishes, culled from the cuisine of many countries and representing excellent value for money. Your meal can be the traditional roast beef dinner or a totally vegetarian meal; it can be as simple as grilled steak or as elaborate as 'John's poulet', where fresh chicken breast is stuffed with apple and paw paw then topped with almonds, breadcrumbs and sesame seeds before being fried and served with a sauce of port wine and chervil. Whatever your decision, fresh ingredients will have been used wherever possible in its preparation.

Lunch/dinner td fr £5.25 or alc £11
Last dinner 11pm
Credit cards [1] [2] [3] [5]
No parking on premises

DIRLETON Lothian *East Lothian* Map 12 NT58

★★★ H
Open Arms
✆ (062085) 241
Tx 727887

Situated at the side of the green in a pretty little East Lothian village, this hotel of quality and distinction maintains fine standards of housekeeping and hospitality. The well-equipped bedrooms are comfortable, and refurbishment is gradually upgrading them to a chintzy, country-house style. Traditional

Price band C
Bar lunch alc £5
Lunch alc £8
Dinner alc £12.50
Last dinner

lounges are at their most attractive in the winter months when log fires roar, and the dining room has been tastefully modernised. Meals are enjoyable — the traditional Sunday lunch being particularly popular.

10pm
Credit cards [1] [2] [3] [4] [5]
Parking on premises

DITCHLING East Sussex Map 4 TQ31

INN **Bull Hotel**
2 High St
☏ Hassocks (07918) 3147

Recently renovated, this pleasing Sussex tile-hung inn stands at the crossroads in Ditchling. Three prettily decorated rooms are available for bed and breakfast; all have private bathrooms (fully tiled and carpeted) and are equipped with CTV and tea/coffee-making facilities. Breakfast is served in a small dining room where an à la carte dinner menu is also usually available. Bar meals are served here and in the large bar, which has a welcoming log fire, polished oak furniture and antique clocks. There is a garden with tables and chairs for drinks and meals in fine weather.

Price band B
Bar lunch 70p–£5
Dinner alc fr £5
Last dinner 9.30pm
Credit cards [1] [2] [3] [5]
Parking on premises
Restaurant closed to non-residents Sun, & Mon dinner

DONYATT Somerset Map 3 ST31

×× **Thatcher's Pond**
☏ Ilminster (04605) 3210

The atmosphere is friendly and informal at this charming restaurant, created from an attractive beamed farmhouse which dates back to the 15th century. A tempting cold buffet, laid out on a large central table, is the basis of most meals here, though a hot dish of the day is always available as well. Different salads may be accompanied by a choice of cold meats such as beef, ham, turkey and tongue, or fish including salmon and trout, and pâtés and vegetarian items are also usually on offer. Sweets, chosen from the trolley, are excellent.

Lunch alc £10
Dinner alc £11
Last dinner 9.30pm
Credit cards [1] [3]
Parking on premises
Closed 26 Dec–10th Feb
Closed Mon, & Sun dinner

DORCHESTER-ON-THAMES Oxfordshire Map 4 SU59

❀ ★★ B
George Hotel
High St
☏ Oxford (0865) 340404

Dominated by its remarkable Norman abbey, Dorchester's main street is lined by a fascinating collection of old cottages and shops. The George has been part of the scene here since long before its heyday as a coaching inn: its origins can be traced back over eight centuries. Not surprisingly, it retains a wonderful old-world atmosphere. Oak beams, higgledy-piggledy floors and ceilings, and intriguing nooks and crannies are everywhere, and open log fires ensure that the welcome is as warm for today's travellers as it was for those of centuries ago. Each bedroom is furnished and fitted to make the most of its individual features. Much of the furniture is antique (two rooms have four-poster beds), but modern facilities such as CTV and tea/coffee-making equipment are also provided, and nearly all the 17 rooms (eight of them in converted stable block) have private bathrooms. Public rooms are charming and comfortable, and the attractive beamed restaurant is a congenial place where fine fresh food in season (sometimes from the hotel's own garden) is served.

Price band C
Lunch alc £17
Dinner td £12 or alc £17
Last dinner 9.45pm
Credit cards [1] [2] [3] [5]
Parking on premises

DOVER Kent Map 5 TR34

GH **Peverell House**
28 Park Ave
Folkestone (0304) 202573/205088

Extensive views of Dover Castle and the town are a feature of this imposing late Victorian house, which is situated next to Connaught Park and conveniently placed for the cross-Channel ferry port. Comfortable accommodation is offered here for a reasonable price. Six bedrooms, all with washbasins, includes two family rooms, while downstairs there is a cosy TV lounge and a sun lounge. Guests also have the use of the garden. A full English breakfast is available, and for those who need to leave early to catch a ferry, arrangements for Continental breakfast can be made. Dinner should be ordered by noon if required. Peverell House does not accept dogs.

Price band A
Dinner, b&b £18–£21
Last dinner 6.30pm
Parking on premises

DOWNHAM MARKET Norfolk Map 5 TF60

GH **Cross Keys Riverside Hotel**
Hilgay (3m S on A10)
(0366) 387777

This small hotel stands beside the River Wissey in the village of Hilgay. It was once a coaching inn, and today most of the traffic noise from the busy A10 is excluded by secondary glazing. Indeed, the owners, Mr and Mrs Lamb, ensure that the Cross Keys still retains the atmosphere of an inn. The five spacious bedrooms all have private bathrooms and CTV; one is suitable for family occupation. A large garden gives guests access to the river where they may fish. Dogs are not accepted in the hotel.

Price band B
Dinner, b&b £22.60–£29.90
Last dinner 8.30pm
Parking on premises
Closed 23 Dec–21 Jan

DRIFFIELD Humberside Map 8 TA05

× **Queen's Head Inn**
Kirkburn
(3 miles SW on A163)
(0377) 89261

This delightful little village inn with restaurant was once a farmhouse and granary. Today, it retains its simple country character with beams, cream walls hung with dog and horse sketches, lighted candles and fresh flowers. Menus are varied, the chef demonstrating flair and style in the preparation of English and international dishes including a choice of vegetarian meals. Your meal will be served in immaculate surroundings by courteous and attentive staff. Bar meals are also available. A full lunch is served on Sundays only.

Bar lunch alc £4.14–£6.20
Dinner alc £9.35
Last dinner 9.15pm
Credit card [5]
Closed Mon

DROITWICH Hereford & Worcester Map 3 SO86

FH **Phepson Farm**
Himbleton
Himbleton (090569) 205

Featured on a TV travel programme on English farm holidays, Phepson Farm is ideal for a family stay. Guests are free to explore the peaceful 175-acre holding, and children will be enchanted by the lambs and waterfowl, and by feeding-time in the central farmyard. The farm is set on the Wychavon Way, a 66-mile long-distance footpath running through the Worcestershire countryside to Winchcombe in the Cotswolds. Mrs Havard lets three rooms (including one family room) in the farmhouse, all with washbasins and tea-making facilities. Traditional English breakfasts are served, and three or four-course home-cooked dinners are avilable to order.

Price band A
Parking on premises
Closed Dec–Mar

DRUMNADROCHIT Highland *Inverness-shire* Map 14 NH53

❀ ★★ HBL
Polmaily House
(3m W of Drumnadrochit on A831)
✆ (04562) 343

Extensive grounds provide a peaceful setting for this charming country house hotel, which is an ideal base for exploring the beautiful western Highlands. Caring hosts Mr and Mrs Parsons and their attentive, well-motivated staff make guests feel thoroughly at home. Bedrooms are thoughtfully equipped and have many homely touches such as fresh flowers. Seven of the nine have private bathrooms, and one a four-poster bed, and there are two family rooms. All are individually furnished and decorated. A friendly, relaxed atmosphere pervades the public rooms; as well as an inviting drawing room with comfortable armchairs, there is a smaller 'book room'. The attractive dining room offers a short à la carte dinner menu featuring the kind of imaginative dishes created by Alison Parsons that have recently earned Polmaily House our rosette. The hotel has good recreational facilities including an open-air swimming pool, a hard tennis court and a croquet lawn. Dogs are not accepted.

Price band B
Dinner alc £15
Last dinner 9.30pm
Credit cards [1] [3]
Parking on premises
Closed mid Oct–March

DULVERTON Somerset Map 3 SS92

★★ RED
Ashwick House
(3m NW of Dulverton off B3223)
✆ (0398) 23868

Nothing seems to be too much trouble for the Sherwood family, proprietors of this delightful, peaceful Edwardian house whose six-acre grounds slope down towards the lovely River Barle. The six spacious bedrooms (all with bathrooms) are provided with every comfort: not only the more ususal facilities such as CTV and hairdriers but also trouser-presses, radio/cassette-players (with cassettes) and even bathroom scales. The lounges retain many stylish original features such as marble chimneypieces, and are tastefully and comfortably furnished. Flowers and plants abound, and a wood fire in the hall adds a homely touch in winter. The dining room, overlooking the gardens, it equally attractive and provides a relaxing setting for excellent, expertly prepared meals. The fixed-price menus offer a limited but well-planned choice, and fresh local produce is used in abundance. Ashwick House does not accept dogs, or children under eight.

Price band C
Lunch td fr £8
Dinner td fr £12.50
Last dinner 8.45pm
Parking on premises

DUNBAR Lothian *East Lothian* Map 12 NT67

GH **St Beys**
2 Bayswell Rd
✆ (0368) 63571

Though the exterior of this guesthouse is unassuming, its attractive interior is well-appointed, and upstairs rooms have spectacular sea views. Public areas — a cosy lounge with wood-burning stove and a pretty, modernised dining room — are homely and comfortable, while the tastefully decorated bedrooms are thoughtfully equipped with modern appointments. The house is situated within easy reach of the town centre, providing a good base for a touring holiday, and new roads now bring it within striking distance of Edinburgh.

Price band B
Lunch td £3
Dinner td £7
Last dinner 7pm
Credit card [3]
No parking on premises

DUNMOW, GREAT Essex Map 5 TL62

×× **The Starr** Market Place ✆ (0371) 4321	Fresh local ingredients are the basis of many of the dishes at the Starr, a 14th-century building in the centre of this busy country town. Diners can relax over pre-dinner drinks in a cosy lounge-bar while proprietor Mr Jones is on hand to discuss or explain items on the blackboard menu. Cuisine is mainly French or English; old favourites such as home-made steak and kidney pie are available on occasion, but the menu also includes innovative specialities, as well as vegetarian dishes. A comprehensive wine list will cover most customers' requirements, and staff are cheerful and efficient.	Lunch td £10–£15 Dinner td £20–£25 Last dinner 9.30pm Credit cards [1] [3] [5] Parking on premises Closed 3 wks Aug & 2 wks after Xmas Closed Sat lunch & Sun dinner

DUNOON Strathclyde *Argyllshire* Map 10 NS17

★★ H **Enmore Hotel** Marine Parade, Kirn ✆ (0369) 2230	A seafront setting, a warm welcome and good recreational facilities make the Enmore a delightful family holiday hotel. Genial hosts Angela and David Wilson and their team of friendly young staff spare no effort in ensuring that their guests are attentively cared for. The bedrooms, most of them recently refurbished, are bright and cheery and thoughtfully equipped with extras like flowers, chocolates and bathrobes. Most of the 11 rooms have private facilities and CTV; three have four-poster beds and two are family rooms. Public rooms include a comfortable main lounge, a lounge/foyer with period furnishings, a snug cocktail bar and a small TV lounge. The dining room is well-appointed and offers interesting Scottish cooking. Vegetarians can be catered for. Children are welcome at the Enmore, which has a games room, a garden and also its own squash courts.	Price band B Bar lunch £1–£7 Dinner td £13 Last dinner 8.30pm Credit cards [1] [3] [5] Parking on premises

DUNSTABLE Bedfordshire Map 4 TL02

★★★ B **Old Palace Lodge** Church St ✆ Luton (0582) 62201	This ivy-clad red-brick building, part of which was originally Dunstable Palace, where Henry VIII is believed to have stayed, is now a very comfortable 50-bedroom hotel. Welcoming public rooms are harmoniously furnished and have a cheerful atmosphere. The bedrooms, all with private bathrooms, are extremely well-appointed and equipped. Furnishings and décor are of a very high standard, and facilities in all rooms include CTV and telephones. Two rooms have four-poster beds and there are six family rooms. The restaurant, staffed by a professional and hard-working young team, offers an à la carte selection supplemented by daily specialities and roasts from the trolley. Flambé dishes are skilfully and swiftly prepared, and vegetarians can be catered for. Willing and pleasant service is characteristic of the whole establishment, and the hotel has an air of warmth and friendliness. Dogs are not accepted.	Price band C/D Lunch/dinner alc £12 Last dinner 9.45pm Credit cards [1] [2] [3] [5] Limited parking on premises

DURHAM Co Durham Map 12 NZ24

★★★ L
Hallgarth Manor
Pittington
(Off A690, SP Pittington, approx 1m E of AIM/A690 junct)
✆ (091) 3721188

Four and a half acres of grounds surround this elegant listed building, which was a family home until 1984. Now a 23-bedroom hotel, it has retained many of its original features, such as its sweeping staircase and its country-house atmosphere. Bedrooms, all with bathrooms en suite, are tastefully furnished and equipped with CTV and telephones. The comfortable lounge is supplemented by two bars — one of them the beamed Village Tavern, where bar snacks are available at lunch-time. The stylish, split-level Elemore Restaurant offers inventive, modern cuisine, using only fresh produce, at both lunch and dinner. Dishes can be as simple as roast beef or as exotic as the lavishly described specialities on the à la carte menu, for example 'pillows of smoked salmon filled with shell-picked crabmeat rested on a refreshing yogurt and cucumber sauce accompanied by a flower of seasonal salad leaves'. The wine list is extensive and includes a 'directors' bin' of higher-priced wines and, at the other end of the scale, red or white house wine at £4.75 per bottle.

Price band C
Lunch td fr £7.50
Dinner td fr £12.50 or alc £18
Last dinner 9.15pm
Credit cards [1] [2] [3] [5]
Parking on premises

★ **Redhills**
Redhills Ln, Crossgate Moor
(Off A167 just S of Durham roundabout)
✆ (091) 386 4331

This friendly, informal small hotel is popular with both business people and tourists visiting Durham. The six bedrooms, while not large, have been carefully planned to achieve good use of space, and are equipped with CTV and a beverage tray. The comfortable, conservatory-style lounge adjoins the lounge bar and the restaurant, a homely room with a log fire in winter and decorated with copper and brass bric-à-brac. Our Inspector found the four-course table d'hôte dinner menu especially good value, since it offers a good choice with coffee included in the price. Main courses are dishes such as steaks, roast chicken or poached halibut, while sweets might include home-made fruit pie or cheesecake. The lunch menu consists of an extensive range of bar meals. Soups are all home-made, and fresh vegetables are used whenever possible. Redhills does not accept dogs.

Price band B
Lunch td fr £3.95
Dinner td £6.95
Last dinner 10pm
Credit cards [1] [2] [3] [5]
Parking on premises

× **Squire Trelawney**
80 Front St, Sherburn Village
(3m E, off A181)
✆ (091) 372 0613

This small, family-run restaurant offers friendly service and very good value for money. The dinner menu is designed to suit most tastes: main courses include a range of plain steaks, chicken and fish as well as speciality dishes such as steak Diane, scampi au gratin and tournedos Rossini. First courses include cheese and ham croissants, particularly enjoyed by our Inspector. The lunch menu is a more homely and simple affair, with home-made Scotch broth, perhaps, followed by roast pork or braised liver and onions, and apple crumble or jam roly-poly for pudding. Fresh seasonal vegetables are always used. All this is outstanding value, and a good wine list is offered including house wines at £5.95 per litre. The dining room, with its balcony-style seating, is complemented by a small lounge-bar with roughcast walls and interesting bric-à-brac.

Bar lunch fr £1.50
Lunch td fr £4.50
Dinner alc £10
Last dinner 9.30pm
Limited parking on premises

DUROR Highland *Argyllshire* Map 14 NM95

★★ L **Stewart**
✆ (063174) 268

The hotel is set well back from the road in its own woodland and gardens, looking down Glen Appin towards Loch Linnhe and the Hills of Morvern beyond. Privately-owned, it has recently changed hands, and the friendliness and enthusiasm of Mr and Mrs Lang are already making their mark. Accommodation is comfortable, and spacious in the case of front-facing bedrooms, where the simplicity of décor enhances spectacular views. The first-floor residents' lounge has been made most attractive and is well-provided with books and magazines, while the popular ground-floor lounge is used by residents and non-residents alike. In the recently redecorated restaurant, menus offer an interesting range of dishes, all based as far as possible on fresh local produce.

Price band B
Bar lunch alc £3.75
Dinner alc £15
Last dinner 9.30pm
Credit cards [1] [2] [3] [5]
Parking on premises

DUXFORD Cambridgeshire Map 5 TL44

★★★ L
Duxford Lodge
Ickleton Rd
✆ Cambridge (0223) 836444
Tx 817438

Duxford Lodge was a fighter base HQ in World War II. Now a comfortable and carefully converted hotel, it is a fitting and convenient place to stay for visitors to the Imperial War Museum's collection of historic aircraft at Duxford Airfield. Friendly, professional staff, well-equipped accommodation, and some of the best hotel food in the county have boosted the hotel's popularity in recent years. The 11 bedrooms in the main house are supplemented by a further five in an annexe. All have private facilities, CTV, telephones, hairdriers and trouser-presses, and the de-luxe rooms also have mini-bars. Annexe rooms are smaller and more functional than decorative, while those in the main house are individually furnished. The lounge, bar and restaurant have the cosy atmosphere of a grand private house rather than a busy hotel. Food is imaginative and well-presented, with vegetarian meals available.

Price band C
Lunch td fr £9.50 or alc £15
Dinner td fr £12.50 or alc £15
Last dinner 10pm
Credit cards [1] [2] [3] [5]
Parking on premises

EASDALE Strathclyde *Argyll* Map 10 NM71

★ **Easdale Inn**
✆ Balvicar (08523) 256

The pleasant country inn, standing in its own grounds at the edge of the village and commanding sea views, has welcomed guests since Victorian times. Highland hospitality is still very much the norm today, especially in the traditional dining room, where good home cooking makes a speciality of fresh seafood caught by local fishing boats. Considerable refurbishment over the years has resulted in comfortable, well-equipped bedrooms, several of which have en suite facilities, but this has been achieved without sacrificing the original character and atmosphere of the establishment.

Price band B
Bar lunch alc £5.50
Dinner alc £9.25
Last dinner 8.30pm
Parking on premises
Closed Nov–Feb

EASTBOURNE East Sussex Map 5 TV69

× **Byron's**
6 Crown St,
Old Town
✆ (0323) 20171

Tiny, candlelit rooms, warmed by a large log fire in winter, create a relaxed, leisurely atmosphere in which to enjoy Simon and Marion Scrutton's delicious food. Indeed this is not an eating place for those in a hurry,

Lunch alc £7.80
Dinner alc £12.50
Last dinner

since the Scruttons run their little restaurant with a minimum of help, so service can be slow at busy times. However, dishes like halibut with a sauce of white wine, vermouth and chives, or the orange Bakewell tart, are worth waiting for. Everything is freshly cooked to order. Fish dishes are especially recommended, and vegetables are also fresh and good. Vegetarian food is available, and the restaurant has a no-smoking area. Booking in advance is strongly recommended, since Byron's is popular and seats only 22 diners. Lunch is served only by prior arrangement.

10.30pm
Credit cards [2] [3] [5]
No parking on premises
Closed 1 wk Xmas
Closed Sun, & Sat lunch

GH **Mowbray Hotel**
2 Lascelles Ter
✆ (0323) 20012

Seafront and theatres are within easy reach of this welcoming 16-bedroom guesthouse. Furnished in traditional style, the bedrooms are fresh, neat and clean and all have CTV and tea/coffee-making equipment. Four rooms have shower and WC en suite, and there is one family room. The comfortable lounge has books to borrow as well as a good collection of local tourist information. Breakfast and dinner are served (to residents only) in a bright basement dining room. Care is taken over the good, wholesome meals, and guests are asked to order dinner by 5.30pm. The Mowbray does not take children under six.

Price band A
Dinner, b&b £18.25–£19.50
Last dinner 6.30pm
Credit cards [1] [3]
Parking nearby
Closed Jan–Mar

★★ L
West Rocks Hotel
Grand Parade
✆ (0323) 25217

A fine seafront position, a cheerful atmosphere and several spacious public rooms are what attract guests to this family hotel. More than half of the 54 bedrooms have private shower and WC, and a few have private bathrooms. Rooms vary in size and style, and are priced accordingly, but all are fresh, clean and well-maintained; CTV and radio is standard in all. There are five family rooms, but the hotel does not take children under three. Four lounges include a sun lounge and a TV room. There is no bar as such, but drinks can be ordered from the lounge waiter or the porter. Meals, including lunch, are served by cordial, courteous staff in the large, bright dining room. The hotel does not accept dogs.

Price band B
Lunch td £4.50
Dinner td £6
Last dinner 7.30pm
Parking nearby
Closed Nov–Mar

EAST GRINSTEAD West Sussex Map 5 TQ33

★★ **Woodbury House**
Lewes Rd
✆ (0342) 313657

This small, family-run hotel on the southern edge of East Grinstead provides well-equipped bedrooms and good food, and, in our Inspector's opinion, has much to commend it. Of the seven bedrooms (including one family room) six have showers en suite and one has a bathroom. Rooms are of a good size, and some have fine countryside views. Furnishings are mostly traditional (one room has a four-poster bed), and décor is fresh and bright. Room facilities are good, and include CTV, clock/radios, direct-dial telephones and tea/coffee-making equipment. Downstairs, a cosy bar with a coal fire is complemented by an elegant and comfortable lounge for residents and diners. The attractive restaurant, with its pastel décor and lace tablecloths, offers particularly good value in its special table d'hôte menu for residents. Chef Harvey Arann (formerly of the rosetted Spindlewood at Wadhurst) cooks skilfully in a light, modern style.

Price band C
Lunch td fr £10.50 or alc £17
Dinner td fr £12.50 or alc £17
Last dinner 9.30pm
Credit cards [1] [2] [3] [4] [5]
Parking on premises
Closed Dec 25–6

EDINBURGH Lothian *Midlothian* Map 11 NT27

×× **Alp-Horn**
167 Rose St
✆ 031-225 4787

This attractive and intimate Swiss restaurant is now firmly established as the best of its type in Scotland. Situated in the city centre, it has recently been extended to provide a 'no-smoking' dining area, and its appealing décor is very much in the 'Alpine' style. Attentive service is provided by uniformed, professional waiters, and the cuisine is most enjoyable, not over-ambitious, but making good use of fresh produce. Veal and venison, as might be expected, are popular menu items and appear in some delectable variations. Starters and desserts are not quite in the same league of excellence, but the wine list is well-chosen, featuring Swiss and Austrian wines. It is important to book in advance, especially at weekends.

Lunch alc fr £5
Dinner alc fr £12
Last dinner 10pm
Credit card [1]
No parking on premises
Closed 1st 3wks Jul, 2 wks Xmas

GH Dorstan Private Hotel
7 Priestfield Rd
✆ 031-667 6721

Set in a pleasant residential area close to the city's Holyrood Park, and convenient for access to the city centre, this tastefully appointed and thoughtfully equipped guesthouse offers a warm and cheerful welcome. Enjoyable breakfasts are served by friendly staff, and dinners can also be arranged. Bedrooms have been refurbished to a high standard, with attractively coordinated soft furnishings and modern amenities including direct-dial telephones. The public areas of the house, bright with fresh flowers, are well-maintained and comfortable — and the proprietors have provided a good supply of informative reading material for visitors to Edinburgh.

Price band A/B
Dinner, b&b £20–£26
Last dinner 6pm
Parking on premises
Closed Xmas & New Year

★★★ BL
The Howard
Great King St
✆ 031-557 3500

The Howard, an elegant and refined hotel, is situated in the heart of Edinburgh's Georgian New Town. There is a relaxed, club-like atmosphere in its public areas, where traditional décor forms a fitting background to some fine pieces of period furniture, and individually-styled bedrooms are well-furnished and thoughtfully equipped. The basement 'Claret Jug' has long been a popular meeting place of the city's 'smart set', offering a good range of ales and interesting bar food. Dinner menus are enterprising, detailing such dishes as 'A lightly poached egg, encased in puff pastry, on a leek pâté' or 'Breast of duck served with a brandy and honey essence'.

Price band D
Bar lunch fr £2
Lunch alc £7
Dinner alc £14
Last dinner 9.30pm
Credit cards [1] [2] [3] [4] [5]
Parking on premises

×× **Lancers Brasserie**
South Hamilton Place
✆ 031-332 3444

This smart, modern restaurant, specialising in Bengali and North Indian cuisine, has done much to change the Edinburgh public's idea of an Indian meal as the obligatory end to an evening's drinking! Instead of flock wallcovering and paper tablecloths, you will find attractively tiled floors and rosewood furniture, while the more rowdy element is channelled into the basement 'Officers' Club' so that discerning customers may enjoy the authentic cuisine in a restrained atmosphere. Restraint is the keynote of the cooking, too, with flavours carefully balanced in subtle combinations. Particularly recommended is the 'Thali', a set meal which is prepared in both vegetarian and non-vegetarian varieties. Traditional favourites appear

Lunch td & alc fr £4.95
Dinner td & alc fr £6.95
Last dinner 11.30pm
Credit cards [1] [2] [3]
No parking on premises

alongside such innovative dishes as shrimp balls with a mild yogurt sauce, and fresh herbs are used to good effect.

×× **Merchants**
17 Merchant St
✆ 031-225 4009

A smart French restaurant tucked away among the streets and lanes of the city's famous old town offers a background of discreet jazz and the efficient services of polite, aproned staff. Cuisine is robust and provincial in style — simple, yet interesting enough to please most palates. Starters like wild mushrooms and basmati rice with leek and white wine sauce or lamb terrine with garlic and rosemary can be followed by such main dishes as poached queen scallops in champagne sauce or saddle of hare with a rich red wine sauce. A choice of vegetarian dishes is available. Desserts are delicious, and a good wine list offers a suitable accompaniment to every meal.

Lunch td £6.95
Dinner alc £17.50
Last dinner 10.30pm
Credit cards [1] [2] [3] [5]
No parking on premises
Closed Sun

❀× **North Sea Village**
111-3 Buccleuch St
(Close to Edinburgh University)
✆ 031-667 5576

Staff are friendly and the standard of service is particularly good in this modestly appointed little Chinese restaurant, which is situated near the University, to the south of the city centre. The seafood specialities include a fish of the day, usually turbot or monkfish, braised in a pot with oyster sauce or steamed Cantonese-style, and delights like a starter of fresh scallop with black bean sauce, served in its shell. Such favourites as Peking duck and Szechuan fried shredded pork represent the cuisine of other regions. Vegetarian meals are available, and the premises are fully licensed.

Lunch td fr £3.20 or alc £9
Dinner td fr £6 or alc £9
Last dinner 2am
Credit cards [2] [3]
Parking nearby

★★★ HBL
Roxburghe
Charlotte Sq
✆ 031-225 3921

The Roxburghe, a city centre hotel of great character and distinction, stands in one of Edinburgh's grand Georgian squares. The atmosphere of its flower-decked foyer and main lounge is almost club-like, though the new, informal Buttery Restaurant is a departure from tradition. The Consort Bar and Restaurant remain popular, nevertheless, many regular customers appreciating the straightforward cuisine. Bedrooms are individually styled — some already absolutely splendid and others undergoing refurbishment — but all have comfortable, traditional furniture. Standards of hospitality and service throughout the hotel are a credit to Scottish tourism.

Price band D
Lunch/dinner td £11 or alc £17
Last dinner 10pm
Credit cards [1] [2] [3] [5]
No parking on premises

EDWINSTOWE Nottinghamshire Map 8 SK66

★★ B
Forest Lodge
2 Church St
✆ Mansfield (0623) 822970

Although this 18th-century coaching inn cannot claim a long enough history to have Robin Hood associations, it is in the heart of the area that is always linked with his name, and is close to the Sherwood Forest Visitor Centre. However, Forest Lodge does have a wealth of old-world charm, as well as well-equipped modern accommodation. Seven bedrooms, attractively furnished in pine, all have private facilities, CTV and telephones. There is one family room and one four-poster room. The beamed restaurant offers something for everyone. Two table d'hôte menus, at different prices, offer meals to suit

Price band B
Lunch/dinner £2.50–£9.95 & alc
Last dinner 10pm
Credit cards [1] [2] [3] [5]
Parking on premises

most tastes and appetites, and there are special menus for children and vegetarians. There is a discothèque on Thursdays. Hotel and restaurant staff are efficient, courteous and friendly.

EGLINGHAM Northumberland Map 12 NU11

FH **West Ditchburn Farm**
✆ Powburn
(066578) 337

Tranquillity and comfort are assured at this handsome stone farmhouse, which stands in walled gardens on a large livestock farm. The four bedrooms, two with en suite shower, include two family rooms, and are all equipped with CTV, hairdriers and tea/coffee-making facilities. Décor and furnishings are most attractive, and even the towels are selected to match each room. The lounge is comfortable and elegant, while the impressive dining room has an enormous sideboard gleaming with polished silver. Good, wholesome dinners, including delicious sweets, are produced by Mrs Easton, who also makes excellent cakes and biscuits for afternoon tea. Dinner should be ordered by 5pm. The whole family — Mr and Mrs Easton and their daughter, Heather — seem to enjoy their role as hosts, and guests can be confident that they will be well-looked after here. Children under four are not accepted.

Price band A
Dinner, b&b £19–£20
Last dinner 7pm
Parking on premises
Closed Nov–Feb

EGLWYSFACH Gwynedd Map 6 SN69

★★★ ♣♣
Ynyshir Hall
✆ Glandyfi
(065474) 209

The large RSPB reserve of Ynys-hir, rich in bird and plant life, is very near this elegant manor house. Standing in beautiful, secluded grounds, Ynyshir Hall has been revitalised by its present proprietors, the Allison family, and now offers comfortable accommodation and friendly, hospitable service. Of the 11 bedrooms, eight have private facilities. There is one family room and one four-poster room, and several of the rooms are set aside for non-smokers. A good selection of bar meals supplements the small table d'hôte menu, and vegetarians can be catered for. Dogs are not accepted.

Price band B
Lunch/dinner td £12
Last dinner 8.45pm
Credit cards [1] [2] [3] [5]
Parking on premises
Closed Nov 15–Mar 1

ELGIN Grampian *Morayshire* Map 15 NJ26

★★★ HB
Mansion House
The Haugh
✆ (0343) 48811

Once derelict, this historic Scottish mansion has been skilfully restored by its dedicated and enthusiastic owner, Mr Oliveira. Popular with both business people and tourists, the Mansion House is tucked away in its own grounds beside the River Lossie, and has all the attractions of a country house hotel, yet is only minutes from the town centre. Staff here are attentive and sincere, and their efforts are largely responsible for the friendly, hospitable atmosphere. There are 12 bedrooms, varying in size but all with private bathrooms and equipped with almost every conceivable 'extra'. As well as the usual CTV, telephones and tea/coffee-making equipment, guests are likely to find fresh fruit, flowers and a welcoming glass of sherry on arrival in their rooms. Other thoughtful touches include fresh milk in the fridge/bar

Price band C
Lunch td £7.50
Dinner td fr £14 or alc £18
Last dinner 9pm
Credit cards [1] [2] [3] [5]
Parking on premises

and individual boxes of non-sugar sweeteners. Two rooms have four-poster beds and there are three family bedrooms: the hotel welcomes children of any age. Public rooms include an elegant cocktail lounge for residents and diners. Here one can study the dinner menu. A choice of fixed-price menu or à la carte is available, the former more reasonably priced, but the latter more likely to appeal to the discerning palate. Cooking is in the modern style, using the best of fresh produce and with the emphasis on artistic presentation. Vegetarian dishes are available. The Mansion House does not accept dogs.

ELSTEAD Surrey Map 4 SU94

The Woolpack
✆ (0252) 703106

The Woolpack is a very pretty, friendly country pub, its deceptively large interior containing dining accommodation for 44 people plus a bar area where food is also available. Daily menus (sometimes offering a rather limited choice) are displayed on a blackboard and orders are taken at the salad bar; there is also a children's menu. The well-presented meals represent excellent value for money, and service is both cheerful and reasonably speedy. The pleasant garden at the rear of the pub is an attraction in summer.

Lunch/dinner alc £6
Last dinner 9.45pm
Credit card [1]
Parking on premises & nearby

ELY Cambridgeshire Map 5 TL58

❀ × **Old Fire Engine House**
25 St Mary's St
✆ (0353) 2582

Hanging on the wall of the bar in this 18th-century house is a portrait of the fire engine that was once kept here. Today the building, in the shadow of Ely Cathedral, is a popular restaurant, where sound British country cooking turns fresh Fenland produce into all kinds of tempting dishes. Main courses on our Inspector's last visit included jugged hare with forcemeat balls, pike with a piquant sauce, and casserole of rabbit. The simply furnished dining room seats only 36, so booking in advance is recommended.

Lunch alc £10
Dinner alc £11
Last dinner 9pm
Limited parking on premises
Closed 2wks Xmas & Bank Hols
Closed Sun dinner

EMPINGHAM Leicestershire Map 4 SK90

Inn **White Horse**
High St
✆ (078086) 221

Recent improvements at this stone-built village inn near Rutland Water have included the conversion of the former stables to give eight bedrooms, all with private facilities. Three further rooms are available in the main building. All are prettily decorated and furnished, and have CTV and telephones. The White Horse is becoming increasingly popular for its food; in addition to bar meals and a full à la carte restaurant service, a good fixed-price Sunday lunch is available. This offers a good choice for each course: roast beef, or turkey, ham and mushroom pie, or salmon with cucumber and tarragon sauce were the main courses offered on our Inspector's visit, with five starters and five desserts to choose from. Bar food ranges from freshly made soup with home-baked bread to casseroles, chicken Kiev or saddle of lamb. A vegetarian choice is also available, and there is a good sweet list.

Price band B
Bar meal £2.50–£5.50
Lunch td fr £9
Dinner alc £12
Last dinner 10pm
Credit cards [1] [2] [3] [5]
Parking on premises

EMSWORTH Hampshire Map 4 SU70

★★★ Brookfield
Havant Rd
✆ (0243) 373363

Proprietors, the Gibson family, have steadily improved their hotel over several years, and their high standards of accommodation, housekeeping and service make Brookfield a comfortable, pleasing place to stay. The 31 bedrooms (25 with bath en suite and six with shower) have all modern facilities, including CTV and direct-dial telephones. One room has a four-poster bed. Public rooms comprise an elegant lounge, a cosy bar and a spacious restaurant offering either set dinner or an à la carte menu. Dishes are usually French or English in style, and vegetarians can be catered for. A more limited menu is available at lunch-time. Service is pleasant and helpful. Brookfield does not accept dogs.

Price band C
Lunch/dinner td £7.95 or alc £11
Last dinner 9.30pm
Credit cards 1 2 3 5
Parking on premises
Closed 1 wk Xmas

GH **Chestnuts**
55 Horndean Rd
(2m NW of Emsworth on B2148)
✆ (0243) 372233

Four letting bedrooms are available at this quiet guesthouse run by Mr and Mrs Hobbs. Fronted by mature chestnut trees, the detached house has a lovely garden and a swimming pool. Rooms are of a good size and well-equipped, and have older-style furnishings and some antiques. As well as the shared bathroom, there are two shared shower rooms. There is a peaceful, old-world style lounge with plenty of seating and a good range of books, and a dining room furnished with antique tables and chairs. Chestnuts is convenient for the railway station and is an ideal base for touring along the south coast.

Price band A
Dinner, b&b £18–£22
Last dinner 6pm
Parking on premises

ENFIELD Greater London

×× The Norfolk
80 London Rd
✆ 01-363 0979

The finer aspects of traditional restaurant-keeping can be enjoyed at this old fashioned and popular eating house. Roasts are served from a large silver-domed trolley, and flambé dishes are prepared skilfully and with a flourish. The cooking, mainly traditional English and French, features fresh ingredients in season, and sauces are well-prepared and tasty. Vegetarian dishes are available. There is a good choice of sweets from the trolley, and the thoughtfully chosen wine list is reasonably priced. Service is by an enthusiastic team of staff under the personal supervision of a charming and cordial restaurant manager.

Lunch/dinner alc £12.50
Last dinner 10pm
Credit cards 1 2 3 4 5
Closed 3 wks Aug & Bank Hols
Closed Sun, Sat lunch & Mon dinner

ERBISTOCK Clwyd Map 7 SJ34

× Boat Inn
✆ Bangor-on-Dee (0978) 780143

This 16th-century building enjoys a lovely setting near an attractive church, and fronted by the River Dee. A flagstone-floored bar, where a large fire is usually burning, leads through to the oak-beamed restaurant. Here is served an extensive range of well-prepared French and English dishes which have earned the Boat an excellent reputation locally. Diners in search of lighter meals will find a choice of more modest dishes served in a separate building from the main restaurant, but this is open only during summer.

Lunch td fr £5.50 or alc £15
Dinner td £11.95 or alc £15
Last dinner 9pm
Credit cards 1 2 3 5
Parking on premises
Closed 4 wks Jan–Feb

ESKDALEMUIR Dumfries and Galloway *Dumfriesshire* Map 11 NY29

★★ H **Hart Manor** ✆ (05416) 217	This attractive little country hotel, standing in a beautiful, remote situation, offers a high standard of hospitality and a very warm welcome. The seven bedrooms (most of which have en suite shower facilities) are comfortable and modern and thoughtfully provided with reading material. Lounges, bar and dining room, though conservatively decorated, are all well-appointed, with open fires in cold weather. The chef makes good use of fresh produce in the preparation of enjoyable meals; soups are home-made, and a good range of carefully cooked vegetables accompanies such main courses as stuffed poussin with apple and herbs, or entrecôte or beef with whisky sauce.	Price band B Bar lunch alc £3.45 Dinner td fr £10.50 Last dinner 8pm Credit card 3 Parking on premises Closed Xmas day

ETON Berkshire Map 4 SU97

Eton Buttery 73 High St ✆ Windsor (0753) 854479	Our Inspector found the buffet-style lunches especially good value at this licensed riverside restaurant, which has marvellous views of the Thames and Windsor Castle. Traditional lunch dishes usually include a roast and a home-made pie of the day, and there is a fine display of cold first courses and salads as well as cakes, pastries and gâteaux to follow. The dinner menu is à la carte, with waitress service, and prices are accordingly higher.	Lunch/dinner alc £10 Last dinner 10.30pm Credit cards 1 2 3 5 Parking nearby Closed Xmas

EVESHAM Hereford and Worcester Map 4 SP04

★★★ **Evesham Hotel** Coopers Ln ✆ (0386) 49111	There is reputed to have been a building on the site of the Evesham Hotel since the Roman occupation. During the twelve years that the present owners have operated the establishment they have made many improvements — including the introduction of rubber ducks into guests' bathrooms! Orders for meals are taken in the cocktail bar from a menu that is changed daily and takes account of seasonal specialities, and the extensive wine list incorporates the owners' (sometimes merciless) comments. Coffee in the stylish lounge may be accompanied by your choice of liqueur from an amazingly comprehensive list that extends to 63 different types of brandy.	Price band C Lunch td £7.50 or alc £12 Dinner alc £14 Last dinner 9.30pm Credit cards 1 2 3 5 Parking on premises Closed 25–6 Dec

EXETER Devon Map 3 SX99

★★★ H **St Olave's Court Hotel** Mary Arches St ✆ (0392) 217736	In a quiet road just outside the city centre stands this delightful Georgian house, enclosed in a small walled garden. It was built by a local merchant, James Golsworthy, and it is particularly for the cosy restaurant named after him that the hotel is recommended by our Inspector. The cooking, modern and French in style, shows flair and imagination, and value for money is excellent. Table d'hôte menus are supplemented by a wider à la carte choice. Favourite first courses include a delicate mould of smoked salmon, sour cream, cottage cheese and mustard, garnished with lumpfish caviar and lime; or a light mousse of asparagus and chicken wrapped in poached	Price band C Lunch td fr £7.50 or alc £15 Dinner td fr £10.95 or alc £15 Last dinner 9.30pm Credit cards 1 2 3 5 Parking on premises

leeks, served in a creamy sauce. Main courses might be escalopes of duck breast grilled and served with an apple and calvados sauce, or saddle of lamb cut into small steaks and sautéed with rosemary, served on croustades with artichoke hearts. Home-made sweets are carefully prepared, and vegetarian dishes are available. The hotel is privately owned and personally managed by Donald Clarke, assisted by his small team of equally hospitable staff. Most of the 17 cosy, well-furnished bedrooms (four in an annexe) have private facilities, and all have CTV and telephones. Dogs are not accepted.

EXFORD Somerset Map 3 SS83

★★★
Crown Hotel
✆ (064383) 554

This former coaching inn, set in a village at the heart of Exmoor, still offers not only well-appointed bedrooms for guests, but also stabling facilities for their horses. The relaxed, convivial atmosphere of the Crown is ideally suited to the riding, hunting and walking holidays that are so popular in the area. A good range of bar meals is served, and an extensive menu, including vegetarian dishes, is available in the restaurant. Service is friendly and efficient. All 18 bedrooms have bathrooms, CTV and telephones, and are comfortably furnished.

Price band B/C
Lunch td fr £3
Dinner td £14.95
Last dinner 9.30pm
Credit cards [1] [2] [3]
Parking on premises

EXMINSTER Devon Map 3 SX98

Swan's Nest Inn
Station Rd
✆ Exeter (0392) 832371

Convenient for travellers on the busy M5/A38 route, this popular free house just outside Exeter is recommended for its wide selection of traditional cooking, which represents excellent value for money. The spacious, beamed bars are full of character and charm and, in addition to a good range of well-kept draught beers and lagers, cocktails both alcoholic and non-alcoholic are served. The basic cold menu includes crab, prawns, smoked salmon, home-cooked ham, Devon turkey pie, pâtés and cheeses, and is supplemented by hot dishes of the day. There is also a carvery, offering traditional roasts, as well as an à la carte menu for dinner. Sweets are home-made, and helpings generous.

Lunch/dinner £6–£10
Last dinner 10pm
Credit cards [1] [2] [3] [5]
Parking on premises

> The price band indicates the price of bed and breakfast for a single person or room. Price band A = £15 or less; price band B = £16–£30; price band C = £31–£50; price band D = more than £50.

FALKIRK Central *Stirlingshire* Map 11 NS87

× **Pierre's**
140 Graham's Rd
✆ (0324) 35843

Business always seems brisk at this popular little French restaurant, with its attractive décor and cosy atmosphere. Imaginative use has been made of space in the long, narrow room — and the quality of food and service amply compensate for such minor peculiarities as access to the gentlemen's toilet being through the kitchen! A tempting menu offers interesting, wholesome food at realistic prices, with table d'hôte meals representing particularly good value, and the ambience of unhurried calm enables one to do the cuisine full justice.

Lunch td fr £4.40 or alc £8.75
Dinner td fr £9.75 or alc £14.25
Last dinner 9.30pm
Credit cards [1] [2] [3] [5]
Limited parking on premises
Closed Dec 25–6 & Jan 1–2
Closed Sat lunch

FALMOUTH Cornwall Map 2 SW83

★★ HB
Crill House Hotel
Golden Bank
(2½m W of Falmouth on unclassified rd)
✆ (0326) 312994

An acre of garden filled with flowering shrubs shelters this friendly and informal country hotel, which is tucked away down a peaceful country lane. It is run by the hospitable Fenton family, for whom nothing seems to be too much trouble in ensuring guests' comfort. Each of the 11 bedrooms (including three family rooms) has a private bathroom, CTV, radio/intercom and tea/coffee facilities. There is a heated swimming pool in the garden, and afternoon tea can be served by the poolside or on the sun terrace. Hot or cold snacks are available either in the bar or outside at lunch-time, while for dinner there is a five-course table d'hôte menu, with some choice, planned to suit most tastes. Portions are generous, and everything is home-made. In spring and autumn, Crill House offers special one-week packages which include conducted tours to various Cornish gardens and historic houses. Hotel guests are honorary members of the Falmouth Club, whose amenities include tennis, table tennis, squash, billiards and bridge. Falmouth Golf Club is only a few minutes' drive from Crill House.

Price band B
Bar lunch £1–£3.50
Dinner td £9.25
Last dinner 8pm
Credit cards [1] [3]
Parking on premises
Closed end Oct

FAVERSHAM Kent Map 5 TR06

❀×× **Read's**
Painter's Forstal
✆ (0795) 535344

A consistently high standard of French-style cuisine distinguishes this welcoming restaurant, which is tucked away in a sleepy village surrounded by unspoilt countryside. The fixed-price meals are very good value: the chef/proprietor uses only good-quality fresh ingredients, which are put together with skill and imagination. The menu is supported by an interesting wine list. Service is efficient and pleasant, inviting relaxed and enjoyable dining. Background music and subdued lighting in the evening help to maintain a cosy atmosphere.

Lunch td £10 & alc
Dinner alc £19
Last dinner 10pm
Credit cards [2] [3] [5]
Parking on premises
Closed 2 wks Aug
Closed Sun

FLEET Hampshire Map 4 SU85

★★★
The Lismoyne
Church Rd
☏ (0252) 628555

Older-style accommodation with modern facilities are combined with traditional, friendly service at this well-run Victorian hotel. Set in lovely secluded gardens, the Lismoyne is conveniently placed adjoining the North Hants Golf Club and within a few minutes' drive of Windsor Great Park. Bedrooms vary, though most are of good size and have well-maintained private bathrooms. All 40 rooms are equipped with CTV and telephones. The restaurant is very popular locally, and offers particularly good value at lunch-time, when the fixed-price menu usually includes home-made soup, good roasts and a choice from a well-stocked sweet trolley. There is dancing on Saturday evenings in winter.

Price band C
Dinner td fr £8.90 or alc £15
Lunch td fr £7.90 or alc £13
Last dinner 9.30pm
Credit cards [1] [2] [3] [4] [5]
Parking on premises

FLIMWELL East Sussex Map 5 TQ73

× **Woods**
High St
☏ (058087) 342

Opened in late 1986, this new restaurant, run by Elkie and Robin Woods, is already being enjoyed by local customers for its informal atmosphere, uncomplicated service and well-balanced, interesting cooking. The menu is à la carte, though choice is limited, but simple starters complement more innovative main courses, such as fillet steak stuffed with anchovy and onion and served with a chasseur sauce. Special attention is given to vegetables, which are beautifully fresh and interestingly seasoned. The restaurant is comfortable and cosy, and attractively decorated in warm autumn colours.

Dinner alc £12.50
Last dinner 9.30pm
Credit cards [1] [3]
Closed Mon, & Sun dinner
Closed lunch

FOLKESTONE Kent Map 5 TR23

× **Emillo's Portofino Restaurant**
124A Sandgate Rd
☏ (0303) 55866

Traditional Italian dishes plus a small selection of other Continental favourites are the basis of the menu at this popular restaurant. Seating 55 diners, Emillo's Portofino is open for lunch and dinner; our Inspector recommends the fixed-price lunches as particularly good value. Vegetarian dishes are available. The premises are fully licensed and there is a choice of reasonably priced wines. The Italian staff are efficient and cheerful, and the atmosphere is lively and cosy.

Lunch td fr £7.50 or alc £12.80
Dinner alc £12.80
Last dinner 10.30pm
Credit cards [1] [2] [3] [5]
Parking nearby
Closed Mon

★★ **Garden House Hotel**
142 Sandgate Rd
☏ (0303) 52278

This refurbished and modernised Victorian hotel offers comfortable accommodation at reasonable rates. Nearly all the 42 bedrooms have en suite facilities, and all have telephones and CTV. There are seven family rooms and a four-poster room, and the hotel has a lift. A well-appointed lounge-bar, with pretty décor and elegant long drapes, is supplemented by an additional cosy lounge area. The split-level restaurant's table d'hôte lunch and dinner menus usually feature French and English dishes. Service is friendly and cheerful, and proprietor Mr Gregory takes an active interest in his guests' well-being.

Price band C
Lunch td fr £5
Dinner td fr £9.50 or alc £12
Last dinner 8.45 pm
Credit cards [1] [2] [3] [5]
Limited parking on premises

Pullman Wine-Bar 7 Church St ✆ (0303) 52524	Delicious home-made meals at very sensible prices have earned an entry here for this town-centre wine-bar, which is as popular with local business people as it is with holidaymakers. The blackboard menu features traditional casseroles, ploughman's lunches and salads as well as more modern dishes such as burgers, moussaka and chilli. Vegetarian dishes are also included. A daily special dish is always available: on our Inspector's visit it was lamb's liver and onion with vegetables and Lyonnaise potatoes, served in generous helpings, and excellent value at £2.75. The Pullman has a garden where meals can be eaten in fine weather.	Lunch/dinner alc £4.50 Last dinner 9.30pm Credit cards [1] [3] Parking nearby

FORDOUN Grampian *Kincardineshire* Map 15 NO77

FH **Ringwood** (Turn off dual-carriageway at Fordoun and follow signs) ✆ Auchenblae (05612) 313	This modernised villa, surrounded by woodland, has clear views across farmland. The bedrooms are of a high standard, and the provision of en suite toilets is particularly useful as the bathroom is on the ground floor. Guests can relax in a neat little sun lounge or in the television lounge with its homely coal fire. The atmosphere is one of friendly welcome, you will enjoy home baking with your 'cuppa', and a splendid country breakfast is provided.	Price band A Parking on premises Closed Nov–Mar

FORTINGALL Tayside *Perthshire* Map 14 NN74

★★ Fortingall Hotel ✆ Kenmore (08873) 367	A hamlet of thatched cottages lying amid lovely countryside on the River Lyon is the setting for a traditional coaching inn with crow-stepped gables. The hotel has 11 high-ceilinged bedrooms containing heavy Victorian furniture, hand-crafted in walnut or mahogany, and pieces in similar style are interspersed with some interesting antiques in the spacious lounge. The dining room serves a set-price, four-course meal, offering a range of well-cooked British dishes. Fortingall itself is not devoid of interest, for it is reputed to have been the birthplace of Pontius Pilate, and its churchyard contains the oldest yew tree in Britain.	Price band A Bar lunch td fr £4 Lunch td fr £4 or alc £5.75 Dinner td fr £9.50 or alc £10 Last dinner 8.30pm Credit card [3] Parking on premises
GH **Rose Villa** ✆ Kenmore (08873) 335	This delightful Scottish stone villa, tucked away in a lovely village of thatched cottages, provides a house-party atmosphere as guests eat superbly in a small but elegant period dining room with antique furniture, silverware and crystal glasses, the set four-course dinner reflecting both quality ingredients and skilful preparation. Bedroom décor and soft furnishings are based on varieties of roses to be found in the gardens, and the furniture is a blend of traditional and antique. Flower arrangements add a homely air, as do a wealth of thoughtful personal touches.	Price band A/B Dinner, b&b £27.50–£44 Last dinner 8pm Parking on premises Restricted service 25 Oct–Mar

À la carte prices are based on an average for three courses without wine.

FORT WILLIAM Highland *Inverness-shire* Map 14 NN17

❀ ★RED
The Factors House
Torlundy
✆ (0397) 5767

A keen young staff ensure that guests are made thoroughly welcome at this delightful little hotel. It stands in a sheltered corner of the grounds of Inverlochy Castle, which is owned by the proprietor's family. The Factors House offers fine standards of comfort as well as hospitality. Two small lounges provide a relaxing atmosphere with soft music, comfortable armchairs and open fires, while compact bedrooms are charming in appearance and thoughtfully equipped. In the dining room, home-made terrines, mousses and casseroles are regular features of the menu. Tennis, riding and fishing are available.

Price band C
Dinner td fr £14
Last dinner 9.30pm
Credit card [4]
Parking on premises
Closed 15 Dec–Mar

FOWEY Cornwall Map 2 SX15

★★ H
Marina Hotel
Esplanade
✆ (072683) 3315

This four-storey Georgian house occupies a fine position on the waterfront, overlooking both the Fowey River and the open sea. As well as fine sea views from the restaurant and some of the bedrooms, the hotel has a secluded walled garden with access to the water, and a mooring that is available to guests (booking advisable). The 11 bedrooms all have en suite facilities and CTV, and they include one family room. Front bedrooms have attractive sun balconies. The elegant lounge is furnished in keeping with the style of the house. The restaurant, popular with non-residents and residents alike, serves an excellent four-course table d'hôte dinner. An à la carte menu is also offered, and vegetarians can be catered for. Bar meals are available at lunch-time.

Price band B
Bar lunch £1–£4
Dinner td £10.50 or alc £12.50
Last dinner 8.30pm
Credit cards [1] [2] [3] [5]
No parking on premises
Closed Nov–Feb

FOWNHOPE Hereford & Worcester Map 3 SO53

GH **Bowens Farmhouse**
✆ (043277) 430

Guests are made to feel very welcome at this comfortable 17th-century farmhouse set in 1½ acres of gardens in a quiet village. Traditional English home cooking is a highlight of one's stay here; dinner usually consists of home-made soup, followed perhaps by Herefordshire beef and an old-fashioned pudding such as mixed fruit baked sponge. Vegetarians can be catered for by arrangement. Much of the fresh produce comes from the kitchen garden. Bowens has 10 bedrooms, two of which (with private facilities) are in a converted coach house. There are two family rooms, though children under 10 are not accepted. Leisure amenities include a croquet lawn and a putting green. In winter the sitting room, with its wood-burning stove, large comfortable chairs and good supply of books, may have more appeal. Dogs are not accepted.

Price band A
Dinner, b&b £21–£25
Last dinner 7.30pm
Parking on premises
Closed Xmas & New Year

FOYERS Highland *Inverness-shire* Map 14 NH42

★ **Foyers Hotel**
✆ Gorthleck
(04563) 216

This pleasant, unpretentious little family hotel is quietly situated, commanding extensive views over Loch Ness. It offers accommodation in compact but cheerfully decorated bedrooms, the opportunity to relax in a comfortable lounge with colour television or

Price band A
Bar lunch fr £1.75
Dinner td £6
Credit cards [1]

	in one of the bars, and good Scottish cooking. Boats are available for brown trout and salmon fishing in Loch Bran or Loch Farraline, and there is a good choice of hill or forest walks in the area.	[2] [3] [4] [5] Parking on premises

FRAMLINGHAM Suffolk Map 5 TM26

FH **Broadwater Farm** Woodbridge Rd ✆ (0728) 723645	Home-produced wine is an unusual touch at this fine Georgian farmhouse. A four-acre vineyard forms part of the property, and its light, dry wine, bottled under the home label, is requested by many guests at dinner. More conventional home-grown produce goes into Mrs Stocker's simple English cooking, and she also prepares hearty breakfasts. Five spacious and comfortable bedrooms include one twin room with a private bathroom, a family room and one room with a four-poster bed. The drawing room, large and comfortably furnished, has a CTV, a piano and a good selection of books. The log fire will be readily lit when the weather is chilly. Guests are asked to order dinner by 10am.	Price band A Dinner, b&b £17–£20 Last dinner 7pm Parking on premises Closed Xmas

FRINTON-ON-SEA Essex Map 5 TM21

★★ **Maplin Hotel** Esplanade ✆ (02556) 3832	Good sea views and a heated outdoor swimming pool are features of this welcoming, family-run hotel. Staff are warm and hospitable and guests here can be sure of being well-cared for. English home cooking of a high standard, including a good selection of fresh vegetables, is offered at lunch and dinner in the dining room. Bar snacks are also available at lunch-time, and may be eaten outside by the pool. The oak-panelled lounge and cocktail bar are comfortably and tastefully furnished, and bedrooms are spacious and impeccably kept. Most have private bathrooms, and all 12 have CTV and telephones. Two are family rooms, but the hotel does not take children under ten.	Price band B Lunch td £11.25 Dinner td £13 Last dinner 9.30pm Credit cards [1] [2] [3] [5] Parking on premises Closed Jan
GH **Montpellier Private Hotel** 2 Harold Grove ✆ (02556) 4462	Town centre and seafront are both within walking distance of this attractive three-storey house, which is located in a quiet residential area. The six spacious bedrooms include one family room. All are prettily decorated, clean and fresh. Private bathrooms (with shower) and CTV are standard. There is a comfortable lounge, as well as a small sun lounge at the front of the house, and a neatly kept garden. Wholesome home cooking is served by welcoming hostess Mrs Howelett in the well-appointed, licensed dining room.	Price band B Dinner, b&b £25–£30 Last dinner 7pm Credit card [3] Parking on premises
★ **The Rock Hotel** 1 Third Ave ✆ (02556) 77194	A warm welcome from hospitable hosts Mr and Mrs Benmore is to be found at this detached Victorian house overlooking the sea. The Benmores pride themselves on their home cooking, and both à la carte and table d'hôte lunch and dinner menus are offered in the elegant wood-panelled dining room. Vegetarians can be catered for. Residents may relax in a comfortable lounge-bar. The six bedrooms are simply decorated but well-equipped and clean. All have CTV and tea/coffee-making facilities. All but one have private showers, and three of the rooms can accommodate families.	Price band B Lunch td fr £7.50 Dinner td fr £7.50 or alc £10.50 Last dinner 9pm Credit cards [1] [2] [3] [5] Parking on premises Closed Jan

GAIRLOCH Highland *Ross and Cromarty* Map 14 NE87

GH **Horisdale House** Strath ☏ (0445) 2151	Quietly situated to the west of Gairloch and commanding impressive views across the bay to the Torridon Mountains, this modern, purpose-built guesthouse is comfortable and well-appointed. Bedrooms are well-furnished and attractively decorated in pastel colours, while the spacious lounge, with its raised stone fireplace, offers the opportunity to chat or read without interruption from television. Imaginative evening meals are served by prior arrangement. Children under seven years of age are not accepted.	Price band A Dinner, b&b £17–£18 Last dinner 7pm Parking on premises Closed Oct–Apr

GATEHOUSE OF FLEET Dumfries and Galloway *Kirkcudbrightshire* Map 11 NX55

★★★★ L **Cally Palace** ☏ Gatehouse (05574) 341 Tx 777088	This imposing country hotel is set in a hundred acres of immaculate grounds and offers guests the use of a range of leisure activities, tennis courts, an indoor heated swimming pool and a sauna. Efficient management is reflected in the particularly high standards of service, and a stay here represents excellent value for money. Most of the admirably-maintained bedrooms are spacious and all are well-equipped, while a marble-floored, pillared foyer and series of elegant lounges are very much in the grand style. Cuisine, though predictable, is good, and meals are reasonably priced.	Price band C Lunch td £5.75 Dinner td £11 Last dinner 9.30pm Credit card 3 Parking on premises Closed 3 Jan–Feb
★★★ **Murray Arms** ☏ Gatehouse (05574) 207	This attractive former posting inn stands at the centre of the town, as much a focal point in the life of the local community now as when it was first built in the 17th century. Many traditional features have been retained throughout the hotel, including the Burns Room, where the poet reputedly penned 'Scots Wha Hae'. Cheerful bedrooms blend individual styling with modern facilities, and there is some additional accommodation in a delightful chalet-style cottage in the grounds. Adherence to the old values is demonstrated in the four-course, home-cooked dinner which is served each evening by courteous and attentive staff.	Price band B Bar lunch £2–£7 Dinner td £11 Last dinner 8.45pm Credit cards 1 2 3 5 Parking on premises

GATWICK AIRPORT West Sussex Map 4 TQ24

★★★ B **Chequers Thistle Hotel** Brighton Rd, Horley ☏ Horley (0293) 786992	This one-time Tudor coaching house has been tastefully modernised and extended to provide 78 comfortable and well-equipped bedrooms. All have bathrooms en suite, CTV and telephones, and 16 rooms are set aside for non-smokers. Facilities at the hotel include a swimming pool. Good food is available in the elegant restaurant, where the menu is varied and prices are reasonable. Breakfasts offer a wide choice and are well-prepared. Lounges include the attractive reception area, furnished as a library and kept cosy by a fire in winter. The atmosphere is informal and friendly, and staff are helpful and willing.	Price band D Lunch fr £7.25 or alc £16 Dinner td fr £11.25 or alc £16 Last dinner 10pm Credit cards 1 2 3 4 5 Parking on premises

GAYHURST Buckinghamshire Map 4 SP84

FH **Mill Farm** ✆ Newport Pagnell (0908) 611489	Rural peace and quiet, only a few miles from busy Milton Keynes, will be found at this pretty little riverside farmhouse. The homely atmosphere created here by Mrs Adams appeals to families and tourists as well as business travellers. A warm and friendly welcome is extended to all. There are only three bedrooms, but they are full of character, with attractive cottage-style décor and furnishings. Although none has en suite facilities, they are well-served by separate modern bath and shower rooms, and are equipped with TV. A cosy lounge is well-supplied with magazines, books and games. Good farmhouse breakfasts are served in the adjoining elegant dining area; dinner may be ordered by prior arrangement with Mrs Adams. Children are welcome, and riding and fishing are available on the farm.	Price band A Dinner, b&b £15.50–£17.50 Last dinner 8pm Parking on premises

GIFFNOCK Strathclyde *Renfrewshire* Map 11 NS55

× **Turban Tandoori** 2 Station Rd ✆ Glasgow 041-638 0069	This attractively decorated and smartly appointed Indian restaurant will offer you not only the traditional wide range of curries but also a good selection of dishes that are more subtly flavoured, and of these the Tandoori specialities are particularly good. Attentive service and advice are provided by a young team of waiters and waitresses, the girls charmingly dressed in saris. It is advisable to book a table in advance, for space is limited and the establishment is — justifiably — becoming increasingly popular.	Dinner fr £7 Last dinner 12 mdnt Credit cards [1] [2] [3] Parking on premises Closed 25 Dec & 1 Jan Closed lunch

GIGGLESWICK North Yorkshire Map 7 SD86

GH **Woodlands** The Mains (At the end of a cul de sac just off the A65) ✆ Settle (07292) 2576	Visitors to Woodlands, a Georgian-style residence peacefully located in one and a half acres of private grounds, enjoy a country house atmosphere which combines true Yorkshire hospitality with excellent modern facilities. The guesthouse makes a good base for exploring Settle and the hills and dales beyond the River Ribble. Well-appointed bedrooms provide CTV and electric blankets — and, in one case, the more traditional luxury of a four-poster bed — while the comfortable lounges are equipped with guide books to help you discover the beauties of the area. Excellent standards of English cooking are maintained, and a set dinner menu is available.	Price band B Dinner, b&b £27.25–£29.75 Last dinner 6.30pm Parking on premises

GIGHA, ISLE OF Strathclyde *Argyllshire* Map 10 NR64

★★ HL **Gigha Hotel** (Car ferry from Tayinloan, mainland) ✆ (05835) 254	Sound, caring management and the services of friendly staff are important elements in the success of this delightful island hotel — and once guests have experienced a stay here they tend to return time and time again! In a magnificent natural setting, they can relax in comfortable accommodation and enjoy excellent, traditional Scottish cooking which makes full use of fresh produce and regularly features locally-caught seafood. Soup and sandwiches or a buffet lunch are available.	Price band B Lunch td £4 Dinner td £12 Last dinner 8pm Credit cards [1] [3] Parking on premises Closed Nov–Mar

GILLINGHAM Dorset Map 3 ST82

★★ RED ♣♣ H
Stock Hill House
Wyke
✆ (07476) 3626

A gracious atmosphere prevails at this delightful small hotel, set in extensive and lovely grounds. The comfortable and tastefully furnished drawing room and hall/lounge invite relaxation, and most of the six bedrooms are very attractive. All have private facilities, CTV and telephones. Good leisure amenities here include an indoor swimming pool, a sauna, a gymnasium and a croquet lawn. The cooking at Stock Hill House is as polished as the hospitality: proprietors Peter and Nita Hauser gained a good reputation for their restaurant in Sark, and their high standards continue here. The restaurant is open for lunch and dinner, and menus change daily. The cuisine is best described as international, though Austria has a strong influence, especially in the desserts. Ingredients are fresh and of top quality. Fish dishes worth a try include Devon crab quenelles and wing of skate cooked in cider. Coffee and sweetmeats are included in the set meal price. Stock Hill House does not accept dogs, or children under seven.

Price band C
Lunch td £11
Dinner td £18
Last dinner 9pm
Credit cards [1] [3] [4]
Parking on premises
Closed 2 wks Nov & Feb

GISLINGHAM Suffolk Map 5 TM07

GH **Old Guildhall**
Mill St
✆ Mellis (037983) 361

Beautiful beamed rooms characterise this guesthouse in a quiet Suffolk village. Dating back to the 15th century, the Old Guildhall has four comfortable bedrooms with modern private bathrooms, CTV, radio and tea/coffee-making facilities. All the rooms are full of character; tall visitors should be careful of the beams! The Old Guildhall is run by Ray and Ethel Tranter, hospitable hosts who make their guests very welcome. Traditional English home cooking is available in the licensed dining room, and there are two lounges. One, a quiet reading and writing room, equipped with stationery and a desk, overlooks the lovely garden from the first floor. The other is a very comfortable open-plan area on the ground floor. It still has its original inglenook fireplace and bread oven. Guests have the use of an electric organ and a half-size snooker table in an adjacent room.

Price band B
Dinner, b&b £20–£24
Last dinner 8pm
Parking on premises

GLASGOW Strathclyde *Lanarkshire* Map 11 NS56

★★★
Crest Hotel Glasgow-City
Argyle St
✆ 041-248 2355

A central position near bus and railway station makes this hotel a popular meeting place. Completely refurbished over the last 18 months, it offers accommodation in exceptionally well-equipped bedrooms with attractive modern furnishings and coordinated colour schemes — those designed for ladies even featuring fresh flowers and elegantly perfumed soaps. The public rooms are similarly transformed, the previously functional bar and reception area now replaced by a comfortable lounge in Egyptian mood where morning coffee and afternoon tea are served, and the first-floor restaurant and cocktail bar similarly upgraded.

Price band D
Lunch td £7.60 & alc
Dinner td £11.15 & alc
Last dinner 10pm
Credit cards [1] [2] [3] [5]
No parking on premises

GH **Dalmeny Hotel** ✆ 041-427 1106	Though set in a residential area on the south side of Glasgow, this attractive, stone-built private hotel is conveniently situated for access to both the city centre and the motorway system. Catering mainly for the businessman, its 10 bedrooms are compact, though comfortably furnished and very well-equipped, while the ground floor lounge is particularly pleasant, with bright, clean décor and good seating. The warm, friendly atmosphere and a flexible attitude to mealtimes both contribute to the Dalmeny's popularity.	Price band B B&b only Parking on premises
× × **Kensingtons** ✆ 041-424 3662	The external appearance and surroundings of Kensingtons belie its interior décor and standard of cuisine, for attractively appointed tables and an array of paintings against red felt wallcoverings provide a pleasant setting in which to enjoy fine meals. The food is emphatically British, the 'Taste of Scotland' menu making good use of seasonal game and fresh produce in such dishes as mussels with white wine, onion and tomato sauce, or a richly-flavoured venison casserole.	Lunch td fr £7.50 Dinner td £17.50 Last dinner 9.30pm Credit cards 1 2 3 5 Parking on premises Closed Sun, & Sat lunch
× **Peking Inn** 191 Hope St ✆ 041-332 8971	The Peking Inn was the first Chinese restaurant in Glasgow to abandon the traditional décor, and its cuisine is equally unstereotyped. An attractive menu features both Pekinese and Cantonese dishes, while a blackboard displays such daily specialities as fish with ginger and spring onions or crispy shredded beef with a tangy red-pepper sauce. First-rate service by a young, friendly staff complements the excellence of the food, making a meal here a thoroughly enjoyable experience.	Lunch td fr £3.90 & alc Dinner td fr £5.50 & alc Last dinner 11.30pm Credit cards 1 2 3 5 No parking on premises Closed Sun & Chinese New Year
White House 11–3 Cleveden Cres ✆ 041-339 9375	The White House is hardly an hotel as such, having neither lounge nor dining room; what it does offer, however, is 32 very attractive suites, each individually decorated and equipped to an exceptionally high standard with remote control television (including teletext and in-house movie facilities), direct-dial phone, trouser-press, en suite private facilities and its own fitted kitchen. Although listed by the Association in its self-catering guide, the White House offers much more than this would suggest: though there is no dining room, breakfast is served en suite and a table d'hôte room service is available until 9.30pm. Alternatively, the staff will make a reservation for you at any of the city's three best restaurants, in which case a courtesy car will be available to carry you to and from your meal. Transport is also provided to the city centre in the mornings.	Price band C Breakfast £4.50–£5.95 Snack meals £4.85–£11.50 Lunch/dinner td £11.50–£13.50

GLASTONBURY Somerset Map 3 ST53

FH **Berewall Farm**
Cinnamon Ln
(0458) 31451

The feel of Somerset — as regards both scenery and good farmhouse food — is much in evidence here. Panoramic views include Glastonbury Tor to the north, and guests can either spend time exploring this fascinating area or make use of the farm's excellent leisure facilities which include an outdoor swimming pool and a tennis court. There are also horses and ponies to ride, and guests and their children are welcome to help feed the animals on the farm. Bedroom accommodation, recently extensively altered and improved, now comprises nine rooms, all with bathrooms en suite and CTV, and three will accommodate families. A log fire blazes on chilly days in the cosy lounge, and the licensed restaurant is large and caters for both residents and non-residents in the evenings. Food is freshly prepared and plentiful.

Price band A/B
Dinner, b&b
£20–£23
Last dinner
10pm
Credit cards [1]
[3]
Parking on
premises

GLENDEVON Tayside *Clackmannanshire* Map 11 NN90

×× **Tormaukin Hotel**
Muckhart
(025981) 252

This little restaurant stands by the roadside at the heart of winding Glen Devon. Once a drovers' inn, it dates from the 18th century, and careful conversion and modernisation have preserved low, beamed ceilings, natural stone walls and highly polished woodwork. Bedrooms are small but tastefully appointed, with en suite facilities. An à la carte menu offers a very pleasant range of skilfully prepared dishes with the accent on local produce, and meals are cheerfully served by attentive staff. Vegetarian food is available.

Bar lunch alc £6
Lunch alc £11
Dinner alc £14
Last dinner
9.30pm
Credit cards [1]
[2] [3]
Parking on
premises
Closed 1st 2wks
Jan

GLENSHEE (SPITTAL OF) Tayside *Perthshire* Map 15 NO16

★★ L
Dalmunzie House
(025085) 224

This imposing gabled and turreted Scottish stone mansion stands in the Perthshire Hills, its six thousand acres offering facilities for golf, tennis, putting, fishing, and ski-ing in season, for it has easy access to the nearby ski slopes. The hotel is ably run on country house lines, with both owners and staff providing warm and friendly attention and fine service in all areas. Bedrooms are very comfortable, with en suite facilities which, like the rooms themselves, vary from the roomy appointments of the original house to more compact modern amenities. The lounges, which vary in design, are all pleasantly furnished and decorated, and a wood-panelled dining room provides a fitting background for the enjoyment of well-prepared Scottish food.

Price band B
Bar lunch td £3–
£8
Dinner td fr £10
Last dinner 8pm
Credit cards [1]
[5]
Parking on
premises
Closed 1 Nov–26
Dec

GLOSSOP Derbyshire Map 7 SK09

GH **Wind in the Willows**
Derbyshire Level
(Off Sheffield Road)
(04574) 68001

This early Victorian country house stands on high ground adjacent to the golf course, with attractive views on all sides. Elegant public rooms, like the oak-panelled study, with its range of newspapers and magazines and its open fire on colder days, provide a friendly, relaxed atmosphere that is appreciated

Price band A/C
Dinner, b&b
£28–£58
Last dinner 7pm
Credit cards [2]
[3]

equally by the tourist and businessman. Individually designed and well-furnished bedrooms incorporate some antique pieces in keeping with the character of the house. A set meal in the attractive dining room is followed by coffee in a comfortable lounge, but there is no licensed bar.

Parking on premises
Closed Xmas & New Year

GLOUCESTER Gloucestershire Map 3 SO81

★★★ H
Hatton Court
Upton Hill,
Upton St Leonards
(3m SE B4073)
✆ (0452) 617 412
Tx 437334

Standing in seven acres of well-maintained grounds with splendid views of the Severn Valley and Malvern Hills, this Cotswold-stone house has recently been refurbished to a very high standard, and a new wing of excellent bedrooms has been added. All 53 bedrooms have high quality, individually designed décor and furnishings, a luxurious private bathroom or shower, CTV, in-house video, telephone and many extras including fresh fruit. Some of the rooms have jacuzzis and four-poster or canopied beds. The public rooms are equally well-appointed, including the restaurant which offers panoramic views. Food is in the modern French style, well-cooked and attractively presented, and vegetarian meals can be prepared. A flower is presented to women guests. The hotel possesses a heated outdoor swimming pool and there are future plans for a fully equipped leisure centre. Dogs are not accepted.

Price band C
Lunch td £10.50 or alc £19
Dinner td £13.50 or alc £19
Last dinner 10pm
Credit cards [1] [2] [3] [5]
Parking on premises

GOOLE Humberside Map 8 SE72

★★ **Clifton Hotel**
1 Clifton Gdns
✆ (0405) 61336

The charming 17th-century country house stands on the edge of Goole, conveniently located for access to motorway or to town centre and docks. Its lounge is always inviting, with magazines to read and a coal fire burning, and your welcome is constantly reinforced by the friendly and helpful service you meet at every turn. The freshly prepared and well-cooked meals (in English and international style) served in the comfortable dining room are accompanied by a moderately priced wine list — or you may prefer to eat and drink less formally at the bar.

Price band B
Lunch alc £3.50
Dinner td fr £10 or alc £10
Last dinner 9pm
Credit cards [1] [2] [3] [5]
Parking on premises

GOOSNARGH Lancashire Map 7 SD53

× **Ye Hornes**
✆ Broughton (0772) 865230

Ye Hornes is a delightful little pub/restaurant of 17th-century origin which specialises in good, old-fashioned English fare. Several small dining rooms are available, all decorated and furnished in typical inn style, and the owners maintain a friendly atmosphere, offering a warm welcome to guests. The à la carte menu is short, but the popularity of such skilfully cooked, attractively presented specialities as home-made soups and roast duckling is vouched for by a regular local clientele.

Bar lunch 80p–£5.50
Lunch £7.75–£8.50
Dinner £10.50–£11.50
Last dinner 9.15pm
Credit cards [1] [2] [3] [5]
Parking on premises

GRANGE-OVER-SANDS Cumbria Map 7 SD47

★★ HL
Graythwaite Manor
Fernhill Rd
(04484) 2001

Staying at Graythwaite Manor is like stepping back in time, for the warmth of welcome and standard of service found there have died out in most places. Throughout your stay you will be cossetted in every conceivable way — your cases carried, early morning tea brought to you and dinner served by waitress in 'upstairs downstairs' uniforms. There is an abundance of lounges in which to relax: one cosy little room leads onto a terrace overlooking delightful gardens, a more spacious one contains lots of really comfortable seating, and there is also a snooker room. Good, home-cooked meals based on fresh produce meet with the evident approval of guests — but what they probably value above all else is the peace.

Price band B/C
Lunch td £6.50
Dinner td £12.50
Last dinner 8.30pm
Credit cards [1] [3]
Parking on premises

GRANTOWN-ON-SPEY Highland *Morayshire* Map 14 NJ02

× **Craggan Mill**
(0479) 2288

A white-painted mill, commanding splendid views of Highland scenery from an elevated position just outside the town, has been modernised to provide the setting for this popular little restaurant. Bar and dining room are rustic in style, their beamed ceilings and polished wooden floors creating a farmhouse atmosphere. The furniture is mostly pine, and the overall impression is refreshing and relaxing. Comprehensive menus range from such Italian dishes as pollo alla Romana and scalopina al vino bianco to traditional steaks. All in all, this is a very pleasant little character restaurant, offering simple but cheerful service and value for money.

Lunch td £2.90–£4
Dinner alc £10.95
Last dinner 10pm
Credit card [3]
Parking on premises
Closed Mon Oct–May & lunch winter months

GH Riversdale
Grant Rd
(0479) 2648

Set in a quiet residential area of the Highland town, this granite house in its own grounds offers a friendly and relaxing atmosphere for an overnight stop or extended stay. Guests receive a warm welcome, and a good standard of comfort is maintained in the spacious, traditional-style bedrooms and residents' lounge. A four-course dinner is served in the cheerful, informal dining room, and this, like everything else about Riversdale, represents good value for money.

Price band A
Dinner, b&b £13–£13.50
Last dinner 7pm
Parking on premises
Closed Xmas

GRASMERE Cumbria Map 11 NY30

Baldry's
Red Lion Sq
(09665) 301

In the middle of the attractive little village of Grasmere stands this very pleasant teashop/restaurant — ideal for afternoon tea after a satisfying walk on the fells, or for lunch on one of the Lake District's less good days! Everything here is home-made, even the ice-cream and the tea-bread, and a range of such luxuries as hot, sticky gingerbread with rum butter and cream or delectable apple pie is available. Interesting savouries are on offer at lunch-time, together with such daily specials as chestnut and mushroom roast, chicken and leek pie and sugar-roast ham, all accompanied by interesting side salads. Wine is available, by the glass if required.

Lunch alc £4.75
Last meal 5.30pm
Parking nearby
Closed Nov–Dec, & Thur till Jul

GRASSINGTON North Yorkshire Map 7 SE06

GH **Ashfield House** ✆ (0756) 752584	This small hotel, dating back to the 17th-century, stands in a secluded position only a short walk from the village square. Attractively furnished and sparkling clean, it provides a warm, relaxing atmosphere in which to enjoy the hospitality of friendly hosts while exploring the beautiful Dales. The English style meals served in the cosy dining room exceed one's highest hopes, lounges are comfortable, with open fires, and bedrooms are charmingly decorated and well-equipped.	Price band A/B Dinner, b&b £19–£26.70 Last dinner 7pm Parking on premises Closed Nov–Mar
★ **Grassington House** 5 The Square ✆ (0756) 752406	Rebuilt early in the 18th century and now scheduled as being of special architectural or historic interest, Grassington House stands proudly on the village square. Family-owned and run, it is comfortably furnished throughout and offers very good value for money: the 18 bedrooms are cosy and attractively decorated, two welcoming lounges invite relaxation, and good, honest, home-cooked food is served in a pleasant dining room.	Bar lunches alc £5.50 Dinner td £8.62 Last dinner 7pm Parking on premises Closed Nov–Feb

GRAYSHOTT Hampshire Map 4 SU83

❀ × **Woods** Headley Rd (1m SW of Grayshott on B3002, off A3) Hindhead (042873) 5555	Clinical tiling and meat-racks recall the fact that this was formerly a butcher's shop, but a tasteful conversion job is set off by attractive, simple pine furniture and pots of fresh wild flowers. Competent cooking is by Swedish chef Eric Norrgren, who runs Woods with his Czechoslovakian wife Dana. Quality ingredients are prepared with unfailing skill and flair to give a varied Continental-style menu, often featuring unusual combinations of flavours.	Dinner alc £18 Last dinner 11pm Credit cards 1 2 3 4 5 No parking on premises Closed Sun & Mon Closed lunch

GUILDFORD Surrey Map 4 SU94

GH **Quinns Hotel** 78 Epsom Rd ✆ (0483) 60422	This imposing Victorian house, shaded by tall cedars, is only a few minutes' walk from the town centre. Now a 10-bedroom hotel offering a high standard of service, it is personally managed by resident proprietor Mr Neil Denny. Bedrooms are pleasant and well-equipped with modern facilities, including private bath or shower in most cases. Soft furnishings are coordinated with décor, and all rooms have CTV. Two of the rooms are suitable for families. Dinner is not served, but there are plenty of restaurants nearby. Breakfast is served in a Victorian-style dining room with fine wood panelling and an ornate fire surround. There is no lounge, but each landing has a quiet and comfortable seating area. Fresh flower arrangements are used liberally, and give the hotel a homely atmosphere.	Price band B/C Credit cards 1 2 3 5 Parking on premises
Richoux Restaurant Friary Centre ✆ (0483) 502998	Flagging shoppers can restore their spirits at this stylish restaurant where there is a choice between the Edwardian-style décor of the interior, and al fresco seating that is more reminiscent of a French café. The menu is short but well-thought out. Hot meals might	Lunch alc £7 Last meal 5.30pm Credit cards 1 2 3 4 5

include steak and kidney pie, charcoal-grilled dishes and various toasted savouries. Vegetarian dishes are available. A tempting selection of puddings includes various ice-cream specialities and fresh cream cakes. Service is pleasant and attentive; a welcome little extra touch is the selection of newspapers offered on a rack by the entrance. The Richoux is fully licensed.

No parking on premises
Closed Sun & Bank Hols

GUIST Norfolk Map 9 TF92

×× **The Tollbridge**
✆ Foulsham
(036284) 359

The River Wensum provides a magnificent backdrop for this former toll-house. It also provides some of the fare to be found on the imaginative menu: pike mousseline is a favourite, and eels are served occasionally. Proprietor/chef William Stark uses the freshest of local produce in his cooking. Fish, shellfish and game figure prominently. The style is light and modern, with much emphasis on attractive presentation. Pastry dishes are especially good — sometimes creamed pheasant in a pastry case is served as a starter, and sometimes pastry is used as a complement to a wonderful range of soft fruits to end your meal. Wines are well-chosen to suit most tastes, and prices are surprisingly modest.

Lunch td fr £7.50
Dinner td fr £9 & alc
Last dinner 9.30pm
Credit card [3]
Parking on premises
Closed Sun & Mon

GULLANE Lothian *East Lothian* Map 12 NT48

❀× **La Potinière**
✆ (0620) 843214

A good range of skilfully-prepared, flavoursome French dishes and a list of over 400 French wines have made this charming little restaurant so popular that Saturday dinner is fully-booked for years ahead — despite the fact that meals are served at a set time and no choice is offered! Undoubtedly an element of food snobbery is involved but La Potinière is, nevertheless, well worth a visit, for the inclusive price offers excellent value for money: delicious soups are followed by a light dish such as mousseline, a substantial meat course and tempting desserts, all enjoyed at leisure in an attractive, comfortable dining room.

Lunch td £11.50–£12.50
Dinner td £17.50 (Sat only)
Closed 1 wk Jun and Oct
Closed Wed and Sat lunch

GULWORTHY Devon Map 2 SX47

❀×××
Horn of Plenty
✆ Tavistock (0822) 832528

Drive down quiet lanes to reach this peacefully situated delightful country house-style 'restaurant with bedrooms', noted for its superb cuisine. The comfortable lounge with a bar area, cheered by a log fire in winter, is a relaxing place in which to enjoy an aperitif and browse through the interesting wine list before dining in the bright restaurant with large windows overlooking the Tamar Valley. The English and French-style food is prepared with care from excellent ingredients and proprietor Sonia Stevenson likes to use local produce where possible. Vegetables are fresh and crisp, and sauces well-made. Vegetarian meals are available. The service is pleasant and informal. A converted barn close to the main building houses six well-equipped, tastefully furnished bedrooms, and residential courses on cooking, including the preparation of sauces, are offered.

Lunch td £12.50 or alc £25
Dinner td fr £17.50 or alc £25
Last dinner 9.30pm
Credit cards [1] [2] [3]
Parking on premises
Closed Xmas Day & lunch Thur & Fri

HACKNESS North Yorkshire Map 8 SE99

★★★ **Hackness Grange Country Hotel** (A170 to East Ayton then follow Forge Valley) ✆ Scarborough (0723) 369966 Tx 527667	This fine country residence stands in its own extensive grounds on the banks of the River Derwent, only 5 miles from Scarborough and within the North Yorkshire National Park. It offers a wide range of leisure facilities, notably the indoor heated swimming pool, an all-weather tennis court, a pitch-putt course and 11 miles of trout fishing. Cuisine is of a very high standard, the fixed-price menu offering four courses which might include rainbow trout, salmon or veal, all skilfully prepared and attractively presented. Accommodation is available in thoughtfully equipped bedrooms, and a warm, friendly atmosphere permeates the whole hotel.	Price band C Lunch td fr £5 Dinner td fr £13.50 Last dinner 9pm Credit cards [1] [2] [3] [5] Parking on premises

HALLAND East Sussex Map 5 TQ41

★★ **Halland Forge** ✆ (082584) 456 Tx 8951994	Convenient for the coast, the South Downs and Ashdown Forest, this hotel and restaurant complex provides a comprehensive meals service and 20 well-equipped bedrooms. Snacks and meals, including breakfast, are served from 8am to 6pm in the licensed Coffee Shop, where the buffet lunch selection includes a carvery and a cold table. The beamed Forge Restaurant, open for lunch and dinner, offers three or four-course table d'hôte menus with a good choice of dishes. There is also an à la carte menu. In a separate block from the restaurants and the comfortable Anvil Lounge Bar are the bedrooms, some of which are on the ground floor. All have private bathrooms, CTV, radio and telephones. There are two family rooms, but children under five are not accepted.	Price band C Lunch td £8.50 (Coffee Shop fr £2.20) Dinner td £10.50 or alc £14 Last dinner 9.30pm Credit cards [1] [2] [3] [5] Parking on premises

HALTWHISTLE Northumberland Map 12 NY76

FH **Ald White Craig** Shield Hill (¾ mile N of town on the Hadrian's Wall Road) ✆ (0498) 20565	Situated in an attractive rural location within a short distance of Scottish and Cumbrian borders, close to both town and Hadrian's Wall, this 17th-century, croft-style farmhouse has been tastefully modernised to offer accommodation in three attractive, comfortable bedrooms. Two of the rooms have en suite facilities (the third having sole use of a separate bathroom) and all are equipped with CTV and tea-making facilities. The spacious, open-plan lounge and dining room retain much of the original character of the house, with beamed ceilings, an old stone fireplace and a wealth of bric-à-brac. Dinner must be ordered in advance, but the home-cooked, traditional farmhouse fare can be recommended. The farm itself may well add interest to your stay, for the proprietor raises prizewinning pedigree sheep and some rare breeds of cattle as well as the more usual livestock. The single-level design of the farmhouse makes the accommodation particularly suitable for disabled visitors.	Price band A Dinner, b&b £18.50 Last dinner 6pm Parking on premises Closed Oct–Mar

FH **Broomshaw Hill**
Willia Rd
✆ (0498) 20866

Though close to the town centre, this 18th-century, stone-built farmhouse enjoys an attractive rural setting only a mile from Hadrian's Wall. It has been extended and modernised over the years, but much of its original character is still evident — in the comfortably furnished sitting room, for example, with its chunky stone walls and interesting old fireplace. Farmhouse-style bedrooms are spacious and comfortable, while the period furnishings and antique bric-à-brac of the impressive dining room form an interesting background to your enjoyment of a traditional country breakfast and dinner.

Price band A
Dinner, b&b £15–£16
Last dinner 7pm
Parking on premises
Closed Nov–Mar

HAMBLEDEN Buckinghamshire Map 4 SU78

INN **The Stag and Huntsman**
✆ Henley-on-Thames (0491) 571227

A pretty, rural village at the edge of the Chiltern Hills is an apt setting for this 17th-century inn, which has been used for location shooting for a number of historical films. The three bars, wood-panelled and low-ceilinged, are full of character, and offer a good selection of both beers and bar meals. For a more formal menu, try the small restaurant, and sample the expert cooking of the proprietor's well-travelled son. Bed and breakfast accommodation is available, and the three bedrooms are cosy and attractively furnished. Children and dogs are not accepted.

Price band B
Lunch/dinner alc £8
Last dinner 10pm
Credit cards [1] [3]
Parking on premises

HAMILTON Strathclyde *Lanarkshire* Map 11 NS75

×× **Costa's**
17–21 Campbell St
✆ (0698) 283552

The effort involved in searching out this friendly little restaurant, tucked away in a side street of the town's one-way system, is well worthwhile. Its attractive décor is both unusual and modern, in contrast to a menu which includes such traditional specialities from the proprietor's Cypriot background as hummus (a chick pea paste) and taramosalata (a spread made from cod's roe) with pitta bread among the most widely-known European dishes.

Lunch td fr £4 or alc £15
Dinner alc £15
Last dinner 10.15pm
Credit cards [1] [2] [3] [5]
No parking on premises
Closed last 2 wks Jul, 1st wk Aug, 25 Dec, 1 & 2 Jan
Closed Sun

HAMPTON COURT Surrey Map 4 TQ16

★★ B **The Liongate**
Hampton Court Rd
✆ 01-977 8121
Tx LIONGT 928415

Set between Hampton Court Palace and the peaceful expanse of Bushy Park, this lively hotel has recently undergone a facelift. Bedrooms are tastefully furnished and decorated, with all modern facilities, and there is a choice of restaurants. On the first floor is the Paris Brasserie, where a variety of popular starters precede a cosmopolitan range of main courses that include tandoori chicken, coq au vin, Chinese stir-fry and Cossack kebabs. Downstairs is the Greyhound Pub and Crêperie, where a wide choice of savoury and sweet pancakes is available all day, together with drinks that include several draught beers, pitchers of wine, or frothy cappuccino. Prices are reasonable and service is amiable.

Price band D
Lunch alc £7.50
Dinner alc £7.50
Last dinner 10pm
Credit cards [1] [2] [3] [5]
Parking on premises

HAMPTON WICK Surrey Map 4 TQ16

Al Pante 53 High St ✆ 01-977 4895	This intimate little restaurant offers conventional, authentic Italian cuisine with friendly personal service by proprietor Pietro Perino, assisted sometimes by his Scottish wife. The reasonably priced set menu might offer home-made pâté or antipasto della casa followed by chicken paesana or escalope milanese. Fish, salads, grills and vegetarian choices are also available, as (of course) are pasta dishes, which can be ordered as either a starter or a main course. For a meal in itself, try the delicious, thick minestrone, home-made using fresh vegetables.	Lunch/dinner td £5.90 or alc £11 Last dinner 11pm Credit cards 1 2 3 Parking nearby Closed Sun, & Sat lunch

HARBERTONFORD Devon Map 3 SX75

×× **The Hungry Horse** ✆ (080423) 441	Close to the river, in the centre of the village, stands this stone-built cottage restaurant where hospitable service and a high standard of fresh food go hand in hand. A wide choice of imaginative dishes makes up the daily menu, which is advertised on a blackboard. A first course might be a deliciously light avocado mousse sprinkled with caviar, followed by moist roast guinea fowl in Calvados sauce. Generous helpings of attractively presented home-made sweets are served to finish. All the cooking shows considerable flair, and only quality ingredients are used. A worthy wine list complements the food, and prices are generally reasonable.	Dinner alc £14 Last dinner 9.30pm Credit cards 1 2 3 Limited parking on premises Closed Sun & Mon Closed Lunch

HAREWOOD West Yorkshire Map 8 SE34

★★★ **Harewood Arms** Harrogate Rd ✆ Leeds (0532) 886566	A traditional roadside inn has been delightfully restored and stylishly refurbished to provide old-fashioned comforts with the advantage of modern facilities. The 13 bedrooms all have en suite facilities, CTV and telephones. The hotel is professionally run, boasting an excellent restaurant and a pleasant lounge-bar (decorated with interesting pictures of past Earls) where snacks are available at lunch-time. Friendly, helpful staff provide a relaxed atmosphere, and the whole ambience is of ease and comfort.	Price band C Bar lunch £2.50–£4 Lunch td £7.50 Dinner alc £15 Last dinner 10pm Credit cards 1 2 3 4 Parking on premises

HARLOW Essex Map 5 TL41

★★★ **Churchgate Manor** Churchgate St, Old Harlow ✆ (0279) 20246 Tx 818289	Churchgate Street is in fact a small village, set in unspoilt Essex countryside. Here will be found this large, well-equipped hotel, which has been converted from a 17th-century chantry house. The Chantry Bar and the Manor Restaurant retain many original features, while, by contrast, the new wing offers modern bedroom accommodation with all up-to-date facilities. All 71 bedrooms have private bathrooms, CTV and telephones. Churchgate Manor also has a good indoor leisure complex comprising swimming pool, sauna, solarium and gymnasium, and there is a games room. Attractive landscaped gardens surround the hotel.	Price band C/D Lunch alc £15 Dinner td fr £10.50 or alc £17 Last dinner 9.45pm Credit cards 1 2 3 5 Parking on premises

HARROGATE North Yorkshire Map 8 SE35

★ **Alvera Court** 76 Kings Rd ✆ (0423) 505735	A Victorian building has been completely renovated and restored to combine modern amenities with the original architectural features of the era. The hotel stands opposite the Conference Centre, offering 10 individually furnished bedrooms equipped to a good standard with private facilities. There is a comfortable television lounge, a smart lounge-bar and an attractive restaurant (with vegetarian food available on request). Guests can be sure of a warm welcome on arrival and friendly service throughout their stay.	Price band B Bar lunch £3–£5 Dinner td fr £7 Last dinner 7pm Credit card [1] Limited parking on premises
× **Burdekin's** 21 Cheltenham Cres ✆ (0423) 502610	An unassuming, under-rated small restaurant near the Conference Centre, Burdekin's offers a range of English dishes with international overtones, beautifully prepared and served in a relaxed atmosphere and delightful surroundings. Every care is taken to ensure that food is brought to the table at its best, and the comfort and happiness of guests are regarded as priorities. There is no bar, but an excellent wine list accompanies your meal.	Dinner td £7.85 or alc £15 Last dinner 9.30pm Credit cards [1] [2] [3] Parking nearby Closed lunch & Sun dinner
×× **Emilio's** 3 Ripon Rd ✆ (0423) 65267	This comfortable restaurant, where smart waiters provide helpful, courteous service, is set in an adapted — but still impressive — Victorian house. The table d'hôte lunch menu is very reasonably priced and has an element of exotic Spanish style about it, while the à la carte selection, though more expensive, still represents value for money. Vegetarian food is available, and seafood is a speciality. There is a wine list of about 100 wines; many of them are of fine quality, but others have been included to suit the more humble purse.	Lunch td £5.90 or alc Dinner td £10.80 or alc fr £15 Last dinner 11pm Credit cards [1] [2] [3] Parking on premises Closed Bank Hols Closed Sun
★ B **Gables** 2 West Grove Rd ✆ (0423) 505625	A private house dating from 1896 has been converted into this very pleasant and welcoming hotel, conveniently situated for the town's amenities. It offers nine exceptionally well-fitted and equipped bedrooms, two of which are suitable for families. All rooms have CTV and tea and coffee-making facilities, and most have bath or shower en suite. They are tastefully and comfortably furnished. A well-balanced menu of home cooking, based on fresh produce, is served in the attractive dining room, and guests can relax in a very comfortable lounge and lounge-bar.	Price band B Bar lunch £3.10–£4.50 Dinner td £8.50 Last dinner 8pm Credit cards [1] [3] Limited parking on premises

HARROP FOLD Lancashire Map 7 SD74

FH **Harrop Fold** (Signposted from top of lane) ✆ Bolton-by-Bowland (02007) 600 Tx 635562	This delightful farmhouse, a Norse Longhouse built of local stone, nestles in a secluded valley. It has been lovingly furnished throughout and offers seven carefully designed bedrooms with every comfort and a wealth of personal touches. Two attractive, low-beamed lounges have extensive views over fell and lowland, including the farm's own sheep-raising pasture. Meals are excellent, flair and skill have been brought to bear on good local produce. The quality of	Price band B Dinner, b&b £31.50–£42.50 Last dinner 9pm Credit cards [1] [3] Parking on premises Closed Jan

the food, attentive service and a pleasant atmosphere combine to ensure a truly relaxing break here.

HASLEMERE Surrey Map 4 SU93

❀×× **Morel's**
25–7 Lower St
✆ (0428) 51462

In our Inspector's opinion this is probably the best French restaurant in Surrey, Classical French Cuisine, sound and uncomplicated, is the basis of the menu, which changes monthly. Cooking and preparation are carried out skilfully and service is formal and efficient. The menu is complemented by a sensibly chosen and reasonably priced wine list.

Lunch td fr £11
Dinner td fr £14
Last dinner 10pm
Credit cards [1] [2] [3] [5]
No parking on premises
Closed 2 wks Feb, last 2 wks Sep
Closed all day Mon, Sat lunch & Sun dinner

× **Simla Tandoori**
84 Weyhill
✆ (0428) 3885

This small but popular restaurant offers traditional Bangladeshi cooking and specialises in tandoori dishes. Service is by a team of polite and friendly waiters, who willingly explain and discuss dishes on the menu to assist customers in choosing. Everything is cooked to order, so this is not the place for those in a hurry. The home-made sauces are particularly commended by our Inspector. The restaurant is well-appointed and attractively decorated and there is a rear terrace where meals may be eaten in fine weather.

Lunch td £4.25
Dinner alc £7.50
Last dinner 11.30pm
Credit cards [1] [2] [3] [4] [5]
No parking on premises

HASTINGS East Sussex Map 5 TQ80

GH **Argyle**
32 Cambridge Gdns
✆ (0424) 421294

The railway station, main shops and seafront are all conveniently close to this homely guesthouse, run by welcoming proprietors Mr and Mrs Jacobs. Standards of housekeeping and maintenance are high and the eight bedrooms, while of varying sizes, are neat and cosy. Three are family rooms. Two bedrooms are on the ground floor, and three rooms have shower and WC en suite. There is no general bathroom, but there is a spacious shower room. A comfortable TV lounge is available, and breakfast is served in the half-basement dining room. The Argyle does not accept dogs, or children under five.

Price band A
No parking on premises
Closed Xmas

HATTON Warwickshire Map 4 SP26

FH **Northleigh Farmhouse**
✆ Haseley Knob (092687) 203

Northleigh is an elegant country house offering something special in the way of hospitality. The four comfortable bedrooms are an indication of the thought that has gone into furnishing and décor; everything is of the highest quality in these cheerful, light rooms with their attractive floral fabrics and welcoming personal touches. Meals are excellent, deliciously satisfying and created from the very best of fresh local produce, while the atmosphere is so relaxed that this really is a 'home from home'.

Price band A/B
Dinner, b&b £22.50–£30.50
Dinner by arrangement
Parking on premises

HAWICK Borders *Roxburghshire* Map 12 NT51

× **Old Forge Restaurant** Newmill-on-Teviot (On A7 4 miles S of Hawick) ☎ Teviotdale (045085) 298	This small country restaurant retains the natural stonework of the smithy that it once was, and the blacksmith's forge and bellows have also been retained; a homely touch is added by the attractively laid light pine tables and matching dressers. Inventive cuisine, including a choice of vegetarian dishes, is based on fresh produce, is Cordon Bleu standard, and cheese lovers will wax ecstatic over the carefully chosen selection of British cheeses. Much of the allure of the establishment must lie in its ability to provide such a high standard of food at a very reasonable price, both at lunch-time (when one pays for the number of courses taken) and in the fixed-price three-course evening meal.	Lunch td fr £4.95 Dinner td £9.50 Last dinner 9.30pm Credit cards 1 2 3 Limited parking on premises Closed 1st 3 wks Jan and mid 2 wks May Closed all day Sun & Mon

HAWKHURST Kent Map 5 TQ73

★★ **Tudor Arms** Rye Rd ☎ (05805) 2312	The facilities of a small hotel are combined with the warmth of a country pub at the Tudor Arms, which stands in its own extensive and well-kept gardens in the lovely Weald of Kent. The two bars are supplemented by a comfortable, well-appointed lounge, and the bedrooms have been tastefully renovated to provide modern facilities. Eleven of the 14 rooms have bath or shower en suite, and all have CTV and telephones. Two rooms have four-poster beds and there is one family bedroom. Good, honest home cooking is available in the restaurant, which offers a choice between fixed-price and à la carte menus.	Price band B Lunch td fr £8 or alc £14.50 Dinner td fr £9 or alc £17 Last dinner 9.15pm Credit cards 1 2 3 5 Parking on premises

HAWKSHEAD Cumbria Map 7 SD39

★★ 👪 L **Field Head House** (From Ambleside take B5286 to Hawkshead; ½ mile past Outgate Inn turn R signed Field Head — house ¼ mile on R) ☎ (09666) 240	Dating from the 17th-century, this fine Lakeland country house stands in six acres of mature woodland and gardens, the latter providing flowers and vegetables for use in the hotel. Every guest is greeted like an old friend, and service is caring and attentive. Bedrooms are tastefully decorated and individually furnished with character and charm, while the two comfortable lounges are made cosy by wood-burning stoves. Each evening an interesting five-course dinner is produced, based almost entirely on local produce, and breakfast sees the hearty main course accompanied by home-made rolls, jam and marmalade.	Price band B Lunch td £8 Dinner td £13 — booking essential Last dinner 8pm Credit cards 2 3 4 Parking on premises

HAYLE Cornwall Map 2 SW53

★★ **Hillside Hotel** Grist Ln, Angarrack (1½m E of Hayle on unclassified rd off A30; SP from A30) ☎ (0736) 752180	A home-from-home atmosphere has been created here by sisters Mrs Chadwick and Miss Bill. An imposing Victorian village house built of Cornish granite, the hotel enjoys a peaceful location and has its own walled garden. Several of the ten bedrooms have private facilities. There are three family rooms, one of them very large and with shower en suite. The comfortable lounge is supplemented by a cosy and attractive bar. Imaginative, home-cooked meals, using fresh	Price band B Bar lunch £3.95 Dinner td fr £7.15 Last dinner 7.30pm Parking on premises Closed Xmas

ingredients, are served, and vegetarians can be catered for. Bar lunches are available, and for tea, cakes and biscuits are home-made.

HAYTOR Devon Map 3 SX77

★★★ HL
Bel Alp House
(03646) 217

Tobacco millionairess Dame Violet Wills had this Edwardian house built, high up on the edge of Dartmoor. There are magnificent views from almost every window. A delightful country house-party atmosphere is now nurtured here by hospitable proprietors Captain and Mrs Roger Curnock. The house is comfortably and elegantly furnished, in keeping with its period. The nine bedrooms all have telephones, CTV, radio/intercom and private bath or shower room. Two of the rooms are on the ground floor, and there is a lift. Fresh produce is of paramount importance in Mrs Curnock's cooking. Dinner comprises five courses plus coffee, and one or two alternatives are offered for each course. Children are welcome, but those under six are not allowed in the dining room at dinner. An early supper can be ordered, as can packed lunches.

Price band C
Lunch td £12
Dinner td fr £18
Last dinner 8.30pm
Credit cards [1] [3]
Parking on premises
Prior booking only Dec-Feb

HEDDON'S MOUTH Devon Map 2 SS64

★★ RED
Heddon's Gate
Parracombe (05983) 313

Captivating views over moorland and the wooded valley below are part of the charm of this delightful, quiet hotel set in 15 acres of grounds with a terraced garden. The interior is very much in the country house style, with a comfortable, relaxing sitting room, a writing room and a cosy bar. Bedrooms are individually styled and well-furnished. There are 11 rooms in the main house and three in an annexe, all provided with CTV, radios, telephones, private facilities and several little extras such as fresh fruit. Two rooms have four-poster beds, and there is one family room, though the hotel does not take children under 10. There are fine views from the spacious dining room, where ample breakfasts and excellent five-course dinners are served. Interesting dishes are expertly created from the best ingredients by Anne de Ville, who, with her charming husband Bob, owns and runs the hotel. They are most genial hosts and, assisted by a team of local staff, they provide cheerful, informal service. Our Inspector is firmly of the opinion that, for a quiet, relaxing holiday, with good accommodation and food, it would be hard to find a better hotel.

Price band B
Bar lunch £2–£5
Dinner td £15
Last dinner 8pm
Parking on premises
Closed Nov–Easter

HELMSLEY North Yorkshire Map 8 SE68

★★ BL **The Pheasant**
(2½ miles SE of Helmsley in the village of Harome)
(0439) 71241

This charming family-run hotel is in a delightful situation, overlooking Harome's village pond. The smithy, two cottages and a shop have been completely rebuilt to provide spacious, well-decorated bedrooms, a large, comfortable lounge with full-length windows and a beamed bar where a log fire blazes in cold weather. The proprietor's wife produces an excellent

Price band B/C
Bar lunch fr £1
Dinner td £12.50
Last dinner 8.15pm
Parking on premises

	five-course meal each evening, while the rest of the family ensures that guests are comfortable and well-looked after. For those seeking a really peaceful holiday there is also a 17th-century thatched cottage, full of charm and character, with two bedrooms and two lounges.	Closed Jan & Feb

HELSTON Cornwall Map 2 SW62

★★ L **Nansloe Manor** Meneage Rd ✆ (0326) 574691	Angela and Harry Davy-Thomas formerly owned the Mill House Inn at Trebarwith, winner of our 'Inn of the Year' award in 1985. They are now the charming hosts at this secluded manor house, set in 4½ acres of grounds. Stylish furnishings complement the many original architectural features inside the house, and restoration has been sensitive and tasteful. All of the seven bedrooms have bath or shower en suite, and are equipped with CTV, telephones, hairdriers and tea/coffee-making equipment. The handsome Georgian-style restaurant has a good reputation locally: the à la carte menu is limited but changes frequently. Vegetarian dishes can be provided. Good value winter breaks are offered at £45 per person for two days, inclusive of dinner.	Price band B Lunch td fr £7.10 Dinner alc £12.85 Last dinner 9.30pm Credit cards 1 3 Parking on premises Closed 25–9 Dec

HENFIELD West Sussex Map 4 TQ21

FH **Great Wapses** (3m NE of Henfield off B2116) ✆ (0273) 492544	Bed and breakfast accommodation of a high standard is offered by hospitable hosts Mr and Mrs Wilkin at their peaceful farmhouse in rural Sussex. Part of the house is Georgian, and part dates back to the 16th century. Furnishings are in keeping with the house, and the atmosphere here is homely and appealing. The three comfortably appointed bedrooms are spacious and full of character, and all have private facilities and CTV. Two of the rooms are suitable for families.	Price band A Parking on premises

HENLEY-IN-ARDEN Warwickshire Map 7 SP16

GH **Ashleigh House** Whitley Hill ✆ (05642) 2315	If you are at all interested in antiques and objects d'art, Ashleigh House will prove a real treasure trove. A great deal of loving care has gone into the furnishing of the house to provide luxurious surroundings, and the proprietor is always ready to chat to guests about his acquisitions. The bedrooms (six of which are in the main house and four in an adjacent cottage annexe) combine elegance with comfort, all containing plenty of magazines, CTV tea/coffee-making equipment and en suite facilities. A pretty dining room, decorated in shades of pastel green, looks out on to lawns and beyond to the rolling Warwickshire countryside, providing an idyllic setting in which to start the day with a hearty English breakfast.	Price band A Credit cards 1 3 Parking on premises

À la carte prices are based on an average for three courses without wine.

××**Le Filbert Cottage**
64 High St
(05642) 2700

Midway along the mile-long stretch of the village stands a pretty black-and-white Tudor cottage which has been converted into a very good French country-style restaurant with a cosy, friendly atmosphere. The 'plat du jour' will often consist of the best fresh fish available, purchased from the markets that morning and skilfully prepared by the chef/proprietor. Food here is light, and good portions served; specialities include Cornish scallops wrapped in brill, calves' sweetbreads in a puff pastry case and a variety of well-flavoured soups.

Lunch td fr £9.50
Dinner td fr £14.70 or alc £19.50
Last dinner 9.45pm
Credit cards [1] [2] [3] [4] [5]
No parking on premises
Closed Sun & Bank Hol

HENLEY-ON-THAMES Oxfordshire Map 4 SU78

××**Flohr's Hotel Restaurant**
Northfield End
(0491) 573412

Anglo-German dishes are a speciality at this restaurant, which is part of a small hotel on the edge of Henley. Menus are short and deliberately simple, but quality ingredients are used to good effect. The à la carte menu is supplemented by a fixed-price business menu, and vegetarians can be catered for. Meals are served in a tastefully decorated dining room, and there is also a bar. Personally run by the proprietor, Mr Flohr, the hotel also offers nine modern, simply furnished bedrooms.

Lunch td fr £7.90 or alc £15
Dinner td fr £14 or alc £15
Last dinner 10pm
Credit cards [1] [2] [3] [5]
Limited parking on premises
Closed Sun dinner

The Golden Ball
Lower Assendon
(1¼m NW of Henley on B480)
(0491) 574157

Our Inspector has never been disappointed by a meal at this welcoming country inn. Its popularity is such that it is best to arrive early. The enticing menu offers an interesting range of food both at lunch-times and in the evening, and value for money is excellent. Everything is home-made: soups, pâtés or marinated mushrooms to start may be followed by a choice of pies such as lamb and courgette or steak and oyster, or a filled jacket potato, or one of the pub's specialities such as Golden Ball casserole, a 'chilli bowl', hummus or ratatouille. Several other vegetarian dishes are available. To finish, 'Lorna's home-made coffee and brandy cake' is a highly recommended choice from the range of sweets, which also includes chocolate fudge cake, apple pie or bread pudding.

Lunch/dinner alc £2.50–£10
Last dinner 10.15pm
Credit cards [1] [2] [3]
Parking on premises

HEXHAM Northumberland Map 12 NY96

★★ H **County Hotel**
Priestpopple
(0434) 602030

The County Hotel is quite rightly known as 'Hexham's Homely Hotel', for the proprietors really enjoy having guests and go out of their way to please them. The atmosphere here is one of good humour and enthusiasm, with refreshments available from eight in the morning until midnight. You can enjoy morning coffee and afternoon tea in the comfortable lounge (where a log fire roars on colder days), and there is a tiny cocktail bar which is very popular with local people. The ten bedrooms are comfortable and well-furnished.

Price band B
Bar lunch fr £1.50
Lunch td £7 or alc £7
Dinner td fr £8 or alc £9
Last dinner 9.30pm
Credit cards [1] [2] [3]
Limited parking on premises

HIGH OFFLEY Staffordshire Map 7 SJ72

×× **Royal Oak**
Grubb St
✆ Woodseaves
(078574) 579

The country atmosphere of this little village inn, completely remodelled a few years ago, is very popular with locals. It offers fixed-price three-course lunch and four-course dinner menus, each with a good selection of mainly British dishes, with the emphasis on meat, poultry and game from the region. Portions are very generous and the freshness of the vegetables notable. Wines from a good wide ranging list are modestly priced and the service, by local waitresses, is friendly and attentive.

Bar lunch fr £1
Lunch td fr £6.95
Dinner td fr £8.50 or alc £14.48
Last dinner 9pm
Credit cards [1] [2] [3] [5]
Parking on premises
Closed 2 wks Aug & Bank Hols
Closed Sun dinner

HIGH WYCOMBE Buckinghamshire Map 4 SU89

GH **Clifton Lodge Private Hotel**
210 West Wycombe Rd
✆ (0494) 40095

The past few years have seen a good deal of modernisation and upgrading here, under the guidance of enthusiastic proprietors Mr and Mrs Taylor. All 20 bedrooms have been refurbished, and now have attractive décor, modern fitted furniture and up-to-date facilities including radio and CTV. Many of the rooms have en suite facilities, and two will accomodate families. A quiet and comfortable residents' lounge looks out over the small, well-kept garden, and there is a residents' bar in a corner of the foyer. Breakfast and dinner are served in the elegant, well-appointed dining room, and feature standard English cooking which, like the room charges, represents good value for money. Clifton Lodge is conveniently located for both the M40 motorway and the town centre.

Price band B/C
Dinner, b&b £30–£42
Last dinner 9pm
Credit cards [1] [2] [5]
Parking on premises
Closed 10 days Xmas

HINDHEAD Surrey Map 4 SU83

★★ **Devil's Punch Bowl**
London Rd
✆ (042873) 6565

Standing alongside a stretch of lovely National Trust countryside with spectacular views, this newly refurbished 40-bedroom hotel on the A3 offers easy access to both London and much of the South-East. All rooms (half of them in an annexe) are well-equipped, with private bathrooms, CTV and telephones, and are decorated to a high standard. An attractive sun lounge adjoins Broomsquires Restaurant, whose menu features mainly grills. A table d'hôte menu is available to residents. Bar meals are served in Russell's Bar, a friendly 'local' bar where a wide range of draught beers is also available. A second bar, the Punch Bowl, has a more intimate atmosphere for pre-dinner drinks.

Price band C
Lunch alc £11
Dinner td £8.50 or alc £11.50
Last dinner 9.40pm
Credit cards [1] [2] [3] [5]
Parking on premises

> À la carte prices are based on an average for three courses without wine.

HOLBETON Devon Map 2 SX65

★★★ L
Alston Hall
Battisborough Cross
(075530) 259

This Edwardian country house has kept the style and charm of a more lesisurely era, making it a relaxing place to stay. Mature grounds extending to 4½ acres, and including a swimming pool and tennis courts, surround the house, which stands in undulating countryside between Dartmoor and the sea. Inside, the finest public rooms are the oak-panelled great hall, complete with minstrels' gallery, and the drawing room/ballroom. There is also a cosy bar and a well-appointed restaurant serving freshly-cooked food. The menu is based on quality local produce, cooked with skill and imagination. Vegetables are fresh and crisp, and generous helpings of home-made sweets round off the meals. (It is advisable to book in advance for lunch.) Bedrooms vary in size, but are comfortable and well-equipped. All nine have private facilities, CTV and telephones, combining modern amenities with décor tastefully in keeping with the style of the house. Welcome extras include fresh fruit, iced water and towelling bathrobes. Service is friendly and eager, and the whole hotel has a very pleasing atmosphere.

Price band C
Lunch td fr £9.50
Dinner td fr £13.50 or alc £24
Last dinner 9.30pm
Credit cards 1 2 3 5
Parking on premises

HOLNE Devon Map 3 SX76

FH **Wellpritton**
Poundsgate
(03643) 273

Tucked away in a fold of gentle Dartmoor hills, this small working farm specialises in goats, pigs and sheep. There are breathtaking views from the tastefully modernised farmhouse, an ideal base from which to explore the area. Four of the five bedrooms have private facilities and the farm boasts its own swimming pool. Home-cooked four-course dinners are served in the atractive dining room, using local produce including, of course clotted cream. Proprietor Sue Townsend is always at hand to ensure that her guests experience an enjoyable and relaxing visit. Special arrangements can be made for children, and there is no charge for washing and ironing facilities. Dogs are not accepted. Weekly terms only are available in July and August.

Price band A
Dinner, b&b £15–£17
Last dinner 6pm
Parking on premises
Closed 25–6 Dec

HONITON Devon Map 3 ST10

★★ **New Dolphin**
High Street
(0404) 2377

This recently refurbished town-centre hotel with an inn-style atmosphere has 14 pleasantly appointed bedrooms, including two family rooms, 12 with private bathrooms or showers and all with CTV. On the first floor is a quiet residents' lounge, while on the ground floor is the attractive dining room where guests can enjoy an à la carte lunch or dinner, perhaps sampling the freshly caught local fish. There is an excellent table d'hôte menu at lunch-time too. The aim is to use fresh ingredients as much as possible. Good, well-cooked bar meals are also available at both midday and in the evening in the comfortable front bar-lounge. Vegetarian meals can be provided. The hotel is personally run by the owner, Mrs Rees, aided by charming and friendly staff.

Price band B
Bar lunch fr 95p
Lunch td fr £2.25
Dinner td £7.25 or alc £11.70
Last dinner 9.30pm
Credit cards 1 3
Parking on premises

HOPTON WAFERS Shropshire Map 7 SO67

× **Crown Inn** ✆ Cleobury Mortimer (0299) 270372	Both restaurant and bar meals are recommended at this traditional pub in a village on the eastern side of Clee Hill. The restaurant, open in the evenings only, offers a two or three-course menu. One dish particularly enjoyed by our Inspector was chicken breast stuffed with avocado and wrapped in Parma ham. Vegetarian meals are available. Bar meals, served at lunch-time and in the evening, are chosen from an extensive blackboard menu. Convivial hosts, exposed beams and log fires encourage a cosy, homely atmosphere.	Lunch/dinner alc £12.95 Bar meal fr 95p Last dinner 9.30pm Credit cards 1 3 Parking on premises Closed Sun

HORSHAM West Sussex Map 4 TQ13

GH **Winterpick Corner** (2m SE of town off A281) ✆ (0403) 53882	This lovely, small country house, standing in a superb rural setting two miles south-east of the town, is surrounded by attractive, carefully-maintained gardens which incorporate a heated swimming pool. It offers accommodation in four spacious, well-appointed bedrooms, and the comfortable public rooms are decorated and furnished in traditional country house-style. The hotel, under the personal supervision of the owners, provides guests with a relaxed, informal atmosphere which is much appreciated.	Price band A/B Parking on premises

HORTON Northamptonshire Map 4 SP85

❀ ×× **The French Partridge** Northampton ✆ (0604) 87003	Creative cooking of a consistently high standard, and outstandingly good value for money, draw customers from a wide area to Mr and Mrs Partridge's agreeable little restaurant. He presides over the kitchen, while she organizes the bar and takes the orders. The four-course set menu changes according to seasonal market produce. Recent successes have included beautifully made fresh asparagus soup, or cream of prawn, followed by a delectably light terrine of salmon as a fish course. Main courses consist of meat or fish: lamb is a particular favourite, and there are delicious country dishes like rabbit with tarragon and caramelised garlic. David Partridge excels with his sweets. Pastry is feather-light, and there might be lovely thin pancakes with a hint of coconut and a rich, creamy filling. A savoury is offered, and the well-kept cheeses are also recommended. Value for money extends to the excellent wine list, which covers all the major countries, with the emphasis on France.	Dinner td £15.50–£16 Last dinner 9pm Parking on premises Closed 2 wks Xmas, 2 wks Easter, 3 wks Jul/Aug Closed lunch, & Sun and Mon

HORTON-IN-RIBBLESDALE North Yorkshire Map 7 SD87

INN **Crown Hotel** ✆ (07296) 209	The Crown stands at the centre of the village, beside the river and actually on the Pennine Way. It is set in some of the best walking country in England and is ideally situated for tackling the famous 'Three Peaks'. Believed to be of 17th-century origin, the hotel is full of Dales character, with oak beams reputed to have been ships' timber. The ten bedrooms are warm and comfortable, and there are two relaxing lounges.	Price band A Bar lunch 50p–£2.50 Dinner td £6.33 Last dinner 7.15pm Credit card 5 Parking on

	Honest, home-cooked food is served in the dining room, and the whole atmosphere is genuinely welcoming.	premises

HUDDERSFIELD West Yorkshire Map 7 SE11

× **Weaver's Shed** Knowl Rd ✆ (0484) 654284	This charming restaurant is housed in a converted 18th-century cloth-finishing mill in an interesting Pennine village. Many of the building's original features have been retained, and meals are served against a simple background of stone walls and pine ceilings that preserve the atmosphere of the industry. A blackboard menu offers a selection of traditional English fare which usually comprises five starters and eight or so interesting main courses accompanied by good fresh vegetables; meals are competently cooked, attractively presented and accompanied by a good wine list.	Lunch alc fr £7.50 Dinner alc fr £14 Last dinner 9pm Parking on premises Closed 1wk Jul & 2wks Jan Closed Mon, Sat lunch, Sun dinner

HULL Humberside Map 8 TA02

×× **Cerutti's** 10 Nelson St (On the old ferry quayside) ✆ (0482) 28501	There could not be a more appropriate setting for a specialist seafood restaurant than this former station-master's house which stands on the quayside overlooking the Humber estuary. Its elegant dining room is on the first floor, above a ground floor lounge-bar, and in the relaxed and unhurried atmosphere created by smooth, professional service guests choose from a menu based on fish purchased at the local market. A wide variety is available, cooked in a multitude of ways — simply grilled, served with classic sauces, or in interesting 'specials' which often have an element of surprise — and a selection from the more than adequate wine list will enhance the meal.	Lunch alc £10 Dinner alc £15 Last dinner 9.30pm Credit card [1] Parking on premises Closed Xmas Closed Sun, & Sat lunch

HUNMANBY North Yorkshire Map 8 TA07

★★ HBL **Wrangham House** Stonegate, Hunmanby 3m SW off A165 ✆ Scarborough (0723) 891333	This former vicarage stands in its own well-tended gardens at the edge of the village, only three miles from the sea. Careful restoration has retained much of its original charm and atmosphere, but a high standard of comfort has been provided in the two pleasant lounges (one with small bar) where log fires burn on chilly evenings, and in the quaint but well-equipped bedrooms with their wealth of thoughtful, homely touches. The traditional four-course dinner served in the charming dining room offers home-made pâtés and soups, substanial main courses with fresh vegetables, and mouthwatering sweets, the friendly informality of service being typical of the relaxed atmosphere of the whole hotel.	Dinner, b&b £30 Last dinner 7pm Credit card [1] Parking on premises Closed Dec–Feb

HUNTON North Yorkshire Map 7 SE19

INN **Countrymans** (Signed off A684 between Bedale and Leyburn) ✆ Bedale (0677) 50554	The Countrymans Inn is set in a typical stone-built Dales village, and, despite recent modernisation, its public rooms retain their old world charm, for the big stone fireplace and the wood panelling have been spared. The four modern, comfortable bedrooms have en suite facilities and are well-equipped, having CTV,	Price band A Bar meals alc £7 Last dinner 9.30pm Parking on premises

tea-maker and efficient central heating. Substantial bar meals are served, and although the lunch-time menu is somewhat limited, dishes such as chicken supreme, chilli con carne and beef curry represent excellent value for money; the dinner menu adds fresh fish, steaks and a range of starters and sweets. A very reasonably priced wine list is available.

LAM Staffordshire Map 7 SK15

FH **Beechenhill**
Alstonefield
(033527) 274

Ideally situated for exploring the Peak District, this 92-acre dairy and sheep farm lies in a peaceful and unspoilt rural area. This stone farmhouse, built about 1720, enjoys splendid views of the Manifold Valley. There is one double bedroom and one family bedroom, both of which have recently been refurbished to a good, comfortable standard. The well-furnished lounge/dining room has exposed beams and solid fuel store. Dogs are not accepted.

Price band A
Parking on premises
Closed Xmas

INGLESHAM Wiltshire Map 4 SU29

×× **Inglesham Forge**
Faringdon (0367) 52298

French and Italian dishes form the basis of the cuisine at this pleasant and relaxing cottage-style restaurant. Food is prepared with considerable thought and care, and is freshly made. Specialities include home-made soups, soufflés, eggs florentine and crêpe aux fruits de mer. A good selection of game dishes is available, and there are steaks of various kinds as well as fish. Vegetarian dishes are also served. The table d'hôte lunch menu offers a good choice, but an à la carte selection is also available. A comprehensive wine list is offered, and service is friendly and efficient.

Lunch td fr £9.50 or alc £17.50
Dinner td £14.50 or alc £17.50
Last dinner 10pm
Credit cards 1 2 3 5
Parking on premises
Closed last 2 wks Aug
Closed Sun, Sat & Mon lunch

INVERNESS Highland *Inverness-shire* Map 14 NH64

★★★ **Craigmonie**
9 Annfield Rd
(0463) 231649
Tx 946240

Facilities are continually being improved at this extensively refurbished farmhouse, and it is a popular stopping place for businessmen and tourists alike. The 30 bedrooms are comfortable and well-equipped, with all the extras that a modern, progressive hotel provides. Three have the traditional attractions of a four-poster bed. You can take your ease in a comfortable lounge or a cheerful bar, and the smartly appointed dining room features both French and Scottish cuisine. Special facilities are offered for children.

Price band C
Bar lunch £4–£6
Lunch td fr £5
Dinner td fr £11.50 & alc
Last dinner 9.30pm
Credit cards 1 2 3 5
Parking on premises

GH **Craigside**
(0463) 231576

The welcoming Victorian house overlooks the castle from a quiet residential area within a few minutes' walk of the town centre. It offers accommodation in six bright, cheery bedrooms (four of them with en suite facilities), all nicely furnished and well-equipped. Well-filled bookcases and a range of magazines are provided for the enjoyment of guests relaxing in the comfortable lounge — and their peace is safeguarded by a prohibition on children under 14!

Price band A
(No single rooms)
Parking on premises
Closed Dec–Feb

★★ HBL
Dunain Park
(Off the A82 2½ miles S of Inverness)
(Plan 8 A1)
✆ (0463) 230512

Just a short drive south of Inverness stands this delightful Georgian house, set in six acres of secluded, wooded grounds. Accommodation is provided in six individually furnished and decorated bedrooms of ample proportions which have been equipped with many thoughtful extras. Two rooms are suitable for family occupants. The comfortable armchairs of the charming drawing room, with its welcoming log fire, invite relaxation, and there is a separate lounge-bar. The hotel is rapidly establishing a reputation for sound, country house-style cooking, and the accompanying wine list has been chosen with care that is typical of the establishment. Fishing, shooting, stalking and pony trekking can all be arranged locally.

Price Band C
Bar lunch £5–£7.50
Lunch td fr £9.50
Dinner td fr £15
Last dinner 9pm
Credit cards [1] [2] [3] [5]
Parking on premises

IRVINE Strathclyde *Ayrshire* Map 10 NS33

★★★★
Hospitality Inn
Roseholm, Annick Water
✆ (0294) 74272
Tx 777097

Despite its unpromising brick façade and its position beside the A78, the Hospitality Inn boasts a dining room that is worth a visit. Décor is attractive troughout the hotel, the Moorish-style reception area, complete with fountain, leading on to the Lagoon area, cocktail bar and bedrooms. The theme is continued in the Mirage Restaurant, where an award-winning team presents an interesting range of dishes, excellently cooked and complemented by well-favoured sauces. Meals are attractively presented and served by a cheerful young staff.

Price band C
Lunch td fr £5.50 or alc £19
Dinner td fr £9.50 or alc £19
Last dinner 11pm
Credit cards [1] [2] [3] [4] [5]
Parking on premises

IVINGHOE Buckinghamshire Map 4 SP91

×× **King's Head**
Cheddington
✆ Cheddington (0296) 668264/668388

Reservations are essential for meals at this 17th-century posting house, which is usually busy despite its quiet location in a small hamlet. The ivy-clad building is full of character, and in addition to the attractively furnished restaurant there are two bars and a small, comfortable lounge where after-dinner coffee is served. A set menu and an à la carte selection are offered. Both feature good English and French cuisine: our Inspector particularly enjoyed the steak and kidney pie. A number of fish dishes are also usually available, and vegetarian meals can be prepared. Everything is cooked to order, and helpings are generous. The skilful cooking is matched by professional service at table, and the atmosphere is pleasant and welcoming.

Lunch td fr £12.25 or alc fr £18
Dinner alc fr £25
Last dinner 9.30pm
Credit cards [1] [2] [3] [4] [5]
Parking on premises

IXWORTH Suffolk Map 5 TL97

×× **Theobalds**
68 High St
✆ Pakenham (0359) 31707

Successful team Simon and Geraldine Theobald run this intimate, oak-beamed restaurant in a listed 17th-century house that was previously a village grocery store. Fresh flowers and candles lend atmosphere, and there is a pretty, enclosed patio garden for aperitifs and coffee in summer. In winter, drinks can be enjoyed before a log fire in the cosy bar. Menus change every six weeks to allow for seasonal variations. Only fresh, top-quality produce goes into Simon Theobald's cooking, and he makes good use of

Lunch td £8.50 or alc £8.50
Dinner td fr £14.50 or alc £16.50
Last dinner 10pm
Credit cards [1] [3]
No parking on

fish and game. On our Inspector's visit, dishes included poached mussels with ribbons of pasta tossed in a tomato, garlic and basil sauce, and fillets of hare sautéed in a sherry sauce laced with blackberry jelly. Sweets, ice-creams and sorbets are all home-made, and there is a good cheeseboard. Vegetarians can be catered for. Over 100 wines are featured on the well-chosen list. Children under eight are not admitted in the evenings.

premises
Closed 25-6 Dec
Closed Mon & Sat lunch, & Sun dinner

JEVINGTON East Sussex Map 5 TQ50

×× **The Hungry Monk**
✆ Polegate (03212) 2178

Dining is a delight at this charming, cosy village restaurant. Polished tables, gleaming silverware and a coal fire in winter give the dining room a welcoming atmosphere, and there are three elegant lounges, with deep armchairs and fine pictures, where customers can choose their meal in comfort. The menu is presented on a blackboard, and features good English cooking. Vegetarian dishes are available. A welcome extra touch is the glass of port included in the fixed-price menu. Children under three are not admitted.

Lunch/dinner td fr £12.70
Last dinner 10.15pm
Parking on premises
Closed 24-6 Dec
Closed lunch, except Sun

KELSO Borders *Roxburghshire* Map 12 NT73

★★★ HBL
Sunlaws House
(3m SW of Kelso, off A698 at Heiton)
✆ Roxburgh (05735) 331
Tx 728147

Sunlaws House has been carefully converted by its owners, their Graces the Duke and Duchess of Roxburgh; now, in the best traditions of the country house hotel, it offers good, old-fashioned hospitality — unpretentious, but providing first-rate service with a meticulous attention to detail. Bedrooms (six of the pleasantest being contained in the stable courtyard annexe) are well-equipped and include such niceties as attractive toiletries and capacious bath sheets. Log fires burn in the public rooms on colder days, providing a cheerful focal point for guests who do not wish to play tennis, to indulge in clay pigeon shooting, to fish in the nearby River Teviot or to walk in the magnificent parkland that stretches from the house to its banks. Meals, however, must be the highlight of most visitors' stay, as delicate cooking makes full use of local game, meat, fish and fresh produce.

Price band C
Bar lunch alc £6.50
Lunch alc £9
Dinner alc £17
Last dinner 9.30pm
Credit cards 1 2 3 5
Parking on premises
Kennels provided

KENDAL Cumbria Map 7 SD59

× **The Lord Ted**
21A Stramongate
(Town centre off A65)
✆ (0539) 33826

Cooking is done in full view of the customer in this shop-fronted restaurant close to the town centre. Fresh ingredients are the basis of its success, and meals respresent exceptionally good value for money. Such exotic items as baby squid and oysters appear on the dinner menu alongside the more predictable roast beef and Yorkshire pudding, and there are always fresh vegetables, home-made soups and a selection of sweets ranging from fresh fruit salad to baked rice pudding. The wine list is reasonably priced, with house wines available by the glass. Vegetarian and children's menus are available on request.

Lunch alc £5
Dinner alc £10
Last meal 9pm
Credit card 1
Parking nearby
Closed Bank Hols

KENTALLEN Highland *Argyllshire* Map 14 NN05

×× **Holly Tree** Kentallen Pier ☏ Duror (063174) 292	A beautifully located and attractively renovated railway station, with spectacular views across the loch to the Morvern Hills, forms the setting for this restaurant where wood panelling, old prints and other relics successfully retain the character of the past. In its simple surroundings guests enjoy a standard of cuisine unusual in this part of the world, based on local seafood, venison, beef and game presented in such imaginative guises as pheasant mousse with apple mayonnaise or breast of pigeon cooked with mustard and demerara sugar. A wine list of reasonable length, realistically priced, complements the meal.	Bar lunch £1–£7.50 Lunch td fr £8.50 or alc £6.50 Dinner td fr £12.50 or alc £15.50 Last dinner 9.30pm Credit cards [1] [3] Parking on premises Closed Nov-mid Feb, except Xmas & New Year

KESWICK Cumbria Map 11 NY22

★★ **Crow Park** The Heads ☏ (07687) 72208	There are magnificent views down the Borrowdale Valley from this friendly, family-run hotel which offers cheerfully efficient service in well-decorated and comfortable surroundings. A marvellous collection of antique photographs of Lakeland scenes and people sheds an interesting sidelight on the area. Comfortable accommodation is provided in particularly well-appointed bedrooms, all of which have en suite bathrooms. Enjoyable home-cooked meals are served, dinner being chosen from a set menu which also offers alternatives.	Price band A Dinner td fr £6.50 Last dinner 7.30pm Credit cards [1] [3] Parking on premises Closed mid Nov–Dec
×× **La Primavera** Greta Bridge, High Hill ☏ (07687) 74621	Classic Italian cuisine is the theme at this tastefully appointed restaurant beside the River Greta. The bright, spacious dining room has a central open fireplace and is very well-furnished and decorated, with elegantly set tables. The extensive menu is à la carte, and features traditional Italian favourites such as Parma ham with melon, home-made minestrone, cannelloni, and a good selection of chicken, veal and steak dishes including house specialities. Vegetarian food is available, and there is a tempting choice of home-made sweets to finish. Aperitifs are served in an attractive lounge, which has a roaring fire in winter. Next to it is a comfortable lounge-bar where bar snacks, ranging from soup or spaghetti to coq au vin or trout carpione, are served at lunch-time.	Bar lunch alc £6.50 Lunch alc £7 Dinner alc £10 Last dinner 10pm Credit card [1] Parking on premises
GH Rickerby Grange (From Keswick take A66 to Cockermouth; ¾ mile turn L — Portinscale; turn R down second lane after Farmers Arms) ☏ (07687) 72344	Set in its own well-tended gardens in a pretty little village, Rickerby Grange offers a warm welcome and a home-from-home atmosphere. After a drink in the cosy little bar with its beams and brasses, you can enjoy an imaginative home-cooked four-course dinner in the restaurant. A comfortable lounge is equipped with colour television and a wealth of books and magazines, while the attractively decorated, well-appointed bedrooms have en suite facilities in most cases. Should you wish to sleep in style, one of the bedrooms is furnished with a four-poster bed!	Price band A Dinner, b&b £20–£23 Parking on premises Closed 23–8 Dec

KETTERING Northamptonshire Map 4 SP87

★★★ Kettering's Royal Hotel
Market Place
☏ (0536) 520732

This former coaching inn has been a convenient stopping place for travellers since it was built in 1720, and continues to attract motorists on the several major routes that by-pass the town centre. Completely refurbished in recent years, the hotel is deceptively large, having 39 bedrooms. All have private facilities, CTV and telephones. There are three family rooms and two four-poster rooms. Comfortable furnishings, with plenty of polished wood, characterise the traditional lounge-bar, where the range of real ales is popular with locals. There is also a wine-bar and a modern, brightly decorated coffee shop, frequented by shoppers, which is open all day for snacks and light meals.

Price band C
Bar lunch £1.95-£5
Lunch td fr £5 or alc £15
Dinner td fr £8 or alc £15
Last dinner 10pm
Credit cards 1 2 3 5
Parking on premises

KILCHRENAN Strathclyde *Argyllshire* Map 10 NN02

★★★ HL Taychreggan
☏ (08663) 211

The atmosphere is informally friendly, efficient service being povided by an able young team, at this tastefully appointed country house which is beautifully situated on the shores of Loch Awe. The log fire in the attractive foyer is a welcoming sight, and guests have a choice of three comfortable lounges (one with CTV) in which to relax. Bedrooms are furnished in a style appropriate to the character of the house, and good food with an international flavour is served in a smart restaurant.

Price band C
Bar lunch £1–£5
Lunch td £10
Dinner td £15
Last dinner 9pm
Credit cards 1 2 3 5
Parking on premises
Closed 10 Oct–28 Mar

KILFINAN Strathclyde *Argyllshire* Map 10 NR97

❀ ★★ HB **Kilfinan**
☏ (070082) 201

This charming little hotel, in a peaceful West Coast setting, offers a warm, spontaneous welcome in a relaxing atmosphere. Service is friendly in the well-stocked bar with its inviting log fire, and in the attractive dining room where the memorable meals are based on fresh local produce and regularly include salmon, seafood, pheasant, duck and venison. Bedrooms (with en suite facilities) are bright and cheerful, thoughtfully equipped with many useful extras. The Kilfinan offers an excellent base for walking, fishing, bird-watching, sea-angling — or just relaxing in a tranquil setting.

Price band B
Bar lunch alc £6
Dinner td fr £14 or alc £15
Last dinner 9pm
Credit cards 1 2 3 5
Parking on premises

KILLIECRANKIE Tayside *Perthshire* Map 14 NN96

❀ ★★ HB **Killiecrankie**
☏ Pitlochry (0796) 3220

Delightful grounds with lawns, shrubs and mature trees provide the setting for this former dower house, now converted into an outstanding small hotel with a wealth of attractive features. Individually decorated pine-furnished bedrooms combine quality and style, offering a wide range of thoughtful extras. You can relax in the charming first-floor residents' lounge, or enjoy the friendly bustle of the intimate little bar with its adjoining sun lounge. The traditional-style restaurant, with its views of the garden, provides a perfect setting in which to sample the quality set-price four-course dinner menu, which offers a selection of

Price band B
Bar lunch alc £6
Dinner td fr £14 or alc £15
Last dinner 9pm
Credit cards 1 2 3 5
Parking on premises

'Taste of Scotland' dishes based on local meat, game and fish. Pleasant, willing service is given throughout the hotel, and the whole atmosphere is welcoming.

KILMARTIN Strathclyde *Argyllshire* Map 10 NR89

× **Cairn Restaurant**
✆ (05465) 254

A well-known and popular Argyllshire restaurant, the Cairn has a reputation for providing both good food and value for money. The menu is international in flavour, with seafood much in evidence during the season. The style is delightfully simple, the service friendly and attentive, while the cobble-stone bar's cosy, intimate atmosphere and the candle-lit tables add to the appeal of a relaxing dinner. Light lunches are also available, and these are served in the ground floor bistro.

Price band B
Bar lunch alc £6
Dinner td fr £14 or alc £15
Last dinner 9pm
Credit cards [1] [2] [3] [5]
Parking on premises

KILVE Somerset Map 3 ST14

INN **Hood Arms**
✆ Holford (027874) 210

Dating from the 17th-century, this pleasant inn is just one mile inland from Kilve beach. The five attractively decorated bedrooms are neat and comfortable, and all have private facilities and CTV. Care is also taken to provide homely little extras such as magazines and fresh flowers. There is a small, well-appointed lounge on the first floor. A good range of bar meals is available and an extensive à la carte dinner menu is offered in the restaurant. Children under seven are not accepted.

Price band B
Bar lunch alc £4.50
Dinner alc £8
Last dinner 10pm
Credit cards [1] [3]
Parking on premises

KIMBOLTON Cambridgeshire Map 4 TL06

× **La Côte d'Or**
✆ Huntingdon (0480) 861587

This tiny 14th-century, terraced cottage in the town's High Street has a delightful old world atmosphere, the background of heavy beams and exposed brickwork enhanced by the delicacy of floral prints and arrangements of fresh flowers. Mrs Beever, who was brought up in rural Burgundy, brings all the exuberance and extravagance of that area's cuisine to her meals, using the best produce she can obtain each day. The à la carte menu offers a good range of dishes and the set lunch represents excellent value, but there is also the 'Menu Degustation', which is undeniably exciting; rich flavours abound and surprises like vegetable soufflés will often be included. The wine list offers a good range of French wines — with Burgundy, of course, as a speciality — and the proprietor is always willing to discuss his guests' choice with them.

Lunch td fr £7.95 or alc £12
Dinner td £19.74 or alc £15
Last dinner 8.45pm
Credit cards [1] [3]
Closed 25 Dec & 1 Jan
Closed Tue & Sun dinner

KINGRAIG Highland *Inverness-shire* Map 14 NH80

GH **March House**
Lagganlia
✆ (05404) 388

Wooded Glen Feshie, backed by the outliers of the Cairngorm Mountains, was once the haunt of wolves and bears, and wildlife still abounds there, but guests can relax peacefully in the pleasant atmosphere of March House. The modern building, with its timber upper floor, stands on a tree-studded site; bedrooms are compact but comfortable (three having en suite facilities), while the ground floor lounge offers magnificent views and is very well-appointed, with

Price band A
Dinner td £5
Parking on premises
Closed Nov

Swedish log-burning fires for the cooler evenings. The small open-plan dining area provides an attractive setting in which to enjoy good home cooking, attractively served.

KINGHORN Fife Map 11 NT28

INN **Long Boat**
107 Pettycur Rd
✆ (0592) 890625

This unusual little inn, a single-storey modern building linked to the proprietor's own villa, is perched on a rocky outcrop which looks across a sandy bay to the Firth of Forth. Six modern bedrooms, each having a fully-tiled private bathroom with shower, are clean, neat and well-equipped. There is no separate lounge, but the comfortable lounge-bar is spacious and, like the attractive restaurant, offers a superb view. The Long Boat's emphasis is on good food rather than elaborate accommodation, its style of operation being similar to that of the French restaurant-with-bedrooms.

Price band B
Bar lunch £2.80 – £4.25
Lunch td £4.50 – £5.50
Dinner td fr £7.95 or alc fr £8
Last dinner 9.30pm
Credit cards [1] [2] [3] [5]
Parking on premises

KINGSBRIDGE Devon Map 3 SX74

GH **Ashleigh House**
Ashleigh Rd,
Westville
✆ (0548) 2893

This small guesthouse, conveniently located just outside the town centre, is a good base from which to tour Devon. Owned and run by the Smith family, it is spotlessly clean and offers excellent value for money. The eight bedrooms, one of them a family room, are bright and well-decorated. The comfortable public rooms include a sun lounge. Service is friendly and helpful. Children are welcome if over five years of age.

Price band A
Dinner, b&b £17.50–£18.50
Last dinner 6.45pm
Restricted accommodation Dec–Mar

★★★HBL
Buckland-Tout-Saints
Goveton
(2½m NE on unclass rd)
✆ (0548) 3055
Tx 42513

Set in six acres of peaceful gardens, this elegant house, a fine example of Queen Anne architecture, enjoys magnificent views. It has been under the same family ownership for some considerable time, and recent upgrading has enhanced its atmosphere still further. There are 12 individually styled bedrooms, all with private facilities, CTV and telephone, one of which contains a four-poster bed. The well-proportioned public rooms are of an exceptionally high standard. Recent staff changes in the kitchen have produced encouraging results: food is imaginative and good use is made of local produce. Particularly worthy of note is the well-kept English cheeseboard, which includes some of the more unusual cheeses of the region. The service is charming and enthusiastic, and an area of the restaurant is reserved for non-smokers. Guests can enjoy croquet and mini-golf in the hotel grounds.

Price band D
Bar lunch td £9–£13.50
Lunch td fr £17
Dinner td fr £21
Last dinner 9pm
Credit cards [1] [2] [3] [4] [5]
Parking on premises
Closed 4–21 Jan

KINGSEY Buckinghamshire Map 4 SP70

FH **Foxhill Farmhouse**
✆ Haddenham
(0844) 291650

This beautiful 17th-century farmhouse is reached by an attractive short drive, with well-tended gardens to either side and a small pond. Farm animals wander freely on the four-acre smallholding, giving the place a friendly, cheerful feeling. Hosts Mr and Mrs Hooper are warm and hospitable, and are keen to ensure their guests have a comfortable and enjoyable stay. Their home is traditionally and tastefully furnished; the

Price band A
Parking on premises
Closed Dec–Jan

three bedrooms are full of character and all have lovely views over the surrounding countryside. Traditional farmhouse breakfasts are the only meals served. The well-appointed dining room incorporates a comfortable seating area. Guests are welcome to use the outdoor swimming pool. Mr and Mrs Hooper do not accept children under five or dogs.

KINGSTON BAGPUIZE Oxfordshire Map 4 SU49

FH **Fallowfields**
Southmoor
✆ Oxford (0865) 820416
Tx 83388

This manorial-style stone residence in 12 acres of ground offers reasonably priced accommodation of a high standard, within easy driving distances of Oxford, Stratford, the Berkshire Downs and the Cotswolds. The house — former home of the Begum Aga Khan — is most tastefully furnished throughout, with many antique pieces in keeping with its style. Bedrooms have all modern comforts including electric blankets, clock/radios, tea/coffee trays and en suite facilities. A croquet lawn and swimming pool in the grounds are available to guests, and riding, tennis, golf, water-sports and fishing can all be found locally. Public rooms include a small library/TV lounge (from which guests are welcome to borrow books) and a larger, comfortably furnished lounge with an open fire. Meals are served in an elegant, licensed dining room. Proprietress Mrs Crowther offers a good four-course dinner menu; please book by 11am and order by 6.30pm. On our Inspector's visit, a choice of four first courses included hot fish ramekin or chicken liver pâté, to be followed by chicken with wine, grapes and yogurt, or lamb chops in plum barbecue sauce, or roast loin of pork with stuffing and pineapple. Sweets are chosen from the trolley. Picnic lunches can be provided by arangement. Fallowfields does not accept children under 10.

Price band B
Dinner td fr £12.50
Last dinner 8pm
Credit card [1]
Parking on premises
Closed Oct–Mar
Closed Wed dinner

KINGSTON-UPON-THAMES Greater London

Clouds
6–8 Kingston Hill
✆ 01-5460559

This busy, friendly restaurant on two floors offers a choice of dining styles. The first floor is a cocktail bar, where a limited menu is usually available. For a wider choice of more substantial meals, eat downstairs. Here, first courses include pasta, stuffed mushrooms, and tortilla chips with dips, while your main course might be spare ribs, a hamburger, a 'Convent Garden' special vegetarian salad, or one of various other specialities, served with french fries or a jacket potato. Desserts include home-made cheesecake, gâteaux and ice-creams. Children's portions of most dishes are available at a reduced price.

Lunch/dinner £10 alc
Last dinner 12 midnt
Credit card [1]
Parking nearby

KINGSWELLS Grampian *Aberdeenshire* Map 15 NJ80

FH **Bellfield**
(4 miles W of Aberdeen off A944)
✆ Aberdeen (0224) 740239

Despite its rural location, and its 200 acres of arable and dairy farmland, Bellfield is conveniently close to Aberdeen. The whole house, which is well-decorated and furnished, accommodates guests in two spacious family rooms and a smaller twin room, all centrally

Price band A
Parking on premises
Closed Dec

heated and served by a modern bathroom. There is an attractive, comfortable lounge with CTV and a trolley provides facilities for making coffee or tea in the evening, together with a supply of biscuits. In the morning you will be served with the good cooked breakfast of your choice.

KINGUSSIE Highland *Inverness-shire* Map 14 NH70

❀ × **The Cross** High Street ✆ (05402) 762	Skilful cooking, warm personal attention and charm and simplicity of appointments come together to make this little restaurant a delight to visit. The à la carte menu, which changes monthly, offers a fairly limited range compiled from the specialities of many countries, prepared and cooked with flair, using local produce to good effect. The proprietor is happy to discuss the dishes with guests, and also to guide them through the extensive wine list. Vegetarian dishes are available.	Dinner alc £12.50 Last dinner 9.30pm Closed 1–24 Dec Closed lunch, & Mon
❀ ★ H **Osprey Hotel** ✆ (05402) 510	The proprietors are very much involved in the running of this small hotel, and their flair and enthusiasm contribute much to its warm and friendly atmosphere. It has a well-deserved reputation for good food, and dinner (a set main course, with a mouthwatering selection of starters and desserts) is a triumph of inventive Cordon Bleu expertise. An impressive wine list accompanies the meal. Quality, fresh produce (often with a Scottish flavour) is always used, and this is evident, too, in the superb standard of the breakfasts. The atmosphere in the dining room is very convivial, with prompt, efficient service. Bedrooms are pretty without being fussy, and provide touches of luxury with good towels and wrapped soap. Lounges are compact, but one has a wood-burning stove and plenty of reading material. Altogether, this unique little hotel offers tremendous value for money and is well worth the detour from the A9.	Price band B Dinner td £14.50 Last dinner 8pm Credit cards [1] [2] [3] [4] [5] Parking on premises Closed Nov–Dec
GH **Sonnhalde** East Ter ✆ (05402) 266	This small Highland guesthouse overlooks the town and has splendid panoramic views across the Spey Valley. It offers warm, value-for-money accommodation, the seven attractively decorated and coordinated bedrooms being served by two well-appointed bathrooms. The pleasant television lounge on the ground floor is traditional in style, while an African theme is reflected in the pictures and carved figures of the dining room. Both porridge and fish are featured at breakfast, and the good, home-made, three-course dinner includes a simple alternative. All aspects of service are particularly good.	Price band A Dinner, b&b £13 Parking on premises Closed Nov

---

KINROSS Tayside *Kinross-shire* Map 11 NO10

★★★ **Windlestrae** The Muirs ✆ (0577) 63217	The small town of Kinross is popular with anglers, having Loch Leven and its famous island castle just to the east. The Windlestrae — its unusual name meaning 'wind grasses' — stands in its own well-landscaped grounds just off the main road. The original house has	Dinner alc £12.50 Last dinner 9.30pm Closed 1–24 Dec

been extended to provide well-appointed bedrooms with en suite facilities and comfortable public rooms. The restaurant provides a pleasant setting in which to enjoy lunch or dinner, while the imposing split-level Pampas cocktail lounge, overlooking patio and garden, is particularly striking. A delightful country-house atmosphere pervades the whole hotel.

Closed Mon, & lunch

KIRKBEAN Dumfries and Galloway *Dumfriesshire* Map 11 NX95

GH **Cavens House**
✆ (038788) 234

Cavens House, standing near the Solway Firth, provides an excellent centre from which to tour the area. The lovely mansion, set in ten acres of garden and pastureland, offers an outstanding level of hospitality, and the accommodation is particularly suitable for disabled people. Both the fresh, airy bedrooms with their spacious bathrooms and the smart, bright public rooms have been subtly adapted for wheelchair users — doors and corridors are widened and smooth-surfaced flooring has been laid. The set dinner is excellent, a home-made soup or broth usually being followed by a roast (perhaps a succulent haunch of vension) with fresh vegetables or salad, an enjoyable pudding and freshly-brewed coffee.

Price band A
Dinner td £8.50
Last dinner 6.45pm
Parking on premises

KIRKBYMOORSIDE North Yorkshire Map 8 SE68

GH **Appletree Court**
Town farm,
9 High St
✆ Lastingham (0751) 31536

Standing at the end of one of the market town's stone-built terraces, Appletree Court was once a working farm. It stands in attractive walled gardens, and cream teas are served outside when weather permits. The house has been modernised with great care to retain much of the original character and atmosphere: both the elegant, comfortable lounge and the dining room boast exposed beams and interesting old fireplaces. Bedrooms are both charming and well-equipped, offering such thoughtful luxuries as toiletries and mineral water. The friendly proprietors provide courteous, helpful service, and the set meal menus cover a range of interesting dishes, with alternatives always available.

Price band A
Dinner td £8
Last dinner 7pm
Limited parking on premises

KIRTON Nottinghamshire Map 8 SK66

GH **Old Rectory**
Main St
✆ Mansfield (0623) 861540

Standing at the centre of the small village, surrounded by tree-lined lawns and pleasant gardens, this lovely old Georgian house which once belonged to the priest now provides spacious accommodation in a relaxed and peaceful atmosphere. Renovations and improvements have resulted in no loss of charm or character, and standards are impeccably high throughout. One of the ten comfortable bedrooms has a shower and toilet en suite, another has shower but no toilet, and the rest are served by modern, well-maintained facilities. Guests can take their ease in a large, pleasant lounge, and meals are served in an attractively decorated dining room.

Price band A
Dinner, b&b £19.75
Last dinner 9pm
Parking on premises
Closed Dec

KNIGHTWICK Hereford & Worcester Map 3 SO75

★ **The Talbot** ✆ (0886) 21235	This old inn beside the River Teme can trace its history back to the late 14th century. A warm welcome, good food and pleasant accommodation can still be found here, with the bonus of up-to-date leisure amenities including a squash court, a skittle alley and a sauna, as well as private fishing. Hearty home-cooked meals are served both in the bar and, in the evenings, in the restaurant. The day's menu is displayed on a blackboard above one of the big open fires. Fish and game dishes are particular specialities, and vegetarian items are also on offer. Traditional English sweets include treacle tart and steamed pudding, and home-made ice-creams are a favourite in summer. The inn has 10 bedrooms, seven of which have private facilities. There are two family bedrooms.	Price band B Bar lunch alc £6.30 Lunch alc £6.50 Dinner alc £7.50 Last dinner 9.30pm Credit cards [1] [3] Parking on premises

KNIPOCH Strathclyde *Argyllshire* Map 10 NM82

★★★ BL **Knipoch** (6 miles S of Oban on A816) ✆ Kilninver (08526) 251	This warmly welcoming and tastefully modernised Georgian house stands in a beautiful position by the shore of Loch Feochan. Its bedrooms are well-appointed and thoughtfully equipped, with views over the loch, while spacious public rooms have inviting leather armchairs and open fires. The flagstone floor and natural stone walls of the dining room provide a suitable setting for meals which are decidedly Scottish in flavour, with grouse and seafood regularly featured.	Price band B Bar lunch alc £8 Dinner td £22.50 Last dinner 9pm Credit cards [1] [2] [3] [5] Parking on premises

LAGGAN Highland *Inverness-shire* Map 14 NN69

★★★ **Gaskmore House** ✆ (05284) 250	This delightful hotel has risen, like a phoenix from the ashes, from the burnt-out shell of the original building. It stands in its own grounds on an elevated site, with panoramic views stretched out before it and the Monadhliath Mountains behind. The interior has been restored to a very high standard, and the bedrooms (all of which have double glazing and en suite facilities) blend quality with taste. The public rooms feature coordinated carpeting and décor; Italian cane furniture and natural wood tables effectively complement the stone walls of the cocktail bar, and leather-upholstered period seating achieves contrast in the small foyer lounge. The dinners served in the lovely dining room are skilfully cooked and thoughtfully presented, their quality reflecting the use of first class ingredients.	Price band B Bar lunch £3.50–£7 Lunch td fr £3.50 Dinner alc £12.50 Last dinner 9.30pm Credit cards [1] [3] Parking on premises

LANARK Strathclyde *Lanarkshire* Map 11 NS84

×× **Ristorante La Vigna** 40 Wellgate ✆ (0555) 4320	Shop premises in the middle of the market town have been thoughtfully converted to create an attractive little restaurant with smart, tastefully simple décor and uncluttered table appointments. Clients receive a friendly welcome from the proprietor and can expect efficient and attentive service from a friendly staff. Well-prepared Italian specialities, including the traditional favourites, reflect the high standards	Lunch td fr £5 or alc £17 Dinner alc £17 Last dinner 10.30pm Credit cards [1] [2] [3] [5] No parking on

maintained in the kitchen, and the emphasis on fresh ingredients is exemplified by the inclusion on the menus of seasonally-available fish. Predictably, the wine list is almost exclusively Italian, though a few French and German wines are included.

premises
Closed Sun lunch

LANGHO Lancashire Map 7 SD73

★★ B
Mytton Fold Farm
(Sited between the villages of Langho and Whalley)
✆ Blackburn (0254) 48255/49577

Mytton Fold Farm Hotel is now a far cry from the stables originally converted in 1982: extensions provide well-furnished bedrooms with lots of thoughtful extras, together with a comfortable lounge and restaurant-bar. Good Lancashire hospitality is still the order of the day, however, and a stay here is a delightful experience — not least because of fine home-cooked meals, based on local produce. The hotel will appeal to the holiday-maker, for it stands at the beautiful Gateway to the Ribble Valley and is close to Pendle Hill, famous for the witch trials of 1612.

Price band B
Lunch td £5.95
Dinner alc £10
Last dinner 9.30pm
Credit cards [1] [3]
Parking on premises

LANGSTONE Gwent Map 3 ST38

★★ B **New Inn**
(Few miles from Newport on Chepstow Road)
✆ Newport (063341) 2426

This old inn, which enjoyed for many years a fine reputation as a traditional hostelry, has now been extended and refurbished to present-day standards. All 34 well-appointed bedrooms have en suite facilities and CTV, and an attractive restaurant offers both table d'hôte and à la carte menus, while lighter snacks can be obtained in the bars. Children are welcome and babysitting services can be provided. Discothèques can be arranged.

Price band B
Bar lunch £2.50 or alc £9
Lunch/dinner alc £9
Last dinner 10.30pm
Credit cards [1] [2] [3] [5]
Parking on premises

LASTINGHAM North Yorkshire Map 8 SE79

★★ ♣ H
Lastingham Grange
✆ (07515) 345

This lovely country house offers a quality of service surpassed by none: you will be served with morning coffee and afternoon tea at no extra charge, your bedroom will be made ready for you each evening, and muddy, wet boots will miraculously become clean and dry. The hotel is delightfully and peacefully situated in its own attractive gardens, which include an adventure playground for children. Bedrooms are all comfortable, and have en suite facilities. They are supplied with such luxuries as hairdriers and trouser-presses. Log fires burn in a lounge which contains (in common with the rest of the house) many interesting antiques. Excellent, home-cooked, 5-course dinners are served — and the toffee cheesecake cannot go unmentioned!

Price band C
Bar lunch £1.25–£5
Lunch td £8.25
Dinner td £12.75
Last dinner 8.30pm
Credit cards [2] [5]
Parking on premises
Closed mid Dec–Feb

LAVENHAM Suffolk Map 5 TL94

★★★ L
Swan Hotel
High St
✆ (0787) 247477

One of a host of beautiful half-timbered buildings in this East Anglian show village, the Swan is very popular with tourists and business visitors alike. The interior has been carefully refurbished to make the most of the 15th-century building's original features. Log fires and antique furnishings enhance the

Price band D
Dinner td £14.50 & alc
Lunch td £8.95–£10 & alc
Last dinner

	atmosphere in the comfortable open lounge area, while the restaurant has a lofty timbered ceiling and a minstrels' gallery. The 48 bedrooms have lots of character, but modern comforts too: all have private bathrooms and CTV. Traditional English and classic French cuisine are the mainstay of the dining room. Afternoon tea is a highlight of the day, and includes an excellent choice of pastries. Gastronomic weekends are sometimes offered, and there is a popular series of winter concerts.	9.30pm Credit cards [1] [2] [3] [4] [5] Parking on premises

LEAMINGTON SPA Warwickshire Map 4 SP36

★ RED **Lansdowne Hotel** 87 Clarendon St ✆ (0926) 21313 Tx 337556	This small, creeper-clad Regency hotel just outside the town centre offers comfort and hospitality at down-to-earth prices. It is amiably run by David and Gillian Allen, who are very good at making their guests feel at home. There are 10 bedrooms, mostly smallish but prettily decorated and comfortably furnished. Four have private facilities and one is a family room. On the ground floor is a well-stocked bar and a cosy TV lounge, as well as the dining room. Menus are short but sensibly planned, and the food is well-prepared, using fresh ingredients, and attractively presented. Vegetarians can be catered for. Dogs are not accepted, and neither are children under five.	Price band B Dinner td fr £9.65 Lunch td £8.95 Last dinner 8.30pm Credit card [1] Limited parking on premises Restricted service 24 Dec-12 Jan
GH **York House Hotel** 9 York Rd ✆ (0926) 24671	This impressive Victorian residence stands in a particularly attractive area of the spa town, overlooking the River Leam and Royal Pump Gardens, with the famous Jephson Gardens close by. The house has been furnished in an elegant and tasteful manner in keeping with its age: a beautiful, original Victorian WC makes a talking point, and the cosy dining room is adorned with Victoriana. The lounge is particularly noteworthy, its pastel shades providing an ideal background for the many antique pieces and objects d'art displayed there.	Price band A Lunch/dinner £7 Last dinner 6.30pm Parking on premises Closed 20 Dec–1 Jan

LECHLADE Gloucestershire Map 4 SU29

× **Weylands** 6 Oak St (On Burford Road out of town) ✆ Farington (0367) 52587	Proprietor/chef Eric Burger describes his charmingly tiny restaurant as 'a continental kitchen'. Set in a delightful, terraced cottage with old beams, exposed stonework and flagstone floors, its simplicity and informality provide an effective foil for the high standard of skilful, ingenious cusine and attentive service that the customer will enjoy. A short but sound wine list adds the finishing touch to a meal that is always good value for money.	Lunch td fr £9.95 Dinner td fr £12.25 Last dinner 10pm Credit card [3] Parking nearby

LEEDS West Yorkshire Map 8 SE33

GH **Aragon** 250 Stainbeck Ln ✆ (0532) 759306	Surrounded by an attractive garden and offering good parking facilities, the Aragon stands in a good residential area ideally placed for the Leeds Ring Road or the town centre. Inside, there is a small, comfortable lounge with a separate licensed lounge	Price band A/B Bar snacks 70p–£3 Dinner td £6.10 Last dinner 7pm

and bar adjacent to the dining room. Bedrooms are comfortable and have tasteful fittings and good facilities — lit shaving mirrors with electric shaver points, for example. The dining room specialises in home-cooked English dishes, and the dinner menu offers a very reasonably priced choice of starters, main courses and sweets.

Credit cards 1 2 3 5
Parking on premises
Closed Xmas & New year

LEIGHTON BUZZARD Bedfordshire Map 4 SP92

★★★ Swan Hotel
High St
✆ (0525) 372148
Tx 825562
CHACOM-G-SWAN

This 18th-century coaching inn, still with its original façade, now offers all the modern facilities expected by 20th-century travellers. It overlooks the square in Leighton Buzzard, which remains a small, quiet market town in contrast to the busy centres of Luton and Milton Keynes nearby. Public rooms at the Swan are cheerful and comfortable. In the oak-panelled Hunters' Bar, guests may enjoy a quiet drink before lunch or dinner in Mr Swan's Restaurant, where good food and wines are served by friendly staff. The restaurant has gained a good reputation locally for its interesting, well-cooked food and pleasant atmosphere. Vegetarian food is available. The Swan has 38 bedrooms, all with private bathrooms, CTV and telephones, and tastefully furnished with comfort in mind. They include four courtyard bedrooms equipped with kitchenettes — ideal for families, or for guests planning a longer stay.

Price band D
Bar lunch £1.20–£3
Lunch td fr £9.75
Dinner td fr £14.50 or alc £15–£18
Last dinner 9.30pm
Credit cards 1 2 3 5
Parking on premises

LEOMINSTER Hereford & Worcester Map 3 SO45

FH **Wharton Bank Farm**
(Off A49 S of Leominster)
✆ (0568) 2575

This fine 18th-century farmhouse overlooks the Lugg Valley from a high spur of land above the A49. The interior combines character and charm with modern comforts. The four bedrooms, one with a bathroom en suite, are spacious and tastefully decorated, and guests have their own comfortable sitting room and dining room. Breakfasts consist of a traditional British farmhouse platter, and although no other meals are available, Mrs Black, the proprietor, will gladly suggest a number of restaurants and inns within easy reach. Guests at Wharton Bank have the use of an outdoor pool and a grass tennis court. No dogs, please.

Price band A
Parking on premises

LETHAM Fife Map 11 NO31

❀ ★★★ ♔ L
Fernie Castle
(4 miles W of Cupar on A914)
✆ (033781) 381
Tx 295141

This charming little castle, dating back to the 16th century, stands peacefully in its own grounds about four miles west of Cupar. Every effort has been made to retain its original character; the existing features of the bedrooms, which are a mixture of shapes and sizes, have been utilized in meeting the standards expected of a modern hotel, and the cocktail bar boasts an unusual vaulted ceiling. The first-floor lounges are large and comfortable, with welcoming open fires and a good selection of books and magazines. The restaurant is rapidly gaining a reputation for modern-style cuisine, though the

Price band C
Bar lunch td £5.50–£8.50 or alc £17.50
Lunch td £9.50 or alc £17.50
Dinner td £16.50 or alc £22.50
Last dinner 9.30pm
Credit cards 1 2 3 5

portions served are on a traditionally generous scale! The chef makes excellent use of local produce and game, and the à la carte menu is particularly extensive and interesting.

Parking on premises

LETHAM Tayside *Angus* Map 15 NO54

★★★ ♣♣
Idvies House
✆ (030781) 787
Tx 76252

This secluded country mansion stands in its own 12-acre grounds and offers lovely views across the Strathmore Valley towards the glens. The owners provide personal attention, and the atmosphere is pleasant and informal. An attractively appointed restaurant provides the opportunity to enjoy good Scottish fare, with fruit and vegetables from the hotel's walled garden. Public rooms, furnished in a style appropriate to the Victorian period of the house, comprise a high-ceilinged drawing room, a small study lounge and library cocktail bar with chintz curtains and leather-upholstered seating. Large, comfortable bedrooms all have en suite facilities and CTV. Squash courts are available.

Price band C
Bar lunch td £3–£5
Lunch td fr £7.50 or alc £15
Dinner td fr £11 or alc £15
Last dinner 9.30pm
Credit cards [1] [2] [3] [5]
Parking on premises
Closed 26 & 27 Dec
Lunches only 24–5 Dec

LETTERFINLAY Highland *Inverness-shire* Map 14 NN29

★★ HL
Letterfinlay Lodge
✆ Spean Bridge (039781) 622

This friendly, family-run hotel, standing on the busy A82 and backing onto Loch Lochy, provides a simple, comfortable accommodation. Five of the 15 bedrooms have en suite facilities. A cosy lounge-bar leads into a well-appointed public lounge with a splendid view across the loch, and this room is very popular for bar lunches. The dining room offers a menu of plain, wholesome dishes in which only the best quality raw ingredients are used. Fishing is available to residents, as is a babysitting service.

Price band B
Bar lunch £1.80–£8
Dinner td £11–£12.50
Last dinner 8.30
Credit cards [1] [2] [3] [4] [5]
Parking on premises
Closed Nov–Feb

LEW Oxfordshire Map 4 SP30

FH **University Farm**
(On A4095, 3m SW of Witney)
✆ Bampton Castle (0993) 850297

Farmer's wife Mrs Rouse takes tremendous pains to make her guests feel thoroughly at home at this lovely 17th-century Cotswold farmhouse several miles west of Oxford. Accommodation is in six spacious and comfortable bedrooms, all of which have CTV and private bath or shower. There are two rooms suitable for familes, and ground-floor rooms suitable for disabled guests. Both breakfast and dinner feature hearty farmhouse cooking, with home-made bread and preserves. Roasts are a speciality, and are sometimes preceded by a sorbet. Meals are served in an attractive oak-beamed, licensed dining room. The equally pleasant sitting room has an inglenook fireplace, and in fine weather guests can enjoy the sun terrace or a walk in the large garden. Dogs are not accepted.

Price band A
Dinner, b&b £25
Last dinner 7pm
Parking on premises
Closed Xmas & New Year

LEWDOWN Devon Map 2 SX48

❀×× **Fox's Earth**
Lewtrenchard
✆ (056683) 256

Improvements are in progress on this interesing manor house, dating from 1629, to restore it to its former glory and transform it into a country house hotel. Currently it is open only for dinner, which is served in the intimate panelled dining room where there are just six tables. Two imaginative set menus are offered, cooked by recently appointed young chef Martin Lyon who continues to maintain former standards. His food is prepared with care in the modern French style, using good fresh ingredients. There is a small well-chosen wine list and the service is friendly and attentive.

Price band C
Lunch td £13.50 (Sun only)
Dinner td £17 & £20
Last dinner 9.30pm
Credit cards [1] [2] [3]
Parking on premises

LICHFIELD Staffordshire Map 7 SK10

GH **Oakleigh House**
✆ (0543) 262688

The large, Edwardian house is situated in a favoured residental area of this famous cathedral city and offers a high standard of accommodation. Its 10 comfortable bedrooms (five of which are located in an annexe) are attractively decorated and well-furnished, the majority having en suite facilities. The dining room, incorporating a conservatory, is particularly pleasant, and guests can take their ease in the relaxed atmosphere of two inviting lounges.

Price band B
Dinner td £8.50 or alc £14.50
Last dinner 9.30pm
Credit cards [1] [3]
Parking on premises
Restricted accomodation Xmas

LIFTON Devon Map 2 SX38

★★★ HL
Arundell Arms
✆ (0566) 84666

This attractive, creeper-clad former coaching inn is famous for its excellent sporting facilities. Visitors may enjoy salmon and trout fishing in a 20-mile stretch of the River Tamar, and courses for beginners are available. An ancient cockpit in the grounds is now a well-stocked tackle room. Shooting and stalking are also offered. The hotel, recently refurbished, provides comfortable accommodation in 24 tastefully appointed bedrooms, nearly all of which have a private bath or shower. Every room is equipped with CTV and telephones. In the lounge, with its fine Cornish blue slate floor, a cheerful log fire brightens winter days. The restaurant boasts good English and French-style food and at lunch-times a cold buffet is served in the split-level bar. Guests may be assured of warm hospitality from proprietor Anne Voss-Bark and her staff.

Price band C
Bar lunch £1.50–£5
Lunch td £9 or alc £20
Dinner td £16 or alc £20
Last dinner 9pm
Credit cards [1] [2] [3] [5]
Parking on premises
Closed 24–7 Dec

LIMPSFIELD Surrey Map 5 TQ45

Brasserie at the Old Lodge
High st
(Entrance from car park at rear of the ❀×× Old Lodge)
✆ Oxted (0883) 717385

The proprietors of the distinguished Old Lodge restaurant offer excellent, though simpler fare in this attractive new brasserie at the rear of their premises. Food here is of the highest quality, and is prepared to order by the chef, who cooks in full view of the customers. Lasagne and garlic bread were enjoyed by our Inspector; other main courses are papillotes of sole and a choice of stews. First courses included home-made soup and marinated mushrooms, and there were

Lunch alc fr £4
Dinner alc £10
Last dinner 9.15pm
Credit cards [1] [2] [3] [4] [5]
Parking on premises
Closed 1st 2 wks

tempting sweets such as cherries jubilee or hot chocolate profiteroles. Service is courteous and attentive but friendly, helping to account for the justifiable popularity of this new venture.

Jan & Good Friday
Closed Mon, Sat lunch & Sun dinner

LINCOLN Lincolnshire Map 8 SK97

★★ The Loudor
37 Newark Rd
(3 miles SW A46)
✆ (0522) 680333

High standards of comfort and cheerful, attentive service have earned the Loudor a well-deserved reputation for excellence. The bedrooms are light and cheerful, thoughtfully furnished and beautifully kept. Meals are well-prepared, every effort being made to cater for guests' individual requirements, while the cosy lounge and small bar provide for after-dinner relaxation. The hotel is popular both with businessmen and with visitors exploring this historic cathedral city.

Price band B
Bar lunch td £4.95–£6.50
Lunch td fr £6.95 or alc £10
Dinner td fr £7.95 or alc £10
Last dinner 8.15pm
Credit cards [1] [2] [3] [5]
Parking on premises

LITTLE HEREFORD Hereford & Worcester Map 7 SO56

FH **Lower Upton Farm**
(1½m S of A456)
✆ Brimfield (058472) 322

Mr and Mrs Williams are welcoming hosts at their peaceful Victorian farmhouse close to the county boundary between Shropshire and Hereford & Worcester. Guests are offered an unusually extensive dinner menu, and asked to make the choice well in advance so that Mrs Williams can shop and cook accordingly. Popular dishes are Shropshire lamb, and chicken in a sauce of mushrooms and local cider. For sweet, there are usually pies or crumbles in winter, trifles or fools in summer — all home-made, of course. No wine list is available, but guests are encouraged to bring their own. Breakfasts are in traditional farmhouse style, and packed lunches are available on request. Three letting bedrooms are available, including one family room, at very reasonable prices. Dogs are not accepted.

Price band A
Dinner, b&b £11.50–£12.50
Last dinner 7pm
Parking on premises
Closed Xmas & New Year

LITTON North Yorkshire Map 7 SD97

GH **Park Bottom**
✆ Arncliffe (075677) 235

Set in the beautiful and unspoiled valley of Littondale, Park Bottom is an attractive, architect-designed, stone house. Its interior is well-furnished and equipped to suit the modern traveller, but the traditional log fire in the comfortable lounge provides a focal point that the central heating cannot rival. A split-level dining room offers good home cooking, and the set dinners are based on top-quality fresh local produce. The guesthouse makes an ideal centre for those touring the delightful Yorkshire Dales that surround it. Children over five welcome.

Price band A
Dinner, b&b £17–£22
Last dinner 8.30pm
Parking on premises
Closed Dec–Feb

> À la carte prices are based on an average for three courses without wine.

LIZARD Cornwall Map 3 SW71

GH **Penmenner House Hotel**
Penmenner Rd
(0326) 290370

Traditional Cornish hospitality is provided by proprietors Marion and Keith Williams here at one of Britain's most southerly hotels. The period granite house is set on the edge of the village, and there are magnificent coastal views from most windows. The eight bedrooms, including two family rooms, are simply furnished but adequate, and all have tea/coffee-making facilities. Five rooms have shower and WC en suite. Local produce, including fresh fish and Cornish cream, features in Mrs Williams' sound home cooking. At dinner (which should be ordered by 6pm), a set menu of freshly prepared dishes is offered. Alternatives can be ordered by prior arrangement. A reasonably priced wine list is available, and local beer is freshly drawn from the cellar. The hotel has a games room where guests can play tennis, darts and pool. There are also three self-catering flats to let.

Price band A
Dinner td £6
Last dinner 7pm
Parking on premises.
Closed Nov-Mar

LLANDDEINIOLEN Gwynedd Map 6 SH56

FH **Ty'n Rhos Farm**
Port Dinorwic (0248) 670489

Magnificently situated, with views of Snowdonia to one side and the rolling countryside of Anglesey to the other, the Kettle family's peaceful farm offers a warm welcome and well-equipped accommodation. The farmhouse has been tastefully extended to give nine bedrooms, all with private bathrooms and including three family rooms. Early-morning tea trays are provided, and CTV is available in rooms on request. The large, beamed lounge is kept cosy by a log-burning stove, and there is a small bar in the dining room. Home-produced meat (including home-made sausages at breakfast), and vegetables and fruit that often come fresh from the kitchen garden, are the mainstay of meals, which are served to residents only. Dogs are not accepted.

Price band A
Dinner td £19.50–£21
Last dinner 7pm
Parking on premises
Closed Xmas & New Year

LLANDUDNO Gwynedd Map 6 SH78

★★★ RED
Bodysgallen Hall
(On A470 Llandudno link rd)
Deganwy (0492) 84466
Tx 617163

This splendidly sited Jacobean country house is highly recommended by our Inspector for its comfort, elegance and high standards of both food and service. The interior is pervaded by a rich sense of history: most features, such as the panelled hall and drawing room, with their stone chimneypieces, date from the 17th century, but part of the house is three centuries older, having been built as a watchtower to defend Conway Castle. Antique furnishings are complemented by carefully chosen fabrics, interesting paintings and objects d'art. Public rooms also include a cosy bar and a library. The handsomely furnished bedrooms are 28 in number, all with private bathrooms, trouser-presses, CTV and telephones. Thoughtful extras include flowering plants, home-made biscuits and mineral water. Nine of the rooms are in a separate building, including three family rooms (but children under eight are not accepted). The hotel has facilities for disabled guests. A choice of

Price band D
Bar lunch £1.50–£3.50
Lunch td fr £7.50
Dinner td £18.50 or alc £22
Last dinner 9.45pm
Credit cards 1 2 3 5
Parking on premises

imaginative and expertly prepared dishes from a fixed-price menu is offered in the distinguished restaurant, where the surroundings are suitably imposing and the service courteous and smiling. Vegetarians can be catered for. Bodysgallen Hall stands in magnificent gardens including a notable knot garden, a walled rose garden. Leisure amenities include tennis, croquet and riding.

GH **Craiglands**
7 Carmen Sylva Rd, Craig-y-Don
✆ (0492) 75090

Ideally situated in the quieter part of the town yet close to the seafront, this large detached Victorian house has been restored and converted into a pleasing private hotel with good facilities. All six bedrooms (including one family room) have showers en suite, CTV, tea/coffee-making equipment and comfortable modern furniture. Public rooms are not large but are cosy and tastefully furnished, and the whole establishment is kept in good order and spotlessly clean by proprietors Colin and Blodwen Mullin. Dinner should be ordered by 5.30pm. Children under four are not accepted.

Price band A
Dinner, b&b £13–£15
Last dinner 6pm
Parking nearby
Closed Dec–Mar

★★★ BL **Empire Hotel**
Church Walks
✆ (0492) 79955
Tx 617161

This privately run hotel offers a high standard of comfort and excellent facilities. There are 56 bedrooms, all with private facilities, CTV and telephone, eight of which are family rooms. These vary in size but all are well-furnished and two have four-poster beds. Extras include a personal video for which guests may borrow tapes from a large in-house library. Good food is served in the Watling Restaurant and the pool-side coffee shop, where a wide range of light meals may be obtained. Vegetarians are also catered for. There are indoor and heated outdoor swimming pools and a very well-equipped health and fitness area with trained staff in attendance. The hotel has live music and dancing on Saturdays.

Price band C
Bar lunch alc £5.75
Lunch td £8.25
Dinner td £12.65
Last dinner 9.30pm
Credit cards [1] [2] [3] [4] [5]
Parking on premises
Closed Xmas & New Year

★★★ **Gogarth Abbey Hotel**
West Shore
✆ (0492) 76211

Alice Liddell, the little girl who inspired Lewis Carroll to write *Alice in Wonderland*, lived in a house that is now part of this pleasant holiday hotel. Set on Llandudno's West Shore, with views of Conway and Snowdonia, the hotel is conveniently placed for walks on Great Orme and for the North Wales Golf Course. Even nearer at hand are the hotel's own indoor swimming pool, croquet lawn, putting green, sauna and solarium, and other leisure activities include dancing in season. All 41 bedrooms are comfortably furnished and have private facilities and CTV. Four will accommodate families. Public rooms include relaxing lounges and a well-appointed bar, as well as an attractive dining room where a good table d'hôte dinner menu is offered. Cooking and presentation are imaginative, and staff and management are always freindly and attentive. Vegetarian food can be provided. The hotel does not accept dogs.

Bar lunches td £5–£8
Dinner td fr £10.50 or alc £15
Last dinner 8.30pm
Credit cards [1] [2] [3]
Parking on premises
Closed 23 Dec–24 Jan

À la carte prices are based on an average for three courses without wine.

★ HL
Gwesty Leamore
40 Lloyd St
☎ (0492) 75552

'Croeso I Leamore' (welcome to the Leamore) proclaims a sign above the bar at this family-run, truly welcoming and very Welsh hotel. Proprietors Beryl and Fred Owen take a pride in the recently refurbished accommodation, warm hospitality and good food that they offer their guests. More than half of the 12 bedrooms have shower or bath en suite, and all are equipped with CTV, clock/radios, hairdriers, tea/coffee-making facilities and even sewing kits. There are four family rooms, and children of any age are welcome (but dogs are not accepted). Downstairs, guests may relax in the comfortable lounge or the small but well-stocked cocktail bar. In the licensed dining room, menus offer a limited choice but the food is always good and made from fresh produce.

Price band A/B
Bar lunch £2.50–£4
Dinner td fr £6
Last dinner 7.30pm
Limited parking on premises
Closed Xmas

★★ **Merrion**
South Parade
☎ (0492) 860022

Situated on the promenade and close to the Victorian pier, this hotel has belonged for three generations to the Bream family who have carried out many improvements. The 67 bedrooms are comfortable and well-equipped with en suite facilities and CTV. Seven of the rooms will accommodate families. The lounges, too, are nicely furnished. In charge of the kitchen is Gareth Bream who, when he is not working at the hotel, travels the country in search of new ideas to improve his culinary skills. Vegetarian dishes are available. Music and dancing are also on offer.

Price band B/C
Bar lunch alc £5.50
Dinner td fr £10.50 alc £13
Last dinner 8.30pm
Credit cards [1] [2] [3]
Parking on premises

★★ RED **St Tudno**
Promenade
☎ (0492) 74411

The friendly atmosphere and bright, tasteful décor of this small Victorian hotel near the pier make it a most pleasant place to stay. The quarter-bottle of sparkling wine that greets guests on arrival in their rooms is a suitable introduction to the excellent hospitality provided by proprietors Janette and Martin Bland. Public rooms are cheerfully and artistically furnished; the dining room, with its bamboo furniture, trellis wallpaper and profusion of plants, has a garden-like atmosphere. The pleasant, modern coffee lounge, non-smoking sitting room and Victorian-style bar are all most attractive places to relax. Leisure facilities include an indoor swimming pool. Bedrooms are compact but well-equipped and prettily decorated. All 21 have private facilities, CTV and telephones. Four of the rooms will accommodate families. Food at St Tudno is in the care of Mr Bland, who produces very good five-course dinners with a choice of dishes including some Welsh specialities. Vegetarians can be catered for.

Price band B/C
Lunch td fr £8.50 or alc £10
Dinner alc £15.50
Last dinner 9.30pm
Credit cards [1] [3]
Limited parking on premises
Closed 19 Dec–21 Jan

LLANFAIR DYFFRYN Clwyd Map 6 SJ15

GH **Eyarth Station**
☎ (08242) 3643

Genuine hospitality and a friendly welcome are extended by hosts Jen and Bert Spencer at this delightful converted railway station. Nothing seems to be too much trouble for the Spencers: they really enjoy looking after their guests, who become part of the family. There are three bedrooms to let, including one family room, all furnished and decorated to a high standard and all with private bath or shower rooms. The original ticket office is now a feature of the hall, and where the trains once ran, a spacious lounge now

Price band A/B
Parking on premises
Closed Xmas

offers comfortable modern seating and the warmth of a wood-burning stove on chilly days. Dinner is available to residents if ordered by 4pm. Guests may use the small outdoor swimming pool in summer, and there are several acres of garden and paddock to explore.

LLANFIHANGEL Powys Map 6 SJ01

FH **Cyfie Farm**
(2 miles S of Llanfihangel on unclassified rd off B4382)
Llanfyllin
(069184) 451

This 17th-century traditional Welsh long house stands in an elevated position with breaktaking views, in the remote and unspoilt heart of mid Wales. There are two rooms in the main farmhouse, with a shared bathroom, and one family suite which has its own lounge and shower room. Décor and furnishings are traditional and of a high standard, with many exposed oak beams in the walls and ceilings. A log fire burns in winter in the cosy lounge, and in the congenial dining room guests eat family-style at one large table. Mrs Jenkins supplies plentiful and wholesome farmhouse fare, using mainly home-produced meats and vegetables in season. Traditional Welsh dishes sometimes served include lamb and leek pie. Guests are welcome to take an interest in the many activities of the 178-acre mixed farm, or, alternatively, this is an ideal location for touring mid Wales. Either way, the Jenkins family's outstanding hospitality and beautiful Welsh home will ensure guests of a memorable holiday. Cyfie Farm does not accept dogs.

Price band A/B
Dinner, b&b £16.50–£17.50
Last dinner 7.30pm
Parking on premises

LLANGATTOCK Powys Map 3 SO21

GH **Ty Croeso**
Dardy
Crickhowell
(0873) 810573

Commanding views over Crickhowell and the River Usk are a feature of this pleasant guesthouse (whose name means 'welcoming house') near the Brecon and Monmouth Canal. A wide selection of good-value, freshly prepared food is available at lunch-times and in the evening in the restaurant, and the bedrooms are modern, comfortable and well-appointed.

Price band B
Bar lunch fr £2.95
Lunch/dinner alc £10
Last dinner 9.45pm
Credit card [3]
Parking on premises

LLANGOLLEN Clwyd Map 7 SJ24

★★ H
Ty'n-y-Wern
(1m E of Llangollen on A5)
(0978) 860252

Proprietors here since 1984, the Fishers have spared no time or expense in ensuring that their hotel offers comfort and good value for money. Ty'n-y-Wern stands in a a commanding position overlooking the Vale of Llangollen and is ideally placed for holidaymakers wishing to explore this lovely area. Traditional standards of hospitality and service are maintained, and dinner, prepared by Sebastian Fisher, is skilfully and imaginatively cooked. Vegetarians can be catered for. The 12 individually furnished bedrooms all have TV, and most have private facilities. Public rooms are comfortable and attractive and are cheered and warmed by open fires in winter. Children and dogs are welcome.

Price band B
Lunch alc £5
Dinner alc £7.50
Last dinner 9pm
Credit cards [1] [3]
Parking on premises
Restaurants closed to non-residents Mon, & Sun dinner

LLANGYNOG Powys Map 6 SJ02

★ **New Inn** ✆ Pennant (069174) 229	This lovely 18th-century inn stands in the heart of the tiny village of Llangynog, surrounded by the beautiful countryside of the Berwyn Mountains and the Tanat valley. There are eight bedrooms, three of them with bathrooms en suite and two suitable for familes. All are comfortably furnished and attractively decorated. Public rooms include a cosy, beamed bar with a wood-burning stove, and a separate television lounge. There is also a pool table. Food is always good, and lunch and dinner (including vegetarian dishes if required) are served both in the bar and in the pretty dining room. The New Inn is owned and run by the hospitable Williamson family, who take pleasure in ensuring that their guests are well-looked after in every way.	Price band B Bar lunch alc £4.58 Lunch td £5.50 or alc £5.80 Dinner td £6.25 or alc £8.73 Last dinner 9.45pm Parking on premises

LLANWRTYD WELLS Powys Map 3 SN84

GH **Lasswade House** ✆ (05913) 515	Conveniently located for exploring the wild uplands of mid Wales, this delightful little family-run hotel has good facilities and a pleasant country house atmosphere. The handsome Edwardian house has eight letting bedrooms, six of them with private bath or shower and all with CTV, alarm clocks, radios and tea/coffee-making equipment. Thoughtful extra touches include fresh flowers and books. Amenities available to guests include an outdoor swimming pool, and good home-cooking is provided in the licensed dining room, which is also open to non-residents for dinner by prior arrangement. Both fixed-price and à la carte menus are available, and guests make their choice over a drink in the lounge, with its fine views and elegant antique furnishings. Lasswade House was a regional winner of the 1986-7 AA Guesthouse of the Year award.	Price band A Dinner td £10 or alc £13 Last dinner 9.30pm Credit cards [1] [3] Parking on premises

LOCHEARNHEAD Central *Perthshire* Map 11 NN52

★ HBL **Mansewood Country House** ✆ (05673) 213	Standing at the roadside on the southern outskirts of the village, this comfortable, efficiently-run hotel offers two relaxing lounge areas and a small bar whose aeronautical theme reflects the previous career of the proprietor. Bedrooms are compact but comfortable, and the cheerfully decorated dining room displays a multitude of pictures, prints and ornaments — all featuring red poppies. This warm, friendly establishment makes an ideal touring base for the Central Highlands of Scotland. Sailing, surfing, water ski-ing and riding are available.	Price band A/B Bar lunch td £1.95–£6.25 Dinner td fr £8.50 Last dinner 8.30pm Credit cards [1] [2] [3] [5] Parking on premises Closed Jan-Feb

LODDON Norfolk Map 5 TM39

FH **Stubbs House** ✆ (0508) 20231	Peacefully situated on the outskirts of Loddon, overlooking Stubbs Green, this delightful Georgian house is easily accessible from the Norwich-Beccles road. Its friendly accommodation differs from that of a conventional farmhouse only in the number of rooms available (some with private facilities) and the	Price band A/B Dinner td £7 Last dinner 6.30pm Closed Nov-Feb Parking

range of services offered. The meals offered in the spacious dining room are English in style, using only the freshest of produce. Two lounges are available for guests' use, one containing a colour television, reading materials, chess and board games, or you are welcome to relax on the putting green in the sheltered gardens.

LONDON BARNES Greater London Map 4 TQ38
Also see Claygate, Hampton Court and Hampton Wick

× **Barnaby's** 39B High St, SW13 ✆ 01-878 4750	French regional fare is the mainstay of this little restaurant close to the Thames. Warm colours, lantern lighting and a Victorian fireplace help create a cosy, welcoming atmosphere, and the brick walls are hung with framed prints of London. The French proprietor/chef cooks reliably, always using fresh ingredients to advantage. His short, well-balanced menu is complemented by a limited but sensibly planned wine list.	Lunch/dinner alc £14 Last dinner 10.15pm Credit cards 1 2 3 4 5 Closed Easter, 3 wks Sep, Xmas & New Year Closed Sun, & Mon & Sat lunch

BATTERSEA

❀ ×× **L'Arlequin** 123 Queenstown Road, SW8 ✆ 01-622 0555	Please see the value-for-money London lunch feature	Lunch td £15.50 or alc £40 Dinner alc £40 Last dinner 10.30pm Credit cards 1 2 3 5 No parking on premises Closed Sat & Sun

BATTERSEA

❀ ×× **Les Fauves** 24 Queenstown Rd, SW8 ✆ 01-720 5199	Please see the value-for-money London lunch feature	Lunch/dinner td £9.95–£17.95 Last dinner 11pm Credit cards 1 2 3 5 No parking on premises Closed 1st 3 wks Aug & 2 wks Xmas Closed Sun & Mon

BLACKHEATH

Bardon Lodge Hotel 15 Stratheden Rd, SE3 ✆ 01-853 4051	This grand Victorian residence is about five miles from central London, but is well-placed for visiting Greenwich and for public transport to the West End. Mr Knutt, the proprietor, continues to extend and improve the accommodation here: all 42 rooms now have private showers, and some also have WCs. There	Price band B Credit cards 1 3 Limited parking on premises

are five family bedrooms; CTV, telephones and double glazing are standard in all rooms. Furnishings are modern, with coordinated décor and quality fabrics, and beds have duvets (though conventional bedding is available on request). The comfortable lounge and the breakfast room retain their Victorian grandeur in their magnificent ceilings and carved wooden fireplaces. Full English breakfast is provided.

COVENT GARDEN

❀ ××× **Boulestin**
1A Henrietta St, WC2
✆ 01-836 3819

Top-class French cuisine, impeccably served in elegant surroundings, draws a distinguished clientele to this very professionally run Edwardian-style restaurant. Seasonal availability of fresh food dictates the make-up of the well-balanced menu, which features classic French dishes. Cooking is sound and imaginative, and presentation is flawless. Vegetarian dishes are available. Smartly dressed French staff provide polished service. All this, of course, does not come cheap — though the set lunches are not too highly priced. The extensive wine list should satisfy most discerning customers.

Lunch td £15 or alc £45
Dinner alc £55
Last dinner 11.15pm
Credit cards 1 2 3 4 5
No parking on premises
Closed last 3 wks Aug, 1 wk Xmas & Bank Hols
Closed Sun

× **Le Café des Amis du Vin**
11–4 Hanover Place, WC2
✆ 01-379 3444

The lively atmosphere of a traditional French café prevails at this popular spot, which is cosmopolitan in its clientele and is much frequented by theatre-goers. Typical French dishes are the basis of the appealing blackboard menu, and service is by French waiters, who manage to glide efficiently among the rather tightly packed tables. Vegetarian meals are also available. The reasonably priced wine list is extensive enough to offer something for most palates.

Lunch/dinner alc £12.50
Last dinner 11.30pm
Credit cards 1 2 3 5
No parking on premises
Closed Sun

× **Le Café du Jardin**
28 Wellington St, WC2
✆ 01-836 8769

Cheerful, aproned French waiters set the tone at this lively brasserie in the heart of theatreland. The very Gallic-style décor completes the impression that you might have been transported to the streets of France. Menus are short, but include a selection of plats du jour which change frequently, and vegetarian dishes. Cooking is honest and wholesome, and draws local business people at lunch-times as well as theatre-goers in the evening.

Lunch td £9.50 or alc £15
Dinner td £6.95 or alc £15
Last dinner 11.30pm
Credit cards 1 2 3 4 5
No parking on premises
Closed 25–6 Dec & Bank Hols
Closed Sun, & Sat lunch

× **The Happy Wok**
52 Floral St, WC2
✆ 01-836 3696

This small Chinese restaurant next to the Royal Opera House offers enjoyable eating before or after the theatre. Dishes of Pekinese or Szechuan origin are the basis of the large and varied menu. It includes many unusual items introduced by the proprietors, who are always eager to apply their expertise to new ideas. Vegetarian meals are available, and good quality fresh ingredients are always used. Service, by smartly dressed staff, is courteous and efficient.

Lunch/dinner td fr £13
Last dinner 11.30pm
Credit cards 1 2 3 5
No parking on premises

Pasta Bar
30 Henrietta St, WC2
✆ 01-836 8396

Authentic Italian dishes are accompanied by self-serve salads at this lively, cheerful pasta restaurant. There are no frills: customers are here for the pasta! If choice is limited, seating a little cramped and the wine list fairly basic, this is amply compensated by friendly service and genuinely good value for money. Vegetarian meals are available.

Lunch/dinner alc £7.50
Last dinner 11.30pm
Credit card [1]
Parking nearby

❀ ★★★★★ RED
Savoy Hotel (River Room)
Strand, WC2
✆ 01-836 4343
Tx 24234

It is for the famous River Room restaurant that our Inspector has chosen to include the Savoy in this book. Opulent, stately surroundings form a suitable backdrop to meals produced by accomplished maître-chef Anton Edelmann. Food consists mainly of classic dishes, using first-rate fresh ingredients. Service is polished, courteous and attentive. In addition to the à la carte menu, which offers a very large range of dishes, there are fixed-price lunch and dinner menus. There is dancing to live music in the evenings.

Bar lunches td £3.20–£8 or alc £15
Lunch td £17.50 or alc £28
Dinner td fr £22
Last dinner 11.30pm
Credit cards [1] [2] [3] [5]
Parking on premises (charge)

Tuttons
11–2 Russell St, WC2
✆ 01-836 4141

This large, bright brasserie next to Covent Garden Market serves everything from a cup of coffee to a full meal. Popular snacks such as chicken liver pâté appear on the menu, and there are some unusual British regional specialities such as Arbroath smokies or Cumberland sausage. Vegetarian meals are also available. Alternatively, customers can choose to have a drink in the Spanish-style bar downstairs, where spicy snacks are also served. Service is by cheerful young waitresses.

Lunch/dinner alc £9
Last dinner 11.30pm
Credit cards [1] [2] [3] [5]
No parking on premises

EALING

× **Maxim Chinese**
153-5 Northfield Ave, W13
✆ 01-567 1719

An extensive menu specialising in Peking cuisine is offered at this large restaurant, which seats about 100 and stays open late. Vegetarian meals are included in the choice, and there are some interesting set meals which give a good introduction to the style of food. Diners with limited experience of Chinese food can also appeal to the helpful young Oriental staff for assistance in choosing their meals. Service is cheerful and willing.

Lunch td fr £5 or alc £15
Dinner td fr £10 or alc £17
Last dinner 12 mdnt
Credit cards [1] [2] [3] [5]
No parking on premises
Closed Sun lunch

ELTHAM

Yardley Court Private Hotel
18 Court Rd, SE9
✆ 01-850 1850

Beautifully maintained accommodation and charming, welcoming proprietors make a stay at this guesthouse well worth travelling the extra distance from central London. The eight bedrooms (including two family rooms) are provided with many thoughtful extras such as hairdriers, alarm clocks, sewing kits and tissues, as well as CTV, and most have private shower rooms (no bathrooms are available). There are duvets on the beds, but conventional bedding can be provided for guests who prefer it. Excellent English breakfasts are served in the dining room, which is in the modern

Price band B
Parking on premises

extension at the back, and there is also a lounge with large, comfortable armchairs and plenty of homely bric-à-brac. Dogs are not accepted, and neither are children under three.

FULHAM

❀ × **L'Hippocampe**
131A Munster Rd, SW6
✆ 01-736 5588

Please see the value-for-money London lunch feature

Lunch td £9.50 & alc
Dinner alc £20
Last dinner 11pm
Credit cards [1] [2] [3]
Parking on premises
Closed 24 Dec–31 Jan
Closed Sat & Sun lunch

HAMPSTEAD

× **Café Flo**
205 Haverstock Hill,
Belsize Park, NW3
✆ 01-435 6744

Simple décor, French posters and helpful, friendly French staff are the accompaniment to authentic French regional cooking here. Choose your menu from fixed-price, à la carte or semanier (a different dish each day of the week). Alternatively, you can opt for the excellent value of 'L'idée Flo' — salad or soup followed by steak with frites and then coffee, offered at £4.95 per person at lunch-times and for evening meals before 8pm or after 10.30pm. Cooking is reliable and skilful, and the best fresh ingredients are used. Of the varied choice of dishes available, our Inspector particularly recommends the terrine maison, made with chicken livers and wild mushrooms, and the confit de canard. Vegetables, served in separate bowls, are specially tasty, and good house salads are offered as an alternative. A wide selection of regional wines complements the food.

Lunch/dinner td fr £4.95 or alc £12
Last dinner 11.45pm
Credit cards [1] [3]
Closed Xmas

GH **Frognal Lodge Hotel**
14 Frognal Gardens, NW3
(Off Church Row)
✆ 01-435 8238
Tx 8812714

This cosy, comfortable little hotel in Hampstead Village is the perfect antidote to the concrete anonymity of many modern hotels. Popular with overseas visitors, Frognal Lodge has a well-established tradition of good old-fashioned hospitality and home comforts. The congenial lounge is furnished with relaxing sofas and easy chairs, as well as thoughtful extras like a writing desk and stationery, and magazines are provided. Several of the 17 bedrooms are large family rooms, and there are some with private bathrooms and CTV. All rooms have telephones and can be reached by lift. Freshly cooked English breakfasts are served by courteous, attentive staff in the small breakfast room. All is well supervised by the manager, Allan McGlashen. Frognal Lodge is within five minutes' walk of Hampstead Underground station, from where Piccadilly Circus can be reached in 20 minutes.

Price band B
Credit cards [1] [2] [3] [5]
No parking on premises

HENDON

Peacehaven Hotel 94 Audley Rd, NW4 ✆ 01-202 9758	Helpful personal service from the friendly owner, Mr Summers, makes this small bed and breakfast hotel worth a mention here, even though comparable accommodation could be found closer to the West End. Bedrooms are brightly decorated and have modern furnishings and CTV; two bedrooms can accommodate families. Only one of the 12 rooms has a private bathroom, but general bathroom facilities are above average. Housekeeping standards are high. There is no lounge, but the small breakfast room, which also serves as the reception, has a sitting area. A good choice of dishes is offered at breakfast. The hotel is quite close to Hendon Central Underground station and a short distance off the A41. Dogs are not accepted.	Price band B Credit cards [1] [3] Limited parking on premises

ISLINGTON

❀× **Anna's Place** 90 Mildmay Park, NI ✆ 01-249 9379	Excellent Swedish and Continental fare is on offer in this small, simply furnished restaurant where potted plants, Victorian lamps and interesting pictures all add to the charm and genuinely warm atmosphere. The cooking is skilful, using very good-quality ingredients. Though there are original dishes on the menu, don't miss a superb gravad lax (salmon marinated with dill), Jansson's fritelse (layers of potato and onion with cream baked in the oven), and oxenllader (beef olives stuffed with Swedish anchovies and bacon flavoured with garlic and allspice). Service is attentive and helpful; the young friendly staff are supervised by Anna herself.	Bar lunch, lunch & dinner alc £16 Last dinner 10.30pm No parking on premises Closed 2 wks Easter, Aug & Xmas Closed Sun & Mon

KENSINGTON

Apollo Hotel 18–22 Lexham Gardens, W8 ✆ 01-373 3236	The Apollo and its sister hotel, the Atlas (see below), are quietly and conveniently located, with gardens nearby, close to the Cromwell Road. Bedrooms at the Apollo are simply furnished but of good size. There are 60 in all, many of which have shower or bathroom en suite, and all with radios and telphones. Breakfast is served in the large, well-appointed basement restaurant.	Price band B/C Credit cards [1] [2] [3] [4] [5] No parking on premises
Atlas Hotel 24-30 Lexham Gardens, W8 ✆ 01-373 7873	Under the same ownership as the neighbouring Apollo Hotel (see above), the Atlas also offers convenient, well-equipped accommodation at modest cost. Most of the 70 airy bedrooms have private bathrooms, and all are comfortable and equipped with radio and telephone. There is a lounge area and a bar on the ground floor, while in the basement is a plesant three-section dining room where full breakfast is served. Service is by friendly staff under the personal supervision of the proprietor.	Price band B/C Credit cards [1] [2] [3] [4] [5] No parking on premises

> À la carte prices are based on an average for three courses without wine.

× **Il Barbino** 38 Kensington Church St, W8 ✆ 01-937 8752	Tiny and crowded, Il Barbino has the warm and informal atmosphere typical of an Italian restaurant. The menus available in its ground and first floor dining rooms offer an extensive à la carte selection which is supplemented by a blackboard display of daily specialities, usually including several temptingly-presented fresh fish dishes. The high standard of cuisine is complemented by a comprehensive wine list to give an enjoyable and value-for-money meal.	Lunch/dinner alc £12 Last dinner 11.45pm Credit cards [1] [2] [3] [4] [5] No parking on premises Closed Bank Hols Closed Sun, & Sat lunch
★★ **Hotel Lexham** 32–8 Lexham Gardens, W8 ✆ 01-373 6471	Reasonably priced accommodation is offered at this traditional family-style hotel in a quiet Kensington square. Most of the 63 bedrooms are of good size; they include a number of large family rooms with facilities for children. Some 30 rooms have private bath or shower, and all have radios and telephones. CTV is available in one of the two lounges. The dining room offers a simple and moderately priced table d'hôte menu. It is not licensed. The hotel does not accept dogs.	Price band B Lunch alc £4.50 Dinner alc £6.50 Last dinner 8pm Credit cards [1] [3] No parking on premises Closed 24 Dec–1 Jan
×× **The Sailing Junk** 59 Marloes Rd, W8 ✆ 01-937 5833	Customers who have hearty appetites, and a liking for a party atmosphere, will enjoy eating at this delightful Chinese restaurant. The fixed-price menu — the 'Dragon Boat Festival Dinner' — is a 10-course feast, and since there is no à la carte menu you have to be hungry to eat here. But the food is beautifully fresh, authentic and well-cooked, and is served with style by Mandarin waitresses. Spices are used skilfully, and sauces are particularly good. A typical meal might consist of meat balls, sesame prawns, steamboat soup, special rice, special noodles, spare ribs, shredded beef, sweet and sour pork, toffee banana and orange sorbet and, finally, tea. Bamboo and candlelight complete the party mood, making a meal to celebrate a special occasion truly an experience to remember.	Dinner td £11.90 Last dinner 11.15pm Credit cards [1] [2] [3] [5] No parking on premises

KNIGHTSBRIDGE

★★★ HL **Basil Street Hotel** Basil St, SW3 ✆ 01-581 3311 Tx 28379	One of only a handful of large London hotels still in private ownership, the Basil Street firmly upholds the old-fashioned virtues of good manners, discretion and friendly service. Traditional afternoon tea and excellent English breakfasts are bastions of the hotel's 78-year tradition. At lunch and dinner, soundly prepared English fare can be chosen from table d'hôte or à la carte menus in the elegant, candlelit dining room. The lounge has some splendid antique furniture, and the 92 bedrooms, many of them newly redecorated, are well-equipped. Most have private bathrooms, and all have CTV and telephones.	Price band D Bar lunch td fr £4.75 Lunch td fr £10.75 or alc £15 Dinner alc £18 Last dinner 9.45pm Credit cards [1] [2] [3] [4] [5] No parking on premises
Claverley Hotel 13–4 Beaufort Gardens ✆ 01-589 8541	This is a very good-value bed and breakfast establishment, conveniently close to Harrods. The Georgian house stands in a quiet, leafy square yet is only a stone's throw from the busy Brompton Road.	Price band C Credit card [3] No parking on premises

Continued on page 153.

L·O·N·D·O·N *lunch*

VALUE FOR MONEY

London Lunch — Value for Money

Eating at London's top restaurants and hotels is not usually a pastime that people associate with 'value for money'. In fact, quite the contrary. When people eat out at restaurants like Le Gavroche or in hotels like the Hilton or the Inn on the Park, not only do they expect to be treated to the ultimate gourmet experience, drink the best wine, enjoy superlative service in sumptuous surroundings, but they also expect to pay a considerable amount of money for the privilege.

Best of Swiss fare at the Chesa Restaurant

That said, our Inspectors have discovered that many of London's top, and up and coming, eating houses, while charging conventional London prices in the evening, often feature exceptional value-for-money set menus as lunch time. This means that a diner expecting to pay around £30 to £40 for a three-course evening meal might only have to pay around £20 for a similar three-course set meal at lunch time in the same restaurant.

Although those living or working in the vicinity of such restaurants tend to know and take advantage of these good lunch time deals, the majority of people remain unaware of the bargains to be found. So our Inspectors have gathered together a list of the London eating houses that in their opinion offer outstanding value-for-money lunches. Read on, we'll try and whet your appetite by telling you just a little about each one of them.

L'Arlequin SW8

This attractive restaurant with its pale green and white décor and pretty pink tablecloths is owned and run by the Delteil family. And not only are the owners of this restaurant and the food they produce French, but so also are all the waiters who serve there. At £14.50 a head the three-course lunch menu, which changes daily, is something of a bargain. Diners can expect a salad, fish dish or some sort of terrine for starter, a delicious meat or fish dish served with a side plate of fresh vegetables for main course and perhaps home-made ice-cream, soft fruit served with a sorbet of the same flavour or a delectable mousse for dessert.

Auberge de Provence SW1

The Auberge de Provence, at the St James Court Hotel, specialises in Provençal cuisine — and accompanying wine. Here in a setting entirely complementary to the cuisine, lunch time diners can savour the very best of Provençal fare for only £15 a head. For starter there might be a choice of fresh vegetable stew or a salad with smoked salmon and poached egg. For main course, perhaps a brill soufflé with a light tomato butter sauce or sliced pork fillet with sage flavoured sauce, and for dessert diners can either make their selection from the wide range of Provençal cheeses or opt for a sweet. Coffee and petits fours, to round off the meal, are also included in the price.

Berkeley Hotel SW1

The elegant and comfortable Buttery and Perroquet Bar, attractively laid out on three levels within the Berkeley Hotel, is a popular meeting place with a cosmopolitan appeal. After having an aperitif in the Perroquet Bar, diners can make their way down to the Buttery for lunch. Here they can help themselves to as much as they want in the way of starters and main course dishes from the buffet — for only £9.50. There are about a dozen dishes, such as avocado and prawns, smoked salmon or egg mayonnaise to choose from for starter, as well as a wide range of hot dishes, which vary from day to day, for main course.

Dukes Hotel SW1

Within the elegant Dukes Hotel lies a cosy and informal restaurant that offers good food, good service and good value for money. The lunch menu, which changes daily, can offer as many as five starters to choose from. For main course diners can opt for the roast; for a fish dish like supreme of salmon with walnuts, grapes and celery; or perhaps breast of duck with fresh blackberry and kirsch sauce. For dessert don't miss the bread and butter pudding made with honey which has become something of a speciality in this restaurant. The three-course lunch costs £17.50 a head, but if diners prefer they need only have two courses, or even just one course, which cost £15.50 and £12.50 respectively.

Le Gavroche, the very best of classical cuisine

Le Gavroche W1

London's famous Le Gavroche Restaurant is believed to be awesomely expensive. But dine there regally at lunch time and the bill for the delectable three-course lunch (wine is extra) will be only £19.50. Here, in a relaxed and gentle atmosphere, diners can sample the very best of classical cuisine adapted to modern times. The luncheon menu has a choice of two starters such as a salad of foie gras, artichoke and guinea fowl or celery with scallop and saffron soup.

For main course there might be a plate of different types of fish (salmon, sea bass, turbot, sole, scallops and lobster) served in a champagne and butter sauce, perhaps rack of lamb roasted with tomatoes and olives or calves livers in breadcrumbs served with a light cream and mustard sauce. There is always a mouth-watering selection of desserts, or, if preferred, diners can make a choice from a cheeseboard that seems to go on forever. Coffee and petits fours are also included in the set luncheon menu price.

London Hilton, best of seasonal British fare.

London Hilton SW1

The British Harvest Restaurant, on the first floor of London's Hilton Hotel, features the very best of seasonal British fare. And extensive research was carried out when this restaurant first opened to find original and unusual British recipes on which the dishes that are served here are based. Each day the chef goes to market to select the best seasonal produce available, returning to the restaurant to write out his menu for the day. The cuisine is simple, using very good ingredients, and the three-course lunch menu, which includes a half bottle of wine, costs £15.50. There is a good and varied choice for each course and diners are also encouraged to drink the English white wine available.

L'Hippocampe SW6

The French chef/patron of this honest and unpretentious restaurant specialises in making excellent fresh fish dishes and delicious sauces and although L'Hippocampe is a little out of the way, because of its good food, and the friendly and attentive service given to each and every customer, it has, nevertheless, become very popular. When the weather is kind, diners can eat out in the restaurant's small courtyard. The lunch time menu is priced at £9.50 a head plus 15 per cent service.

Inn on the Park Hotel W1

Lanes Restaurant, within the Inn on the Park Hotel, is an elegant and yet informal restaurant which has a splendid display of hors d'oeuvres as its centrepiece and focal point. Here there is a choice of three set lunch menus, all of which include unlimited wine, that can only be described as outstanding value for money. The 'Mayfair Choice', which costs £16.75 a head, includes a soup of the day, choice from the hors d'oeuvres table, sweet from the trolley or cheese, and coffee. The 'Park Lane Fayre' menu priced at £19 offers hors d'oeuvres or soup for a starter, a choice of fine hot dishes, such as veal medaillons in a white wine sauce or fillets of beef with caper sauce for main course, as well as sweets from the trolley, or cheese, and coffee. The 'Master's Choice' menu, which at £20 a head is the most expensive option, offers the same starters and desserts as the Mayfair menu, but with even more impressive main dishes.

Les Fauves SW8

A few minutes south of Chelsea Bridge in Queenstown Road, Battersea is a new restaurant called Les Fauves that specialises in fine French food. The understated elegance of the décor and furnishings provide a suitable backcloth for the £9.95 three-course lunch recommended by our Inspectors as excellent value for money. A typical lunch might include a carrot mousse for starter, followed by ballotine de volaille (that's chicken taken off the bone, stuffed, rolled and then cut into slices like a terrine) for the main course, and for dessert le pave trois chocolat (that's a chocolate gateau made from three different types of chocolate), or a choice from this restaurant's outstanding cheeseboard.

Mayfair Intercontinental W1

The Mayfair Hotel has two restaurants that our inspectors feel offer exceptional value-for-money lunch time menus. The gracious and aptly named Château Restaurant, which has a series of alcoves leading off the main room, provides a cosy and intimate ambience in which to enjoy delicious French cuisine served by waiters wearing tails. A three-course lunch here costs £15.50 a head. The Coffee Shop with its waitresses attractively uniformed in pink-striped tunics and little green pinafores has a bustling, up-to-the-minute and informal feel about it. Here diners opting for the luncheon buffet can enjoy a three-course meal, plus a carafe of wine and tea or coffee to follow for only £13.50.

Mijanou SW1

This tastefully decorated small French restaurant, which has smoking and non-smoking levels, has a warm and cheerful ambience that is very appealing. Sonia Blech uses the best of seasonal market produce available, together with her own distinctive style of flavouring, to produce innovative dishes of a consistently high standard. The menu is short but full of variety, and is supplemented by daily specials. Neville Blech, who supervises the service, is only too happy to whet diners' appetites with a full explanation of the ingredients of each dish. The set lunch at Mijanou costs just £10.95 a head.

Portman Intercontinental Hotel W1

With its rich purple and beige décor, heavy curtains, wood panelling and partitions and great bay windows that look out onto Portman Square, Truffles Restaurant at the Portman Intercontinental Hotel, certainly has a period feel about it. On the £16 fixed-price luncheon menu there is usually a choice of hot or cold starters from the buffet table, such as artichoke and chicken salad or sweetbreads with wild mushrooms in puff pastry. For main course there is always a roast of some sort on offer, often meat or fish cooked in pastry or dishes like tournedos served with broccoli mousse. With sweets like passion fruit mousse, eclairs, delicious tarts, fresh fruit salad or bread and butter pudding on the menu, the choice of dessert is an impossible one. Coffee is also included in the price.

RSJ SE1

On London's Southbank is a small and popular French restaurant offering high-quality food at most reasonable prices that, because of its Southbank location, many people might not have heard of. With its beautiful arched windows and sunny yellow and blue Laura Ashley décor, this is a lovely place to enjoy a three-course lunch and coffee for only £12.75 a head (plus 10 per cent service charge).

Here diners have a choice of three starters such as chicken liver terrine, avocado salad or smoked salmon and haddock mousse. This might be followed by cutlets of lamb with two-peppers sauce, stuffed breast of chicken with vegetable mousse or fillet of sole with a shellfish sauce. All dishes are accompanied by fresh vegetables or salad. Pot de chocolat, chestnut parfait ice-cream or cheese (of which there are always at least 20 English and Continental varieties to choose from) are among the desserts that you might find at this restaurant. Coffee and mints are also included in the price.

Swiss Centre W1

Being in the Swiss Centre, its not so surprising that the Chesa Restaurant with its bright, elegant and simple décor, should give diners the feeling that they are eating out in Switzerland. Food is served on Swiss china under silver cloches and the 'Swiss Gourmet Menu' priced at £13.50 is recommended to lunch time diners. Based on Nouvelle Cuisine and featuring the best of Swiss fare it includes starters such as wild mushrooms with a Madeira sauce, followed by slices of breast of duck with Armagnac for main course, and perhaps cold cherry soufflé for dessert. The meal is rounded off with coffee and home-made chocolates.

All the tastefully decorated bedrooms have CTV and telephones, and many also have private facilities. Public rooms include a guests' drawing room — a quiet, comfortable place to read or write — and a spacious reception/foyer area where a good supply of reading matter includes plenty of tourist information. There is also a bright, attractive basement dining room, where substantial breakfasts are served.

× × Maxie's Wine-Bar
143 Knightsbridge, SW1
✆ 01-225 2553

A small but well-chosen menu of Chinese food is offered at this modern wine-bar/restaurant. Meals are served either at the bar counter or in the restaurant area of the tastefully decorated, air-conditioned basement. Food is flavoursome and competently prepared; dishes might include Szechuan shredded pork, crispy chilli sauce beef or barbecued spare ribs, and there is a variety of starters. A reasonably priced and comprehensive wine list is available, and service, by Continental staff, is courteous but unpretentious and friendly.

Bar lunch £2–£5 or alc £6
Lunch td fr £7 or alc £10
Dinner td fr £7 or alc £13
Last dinner 11pm
Credit cards 1 2 3 5
Closed 25–8 Dec

The Stockpot
6 Basil St, SW3
✆ 01-589 6827

This cheap and cheerful restaurant is very popular at lunch-times with tourists, shoppers and local office workers. The menu, changed daily, has something for everyone; there are omelettes, pasta dishes, a good range of salads, and hot specialities such as roast beef with Yorkshire pudding, chicken Madras, or scampi. Few main dishes cost more than £2. To start, there is a short list of popular items like soups, pâté, melon or prawn cocktail, and, to finish, good home-made sweets such as crumble, sponge pudding or banana split, costing well under £1. Service is speedy and efficient. For quick, simple daytime eating at very moderate cost, the Stockpot is ideal.

Lunch alc £3.50
Last meal 5pm
Parking nearby
Closed Sun
Closed dinner

MAIDA VALE

Le Cochonnet
1 Lauderdale Parade, W9
✆ 01-289 0393

Freshly prepared, honest cooking is complemented by a good selection of reasonably priced wines at this lively and popular wine-bar and restaurant. Daily specialities, which usually include a wholesome home-made soup as well as a pasta dish and a fish dish, supplement the short à la carte menu of basic fare including a range of steaks. The premises are fully licensed.

Lunch/dinner alc £10
Last dinner 10.15pm
Credit cards 1 2 3 5
Parking nearby

PADDINGTON

Pembridge Court Hotel
34 Pembridge Gardens, W2
Notting Hill
✆ 01-229 9977

Located in a tree-lined road near Notting Hill Gate Underground station and the Portobello Road antique market, Pembridge Court has well-equipped accommodation and a good restaurant. There are 26 bedrooms (including six family rooms), all with private bathroom or shower, CTV, radio and telephone. Improvements still under way include enlarging some bedrooms and installing a new lift. Good, simple food is served in pleasant surroundings in the licensed basement restaurant.

Price band C
Dinner alc £12
Last dinner 11.30pm
Credit cards 1 2 3 5
Limited parking on premises (charge)
Restaurant closed Bank Hols

ST JOHN'S WOOD

Crockers
24 Aberdeen Place, NW8
✆ 01-286 6608

Also known as Crocker's Folly, this lovely Victorian building is the favourite London pub of one of our Inspectors. The story behind its alternative name is that the pub's original owner meant to build his inn beside the planned Marylebone Station, but miscalculated where the station entrance would be, and ended up with his pub a mile away from the new railway. But 'it's an ill wind . . .', and today customers can enjoy good, hearty bar meals and a range of real ales here in pleasant surroundings. Elaborate Victorian décor includes moulded ceilings, inlaid with bronze relief, and a pillared marble fireplace, as well as opulent fixtures and fittings with mahogany much in evidence. Hot and cold food is served in the central bar. Daily specialities might include home-made soup, beef with noodles, or shepherd's pie, and the treacle tart should not be missed. Children are allowed in the eating area only. The comfortable main lounge has a theatre/music hall, with live entertainment most evenings.

Bar meal alc £4.50
Last dinner 10pm
No parking on premises

SOUTH KENSINGTON

Number Eight
Emperor's Gate, SW7
✆ 01-370 7516

Fourteen comfortable bedrooms are available at this elegant little hotel in a quiet cul de sac a few minutes' walk from the Natural History Museum. Most rooms have bathrooms en suite, and all are fresh, clean and attractive, with coordinated fabrics and décor. Facilities such as CTV, radios, telephones and hairdriers are provided in all rooms, and some have small refrigerators too. The hotel has no lounge, and a buffet-style breakfast is the only meal served. A good range of hot and cold dishes is provided, and the basement dining room is light and attractively furnished. The hotel does not accept dogs.

Price band C
Credit cards [1] [2] [3] [5]
Parking nearby

WATERLOO

× **RSJ** 'The Restaurant on the South Bank'
13A Coin St, SE1
✆ 01-928 4554

Please see the value-for-money London lunch feature

Lunch td £11.25 or alc £20
Dinner td £11.95 or alc £20
Last dinner 11pm
Credit cards [1] [2] [3]
No parking on premises
Closed 25–8 Dec
Closed Sat & Sun

WEST END

Academy Wine Rooms
13–4 Cork St, W1
✆ 01-409 1370

Champagne is a house speciality at this up-market wine-bar close to Savile Row and the Burlington Arcade. Catering very much for business people, the operation here consists of a wine-bar on the ground floor and a grill room, open only at lunch-times, in

Lunch/dinner alc £10
Last dinner 10.30pm
Credit cards [1]

	the basement. A good choice of freshly prepared hot and cold food is available, and is complemented by a well-chosen selection of reasonably priced wines. Décor is in the familiar wine-bar style, with posters on the walls, simple furnishings, and stools at the bar.	2 3 4 5 Parking nearby Closed Sat & Sun Grill room closed dinner
× **Alastair Little** 49 Frith St, W1 ✆ 01-734 5183	Consistently high standards of cooking are maintained by proprietor/chef Alastair Little and his young staff at this small, modern restaurant. The menu, different each day, shows flair and imagination, with influences from France and Japan. Fresh fish is a speciality, and vegetables are carefully chosen and well-prepared. The atmosphere is friendly and informal, and service is pleasant and prompt.	Lunch/dinner alc £18 Last dinner 11pm Credit card 3 No parking on premises Closed last 2 wks Aug & Bank Hols Closed Sat & Sun
×× **Chesa** (Swiss Centre) 10 Wardour St, W1 ✆ 01-734 1291 Tx 8811646	Please see the value-for-money London lunch feature	Lunch/dinner td £13.50 or alc £20.25 Last dinner 12 mdnt Credit cards 1 2 3 4 5 No parking on premises Closed 24-6 Dec
★★★ L **Clifton-Ford Hotel** 47 Welbeck St, W1 ✆ 01-486 6600 Tx 22569	This recently upgraded hotel on the fringes of the West End is popular with business people and tourists alike. Accommodation is generally of a high standard; the bedrooms are of a good size and all have private bathrooms, CTV and telephones. Comfortable and relaxing seating is provided in the spacious, open-plan public areas, where the elegant furnishings and décor are complemented by a baby grand piano. French-style cuisine is offered in the well-appointed restaurant. Food is competently prepared and a well-planned selection of wines is offered at reasonable prices.	Price band D Bar lunch alc £5 Lunch alc £10 Dinner alc £19 Last dinner 10.15pm Credit cards 1 2 3 5 Parking on premises (charge)
❀❀❀×××× **Le Gavroche** 43 Upper Brook St, W1 ✆ 01-408 0881	Please see the value-for-money London lunch feature	Lunch td £19.50–£40 or alc £45 Dinner td £40 or alc £45 Last dinner 11pm Credit cards 1 2 3 4 5 No parking on premises Closed 22 Dec–2 Jan

★★★★★ BL
Inn on the Park
Hamilton Place,
Park Ln, W1
☎ 01-449 0888
Tx 22771

Please see the value-for-money London lunch feature

Lunch td £18.25–£21.50
Dinner td £21.25–£23.75 or alc £24.35
Last dinner 12 mdnt
Credit cards 1 2 3 4 5
Parking for residents only

× **Kerzenstuberl**
9 St Christopher's Place, W1
☎ 01-486 3196

In the Kerzenstuberl you will be able to enjoy the food and wines of Austria while relaxing in an authentically Austrian atmosphere. Cheerful service is offered by staff dressed in national costume, and at some time during the course of the evening the proprietor will burst into song, accompanied by the strains of an accordian, urging customers to 'sing along' with him!

Lunch alc £15.20
Dinner alc £20.25
Last dinner 11pm
Credit cards 1 2 3 5
No parking on premises
Closed Easter, 5 Aug–5 Sep, Xmas & Bank Hols
Closed Sun, & Sat lunch

★★★★★ L
London Hilton
22 Park Ln, W1
☎ 01-493 8000
Tx 24873

Please see the value-for-money London lunch feature

Lunch td £15.50 or alc fr £22
Dinner alc fr £25
Last dinner 1am
Credit cards 1 2 3 4 5
Parking nearby

★★★★★ **Mayfair Inter-Continental**
Stratton St, W1
☎ 01-629 7777
Tx 262526

Please see the value-for-money London lunch feature

Lunch td £13.50–£15.50
Dinner td £23 or alc £25
Last dinner 10.30pm
Credit cards 1 2 3 4 5
No parking on premises
Closed Sat lunch

× **New World**
1 Gerrard Place, W1
☎ 01-734 0677

True Chinese family-style dining in an authentic Chinatown atmosphere can be experienced at this very large restaurant off Shaftesbury Avenue. Its popularity with Chinese customers should be recommendation enough. Flavoursome provincial specialities are the basis of the extensive menu, which is supplemented at lunch-times by a range of enticing snacks served from dim sum trolleys. Vegetarians are well-catered for. Service, in typical Chinese style, is hospitable and courteous.

Lunch td £3
Dinner td £4.80
Last dinner 11.30pm
Credit cards 1 2 3 4 5
No parking on premises
Closed 25 Dec

★★★★ L **Portman Inter-Continental** 22 Portman Sq, W1 ✆ 01-486 5844 Tx 261526	Please see the value-for-money London lunch feature	Lunch td £14.80 or alc £20 Dinner td £17 or alc £25 Last dinner 11pm Credit cards 1 2 3 4 5 No parking on premises

WESTMINSTER

❀××× **Auberge de Provence** (St James Court Hotel) Buckingham Gate, SW1 ✆ 01-821 1899 Tx 938075	Please see the value-for-money London lunch feature	Lunch td £16.75 or alc £26 Dinner alc £30 Last dinner 11pm Credit cards 1 2 3 4 5 No parking on premises Closed Sat & Sun
★★★★★ RED **Berkeley Hotel** Wilton Place, SWI ✆ 01-235 6000 Tx 919252	Please see the value-for-money London lunch feature	Lunch (Buttery) td £15 or alc £30 Dinner alc £35 Last dinner 10.45pm Credit cards 1 2 3 5 Parking for residents (charged)
❀★★★★ HB **Duke's** St James Pl, SW1 ✆ 01-491 4840 Tx 28283	Please see the value-for-money London lunch feature	Lunch/dinner td £19 or alc £30 Last dinner 10pm Credit cards 1 2 3 4 5 No parking on premises
★ RED **Ebury Court Hotel** 26 Ebury St, SW1 ✆ 01-730 8147	Traditional hospitality is the secret of success at this delightful hotel, which has been caringly run by the Tophams for some 50 years. Conveniently situated between the rail and coach stations at Victoria, it is reasonably priced for its location and offers many homely touches. Open fires cheer the sitting rooms in winter, and guests may obtain temporary membership of the club bar. Meals are served in an inviting basement restaurant. Wholesome dishes are prepared using fresh produce, and bread is home-made. Staff are helpful and courteous under the supervision of Mr and Mrs Topham, who go out of their way to make their guests comfortable. Bedrooms vary in size, but are all nicely decorated and equipped with radios. Some of the 39 rooms have private bathrooms, and all	Price band C Lunch alc £11.50 Dinner alc £13 Last dinner 9pm Credit cards 1 3 No parking on premises

front rooms are double glazed. The hotel has a unique and pleasant atmosphere, and continues to please our members, as it has for many years.

×× **Gavvers** 61 Lower Sloane St, SW1 ✆ 01-730 5983 Tx 8813079	This busy restaurant is owned by distinguished restaurateurs the Roux Brothers, best known for their top-class eating places Le Gavroche and the Waterside Inn at Bray. Gavvers offers a value-for-money three-course set menu of most enjoyable fare. The choice is simple: soup or hors d'oeuvres is followed by either fish or an entrée with vegetables, and then dessert or cheese, and coffee. The price includes an aperitif and half a bottle of wine. Service is by charming young French staff, and surroundings are comfortable and pleasant.	Dinner td £19.75 Last dinner 11pm Credit cards [1] [2] [3] [5] No parking on premises Closed lunch & Sun
★★★★ RED **Goring Hotel** Beeston Place, Grosvenor Gardens, SW1 ✆ 01-834 8211 Tx 919166	Owned and run by Mr George Goring, whose family have been proprietors here since the hotel opened in 1910, the Goring maintains a fine tradition of courteous, smiling service and beautifully maintained accommodation. Fresh flowers, open fires in cold weather, and a supply of reading material help to create a homely atmosphere in the main lounge and cocktail bar, which overlook the delightful little garden. The 90 bedrooms vary in size but are elegantly furnished, spotlessly clean and well-equipped. CTV, telephones and private bathrooms are standard in all rooms, and those facing the street are double glazed. Room service is as prompt and pleasant as the service in the dining room, where good à la carte and table d'hôte menus are offered. Cooking is sound and mostly traditional, with the emphasis on fresh raw materials. Vegetarian meals can be provided. The Goring does not accept dogs.	Price band D Bar lunch alc £8 Lunch td fr £13 or alc £25 Dinner td £17.50 or alc £25 Last dinner 10pm Credit cards [1] [2] [3] [5] Limited parking on premises (charge)
❀ ×× **Mijanou** 143 Ebury St, SW1 ✆ 01-730 4099	Please see the value-for-money London lunch feature	Lunch td £11.50 or alc £23.50 Dinner td £19.50–£29.50 or alc £23.50 Last dinner 11pm Credit cards [1] [2] [5] No parking on premises Closed 1 wk Easter, 3 wks Aug, 2 wks Xmas Closed Sat & Sun

WOODFORD

Grovehill Hotel 38 Grovehill, South Woodford, E18 ✆ 01-989 3344	Although some distance from central London, this quietly situated, popular commercial hotel is reasonably close to South Woodford Underground station and is directly off the A11. Only five of the 21 compact bedrooms have private facilities, but all are	Price band B Credit cards [1] [2] [3] Limited parking on premises

well-equipped, and standards of housekeeping are impressive. There are two family rooms, and all the bedrooms have CTV, radio and tea/coffee-making equipment and are double glazed. There is no lounge (though a bar is sometimes available) but the hotel has a pleasant 'home-from-home' atmosphere, cultivated by friendly proprietor Mr Mamelok. Full English breakfast is served, freshly cooked and chosen from a reasonable selection of dishes. Service is generally restricted at weekends.

LONGFRAMLINGTON Northumberland Map 12 NU10

×× **Anglers Arms**
Weldon Bridge
(¼ mile off A697, signed, just N of Longframlington)
✆ (066570) 655

Set on the River Coquet, in the heart of undulating countryside, this is a traditional Northumbrian inn. Whether you are looking for a bar meal, a substantial repast or a comfortable bedroom, the Anglers Arms can oblige. The quaint bar — spacious, comfortable and very popular — provides an extensive menu of appetising dishes, and the small dining room (which extends into an impressively converted Pullman carriage) offers an à la carte selection of soups, seafood, poultry and grills, together with flambé dishes and other specialities in English, French and Portuguese style. At lunch-time, a good table d'hôte menu is offered.

Bar lunches td £3
Lunch td £7.50
Dinner td £8.50 or alc £10.50
Last dinner 9.30pm
Credit cards 1 2 3 4
Parking on premises

INN **Granby**
(On A697 N of Morpeth)
✆ (066570) 228

This 200-year-old inn, formerly a coaching stop, offers every modern comfort while still retaining its traditional atmosphere and charm. The whole Hall family play their part in the running of the inn, aided by charming local staff, and this combination results in friendly and helpful service. Accommodation, whether in the main building or a garden chalet, is cosy and comfortable, and the meals provided in both bar and dining room represent excellent value for money. From here, the holidaymaker is within easy reach of the coast, the Cheviot Hills, Holy Island and the Farne Islands, Alnwick and Roman Wall.

Price band B
Bar lunch td £2.85–£12.50
Dinner td £10.75 or alc £12.50
Last dinner 9pm
Credit cards 1 2 3
Parking on premises
Closed 25 Dec

LONGRIDGE Lancashire Map 7 SD63

FH **Falicon**
Fleet Street Ln
(Just off B6245 between Ribchester and Longridge)
✆ Ribchester (025484) 583

This charming 200-year-old farm — a 13-acre smallholding raising sheep and beef cattle — stands at the end of a lane in a delightful rural setting. Fully centrally heated, it is warm and welcoming, providing hospitality along good old-fashioned lines. Bedrooms are comfortable, furnished to a high standard, and have en suite facilites. The good, home-cooked meals served in the dining room provide very good value for money. Smoking is not permitted in rooms, and children under ten are not accepted.

Price band B
Dinner, b&b £32.50
Last dinner 7pm
Parking on premises

> The price band indicates the price of bed and breakfast for a single person or room. Price band A = £15 or less; price band B = £16–£30; price band C = £31–£50; price band D = more than £50.

LONGSDON Staffordshire Map 7 SJ95

FH **Bank End**
Old Leek Rd
(2 miles SW of Leek on A53)
☏ Leek (0538) 383638

This 15th-century, 62-acre beef farm provides a standard of accommodation and recreational facilities not normally found in its category. Nine spacious, modern and comfortable bedrooms, each with CTV and most with en suite bathroom or shower, are split between the farmhouse and a converted sandstone outbuilding. Outdoor activities include swimming in the heated pool, riding and private fishing, while the house contains a games room as well as the comfortable lounge and licensed bar. Animals, including ducks, calves and dogs, are much in evidence, creating an authentic farmyard atmosphere, and children are welcome to wander among them at will.

Price band A
Dinner, b&b £17–£21
Last dinner 9pm
Parking on premises
Closed Xmas

LOOE Cornwall Map 2 SX25

★★ **Commonwood Manor**
St Martin's Rd, East Looe
☏ (05036) 2929

There are wonderful views from almost every window of this imposing, white-painted house set high above the East Looe River. The hotel stands in three acres of grounds surrounded by rolling Cornish countryside, yet it is only a 10-minute walk from the popular fishing village of Looe. The hotel has been furnished with imagination and taste, from the stylish dining room, with its polished wooden floor, to the comfortable, sunny lounge. There is also a bar and a video room, as well as a sun terrace with a swimming pool. Each of the 11 bedrooms has en suite facilities and CTV, and all are prettily decorated and furnished. Two rooms are suitable for families: children of all ages are welcome, and children's meals are available. The restaurant offers good-value à la carte menus at lunch and dinner, and service is friendly and efficient.

Price band B
Bar lunch alc £5
Dinner alc £7
Last dinner 8.30pm
Credit cards [1] [2] [3]
Parking on premises

LUDDENDEN FOOT West Yorkshire Map 7 SE02

FH **Crib Farm**
(Best approached from Sowerby Br and Sowerby New Road)
☏ Halifax (0422) 883285

This sturdy, Pennine-stone building (listed as a public house in 1625) stands on the side of Blackwood Common with spectacular views over the River Calder in the valley below. Modern bedrooms with up-to-date facilities have been provided, but the mullion-windowed house retains the charm of its period externally, and original fittings have been preserved in the attractive lounge and dining room. The proprietress extends a warm welcome to every guest and personally oversees the preparation of good, traditional, English meals. With children in mind, tours of the farm are available at milking and feeding times.

Price band A
Dinner, b&b £14.50–£15.50
Parking on premises
Closed Nov-Feb

LUDLOW Shropshire Map 7 SO57

★★ **Angel Hotel**
Broad St
☏ (0584) 2581

Lord Nelson visited the Angel Hotel in 1802, and today a succession of visitors make this former posting house a base from which to explore the historic town and its lovely surroundings. It is by no means luxurious, but all 17 comfortable, recently refurbished bedrooms are well-equipped and have en suite facilities. The well-cooked meals are simple but

Price band C
Bar lunch £1.50–£3.50
Lunch td £6.50 or alc £10
Dinner td £9.50 or alc £12

wholesome, and service is informally friendly. In short, this is a comfortable, no-nonsense hotel which offers good value for money.

Last dinner 9pm
Credit cards [1] [2] [3] [5]
Parking on premises

LYME REGIS Dorset Map 3 SY39

★★★ H **Alexandra Hotel**
Pound St
✆ (02974) 2010

This charming, friendly hotel stands in peaceful gardens with views across Lyme Bay, yet is within easy walking distance of the beach and the famous Cobb as well as the shops. The 18th-century building has been carefully restored and fitted with modern facilities while retaining the relaxed atmosphere of its former days as a prestigious private residence. Standards of hospitality and service are high, proprietors Mr and Mrs Haskins and their friendly staff being always very helpful. Food is traditionally English, and our Inspector particularly enjoyed afternoon tea, served in the drawing room or sun lounge or in the garden. The 24 bedrooms include six family rooms, and the hotel welcomes children of all ages. Most rooms have private bathrooms and all have CTV. Spring and autumn bargain breaks are available.

Price band B
Bar lunch £1.25–£1.75
Lunch td fr £6.25 or alc £13.50
Dinner td £10.50 or alc £13.50
Last dinner 8.30pm
Credit cards [1] [2] [3] [5]
Parking on premises
Closed 18 Dec–3 Feb

★★ **Royal Lion Hotel**
Broad St
✆ (02974) 5622

Our Inspector particularly recommends this 16th-century coaching inn, in Lyme's main street, for its wide variety of food. Meals are available both in the convivial, beamed bar and in the Dog House Grill, which is open throughout the year for coffee, lunches, teas and evening meals. The standard menu (mostly grills and salads) is supplemented by a daily blackboard, and there is a good cold display of fresh cooked meats, quiches, etc. A sound wine list (including wine by the glass) and friendly service make this a worthwhile port of call. The hotel also has 25 bedrooms (including some smart new ones), all with private facilities and CTV.

Price band B
Bar lunch £2.50
Lunch alc £3.50
Dinner td £9 or alc fr £10
Last dinner 10pm
Credit cards [1] [2] [3] [5]
Parking on premises

LYMINGTON Hampshire Map 4 SZ39

★★★ 👥 BL
Passford House
Mount Pleasant
(2m N of Lymington on Sway rd)
✆ (0590) 682398
Tx 47502

This comfortable country house hotel stands in nine acres of lovely gardens on the edge of the New Forest. Beautifully appointed public rooms include three lounges and a cocktail bar. Furnishings are tasteful and elegant, and include some antiques. Books and card games, log fires and fresh flowers all contribute to a homely effect. The well-designed restaurant offers a high standard of professional cuisine, with a good choice of dishes and an impressive central display of hors d'oeuvres. The menu is complemented by an extensive and varied list. The hotel has excellent leisure facilities including two swimming pools, a hard tennis court, a croquet lawn and putting green, a sauna and spa, and a children's play area. The 56 bedrooms, including four family rooms and a suite, are equipped and maintained to a high standard. All have private bathrooms, CTV, radio and telephone.

Price band C
Lunch td £8 or alc £10.50
Dinner td £14 or alc £18
Last dinner 9pm
Credit cards [1] [2] [3]
Parking on premises

LYMM Cheshire Map 7 SJ68

Bollin
Mill Lane, Heatley
(1½ miles NW on A6144)
✆ (092575) 3657

When it was opened in 1976, this popular, unpretentious little restaurant was charging £2.30 for a T-bone steak and £2.40 for duckling á l'orange! Unfortunately, times change, but it continues to offer very good value, serving a £6.50 set lunch which includes such items as home-made soups, haggis, black pudding, steak pies and various fish dishes — almost every taste is catered for, helpings are generous and service is friendly. An à la carte menu is also available, as are bar snacks, and wines are reasonably priced, with house wines from £4.75. The restaurant is equally suitable for a business lunch or a family occasion.

Lunch td £6.50
Dinner td £9.50 or alc fr £12
Last meal 10pm
Credit cards [1] [2] [3] [5]
Parking on premises
Closed Bank Hols
Closed Sat lunch

LYTHAM ST ANNES Lancashire Map 7 SD32

★★ H **Chadwick**
South Promenade
✆ (0253) 720061

This modern, well-furnished seafront hotel has been in the hands of the same family for many years, and every season sees further improvements added to the already good facilities. It boasts a heated indoor swimming pool which is treated with ozone, spa bath, Turkish bath and solarium. Playrooms and a games room are provided, and there are extensive lounges and bar areas. Bedrooms are comfortable, with lots of extras, while the newly-furnished restaurant serves good honest meals. It is very much a family hotel, offering excellent value for money, and there are also good facilities for the disabled.

Price band A/B
Bar lunches £2.20–£2.60
Lunch td fr £4.50
Dinner td fr £7.80
Last dinner 8.15pm
Credit cards [1] [2] [3] [5]
Parking on premises

MACCLESFIELD Cheshire Map 7 SJ97

★★ **Crofton Hotel**
22 Crompton Rd
✆ (0625) 34113

Situated in a residential area close to the town centre, this newly-furnished and renovated small hotel operates under the personal management of the resident proprietors. The bedrooms are well-designed, with quality furnishings throughout, and have CTV and en suite facilites. There is a comfortable residents' lounge and a small but well-stocked bar. The attractive dining room serves good, honest food, and here, as elsewhere in the hotel, nothing is too much trouble for the others.

Price band B
Lunch td fr £6.50 or alc £7.50
Dinner td fr £10 or alc £12.50
Last dinner 11pm
Credit cards [1] [3]
Parking nearby

MACHRIHANISH Strathclyde *Argyllshire* Map 10 NR62

GH **Ardell House**
✆ (058681) 235

Winner of the AA's Scottish Guest House of the Year Award for 1986/7, Ardell House is a roomy Victorian residence whose bow windows offer a pleasant outlook across the golf course to the Isles of Islay and Jura. Most of the spotlessly clean bedrooms (three of which are contained in a tastefully converted stable block) are in traditional style and all have been thoughtfully equipped with CTV and tea-making facilities. The comfortable first floor lounge provides a courtesy bar, and the atmosphere throughout the hotel is warm and informal. A stay here is a memorable experience — and much of its special quality is directly attributable to the unstinting efforts of the owners.

Price band A/B
Dinner, b&b £23–£30
Last dinner 7pm
Parking on premises
Restricted accommodation Nov–Jan
Closed Xmas & New Year

MALVERN Hereford & Worcester Map 3 SO74

★★★ Colwall Park Hotel
Colwall
(3m SW of Malvern on B4218)
✆ (0684) 40206
Tx 335626

Built at the turn of the century at the foot of the Malvern Hills, the Colwall Park has been sympathetically modernised by its owners Mr and Mrs Frost. The 20 bedrooms vary considerably in size, but are all fitted out to modern standards, with private facilities, CTV and telephones. Two rooms are suitable for families. A tempting three-course table d'hôte menu is offered in the restaurant. A wide choice of first courses includes imaginative items like Stilton croquettes with tomato and paprika sauce, crab mousseline with sorrel sauce, and avocado terrine set in tomato coulis. There are vegetarian dishes among the main courses, which also include traditional fare like steak and oyster pie, game casserole or roast lamb, as well as more innovative specialities like baked chicken and lime.

Price band C
Bar lunch td £2.50–£6.50
Lunch td £7.75
Dinner td fr £11.75
Last dinner 9.30pm
Credit cards [1] [2] [3]
Parking on premises

★★ ♣♣ Holdfast Cottage
Welland
(4 miles SE of Malvern on A4104)
✆ Hanley Swan (0684) 310288

Polished antique furniture, pretty décor and pot plants bring out the homely, cottage-style atmosphere of this nine-bedroom hotel at the foot of the Malvern Hills. Standing in two acres of lovely gardens, with lawns, shrubberies and a wildlife haven, the house originates from the 17th century but was enlarged in Victorian times. Most of the bedrooms now have private facilities, and all are equipped with CTV and electric blankets. Downstairs, the lounge and bar open onto a wisteria-hung terrace, as does the charming dining room. Here the day begins with a choice of breakfast styles: wholefood, or traditional English. Light snack lunches can be provided on request, and for dinner there is a four-course set menu, changed daily, as well as an à la carte selection. Locally reared meats usually feature, sometimes in inventive dishes like sautéed avocado and lamb's kidney with Cumberland sauce, and there is a vegetarian alternative such as lenten leek and cheese dumpling casserole. Children's meals are also available.

Price band B
Dinner td £9.75 or alc £12.50
Last dinner 8.45pm
Parking on premises

GH Old Parsonage Farm
Hanley Castle
✆ Hanley Swan (0684) 310124

Mr and Mrs Addison's elegant 18th-century house stands in 1½ acres of grounds against a backdrop of the Malvern Hills. Here guests can enjoy a homely, relaxed atmosphere and good food. Two of the three bedrooms have en suite facilities, and downstairs there are two lounge areas, well-supplied with books, and a cosy dining room whose inglenook fireplace still has its original bread oven. Mrs Addison is a competent and creative cook, and her food — frequently local produce — is enhanced by interesting use of herbs and by some unusual sauces. Mr Addison is in the wine trade, so the wine list is above average, and offers a good selection of interesting items. A small conference room is available above the old cider mill.

Price band B
Dinner td £10.50
Last dinner as required
Parking on premises
Closed last 3 wks Dec

À la carte prices are based on an average for three courses without wine.

MANCHESTER Greater Manchester Map 7 SJ89

× **Armenian Taverna** 3–5 Princess St ✆ (061) 834 9025	This basement city-centre Armenian restaurant is set amid the Gothic splendours of Albert Square and provides authentic Middle Eastern cuisine in surroundings characteristic of that area. Such dishes as hummus, judi kebab, shish kebab and cous cous from North Africa are expertly cooked and attractively presented, and one is tempted by desserts like patleva, which consists of layers of puff pastry with cinnamon, walnuts, syrup and rose water. Service is friendly and helpful, and there is a well-balanced wine list.	Dinner alc £8 Last dinner 11.30pm Credit cards [1] [2] [3] [5] Parking nearby Closed 25 Dec & 1 Jan Closed lunch
×× **Assam Gourmet** 17A Bloom St ✆ 061-236 6836	Tucked away behind the bus station, this very comfortable and relaxed basement restaurant is the first in Manchester to provide Assami-style cuisine. The inexpensive businessman's lunch is popular, but the real attraction lies in such delicious authentic dishes are hurrakka gosht kabab (grilled venison with lemon sauce), muchlee sarsoon (trout or lemon sole with mustard and spring onion sauce), or even lobster sarsoon when available. Friendly service is provided by attentive staff, and private parties or banquets can be arranged.	Lunch td £2.95 or alc £10.50 Dinner td £7.50 or alc £10.50 Last dinner 11pm Credit cards [1] [2] [5] No parking on premises Closed 25–6 Dec, 1 Jan & Good Friday Closed Sun lunch
×× **Casa España** ✆ 061-224 6826	Two styles of dining are offered by this typical Spanish restaurant — the less expensive Pizza and Pasta House is upstairs, the popular restaurant downstairs. Décor is characteristically Iberian, featuring rough-cast walls hung with tiles and plates, archways and pine furniture. In the evenings a wide range of Spanish dishes is offered, including a particularly good paella, but lunch is restricted to a good-value table d'hôte menu. The wine list is adequate, with jugs of fruity Sangria available, and service is friendly and attentive.	Lunch td £3.95 or alc £9.50 Dinner alc £9.50 Last dinner 10.30pm Credit cards [1] [2] [3] [5] Parking nearby
× **Kosmos Taverna** 248 Wilmslow Rd, Fallowfield ✆ 061-225 9106	Authentic Greek cuisine is served in this boisterous and happy little restaurant close to the city centre, and it must rate as one of the best of its kind outside London. Decorated in typical taverna style, with helpful, cheery service and food that is well above average, it offers excellent value for money. The special Meze, with its seemingly never-ending succession of items, is particularly recommended, and there is a good wine list. Vegetarian dishes available.	Dinner td £7.50 or alc fr £10 Last dinner 11.30pm Credit cards [1] [3]

The price band indicates the price of bed and breakfast for a single person or room. Price band A = £15 or less; price band B = £16–£30; price band C = £31–£50; price band D = more than £50.

×× **Rajdoot** St James House, South King's St ☎ 061-834 2176	Authentic Indian cuisine is served in a traditional atmosphere at this spacious restaurant in the heart of the city centre. Attentive and friendly service is provided by eager staff, and delicate, pungent spices are used in the preparation of such dishes as rogan josh, chicken moghlai and prawn masalla. Freshly baked nan is available, and there is also a good range of Indian sweets. The set-price menu is particularly recommended.	Lunch td fr £5.50 or alc £6 Dinner td fr £9.50 or alc £9.50 Last dinner 11.30pm Credit cards [1] [2] [3] [5] No parking on premises Closed Sun lunch
× **39 Steps** 39 South King St ☎ 061-834 9155	A colour scheme of bright reds, blues and yellows gives a fresh, modern image to this popular, bustling restaurant set in a city centre basement. Cuisine is noteworthy, and the attractively presented French and Italian food is served by a friendly and courteous young staff. Among the dishes available are mignons of pork maxine (pork fillets with spinach and cream cheese) and rendez-vous de fruits de mer (mixed fresh fish in herb sauce), while the blackboard menu often features fresh oysters.	Lunch td £1.95–£15 & alc Dinner td £3.95–£15 & alc Last dinner 11pm Credit cards [1] [3] No parking on premises Closed Sun, & Mon dinner
×× **Truffles** 63 Bridge St ☎ 061-832 9393	An attractive restaurant in the centre of Manchester, Truffles is decorated and furnished in Victorian style and offers an extensive French menu. The dining room is decorated in pink, with Victorian prints on the walls, and you can enjoy drinks before your meal in an upstairs lounge in drawing room style. High quality fresh ingredients are used in the preparation of high standard dishes, and there is a good wine list available. Service is friendly yet professional. Vegetarian meals available.	Lunch td £7.50 Dinner alc £19.50 Last dinner 10.30pm Credit cards [1] [2] [3] [5] No parking on premises Closed 1 wk Jan, 2 wks Aug & Bank Hols Closed Sun & Mon, & Sat lunch
Wiltons Brasserie 406 Wilmslow Rd, Withington ☎ 061-445 5889	Wiltons, the first brasserie to open in South Manchester, is proving very popular, providing reasonably priced meals in very pleasant surroundings with bright décor and fresh flowers on the tables. Drinks are served with crudités in the small bar, and your meal is chosen from a short à la carte menu which changes regularly, plus daily specials. Some interesting dishes are offered — avocados and prawn remoulade, for example, hot winter salad or chicken Martinique (supreme of chicken with coconut and orange butter). Tempting sweets include Tennessee cheesecake and chocolate and hazelnut torte, and a short, sensibly priced wine list is available, together with a good selection of bottled beers.	Dinner alc fr £9 Last dinner 10.30pm Credit cards [1] [3] Parking on premises Closed lunch

×× **Yang Sing** 34 Princess St ✆ 061-236 2200	The Yang Sing is one of the best-known Chinese restaurants in the city, renowned for its exceptionally high standard of cuisine. It has now moved from its original small basement to much larger premises, where it continues to offer a wide and delicious range of meals. Soups include the traditionally exotic shark's fin and bird's nest, seafood dishes are numerous, and duck, chicken and pork appear in a variety of guises. A meal at this restaurant is a memorable experience from the first moment that you enter its bustling atmosphere through a doorway copied from that of a Chinese temple.	Lunch/dinner td £9.50 Last dinner 11pm Credit cards [1] [2] No parking on premises Closed 25 Dec

MARKET RASEN Lincolnshire Map 8 TF18

★★★ H **The Limes** Gainsborough Rd ✆ (0673) 842357	Our Inspector has chosen this former country house, well-equipped but not luxurious, primarily because of the consistently high standards of hospitality and service he has found here over recent years. The staff are professional and courteous but genuinely friendly. Food, too, is well-above average: imaginative French and English dishes are offered from a short á la carte menu, and vegetarian meals are available. Leisure amenities include squash courts, and the hotel has 3½ acres of grounds. The 17 bedrooms, including four family rooms, all have private facilities, CTV, radios, telephones and trouser-presses. Standards of maintenance throughout the hotel are high, and most guests' needs are anticipated — though anything lacking will be promptly and willingly supplied on request.	Price band C Bar lunch td £1.20–£2.50 Lunch td fr £2.95 or alc £6.50 Dinner td fr £4.50 or alc £8.50 Last dinner 9.30pm Credit cards [1] [3] [5] Parking on premises

MARPLE Greater Manchester *Cheshire* Map 7 SJ98

★ B **Springfield Hotel** Station Rd ✆ 061-449 0721	In 1985 this well-furnished small hotel was completely refurbished to a high standard in Victorian country house-style. The resident owners ensure that your stay here is a delightful experience, akin to being a guest in a private house. The well-equipped bedrooms, with their coordinated soft furnishings and mahogany furniture, all have CTV, there is a comfortable small lounge, and interesting, well-prepared food is served in an attractive dining room. The hotel is conveniently close to Manchester and the famous Marple Canal Locks.	Price band B Dinner td £10 Last dinner 7.45pm Credit cards [1] [2] [3] Parking on premises

MARTON Warwickshire Map 4 SP46

FH **Marton Fields** ✆ (0926) 632410	This large Victorian farmhouse, set amid rolling Warwickshire countryside within easy reach of Leamington Spa and Rugby, offers accommodation in cosy, well-equipped bedrooms with many homely touches. The proprietor, Mrs Dronfield, has furnished the whole house in a stylish, elegant manner, and many of the pictures hanging on the walls are her own, for she is an accomplished amateur artist who enjoys arranging painting holidays at the farm for fellow enthusiasts. She also mills home-grown wheat and bakes bread which is a fitting accompaniment to	Price band A Dinner, b&b £17–£19 Last dinner 8pm Parking on premises Closed Xmas

the fresh local eggs served at breakfast. At dinner-time the long, polished table is transformed by silver candelabra into an elegant setting for a more sophisticated range of dishes, but the emphasis is still on wholesome home cooking. A comfortable, friendly atmosphere prevails, and guests can relax in their own way, whether this takes them to the lounge or the croquet lawn.

MARYPORT Cumbria Map 11 NY03

×× **Retreat**
Birkby
✆ (0900) 814056

A large detached house has been completely redecorated and refurbished with charm and elegance to create this delightful restaurant. Pre-dinner drinks are served in a spacious, comfortable bar, the dining room is particularly tastefully appointed, and you can linger over coffee in a sumptuous lounge. The proprietor is German, so the interesting à la carte menu contains a good selection of German specialities among its international range of dishes. The choice is extensive: Scottish wild game pâté, vegetable soup with herbs, cream and smoked bacon, and beef fillets with paprika sauce and pimentos are just a few of the tempting alternatives. The four-course table d'hôte menu is equally wide-ranging and offers good value for money.

Bar lunch alc £4.50–£5.50
Sunday lunch td £7
Dinner td £11 or alc £8.80
Last dinner 9pm
Credit cards [1] [3]
Parking on premises

MAWNAN SMITH Cornwall Map 2 SW72

★★★ **Budock Vean Golf and Country House Hotel**
✆ Falmouth (0326) 250288
Tx 45266

Luxurious accommodation, a private nine-hole golf course, and excellent indoor swimming pool and a tranquil setting by the Helford River make this professionally run hotel something out of the ordinary. Grounds extending to 65 acres include lush, sub-tropical gardens, private river foreshore and all-weather tennis courts. Much of the hotel's stylish interior has recently been redesigned for added comfort, and further improvements to bedrooms are planned. CTV, radio, telephones and private bathrooms are standard in all of the 53 bedrooms, one of which is suitable for family occupation. Some have adjoining sitting rooms. There are several cosy public lounges and a well-stocked residents' cocktail bar. Both table d'hôte and extensive à la carte menus are offered in the spacious restaurant, where local seafood is among the specialities.

Price band C
Bar lunch td £1.30–£3.40
Lunch td fr £6.50
Dinner td £13.65
Last dinner 9.30pm
Credit cards [1] [2] [3] [5]
Parking on premises
Closed Jan–Feb

★★★ HL
Meudon Hotel
✆ Falmouth (0326) 250541
Tx 45478

Beautiful gardens containing many rare flowering shrubs and sub-tropical plants surround this luxury hotel, which has been carefully developed by present owners the Pilgrims from a turn of the century mansion. Meudon combines present day comforts with the relaxing atmosphere and courteous service more often associated with country houses of yesteryear. The well-appointed restaurant serves English food at its best, with local produce such as fresh lobsters, oysters and crabs a speciality. Many

Price band C
Tray lunch td £5–£12 or alc £15
Lunch td £12 or alc £15
Dinner td £16
Last dinner 8.45pm
Credit cards [1]

vegetables come from the hotel garden. Meals are served in an attractive, glazed terrace restaurant with fine views of the gardens. There are 30 bedrooms, all with en suite facilities, telephones, radio and CTV. Facilities such as trouser-presses, irons, kettles and hairdriers will be provided on request, and full room service is available. Public rooms include three elegant lounges and a cocktail bar.

[3] [5]
Parking on premises
Closed 1 Jan–16 Feb

MAYPOOL Devon Map 3 SX85

★★★ Lost and Found Inn
Ⓡ Torquay (0803) 842442

A peaceful setting high above the River Dart, and splendid views down across the valley, are features of this extensively renovated small hotel, which is reached along quiet Devon lanes. The 16 bedrooms, all with facilities en suite, CTV and telephones, combine modern standards with charm and character, and are spotlessly clean. Public rooms, including a large lounge-bar and well-appointed dining room, are complemented by a pleasant sun terrace which gives lovely views over the gardens. Personally owned and managed by the Giblett family, the Lost and Found offers imaginative, freshly prepared food, all cooked to order, and served in an informal, hospitable atmosphere. The hotel welcomes dogs, but children under 12 are not accepted.

Price band C
Bar lunch td £3–£10
Lunch/dinner td £13.25
Last dinner 10pm
Credit cards [1] [2] [3] [4] [5]
Parking on premises

MELMERBY Cumbria Map 12 NY63

Village Bakery
Ⓡ Penrith (0768) 81515

A 200-year-old barn has been converted into a bakery and a simple but charming restaurant with an interesting menu featuring mainly wholefood dishes. These are of a very high standard, prepared from quality ingredients such as stone-ground wholemeal flour milled from organically grown wheat, free range eggs and naturally grown fruit and vegetables, much of the produce coming from the proprietors' own smallholding. Breakfast, coffee, lunch and tea are served, and everything is very reasonably priced. They also offer an interesting selection of teas, a short wine list and the local draught bitter.

Lunch alc fr £5
Last meal 5pm
Parking on premises and nearby
Closed 25 Dec–wk before Easter
Closed Mon

MELROSE *Borders* Roxburghshire Map 12 NT53

Marmion's Brasserie
Buccleuch St
Ⓡ (089682) 2245

Named after one of the heroes of Sir Walter Scott, who lived just two miles away, Marmion's Brasserie maintains the French connection, its authentic atmosphere enhanced by pictures and prints, original wood panelling, tables with wrought-iron bases and waitresses in crisp, white aprons. At any time of day or evening, one can relax over a cup of coffee or a glass of wine while reading the papers and periodicals provided — or perhaps playing a game of Trivial Pursuit! A selection of pâtisserie is available, while lunch and evening meal menus offer such dishes as smoked trout pâté, Stilton pie and monkfish tails in garlic butter.

Last meal 6.30pm Sun, 10.30pm Mon–Sat
Parking nearby
Closed Sun Oct–Mar
Closed Sun dinner

MELTON CONSTABLE Norfolk Map 9 TG03

FH **Rookery Farm**
Thurning
(Off B1235 at Briston)
✆ (0263) 860357

The visitors' book at this 17th-century farmhouse is a good testimony to the warm welcome, relaxed atmosphere and comfortable accommodation to be found here. The house enjoys a wonderfully peaceful location down a quiet country lane — and, our Inspector notes, can be difficult to find, so pay particular attention to the directions given when you book. Guests are welcome to look round the 425-acre arable farm, though children must be accompanied. Accommodation, comprising a family room (with shower en suite) and a single room, is comfortable, clean and well-maintained. A guests' bathroom is nearby. On the ground floor is the guests' lounge, a comfortable and homely room which has a television and a log fire in winter. Breakfast and dinner are served, on an attractive polished wood table, overlooking the gardens. Dogs are not accepted.

Price band A
Dinner, b&b £12.50
Last dinner as required
Parking on premises
Closed Oct-Apr

MERE BROW Lancashire Map 7 SD41

× **Crab and Lobster**
(At rear of Legh Arms in centre of village)
✆ Preston (0772) 812734

Predictably, this delightful and popular little restaurant specialises in fresh fish, but other dishes are featured on the à la carte menu, and the sweet trolley is particularly tempting. Warm, comfortable and well-furnished, it is a pleasant place to dine, with friendly service meeting your every need. There is a small bar for pre-dinner drinks, and an adequate wine list is available. To avoid disappointment, book a table in advance!

Dinner alc £15
Last dinner 9pm
Credit cards [1] [3]
Parking on premises
Closed Xmas & Jan
Closed Lunch, & Sun & Mon

MIDHURST West Sussex Map 4 SU82

Pummerys Wine-Bar
Knockhundred House,
Knockhundred Row
✆ (073081) 5144

Excellent value for money is to be found in the good, honest cooking here at Michael Turner's simply furnished and informal wine-bar. Candles in wine bottles on the oilcloth-covered tables, and paintings with wine-related themes, all help to set the scene for a range of unpretentious international dishes including daily specials, which are listed on a blackboard. Our Inspector particularly recommends the delicious home-made soups and the Greek lamb casserole. There are home-made puddings to finish, and some good wines are available.

Lunch/dinner alc £8
Last dinner 10.15pm
Parking nearby
Closed Sun

MILFORD-ON-SEA Hampshire Map 4 SZ29

GH **Seaspray**
8 Hurst Rd
✆ Lymington (0590) 42627

You can taste the sea air at this plesant modern guesthouse right on the seafront, away from the village centre. Six bedrooms include one family room and two rooms with showers en suite. All rooms have CTV and are well-furnished, with pretty, coordinated décor. Public rooms include a very comfortable bar/lounge and a dining room where good English breakfasts and freshly cooked evening meals are served. Guests requiring dinner are asked to order by 11am.

Price band A
Dinner, b&b £18.50–£26.50
Last dinner 6.30pm
Parking on premises

MILTON COMMON Oxfordshire Map 4 SP60

★★ Belfry Hotel
Brimpton Grange
✆ Great Milton
(08446) 381
Tx 837968

Only 10 minutes' drive from Oxford, yet in the heart of the countryside, this large hotel on the A40 has good amenities, including an outdoor swimming pool as well as indoor games such as table tennis, darts and pool. There is also a disco on Saturday evenings. The Belfry stands in extensive grounds and enjoys uninterrupted views over south Oxfordshire's rolling countryside. The 60 well-equipped bedrooms all have CTV, radio, telephones and bath or shower rooms en suite. Public rooms include a Tudor-style bar and an oak-panelled restaurant where good English and Continental fare is served.

Price band C
Bar lunch td £1.25–£3
Lunch td £8 or alc £10
Dinner td fr £11 or alc £12.50
Last dinner 9.30pm
Credit cards [1] [2] [3] [5]
Parking on premises
Closed 25–30 Dec

MINEHEAD Somerset Map 3 SS94

★★★ H Benares Hotel
Northfield Rd
✆ (0643) 2340

This friendly holiday hotel stands in pleasant gardens in a fine position overlooking the town and the coast. Resident owner Peter Maskrey and his staff are most anxious to please. The hotel is attractively furnished throughout, especially the excellent lounge. The spacious restaurant has garden views, and offers a five-course dinner with a good selection of well-prepared dishes (including vegetarian food). Bar meals are available at lunch-times. All of the 18 bedrooms have bathrooms en suite, and all have CTV.

Price band B
Bar lunch alc £5
Dinner td £10.50 or alc £15
Last dinner 8.30pm
Credit cards [1] [2] [3] [5]
Parking on premises

MODBURY Devon Map 3 SX65

× The Modbury Pippin
35 Church St
✆ (0548) 830765

Economical lunches and more sophisticated evening meals are served at this popular cottage-style restaurant, converted from a shop in the village centre. Frank and Muriel Mullery have been proprietors here for some time and, helped by their small team of staff, they offer efficient and friendly service and good food. Cooking shows imagination and flair, whether you choose the table d'hôte menu for its excellent value, or the à la carte selection, which is more ambitious and accordingly a little more expensive. Fresh, top quality raw materials are used in the preparation of dishes that are mainly simple, but attractively served. Vegetables are fresh and expertly cooked, while sweets are enticing and come in generous portions. Vegetarian food is available. Wines are well-kept and reasonably priced, with a good selection from lesser-known areas. The Modbury Pippin does not admit children under five.

Bar lunch £2
Lunch alc £6
Dinner td £8.50 or alc £10
Last dinner 9.30pm
Credit cards [1] [2] [3] [5]
No parking on premises
Closed Jan
Closed Sun & Mon (Oct–May), Tues & Wed (Nov–Mar)

MOFFAT Dumfries and Galloway *Dumfriesshire* Map 11 NT00

GH Well View
Ballplay Rd
✆ (0683) 20184

Well View, an attractive house overlooking the popular town of Moffat, was built in 1864 for two brother shoemakers. It has now been converted into a particularly well-run guesthouse where good service is provided by a pleasant young staff. Bedrooms are

Price band A/B
Lunch td £6
Dinner td £9
Last dinner 8pm
Credit card [3]

well-appointed, lounges comfortable, and cuisine of an excellent standard — the dinner menu, for example, offering such dishes as deep-fried mushrooms stuffed with pâté, fennel soup, Annandale trout in Dijon mustard sauce and chicken in a sherry sauce. Special dinners and wine-tastings are held throughout the winter months.

Parking on premises

MONMOUTH Gwent Map 3 SO51

★★★ **King's Head**
Agincourt Sq
(0600) 2177
Tx 497294

A large plaster panel of the crowned head of Charles I, who often visited this 17th-century hotel, is said to have been commissioned by the Royalist landlord of the period, and can still be seen in the hotel bar. The square in which the hotel stands is so called because of this historic town's connections with another king, Henry V, born at nearby Monmouth Castle. Today, the King's Head has been tastefully and imaginatively modernised to meet the needs of the 20th century. The main building contains 28 bedrooms with facilities en suite, and three more rooms, two of which are suitable for families, are in a separate building. All rooms have CTV and telephones. Meals are available both in the hotel dining room and in the Grill Room, which offers popular meals at competitive prices.

Price band C
Lunch td £10 or alc £16.50
Dinner td £15 or alc £16
Last dinner 9pm
Credit cards [1] [2] [3] [5]
Parking on premises

MONTROSE Tayside *Angus* Map 15 NO75

FH Muirshade of Gallery
(5 miles W of Montrose on unclassified rd between A987 & A94)
Northwaterbridge (067484) 209

A stay at this pleasant little roadside farm, set in rolling Angus countryside, represents value for money, and one is assured of the friendly, personal attention of the owner. Accommodation is provided in two pretty ground floor bedrooms with coordinated décor, modern beds and built-in furniture, and there is a cosy, comfortable residents' lounge with CTV. In the dining room, meals are served at a communal table, dinner consisting of a set main couse with a choice of starters and sweets.

Price band A
Dinner, b&b £12–£12.50
Last dinner 6.30pm
Parking on premises
Closed Nov–Mar

MOUNT HAWKE Cornwall Map 2 SW74

★ HBL **Tregarthen Country Cottage Hotel**
Porthtowan (0209) 890399

This small, informal hotel combines peace and quiet with a cottage-like atmosphere and plenty of home comforts. Pretty furnishings and décor complement the beamed interior, and public rooms (which include a bar) are cosy and warm, with a log fire in the lounge in winter. All six bedrooms have bath or shower rooms en suite, and a whirlpool bath has recently been fitted for guests' use. There is a three-bedroom cottage suite separate from the main building. Good home cooking, using fresh local vegetables and produce in season, is the basis of menus here. Proprietors Mr and Mrs Clive Hutton are most solicitous, and, along with their staff, they ensure that all their guests' needs are met.

Price band A
Dinner td fr £7.50
Last dinner 8pm
Parking on premises

> À la carte prices are based on an average for three courses without wine.

MULL, ISLAND OF Strathclyde *Argyllshire* Map 13 NM55
TOBERMORY

★ HL **Tobermory**
53 Main St
✆ (0688) 2091

This delightful little hotel, beautifully positioned on the waterfront and overlooking picturesque Tobermory Bay, provides an ideal base from which to explore the island. The comfortable bedrooms have thoughtful personal touches, two charming lounges decked with an abundance of fresh flowers invite easy relaxation, and good freshly-prepared food is served in the cosy dining room, including vegetarian meals. The hotels yacht is available for sailing.

Price band A/B
Dinner td £10.50
Last dinner 7.30pm
Closed Nov–Mar
Closed lunch Apr–Oct

MUTFORD Suffolk Map 5 TM48

GH **Beulah Hall**
Dairy Ln
✆ Barnby (0502) 76226

Resident proprietors Mr and Mrs Aarons are already gaining a good reputation for their recently opened small hotel. Personal attention and a good choice of home cooking are part of the reason. Dinner usually consists of a choice of half a dozen first courses, followed by a roast, and then one of several puddings. Everything is prepared by Mrs Aarons, who also serves traditional English breakfasts, and will happily arrange an early breakfast on request. The hotel has two lounges and a small cellar bar. All bedrooms are equipped with CTV. Outside amenities include a heated swimming pool and a small, well-stocked fishing lake. The grounds have largely been left natural to encourage wildlife.

Price band B
Dinner, b & b £22–£30
Last dinner 7.30pm
Parking on premises

NAIRN Highland *Nairnshire* Map 14 NH85

★★ H **Carnach House**
Delnies
✆ (0667) 52094

The hotel, standing in its own grounds only yards from the A96, is run in a relaxed country house-style and offers friendly, attentive service. There are some spacious bedrooms with fitted furniture, and smaller ones in more traditional style, all en suite. The cosy cocktail lounge and comfortable bar both have log fires burning in season. Dinner (chosen from two fixed-price menus, one five-course and the other, slightly more expensive, à la carte) will both satisfy the heartiest appetite and appeal to the discerning palate. Vegetarian meals are also available.

Price band B
Bar lunch £3.25–£10
Dinner td fr £9.50
Last dinner 9pm
Credit cards [1] [3]
Parking on premises

NANTWICH Cheshire Map 7 SJ65

×× **Churche's Mansion**
Hospital St
✆ (0270) 625933

This exceptional half-timbered mansion was built in 1577 for Richarde and Margerie Churche, whose name it still bears. Open to the public during the summer months, it is a fine example of the architecture of its period. The house retains many original features; a mantle in an upper room bears the first owner's initials, and much of the old panelling remains. The restaurant offers fixed-price lunch and dinner menus, cuisine being essentially British, with a few Continental additions. Starters include curried cockles and prawns, cream of parsnip soup and slices of smoked beef with leek salad, while for your main course you might choose grilled whiting with peppercorn sauce, steak and oyster pie or jugged saddle of hare. The wine list includes English, New Zealand and Californian wines.

Lunch td fr £6.25
Dinner td fr £12.50
Last dinner 9.30pm
Credit cards [1] [3]
Parking on premises
Closed 25–6 Dec & 1 Jan

NEAR SAWREY Cumbria Map 7 SD39

GH The Garth
☎ Hawkshead
(09666) 373

This delightful Victorian country house stands in its own grounds and offers accommodation of a charm and quality rarely found. The owners have personally redecorated and refurbished it to excellent effect, antique furniture and ornaments retaining the original character. A traditional home-cooked dinner — served in the elegant dining room with its well-appointed tables and silver cutlery — is the highlight of the day, and a healthy breakfast is served too. There is a comfortable lounge where a log fire burns in a most unusual carved wood fireplace, the excellent bedrooms are individually furnished and decorated, and the bathrooms are a delight, with antique marble washstands and quality toiletries.

Price band A
Dinner, b&b £18.50–£19.50
Last dinner 7pm
Parking on premises
Closed Dec

NEEDHAM MARKET Suffolk Map 5 TM05

GH **Pipps Ford**
(Off roundabout at A45/A140 junct)
☎ Coddenham
(044979) 208

Some of the most interesting and charming accommodation in East Anglia is to be found in this collection of timber-framed 16th-century buildings nestling in a hollow off the A45. Original features such as beams and stonework are complemented by comfortable, tasteful soft furnishings, antiques and quality fittings. There are two delightful sitting rooms, and seven bedrooms all of which have private bathrooms. Four of the bedrooms are in a recently converted former cowshed, and have been fitted out with flair and skill in country-style, with stripped, waxed furniture and lovely fabrics. One of the rooms in the main house has an antique French bed and a luxury bathroom with a corner bath and twin washbasins. Meals are served in the conservatory, with views of the pretty, old-fashioned garden. Four-course dinners (which should be ordered by noon) might begin with deep-fried crab parcels, warm chicken liver salad or little mussel pots with butter and garlic. Roast goose, crown of lamb with fresh herbs, home-smoked gammon or beef, fresh fish, pies and casseroles are some of the main-course offerings, while puddings could be traditional steamed treacle sponge, zabaglione or a home-made sorbet or ice-cream. An enormous choice at breakfast might include items as diverse as waffles, kedgeree, muesli with yogurt, or goose eggs — or, of course, a traditional farmhouse breakfast. Leisure amenities at Pipps Ford include an outdoor swimming pool and a hard tennis court. Fishing is also available.

Price band A/B
Dinner, b&b £24–£32.50
Dinner td £12
Last dinner 7.15pm
Parking on premises
Closed Xmas & New Year

NEWBURY Berkshire Map 4 SU46

× **The Red House**
Marsh Benham
(SP off A4, 2m W of Newbury)
☎ (0635) 41637

This pleasant, thatched country inn has both a restaurant and an excellent choice of bar snacks. Whichever you choose, the home-cooked, wholesome food represents excellent value. Typical dishes on the extensive bar menu include home-made pies (such as steak and kidney, venison, or lamb with redcurrant jelly), smoked salmon cheesecake with salad, fresh

Bar snacks £2–£3.50
Lunch td fr £8 & alc
Dinner td £11–£14 & alc
Last dinner

	grilled sardines, scallops in the Venetian manner, tomato and aubergine savoury, or moules normande. Vegetarian dishes are always available. Personally supervised by the proprietor, Mr Bullock, the Red House offers a warm welcome and has a lively, cheerful atmosphere. There is a Wendy house in the garden, but children under 14 are not allowed inside the pub.	9.45pm Credit cards [1] [2] [3] [5] Parking on premises

NEW MILTON Hampshire Map 4 SZ29

GH **Ashley Court Hotel** 105 Ashley Rd ✆ (0425) 619256	Ashley Court is a short walk from the centre of this busy little town, which is set between the New Forest and the sea. Resident hosts Mr and Mrs Davies offer comfortable accommodation and good service, and our Inspector particularly recommends their home cooking. Breakfasts are of an impressive standard, and dinner is available if ordered by noon. The hotel has a residential licence, and there is a small bar, as well as a separate, comfortable TV lounge. Bedrooms, some with duvets, are brightly decorated and have early-morning tea facilities. All of the eight have bath or shower rooms en suite, and one room is suitable for families. Dogs are not accepted.	Price band B Dinner, b&b £22.50–£24.50 Last dinner 6.30pm Credit cards [1] [3] Parking on premises Closed 31 Dec–1 Jan

NEWCASTLE-UPON-TYNE Tyne and Wear Map 12 NZ26

❀××× **Fisherman's Lodge** (Jesmond Dene, off A1058, Newcastle coast road, signed at entrance to Dene) ✆ 091-281 3281	Though not cheap, the Fisherman's Lodge offers very good value, particularly in its table d'hôte menu. Predominantly a fish restaurant, it is appropriately situated alongside the Ouse Burn. Two open-plan dining rooms are tastefully furnished and decorated to create an intimate atmosphere, and there are also two very comfortable lounges where aperitifs and after-dinner coffee are served. A mouthwatering selection of dishes is available, some being changed daily to take advantage of seasonal produce. Meat and poultry are there for those who prefer them to fish, and there is a delicious array of sweets. Whatever you choose, you will be served in generous measure by friendly, courteous and attentive staff.	Lunch td fr £10.50 or alc £16 Dinner alc £16 Last dinner 11pm Credit cards [1] [2] [3] [5] Parking on premises Closed 25 Dec–1 Jan and Bank Hols Closed Sun, & Sat lunch
×× **Great Wall** 35–9 Bath Ln ✆ 091-232 0517	Comfortable and friendly, the restaurant offers a good range of dishes from Canton and Peking. The intimate dining room, with its fabric-draped walls, features a dramatic spot-lit mural, and the small lounge-bar is cosy and inviting. Staff are spontaneously helpful, and the banquet-style set dinner (for 2-8 people) represents excellent value for money while enabling guests to try a wide range of dishes. Vegetarian meals are available.	Lunch td £2.80 Dinner td £9 Last dinner 11.30pm Credit cards [1] [2] [3] [5] Parking nearby (evenings)
× **Ristorante Roma** ✆ 091-232 0612	This long-established Italian restaurant, the first to be opened in the city, continues to give good value without compromising its high standards of comfort, service and quality of food. There is a spacious cocktail bar on the ground floor, and another small bar adjoining the comfortable first-floor dining room with its intimate atmosphere. Cheerful, friendly staff proffer an à la carte menu that features a feast of Italian dishes, meat and fish accompanied by a wide	Lunch td fr £2.95 & alc Dinner alc fr £8 Last dinner 11.30pm Credit cards [1] [2] [3] No parking on premises

variety of sauces and served with pasta made on the premises. A choice from the wine list, perhaps from the good range of Italian wines, will complete your enjoyment.

Closed 25 Dec & 1 Jan
Closed Sun lunch

NEWNHAM BRIDGE Hereford and Worcester Map 7 SO66

FH **Lower Doddenhill**
✆ (058479) 223

The fact that nearly all the bookings at Lower Doddenhill Farm are made by regulars who return year after year speaks for itself! The listed 17th-century farmhouse, which stands majestically overlooking the picturesque Teme Valley, has been sympathetically restored without loss of character, and a renovated oast house nearby now holds a small antique shop. Guests can completely 'wind down' in the friendly, homely atmosphere here, enjoying ample portions of traditional farmhouse fare, then chatting with their hosts in the comfortable lounge.

Price Band A
Dinner, b&b £15.50–£18
Last dinner 7.30pm
Parking on premises
Closed Dec–Feb

NEWPORT Gwent Map 3 ST38

★★★ **Ladbroke Hotel and Conference Centre**
The Coldra
(100 yards from M4 junct 24)
✆ (0633) 412777
Tx 497205

Conveniently situated only a hundred yards from junction 24 of the M4, this modern, purpose-built hotel offers an informal atmosphere which is enlivened by music and dancing each Saturday evening. The 119 bedrooms (22 of them non-smoking) have CTV and en suite bathrooms, spacious split-level public rooms are tastefully furnished and there is air-conditioning throughout the hotel. A sports complex which will considerably enhance the recreational facilities of the hotel is currently under construction in the extensive grounds.

Price band C
Bar lunch td £2.50–£5
Lunch td fr £7.50
Dinner td fr £10.95 or alc £14.50
Last dinner 10pm
Credit cards [1] [2] [3] [5]
Parking on premises

NEWTON ABBOT Devon Map 3 SX87

× H **Hazelwood House**
33A Torquay Rd
✆ (0626) 66130

This small hotel, a few minutes' walk from the town centre, is particularly recommended for its outstanding restaurant. Respresenting excellent value for money, the restaurant is open to residents and non-residents for lunch and dinner. Booking is advisable. Both à la carte and table d'hôte menus are available, and there is a special fixed-price light lunch consisting of a main course with fresh vegetables and ¼ litre of house wine for under £4. Cooking is original and imaginative, and everything is freshly prepared to order. Favourite starters are country pâté or delicate seafood mould, and for main course there might be roast stuffed quail or chicken Stilton supreme. Vegetarian dishes are available, and to finish there are delicious home-made sweets or a choice of English cheeses. The panelled dining room is small but well-appointed, and service is friendly and hospitable. The hotel has six cosy, simply but prettily furnished bedrooms, including one family room. Most have private shower or bathroom, and all have CTV.

Price band B
Lunch td £5.95 or alc £10
Dinner td £5.95 or alc £12
Last dinner 9.30pm
Credit cards [1] [3]
Parking on premises

NEWTONMORE Highland *Inverness-shire* Map 14 NN79

GH **Alvey House** ✆ (05403) 260	As you look out from Alvey House, stands of trees frame superb open views over the Spey Valley and Grampian Mountains. Standing in its own terraced garden, the relaxing little guesthouse assures guests of the personal attention and service of the owners. The fresh décor of the bedrooms is coordinated with their soft furnishings, most of the furniture is modern, and four rooms have en suite facilities. You can take your ease in the sun lounge with its Spanish furniture, or chat to fellow guests in the comfortable residents' lounge — perhaps recalling the day's triumphs or tragedies on the adjacent golf course. Dinners, which take the form of set main courses with a choice of starters and sweets, feature good quality local produce such as Scottish lamb.	Price band A Lunch td £4–£5 Dinner td £7 Last dinner 7pm Parking on premises Closed Nov–Dec (Open Xmas)

NEWTON STEWART Dumfries and Galloway *Wigtownshire* Map 10 NX46

FH **Auchenleck** Minnigaff (From Newton Stewart, cross bridge into Minnigaff. Turn first L and follow street to indoor bowling centre. Take R fork. 2 miles later take sign for Auchenleck) ✆ (0671) 2035	This delightfully turreted farmhouse enjoys an outstanding, remote setting on the edge of Kirroughtree Forest and the Glentrool Country Park, thus making an ideal base for walking, hill-climbing and bird-watching. Cattle and sheep are raised on the 100 acres surrounding the house, and visitors are encouraged to participate in the work of the farm, if they wish. The pristine bedrooms are spacious, with good views, while the lounge and dining room are attractive and individually appointed. Meals are prepared and presented with care, and a thoughtful supply of indoor games and books is a welcome diversion on the inevitable wet day.	Price band A Dinner, b&b £14 Last dinner 6.30pm Parking on premises Closed mid Oct–Easter
★★ **Creebridge House** ✆ (0671) 2121	Once the home of the Earls of Galloway, this tastefully appointed hotel is still operated in the country house style, even though the town centre is only minutes away. Individually styled bedrooms are spacious and provide a good range of equipment, most of them also having well-appointed bathrooms. Public areas are constantly undergoing improvement, and the character bar, with its open fire and good selection of real ales, is deservedly popular. Meals are always enjoyable, for good-quality local produce is taken as the basis for skilful home cooking, and the reasonably-priced four-course table d'hôte menu includes excellent game terrines, wholesome soups, delicately-cooked seafood with subtle sauces and tempting puddings.	Price band B Bar lunch £2.95–£8.50 Dinner td £11.95 Last dinner 8.30pm Credit cards 1 3 Parking on premises

NORTON Shropshire Map 7 SJ70

★★ B **The Hundred House** (On A442 6 miles of Bridgnorth) ✆ (095271) 353	Conveniently situated for access to the M54, and near the tourist attractions of Coalbrookdale and Ironbridge Gorge, The Hundred House is an imposing old hostelry which has been restored and improved to a very high standard. The public areas retain their old world charm, bars having oak-panelled walls and Jacobean fireplaces; bric-à-brac and cast iron articles associated with the history of the area are also very much in evidence. In the simple, cosy setting of the	Price band C Bar lunch alc £5.50 Lunch/dinner alc £8.75 Last dinner 10pm Credit cards 1 2 3 5

	restaurant, with its brick walls and beamed ceiling, guests enjoy well-prepared meals chosen from a range of traditional English dishes.	Parking on premises

NOTTINGHAM Nottinghamshire Map 8 SK54

Ben Bowers 128 Derby St ✆ (0602) 413388	This popular restaurant, a sister to its namesake in Derby, is situated at the western edge of the town centre, in a position convenient for businessfolk and shoppers during the day and visitors to the town's attractions in the evening. Extensive menus offer a wide variety of dishes from all over the world, ranging from the simple steak to such exotic dishes as vegetarian vol-au-vent Hawaii. The table d'hôte menu represents particularly good value, there is an extensive à la carte selection, and the restaurant features an interesting array of cocktails. For those with less time to spare, or smaller appetites, there is Betty's Bar, with its good selection of appetising and unusual snacks. Your well-being is the management's concern, and it prides itself on using fresh ingredients wherever possible and on avoiding artifical flavourings and colourings.	Lunch/dinner td fr £5.95 or alc fr £12 Last dinner 10.15pm Credit cards [1] [2] [3] [5] Parking nearby Closed Sun
GH **Hotel Windsor** 116 Radcliffe Rd (1 mile S on A6011) ✆ (0602) 813773	This large, friendly, and family-run guesthouse has many features that you would not normally expect in an establishment of its category. Though some of the 43 bedrooms are rather small, they are all well-equipped and all of them have en suite facilities and CTV. Constant attention to detail provides comfortable surroundings which, combined with the value-for-money meals served, makes Hotel Windsor an ideal base for tourists and business people alike.	Price band B Dinner, b&b £28.17–£35.07 Last dinner 8pm Credit cards [1] [2] [3] Parking on premises Closed 25–6 Dec

NUNNINGTON North Yorkshire Map 8 SE67

❀×× **Ryesdale Lodge** (Nunnington signed off A170 — pass Nunnington Hall 400 yards R at crossroads 1 mile on R) ✆ (04395) 246	It is hard to believe that this tranquil hotel was once the village railway station! The rambling old stone building has been tastefully converted to offer seven individually styled bedrooms, all having private bathrooms (two with whirlpool baths), equipped with everything that a guest could need and made welcoming with fresh flowers. There are comfortable, inviting lounges where drinks are available before and after dinner, and a charming dining room in which an interesting table d'hôte dinner is served (the menu changing regularly but retaining such popular dishes as Ryedale lamb casserole and fillet of beef).	Price band C Dinner td fr £16.95 Last dinner 9pm Credit cards [1] [3] Parking on premises Closed 1st 3 wks Jan

OAKHAM Leicestershire Map 4 SK80

Oakham Gallery 17 Mill St ✆ (0572) 55094	Oakham is an attractive market town standing amid the beauties of the Leicestershire countryside, close to Rutland Water, and local residents as well as tourists flock to this pretty little tearoom set above an art gallery. Morning coffee, light lunches and afternoon tea are served by a cheerful young staff, the mouthwatering selection of cakes and scones proving particularly tempting.	Parking nearby Closed Xmas Closed Mon

OAKHILL Somerset Map 3 ST64

×× **Oakhill House**
Bath Rd
(On A367 just N of Oakhill)
✆ Shepton Mallet (0749) 840180

Four acres of parkland surround this charming Georgian country-house restaurant, run by the Long family. Cooking and presentation are equally good, and the menu changes frequently. The set lunch is particularly good value and is popular with local business people. Dinner is à la carte. Vegetables are fresh, and dishes are planned with flair and imagination, often using interesting contrasts of flavour. Mousses are light and desserts especially tempting. The dining room has a relaxed and comfortable atmosphere, and there is an open fire in winter. (Oakhill House also offers bed and breakfast accommodation in three bedrooms.)

Lunch td £8.25 or alc £16
Dinner alc £16
Last dinner 9.30pm
Credit cards 1 2 3 5
Parking on premises
Closed mid Jan-mid Feb
Closed Mon, & Sat lunch & Sun dinner

OLD DALBY Leicestershire Map 8 SK62

Crown Inn
Debdale Hill
✆ Melton Mowbray (0664) 823134

Tucked away at the lower end of the village, this delightful inn resembles a squat, comfortable farm cottage. Well-used and polished furniture, small rooms, open fires and quarry-tile floors give the interior a cottage-like feeling too. Rows of casks behind the lovely old-fashioned bar draw the beer connoisseurs, while others come for the garden or the flourishing pétanque league. But perhaps most of all it is the food that gives the Crown such a popular following. A tempting menu of bar meals ranges from speciality snacks such as Stilton dip with crudités, Welsh rarebit, or a 'Crown lunch' (pork pie, ham, cheese, pickles and salad) to very substantial hot dishes like game pie, carbonnade of beef, or steaks. Vegetarian dishes include stuffed tomatoes, or stuffed mushrooms in batter with horseradish sauce. For more formal eating here are two pretty dining rooms offering very good value in a three-course table d'hôte menu, which changes frequently to reflect fresh market produce. A typical starter might be a puff pastry case containing snails with bacon, onions and chives in a cream and wine sauce, while for main course there might be turbot and sea bass served with fresh sorrel, or fillet steak cooked with wild mushrooms, horseradish, whisky and real ale.

Bar meal £1–£6
Lunch/dinner td £15
Last dinner 10.30pm
Parking on premises
Closed Sun & Mon dinner

ONICH Highland *Inverness-shire* Map 14 NN06

★★★ H
Lodge on the Loch
Creag Dhu
✆ (08553) 237

Set back from the roadside, the hotel commands splendid views south towards Argyll and westward across Loch Linnhe to the hills of Movern and Mull. Public rooms are spacious and comfortable, with a lovely open foyer lounge, a smartly-appointed dining room and a small cocktail bar which has recently been attractively redecorated. All bedrooms are well-equipped, those in the new wing being of a particularly high standard. Carefully prepared and interesting meals, making good use of game and local produce, are matched by attentive service throughout the hotel.

Price band B
Bar lunches alc £3
Dinner td £12 or alc £16
Last dinner 10pm
Credit cards 1 2 3 5
Parking on premises
Closed Nov-Mar

ORKNEY Map 16 HY21
STROMNESS

❀ ×× **Hamnavoe**
35 Graham Place
✆ (0856) 850606

The Hamnavoe, standing just off the flagstoned main street of this picturesque Orcadian fishing town, offers a unique combination of good food, friendly service and apparently spontaneous entertainment. The excellent standard of cuisine reflects not only the chef's skill but also the quality of the island's abundant fresh produce in such dishes as stuffed chicken breast or the more exotic poached scallops with mushrooms and pistachio sauce, and the à la carte menu ensures variety by changing with the seasons. As a pleasant end to the evening, you might be lucky enough to be entertained by Peter Pratt — young Orcadian Musician of the Year — on his flute.

Lunch/dinner alc fr £10
Last dinner 10pm
Credit cards [1] [3]
No parking on premises
Closed Mon
Closed lunch except weekends

OSTERLEY Greater London Map 4 TQ16

★★ **Osterley Hotel**
764 Great West Rd
✆ 01-568 9981
Tx 915059

Sound and serviceable accommodation, at a sensible price for the area, commends this modern hotel in West London. Reduced rates are available for two-nights stays at weekends, and a courtesy car to and from Heathrow Airport can be provided. All 60 rooms in the main building have private facilities, and there are additional rooms, including several for families, in an annexe. All rooms have CTV and telephones. Continental breakfast is included in the room rate, but a full English breakfast is available at an extra charge. A regularly changed table d'hôte menu, featuring dishes such as beef Stroganoff or chicken and spring vegetable casserole, is offered in Bramleys Restaurant. Alternatively, grills and popular dishes such as chicken Kiev or steak and kidney pie may be chosen from the à la carte menu. There is dancing to live music on Saturdays. Friendly and willing staff help to ensure enjoyable meals and a comfortable stay.

Price band C
Bar lunches £2
Lunch/dinner £7.95
Last dinner 10pm
Credit cards [1] [2] [3] [5]
Parking on premises

OTLEY West Yorkshire Map 8 SE24

★★★ **Chevin Lodge Country Park**
Yorkgate
✆ (0943) 467818

This interesting hotel, constructed from Scandinavian pine logs, stands in 50 acres of Yorkshire birch forest, set high above the town beside a small lake. Bedrooms and public rooms alike continue the log theme, but they are very well-appointed, with every modern comfort and most attractive soft furnishings. An up-to-date à la carte restaurant offers a good international menu, spiced with a few local specialities such as game in season, and a good wine list accompanies the meal. Woodland walks and a sauna will both help guests to atone for any over-indulgences!

Price band C/D
Bar snacks fr £2.25
Lunch td £7.95
Dinner td £12.75
Last dinner 9.30pm
Credit cards [1] [2] [3]
Parking on premises

> The price band indicates the price of bed and breakfast for a single person or room. Price band A = £15 or less; price band B = £16–£30; price band C = £31–£50; price band D = more than £50.

OXFORD Oxfordshire Map 4 SP50

Le Bistro du Marché/Crêperie Saint Michel
Market Avenue 1,
9A High St
(above covered market)
☎ (0865) 723342

Here, on the first and second floors above Oxford's excellent covered market, two French-style restaurant operations run in tandem. The Bistro du Marché is a coffee house, open in the morning and afternoon for snacks and beverages. Morning coffee comes with a choice of croissant, brioche, pain au chocolat, toast or Danish pastries, and in the afternoon customers can choose from a tempting range of 'gourmandises' including pancakes, ice-creams, home-made fruit tarts and cakes. Traditional English afternoon tea is also available. More substantial snacks include croque monsieur, salads and sandwiches. 'Jus de fruit pressé' — freshly squeezed orange, lemon or grapefruit juice — is one of a wide range of (non-alcoholic) beverages on offer. The second part of the business is the Crêperie Saint Michel, open for lunch and dinner. Here a selection of savoury pancakes, served with side salads, is supplemented by a choice of omelettes, salads and pasta dishes. Several vegetarian dishes are offered and, to finish, there is a good choice of sweet pancakes and other desserts. Fittingly Gallic aperitifs include Kir and Pernod, and a good-value wine list is available.

Lunch/dinner alc £7
Last dinner 11pm
Credit cards [1] [2] [3] [5]
No parking on premises
Crêperie closed Sun

×× **The Paddyfield**
39-40 Hythe Bridge St
☎ (0865) 248835

Good Cantonese and Pekinese food form the basis of the menu at this smart city-centre restaurant. An extensive choice of dishes includes crispy aromatic duck, shredded beef with chilli, chicken with bamboo shoots and Chinese mushrooms, or monkfish in black bean sauce. Vegetarian dishes are also available. The atmosphere is pleasant, and service by young waitresses is friendly and attentive. There is a short but reasonably priced wine list.

Lunch td £3.85
Dinner alc £10
Last dinner 11.45pm
Credit cards [1] [2] [3] [5]
Parking on premises
Closed 25–7 Dec

★ **River Hotel**
17 Botley Rd
☎ (0865) 243475

This small family-run hotel enjoys an attractive setting beside the Thames at Osney Bridge, just west of the city centre. Accommodation including an annexe across the road, comprises 25 compact but well-equipped bedrooms. Most have private facilities and all have CTV and radio/intercom. Three of the bedrooms are suitable for families. Public rooms include a lounge and bar overlooking the river and garden. Good, wholesome fare, priced according to the choice of main course, is served in the River Restaurant.

Price band B
Bar lunch td £3
Dinner td fr £5
Last dinner 7.30pm
Credit card [3]
Parking on premises

GH **Westwood Country Hotel**
Hinksey Hill Top
☎ (0865) 735408
Tx 295141

This comfortable hotel just outside the city is within easy reach of the centre but has a pleasant country house atmosphere and 3½ acres of peaceful gardens and woodlands. The 26 bedrooms (including five family rooms) all have private facilities, CTV and radio/intercom, and some also have hairdriers and trouser-presses. Public rooms, which open onto the gardens, include a restaurant, where lunch and dinner are available to residents. Barbecues are held twice-weekly in summer, weather permitting. Leisure amenities include a keep-fit room and a spa bath. Dogs are not accepted.

Price band B/C
Bar lunch fr £3
Dinner, td £9–£10 or alc £12
Last dinner 8.30pm
Credit cards [1] [2] [3] [5]
Parking on premises
Closed 14 Jun–1 July & 22 Dec–2 Jan

PADSTOW Cornwall Map 2 SW97

❀ × × **Seafood Restaurant** ✆ (0841) 532485	As its name suggests, this charming quayside restaurant specialises in fish and seafood. Choose from the good-value set-price menu or the more comprehensive à la carte. All the dishes are cooked with considerable skill and flair using local produce, and are tastefully presented — in both senses of the word. The extensive wine list includes some very good house wines. The dining area is well-furnished and bright, with cushioned wicker chairs and hanging green foliage, and there is a small bar/lounge area. Accommodation is now also offered in the form of eight comfortable bedrooms, all with private facilities and CTV.	Dinner td fr £14.95 or alc £19.50 Last dinner 9.30pm Credit cards 1 2 3 5 No parking on premises Closed mid Dec-mid Mar Closed lunch, & Sun
GH **Tregea Hotel** High St ✆ (0834) 532455	Mr and Mrs Cowmeadow offer a warm welcome to their 400-year-old house in a quiet street near the shops and harbour. Excellent home-made food is provided; there is no restaurant as such, but dinner is available to residents, and the hotel is licensed. There is a cosy lounge with a friendly atmosphere. The eight bedrooms (all with washbasins) include two family rooms, and all are comfortable and warm.	Price band A/B Dinner, b&b £17.65–£23.30 Last dinner 7.30pm Parking on premises
GH **Woodlands Hotel** Treator (1m W of Padstow on B3276) ✆ (0841) 532426	Nine bedrooms, including three suitable for families, are available at this small, elegant country hotel a mile inland from Padstow. Each bedroom has its own shower room, and all are attractively furnished and decorated, as are the two lounges, one of which has a bar. Proprietors, the Blackhall family, are always on hand to look after their guests. A set dinner is available to residents, but should be ordered by 4.30pm.	Price band A Dinner, b&b £18.50–£20.50 Last dinner 7pm Parking on premises

PARKGATE Cheshire Map 7 SJ27

× × **Mr Chow's** The Parade (W of A540 on B5135) ✆ 051-336 2385	You cannot fail to find this superb and very popular Chinese restaurant, for there is a rickshaw parked in front of it! Though the outside of the building is mock-Tudor, the interior maintains a totally oriental atmosphere, with rotating parasols, gently moving fans, mirrors, dragons and pampas grass. Advance booking is recommended, as it becomes very crowded at times, but you will find the effort well-worthwhile as you enjoy such delicious specialities as fish soup or crispy, aromatic Szechuan duck.	Dinner td fr £8.50 or alc £12 Last dinner 11.30pm Credit cards 1 2 3 5 No parking on premises Closed 25 Dec Closed lunch
★★★ **The Ship** ✆ 051-336 3931	Dating back to the early 19th century, this charming, stone-fronted building enjoys open views over the Dee estuary and marshes towards the Welsh coast and provides a fine base for birdwatchers. Now a comfortably furnished hotel, if offers thoughtfully designed, well-equipped bedrooms, two of which have four-posters, and a small but elegant dining room which serves a high standard of food. Ideally situated for Chester, North Wales and Merseyside, the hotel meets the needs of holidaymaker and businessman alike.	Price range C Bar lunch 95p–£2 Lunch td fr £6.95 or alc £14 Dinner td £10.50 or alc £14 Last dinner 9.30pm Credit cards 1 2 3 4 5 Parking on premises

PATELEY BRIDGE North Yorkshire Map 7 SE16

GH **Grassfields Country House Hotel**
✆ Harrogate (0423) 711412

The gracious Georgian country house, listed as of architectural interest, stands in four acres of garden and woodland, conveniently positioned for exploring the countryside around Nidderdale. Guests are warmly welcomed to the tranquillity of this lovely house, which retains the elegance of its period. Nine comfortably furnished bedrooms have views over the grounds, and you can watch television in a pleasant lounge. The meals served in the attractive dining room represent the best in English home cooking, prepared using vegetables from the garden, free-range eggs and lamb, beef and trout from local producers. A good wine list accompanies the menu.

Price band B
Dinner td £8
Last dinner 7pm
Parking on premises
Closed Nov–Mar

PATTINGHAM Staffordshire Map 7 SO89

★★★
Patshull Park
✆ (0902) 700100
Tx 334849

Once the home of the Earls of Dartmouth, Patshill Hall itself dates back some 250 years and occupies a site where manor houses have stood since the 11th century. Though the magnificent 280-acre park (once landscaped by Capability Brown) offers trout or coarse fishing, riding and walking, it is probably best known for its par 72 golf couse, and the hotel sports shop caters for both fishermen and golfers. The original house has been considerably altered and extended to provide comfortable modern accommodation in 49 well-equipped bedrooms, all with en suite bathrooms. A large, pleasant restaurant, with picture windows overlooking the lake, offers a good selection of English and French dishes, complemented by professional service, while the coffee shop sells a variety of snacks during the day and grill meals in the evening. There are also extensive conference and function facilities available.

Price band C
Bar lunches £2.50
Lunch td fr £5.95
Dinner td fr £8.75
Last dinner 9.30pm
Credit cards [1] [2] [3] [5]
Parking on premises

PEMBROKE Dyfed Map 2 SM90

★★ **Hoyland Hotel**
Hoyland Rd
✆ (0646) 681444

Proprietors the Ward family offer good, comfortable accommodation and friendly service at this fine Georgian mansion in the Pembrokeshire Coast National Park. The building has been completely refurbished to provide 12 bedrooms, all with bath or shower room en suite and equipped with CTV. Two of the rooms will accommodate families. Meals are well-cooked; the dinner menu features English and Continental dishes, and bar lunches are available. Vegetarians can be catered for.

Price band B
Bar lunch £1–£4.95
Dinner td £8 or alc £9
Last dinner 9.30pm
Credit cards [1] [3]
Parking on premises

PENARTH South Glamorgan Map 3 ST17

× **Il Piccolino**
The Esplanade
✆ (0222) 703428

There is a choice of good-value Italian eating at this small restaurant near the yacht club, overlooking the Bristol Channel. The first floor is a restaurant, where a range of expertly cooked, typical Italian dishes is served by friendly staff. A few simple English dishes are also available, as are vegetarian meals. Customers

Lunch/dinner alc £10
Last dinner 11.30pm
Credit cards [1] [2] [3]

	in search of a ligher meal should choose the ground floor, which has been converted into a pizzeria and wine-bar.	No parking on premises

PEN MAEN MAWR Gwynedd Map 6

Le Gallois High St ✆ Llandudno (0492) 623820	Peter and Carol Jones run this small restaurant, centrally situated in a Welsh coastal town. It is called Le Gallois (the Welshman) after Peter himself who was thus nicknamed by a French kitchen team with whom he once worked. Sauté of duck livers with tarragon and Madeira and quails Marcel Provence are two of his specialities which should not be missed, though vegetarians can be catered for. The food is complemented by a small but well-balanced wine list. Carol Jones, who also has a sound knowledge of food and wine, presides over the service in a warm, friendly manner.	Dinner td fr £6.95 or alc fr £11 Last dinner 9.30pm Parking nearby Closed Tue

PENRUDDOCK Cumbria Map 12 NY42

FH **Highgate** (On A66 4 miles W of M6 junct 40) ✆ Greystoke (08533) 339	Attached to this attractive 18th century house with its pretty gardens are 400 hundred acres given over to dairy, beef and sheep farming. It offers accommodation in individually decorated bedrooms with coordinated soft furnishings; all have CTV and two have polished brass bedsteads. The whole house is full of charm and character, with exposed oak beams, shining horse-brasses, attractive ornaments and some quality antiques. There is a comfortable lounge, and the dining-room — where a beautiful dresser displays a fine collection of china — provides traditional farmhouse breakfasts and good, home-cooked, English dinners.	Price band A Dinner, b&b £15–£17 Last dinner 6pm Parking on premises Closed Dec–Jan

PENSHURST Kent Map 5 TQ54

★★ **Leicester Arms** ✆ (0892) 870551	This creeper-clad 17th-century inn in the picturesque and historic village of Penshurst retains much of its original charm and character. It takes its name from Robert Sydney — brother of the Elizabethan poet and statesman Sir Philip Sydney — who was created Earl of Leicester in 1618. Nearby Penshurst Place was the Sydney's family home for two centuries. Worth visiting either for a meal or a stay, the Leicester Arms offers a good selection of wholesome fare (including vegetarian dishes) at lunch and dinner in the split-level restaurant. Drinks before your meal may be enjoyed in the tastefully furnished lounge, and bar snacks are also available. There are seven prettily decorated bedrooms, all equipped with modern amenities including CTV, telephones and en suite bath or shower rooms. Two of the rooms have four-poster beds.	Price band C Bar lunch £1.95–£5 Lunch td £8.50 Dinner td £10.50 or alc £13 Last dinner 9.45pm Credit cards 1 2 3 5 Parking on premises Closed Xmas Day dinner

À la carte prices are based on an average for three courses without wine.

PENZANCE Cornwall Map 2 SW43

★ H **Estoril Hotel**
46 Morrab Rd
✆ (0736) 62468

Florence and Arthur Reardon are genuinely hospitable hosts at this 10-bedroom hotel, conveniently situated between the Promenade and the town centre. All bedrooms have their own facilities, including one family room and one twin-bedded ground-floor room suitable for guests who cannot manage stairs. The rooms vary in size but are well-equipped, with CTV, clock/radios, electric blankets and telephones. Lunch and dinner feature a choice of wholesome, home-cooked food, including speciality local recipes, and using as much fresh produce as possible. The dining room is licensed, and a short wine list is available. Special diets can be catered for by arrangement. Children under seven are not accepted at the hotel.

Price band B
Dinner, b&b £24.50
Lunch td £3.75
Last dinner 7.30pm
Credit cards [1] [3]
Parking on premises
Closed Dec–Jan

★ HL **Tarbert Hotel**
11–2 Clarence St
✆ (0736) 63758

This white-painted Georgian house with its smart, striped awnings stands in a quiet position just outside the town centre. Resident proprietors Delyth and John James are naturally hospitable hoteliers and take a pride in their comfortable accommodation and good food. The homely, candlelit dining room offers a good table d'hôte dinner menu, with a limited choice for each course. There is also an à la carte menu. Mrs James cooks with imagination and flair: typical starters might be carrot and coriander soup, prawns Alabama or Jamaican baked grapefruit, followed by plainer main courses such as roast beef, local crab salad, or sole mornay. Soups, sauces, pies and desserts are all freshly prepared in the hotel kitchen. Special diets can be catered for by arrangement, and packed lunches and lunch-time bar snacks are available. The Tarbert has a charming, cosy lounge-bar, cheered by an open fire on chilly evenings, and a lounge with a writing table. All 12 cottage-style bedrooms have shower rooms en suite, and all have CTV and radio/intercom. There are three family rooms; children of all ages are welcome, and children's high tea can be provided — as can taped bedtime stories!

Price band B
Bar lunches td £3.50
Dinner, b&b £24
Last dinner 7pm
Credit cards [1] [2] [3] [5]
Limited parking on premises
Closed 19–31 Dec

PERRANPORTH Cornwall Map 2 SW75

GH **Villa Margarita Country Hotel**
Bone Mill Rd, Bolingey
(1m S of Perranporth)
✆ Truro (0872) 572063

The peaceful, unspoilt village of Bolingey might be a world away from the hurly-burly of a busy seaside resort, yet the amenities of Perranporth are only a mile down the road. The villa Margarita enjoys a quiet setting here in an acre of well-tended garden. The colonial-style villa has seven large bedrooms, all with showers and most with WCs en suite. The lounge gives fine views of the garden and the Cornish countryside beyond, and there is a small bar adjacent to the dining room. In fine weather dinner can be served outside on the vine-clad patio, and guests can enjoy drinks or snacks during the day beside the swimming pool. Caring resident proprietors Gill and Edmund Jacobs provide good hospitality, and Gill's imaginative and varied meals make full use of fresh local produce. Her flair for cooking even extends to

Price band A
Dinner, b&b £22.50–£24
Last dinner 8.30pm
Parking on premises

breakfasts; eggs Benedict, smoked haddock with poached egg, or porridge with whisky and clotted cream are all available to order. The Villa Margarita does not accept dogs, or children under eight.

PERSHORE Hereford & Worcester Map 3 SO94

★★★ Angel Inn & Posting House
High St
✆ (0386) 552046

Good, fresh food and comfortable, cottage-style bedrooms make a stay here in the heart of this vale of Evesham market town well-worthwhile. Completely renovated in recent years, the attractive bow-fronted building has 16 bedrooms with private bathroom, CTV, radio and telephone. Two four-poster rooms are offered at a special half-board rate which includes flowers and champagne on arrival and free room service. Our Inspector particularly commends the restaurant service at the Angel, which ranges from a full à la carte dinner in the Abbey Restaurant to bar snacks or 'Pershore Cream Teas', served in the lounge, and popular with locals and non-resident visitors as well as hotel guests. Lunches feature a wide choice of hot or cold dishes from the 'Coachman's Table', with a good table d'hôte traditional lunch on Sundays. The day begins with a very good breakfast menu which includes fish dishes. Eggs are free-range, and most vegetables are grown in the hotel's pleasant riverside gardens. Vegetarian food is always available. Smoking is not permitted in the restaurant.

Price band C
Bar lunches alc £4
Lunch alc £11
Dinner alc fr £10
Last dinner 9.30pm
Credit cards [1] [2] [3] [5]
Parking on premises

PERTH Tayside *Perthshire* Map 11 NO12

❀×× Coach House
8–10 North Port
✆ (0738) 27950

You will find this charming little restaurant housed in a Georgian building in the older part of the town. The premises, once the home of an antique shop, have been skilfully and tastefully converted to provide a simple but delightful setting for eating out, and an unusual feature in the spiral staircase which leads up to a small picture gallery on the upper floor. Meals are ably prepared, well-cooked and attractively presented, with clever use of herbs and light sauces, while the fixed-price menu is changed regularly to ensure effective use of fresh ingredients in season. You can also be sure of a warm welcome and friendly, competent service here.

Lunch td fr £8.50
Dinner td fr £12
Last dinner 10pm
Credit cards [1] [3]
Closed 1st 2 wks Jan & 2 wks Jul
Closed Sun & Mon

PITLOCHRY Tayside *Perthshire* Map 14 NN95

GH **Balrobin**
Higher Oakfield
✆ (0796) 2901

Set in its own grounds in a residential district of this popular tourist town, the Balrobin stands high enough to have fine views across to the Perthshire Hills and Tummel Valley. From this 'holiday cottage', built for a wealthy Edinburgh family in 1889, has been created a retreat where guests can enjoy a break in the peace and quiet of charming surroundings. Bedrooms are comfortably appointed, some having en suite facilities, and a restful residents' lounge provides space for relaxation. The pleasant dining room offers the delights of home cooking in the four-course evening meal served by a friendly and attentive host.

Price band A
Dinner, b&b £17.50–£23
Last dinner 7.30pm
Parking on premises
Closed mid Nov-mid Apr

GH **Well House Private Hotel** 11 Toberargan Rd ✆ (0796) 2239	This small, natural stone house, standing on the corner of a road close to the town centre, offers well-organised accommodation and friendly service. Simple but comfortable bedrooms, equipped with central heating and tea/coffee-making facilities, are served by en suite facilities. The spacious residents' lounge blends modern furniture with antiques and has an attractive original fireplace, while the dining room — though rather small and plain — offers good wholesome Scottish cooking.	Price band A Dinner alc £3.50 Last dinner 7.30pm Credit cards [1] [3] Parking on premises Closed Nov–Feb

PLOCKTON Highland *Ross and Cromarty* Map 14 NG83

★★ HL **The Haven** ✆ (059984) 223	The Haven is appropriately named, providing a relaxing break amid some of Scotland's most spectacular Highland scenery. The atmosphere is warm and friendly, and guests have a choice of two comfortable lounges in which to relax or enjoy a quiet drink. Pleasantly decorated, comfortable bedrooms all have CTV and private bathrooms. Specialities offered in the candle-lit dining room include fresh Loch Lomond salmon and prawns, venison and Scottish beef. Boats are available for hire and island picnics.	Bar lunches fr 60p Lunch td fr £4.60 Dinner td £11 Last dinner 8.30pm Credit cards [1] [3] Parking on premises Closed 21 Dec–10 Feb

PLUMTREE Nottinghamshire Map 8 SK63

× **Perkins Bar Bistro** Old Railway Station ✆ (06077) 3695	Situated on the outskirts of the village, the old station was built by the Midland Railway Company in 1880. One hundred and two years later, it was taken over by Tony and Wendy Perkins and converted into a pleasant little bistro-style restaurant which successfully maintains its Victorian character. The centrally-situated bar, gas-lamp fittings and wood-burning stove set an informal scene which is given a Continental flavour by an abundance of Fresh Impressionist prints, painting and posters. A short menu of first-class dishes is changed regularly to take advantage of seasonal availability of fresh produce, and there are also often 'specials', which are displayed on a blackboard.	Bar lunches alc £4.50 Lunch alc £10.50 Dinner alc £11.50 Last dinner 10pm Credit cards [1] [2] Parking on premises Closed wk after Xmas & Bank Hols Closed Sun

PLYMOUTH Devon Map 2 SX45

GH **Georgian House Hotel** 51 Citadel Rd, The Hoe ✆ (0752) 663237	This recently refurbished Georgian town house is an ideal base for exploring most places of interest in historic Plymouth. Accommodation is of a high standard; the 10 bedrooms all have CTV and private facilities. The licensed Fourposter Restaurant offers a good à la carte dinner menu, and the hotel has a convivial bar. Friendly service and hospitality are provided by resident proprietors Mr and Mrs Radford.	Price band B Dinner, b&b £30–£32 Last dinner 9.30pm Credit cards [1] [2] [3] [5] Limited parking on premises

POLMASSICK Cornwall Map 2 SW94

GH **Kilbol Country House Hotel** ✆ Mevagissey (0726) 842481	Home-produced meat, cream, milk and eggs are a bonus at this friendly guesthouse on a country smallholding — braver guests can even try their hand at milking the house cow! Home-cooked meals are served, to residents only, in an attractive licensed dining room (please order dinner by 5pm). There are two lounges in which to relax — one with a bar — and other amenities include an outdoor swimming pool. There are nine warm, well-decorated bedrooms, some with bath or shower en suite, and one suitable for families.	Price band B Dinner, b&b £19.55–£21.85 Last dinner 7pm Credit cards 1 2 3 5 Parking on premises

POOLE Dorset Map 4 SZ09

★ **Fairlight Hotel** 1 Golf Links Rd, Broadstone (3m NW of Poole on B3074) ✆ Broadstone (0202) 694316	This small, secluded hotel offers comfortable, attractive accommodation and a friendly atmosphere. There are 10 bedrooms (some with private bathrooms), a pleasant lounge and small, convivial bar. The hotel is personally run by its owners, Mr and Mrs Marshall, who offer a carefully planned set dinner menu. There is no choice, but the food is well-prepared, and vegetarians can be catered for. Bar snacks are available to residents at lunch-time.	Price band B Dinner td fr £10 Bar lunch £2–£5 Last dinner 7.30pm Credit cards 1 3 Parking on premises Closed 23 Dec–3 Jan
★★ **Sea-Witch Hotel** 47 Haven Rd, Canford Cliffs ✆ (0202) 707697	Situated close to the famous gardens of Compton Acres, this small, friendly hotel has nine well-equipped bedrooms (including two family rooms), all with private facilities, CTV and telephones. Our Inspector particularly recommends Renoirs, the hotel's busy and attractive restaurant. Ian and Kathleen Symons, the proprietors, run the catering side of their business with enthusiasm. Menus feature mainly French dishes, carefully cooked and using good fresh ingredients. Both lunch and dinner are served, with a choice between table d'hôte and à la carte menus. The wine list is extensive and unusual, wine being a keen interest of Mr Symons. 'Gourmet weekend' packages are offered at special rates.	Price band B Dinner td £9.95 or alc £12 Lunch td fr £7.50 or alc £12 Last dinner 9.45pm Credit cards 1 3 Parking on premises Closed 25 Dec–3 Jan

POOLEY BRIDGE Cumbria Map 12 NY42

❀❀★★★ RED ♣♣ **Sharrow Bay Country House** (About 1½ miles from Pooley Bridge, take unclassified road to Howton which leads off the B5320 in the centre of the village) ✆ (08536) 301	Idyllically situated in its own grounds and gardens on the edge of Ullswater, this internationally acclaimed country house hotel has splendid views across the lake to the Helvellyn mountains. Here you will be cosseted in luxury and enjoy cuisine of the highest standard — hearty breakfasts being followed by five-course lunches and six-course dinners which, though not cheap, all provide excellent value for money. Cuisine is predominantly classical, though with some modern influence and the inclusion of a certain number of British dishes, and many fine wines are offered at realistic prices.	Price band D Lunch td fr £14 Dinner td £29.50 Last dinner 8.45pm Parking on premises Closed early Dec-early Mar

PORLOCK Somerset Map 3 SS84

★★ H **The Oaks** ✆ (0643) 862265	This attractively located Edwardian country house is conveniently situated for exploring Exmoor and the coast of Somerset and North Devon. Fine views of the sea and Porlock are a feature of several rooms, and the hotel stands in its own pleasant grounds. The resident owners, Tim and Anne Riley, offer a warm welcome and personal attention. They take a particular pride in their freshly prepared food, chosen from a well-balanced menu. Light lunches are available and the restaurant is open daily for dinner. Accommodation is in 11 bedrooms, all with private facilities and CTV, and including two family rooms.	Price band B Lunch fr £6 Dinner td fr £10.25 Last dinner 8.45pm Parking on premises

PORT APPIN Strathclyde *Argyllshire* Map 14 NM94

❀★★ RED **Airds Hotel** ✆ Appin (063173) 236	A truly charming little hotel has been created from the Old Ferry Inn, in its picture-postcard setting on the shores of Loch Linnhe. It features excellent four-course dinners, skilfully prepared from such top quality ingredients as local venison, beef and lamb, together with a variety of fresh seafood. An outstanding and comprehensive wine list will accompany your meal. Afternoon tea can be enjoyed among the colourful plants of a cheerful sun lounge. Service is unobtrusively attentive, and it is easy to relax in either of the two pleasant lounges, especially in front of the roaring log fires that burn on colder days. Some bedrooms are rather compact, but all are comfortable and spotlessly clean, each having its own individual charm and character.	Price band D Bar lunch td fr £3 Lunch td fr £8 Dinner td fr £22 Last dinner 8pm Parking on premises Closed mid Nov-mid Mar

PORTESHAM Dorset Map 3 SY68

GH **Millmead Country Guest House** Goose Hill ✆ Abbotsbury (0305) 871432	Standing in attractive gardens of over one acre, which produce most of the vegetables and fruit featured on the dining room menu, is this small guesthouse. The building, Victorian in origin, has been sympathetically refurbished and extended to provide eight bedrooms (four with private facilities), including one family room. All rooms have CTV. The owners, Peter and Marion Cox, foster a friendly, hospitable atmosphere. The menus, though short, are well-chosen and presented. All dishes are home-cooked and the wine list, being varied, imaginative and reasonably priced, complements the food. Children over 10 years of age are welcome. No smoking is allowed on the premises.	Price band A Dinner, b&b £24.25 Last dinner 7.30pm Credit cards [1] [3] Parking on premises Closed Dec-Jan

PORT ISAAC Cornwall Map 2 SW98

★★ H **Port Gaverne Hotel** ✆ Bodmin (0208) 880244	Nestling in the valley at the head of a deep cove, this 17th-century inn has a long tradition of hospitality. Present owners Fred and Midge Ross have a 20-year tradition of caring service here, helped by their hand-picked team of staff. The 19 bedrooms, 18 with CTV, telephones and private bathrooms, have recently been supplemented by seven self-catering cottages set round a sunny, lawned courtyard. Food is a priority at the hotel, be it a bar snack or a three-course dinner.	Price band B Bar lunch £1.50-£3.15 Lunch alc £6 Dinner td £10.50 or alc £12.50 Last dinner 9.30pm Credit cards [1]

Cooking shows imagination and care, and uses local produce. The table d'hôte dinner menu changes daily, and features hearty dishes such as coq au vin, sea trout with hollandaise sauce or sirloin steak forestière. A vegetarian choice (usually an omelette) is included. First courses include a home-made soup, and desserts are chosen from the trolley. The bar menu offers Cornish crab soup, pâté, a range of sandwiches and several more substantial dishes such as home-made beef curry, cottage pie and basket meals. The front bar usually features an exhibition of work by local artists.

[2] [3] [5]
Parking on premises
Closed 11 Jan–19 Feb

PORT-NA-CON Highland *Sutherland* Map 14 NC46

GH **Port-na-Con House**
(6 miles E of Durness on A838 Durness-Tongue Road — ¼ mile off main road — E towards loch)
✆ Durness (097181) 367

The guesthouse enjoys a unique position, almost as far north as one could stay on the western side of Britain, and the warmth of its hospitality rivals the splendour of the surrounding mountain and sea lochs. Once a harbour store, it stands on the landward end of the quay that formed the westerly terminal point of the Loch Eriboll Ferry, and it has now been renovated to provide pleasant accommodation with beautiful sea views. Guests gather in the friendly residents' lounge to drink and chat, then move on to the dining room to enjoy a good table d'hôte meal that often features local seafood; an à la carte menu is also offered, and meals are available to non-residents, but it is advisable to book in advance.

Price band A
Lunch alc £9.50
Dinner td £7.50 or alc £9.50
Last dinner 7pm
Credit card [3]
Parking on premises
Closed Dec—Jan
Restricted service Feb & Nov

PORTPATRICK Dumfries and Galloway *Wigtownshire* Map 10 NX05

❀❀★★ RED ♣♣
Knockinaam Lodge
(2 miles S on unclassified road)
✆ (077681) 471

This delightful Victorian stone lodge, attractively set against cliffs in a remote bay, was built in 1869 as a holiday retreat for Lady Hunter Blair. It still provides an escape from the hustle and bustle of modern life for the discerning holidaymaker, providing attentive service and a warm and relaxing atmosphere. Quality and character are combined in the cosy bar and wood-panelled drawing room and reception hall, the latter having a red flagstone floor. Antiques and stripped pine furniture blend harmoniously in bedrooms with charming floral décor, and modern facilities are enhanced by such thoughtful touches as pot pourri, tissues and wrapped soaps. In the restful setting of the charming dining room you can enjoy expertly-prepared French dishes such as noisette de veau aux champignons or filet de turbot à la moutarde et aux amandes, all based on high quality fresh produce.

Price band D
Bar lunch £2–£4.50
Lunch td fr £2
Dinner td £18
Last dinner 9pm
Credit cards [1] [2] [3] [5]
Parking on premises
Closed mid Jan–mid Mar

PORTSONACHAN Strathclyde *Argyllshire* Map 10 NN01

❀ ★★ H
Portsonachan Hotel
Lochaweside
✆ Kilchrenan (08663) 224

This popular little family-run hotel, delightfully situated on the eastern shore of Loch Awe, is especially noted for its warm, friendly, informal atmosphere and its good food. Simple but comfortable bedrooms vary both in size and style, but they are all attractively decorated and some have private bathrooms. The traditionally furnished lounge with its

Price band C
Bar lunch td £1–£5
Dinner td £14.50
Last dinner 9pm
Credit cards [1] [3] [4] [5]

	open fire is an ideal place to relax, and there are also a separate television lounge and snug cocktail bar. Imaginative cooking, coupled with the excellent use which is made of fresh produce, means that a meal at the Portsonachan is a memorable experience. Good fishing is available, and the hotel has boats and outboards for hire on Loch Awe.	Parking on premises Closed Dec–Feb (except Xmas & New Year)

POWBURN Northumberland Map 12 NU01

❀ ★★ RED **Breamish House** (On main A697 through village ✆ (066578) 266	A charming country house set in five acres of gardens and woodland, Breamish House is cosy and comfortable, surrounding guests with a wealth of books, paintings and fresh flowers. The 10 bedrooms all have en suite facilities. There is a pleasant, spacious sitting room and a smaller lounge at the back of the hotel, both with the same peaceful and relaxing ambience, while the elegant dining rooms are candle-lit to create an intimate atmosphere. The excellent dinner menu offers a wide choice of unpretentious dishes, prepared with care from quality produce and attractively presented; service is unobtrusively attentive and very courteous.	Price band B Lunch td fr £8 (Sun only) Dinner td fr £14 Last dinner 8.30pm Parking on premises Closed Jan

PRESTON Lancashire Map 7 SD52

★★★ **Broughton Park** Garstang Rd (On A6 N of Preston close to M55 motorway ✆ (0772) 864087 Tx 67180	Broughton Park combines effectively the splendour of the Victorian age and the requirements of the modern hotel user. Bedrooms are good, well-furnished and comfortable, equipped with the sort of facilities that will appeal to the busy travelling executive. There are two restaurants, the smaller and more intimate of them offering a more elegant style of cuisine and service. An excellent health and leisure club is available to guests, providing a swimming pool with two jacuzzis, a sauna, a solarium and two well-equipped gyms. Well-trained staff render efficient yet friendly service.	Price band C Lunch td fr £6.50 or alc £8.50 Dinner td fr £11.50 or alc £16 Last dinner 10.30pm Credit cards 1 2 3 5 Parking on premises Closed Sat lunch

PULBOROUGH West Susex Map 4 TQ01

★ BL **Chequers Church Place** ✆ (07982) 2486 Tx 67596	This delightful family-run country hotel offers good, well-equipped accommodation and a friendly atmosphere. Basic, sound English fare is served in the small but well-appointed dining room; fresh flowers, together with a log fire in winter, cheer the comfortable, cosily furnished lounge. There are nine bedrooms, including one family room. All have CTV and private facilities, and are generally spacious and prettily furnished.	Price band B Bar lunch fr £1 Lunch td fr £5 Dinner td fr £8.50 Last dinner 8pm Credit cards 1 2 3 5 Parking on premises Restricted menu Sun dinner
❀× **Stane Street Hollow** ✆ (07982) 2819	Stane Street Hollow is a charming, cosy restaurant standing just south of the village, and a warm welcome is extended to guests by its Swiss chef and his wife. The range of dishes on the menu (which, not surprisingly, shows a Swiss bias) is changed monthly	Lunch td fr £8 Dinner alc £15.20 Last dinner 9pm Parking on

to take advantage of seasonal local produce, but the standard of cuisine is consistently high. The comprehensive, reasonably priced wine list contains a few Swiss wines. Vegetarian meals are available.

premises
Closed Sun & Mon

RAASAY, ISLE OF Highland *Inverness-shire* Map 13 NG53

★★ Isle of Raasay Hotel
✆ (047862) 222

The Isle of Raasay is easily reached by car ferry from Sconser, and the diversion is well-worthwhile, for it is steeped in history and abounds in wildlife (including a species of vole unique to it). The heart of the hotel is an old stone mansion, and two stylish modern wings provide smart, well-equipped bedrooms, all having CTV and private bathrooms. Service is attentive, and the satisfying dinners served in the bright dining room, based as far as possible on local produce, include such specialities as fresh crab soup with good roasts and home-made puddings, though choice is restricted. The attractive, pine-clad bar is a pleasant place to relax after an energetic day on the hills. Bar lunches are available.

Price band B
Dinner td £13
Last dinner 7.30pm
Parking on premises

RANGEMORE Staffordshire Map 7 SK12

★★ HL
Needwood Manor Hotel
✆ Burton-on-Trent (028371) 2932

Mr and Mrs George have the knack of making their customers feel like house guests at their beautifully restored Victorian manor house. Two acres of garden and parkland in the heart of Needwood Forest provide a peaceful rural setting, and log fires, fresh flowers and period furnishing reinforce the country house atmosphere. Spacious public rooms have preserved many notable features — not least the magnificent staircase and gallery, constructed of pitch pine and now painstakingly restored. Most of the 11 bedrooms (including two family rooms) have private facilities, and CTV and private telephones are available on request. Dinner is chosen from a good à la carte menu of mainly classic dishes such as steak Diane, veal Cordon Bleu or roast duck, but with some imaginative touches like mango with prawns, as a first course, or chicken with avocado in a paprika sauce to follow. Dogs are not accepted.

Price band B
Dinner td fr £10 or alc £13.50
Last dinner 9pm
Credit cards 1 3
Parking on premises
Closed 24-30 Dec

RAVENSTONEDALE Cumbria Map 12 NY70

★★ H **Black Swan**
✆ Kirkby Stephen (05873) 204

Built of Lakeland stone at the turn of the century, the Black Swan stands at the centre of this peaceful little village, still offering visitors a warm welcome and the assurance of excellent service. Recently refurbished and upgraded, it provides accommodation in bedrooms which are all different but all equally comfortable. On colder days you can enjoy your afternoon tea by a roaring fire in the first-floor lounge (though in summer you will probaby prefer to take it in the pretty garden at the back of the hotel), and there is also an open fire in the character lounge-bar. The home-cooked meals served in the attractive restaurant make good use of locally-raised beef, lamb and game, all prepared to traditional recipes, and even the rolls are baked on the premises.

Price band B/C
Bar lunch td £3-£9
Lunch td £8.50
Dinner td £14
Last dinner 8.15pm
Parking on premises
Closed Jan-Feb

READING Berkshire Map 4 SU77

The Hideaway (At the White Hart Hotel, Main Rd) ✆ (0734) 692277	The Hideaway is described as a bistro, but it has more the relaxed atmosphere of a cottage-style restaurant. Décor is traditional, with dark oak furniture, comfortable chairs and beamed brick walls. The large dining room has two alcoves (suitable for small private parties) on different levels, the larger housing a generously supplied salad bar. Tables are adorned with fresh flowers, and candles supplement the subdued lighting. The menu offers a set priced 'chef's special' each day, and a typical main course would be liver in red-wine sauce with either vegetables or salad. You can then choose from six freshly-made desserts, and complete your meal with a generous Elizabethan-style mug of coffee — replenished at no extra charge!	Lunch/dinner td £5.95 or alc fr £9 Last dinner 10pm Credit cards 1 2 3 5 Parking on premises
Nino's Market Place ✆ (0734) 588966	Nino has established a small group of restaurants in Reading, each with its own individual character and atmosphere. The first, at Market Place, has earned a fine reputation among local residents and is always busy, so booking is recommended. The smallest of the group, it achieved a relaxed atmosphere which is due in no small part to the services of a cheerful, hardworking Italian staff. The menu features not only a variety of pasta dishes but also veal, chicken and a good range of very large, freshly-made pizzas; both vegetables and side salads are always available, and the sweet trolley offers a tempting display of desserts. A well-chosen list of Italian wines gives scope for choice, but the house wine is very acceptable.	Lunch/dinner alc fr £10 Last dinner 10pm Credit cards 1 2 3 5 Parking nearby Closed Xmas Closed Sun
Wine Butts 61 St Mary's Butts (Opposite Butts Shopping Centre) ✆ (0734) 509363	This up-to-the-moment, stylish combination of wine-bar and restaurant in the town centre offers seating for approximately eighty people and is always bustling and lively. Stripped pine furniture blends well with modern décor, an array of framed prints and large green plants softening the general effect. The menu offers a range of popular dishes, such as Mexican pancakes, moussaka and a wide range of pastas including both meat and vegetable lasagnes, and efficient service allows you a breathing space between courses. A good, reasonably-priced list of wines is available, sold by the bottle or the glass.	Lunch/dinner alc fr £7.50 Last dinner 10.30pm Credit cards 1 2 3 5 Parking nearby Closed Sun & Mon

REDDITCH Hereford & Worcester Map 7 SP06

GH **Old Rectory** Ipsley Ln Ipsley ✆ (0527) 23000	Within the Redditch new town development scheme, there lies an extremely hospitable small country house-style hotel. Standing in 2½ acres of grounds, the Old Rectory offers guests a peaceful and comfortable stay with bedroom facilities that can equal a more highly classified hotel and all have telephones and bathrooms en suite. Mr and Mrs Moore have worked hard to convert this part-Elizabethan house into a hotel of character and warmth.	Price band B Dinner £9 Last dinner 7.30pm Closed Sun dinner

REDHILL Surrey Map 4 TQ25

GH **Ashleigh House Hotel** 39 Redstone Hill ✆ (0737) 764763	Good-value accommodation is to be found at this Edwardian-style town-house in a residential area on the outskirts of Redhill. Proprietors Mr and Mrs Warren take a great personal interest in the running of their hotel. They particularly pride themselves on their wholesome, hearty breakfasts. No other meals are served. The hotel has nine comfortable and well-equipped bedrooms, each one individually decorated, with coordinated colour schemes. Rooms are of a good size, and all have washbasins, though only one has a shower en suite. There is one family bedroom. The lounge is homely and attractive, and there is a heated swimming pool in the garden. Dogs are not accepted.	Price band A/B Parking on premises Closed Xmas

REDLYNCH Wiltshire Map 4 SU22

×× **Langley Wood** ✆ Romsey (0794) 390348	A restaurant worth visiting is located in this interesting house in a lovely woodland setting which also offers accommodation. Well-cooked English or French dishes may be chosen from an imaginative menu, vegetarian meals are available, and there is a good short wine list. Guests can enjoy pre-dinner drinks or after-dinner coffee in one of the pleasant lounges. The three comfortable bedrooms are decorated in an attractive homely style, completing Langley Wood's qualification as a very good base from which to tour the surrounding countryside. Booking is essential.	Lunch td £9.50 (Sun) Dinner alc £13.50 Last dinner 11pm Credit cards [1] [2] [3] [5] Parking on premises Closed Mon, Tue & Sun dinner

REDRUTH Cornwall Map 2 SW64

★ HB **Aviary Court** Mary's Well, Illogan (2m NW of Redruth on unclassified rd) ✆ (0209) 842256	The Studley family are charming, helpful hosts at their attractive Cornish country home, which stands in 2½ acres of lovely gardens, and is about a 20-minute walk from the sea at Portreath. All six bedrooms (including one family room) have garden views and are equipped with CTV, clock/radios, hairdriers and tea/coffee-making equipment. Three have private facilities. A daily supply of fresh fruit is provided in rooms. The comfortable lounge, which opens onto the terrace, has a bar, and is warmed by a log fire in winter. Fresh Cornish produce is a speciality in the restaurant, where table d'hôte and à la carte menus are complemented by a short wine list. Aviary Court does not accept dogs, or children under three.	Price band A/B Dinner, b&b £23.75 Last dinner 9pm Credit cards [2] [5] Parking on premises
×× **Basset Count House** Carnkie ✆ (0209) 215181	Tin-miners were once paid in the 19th-century building, the former head office of a mining company, which is set among now disused mine workings. The interior has been completely reconstructed. A semi-circular bar and elegant period furnishings are features of the charming ground-floor drawing room, while the restaurant is sited above to give panoramic views of the surrounding area. The menu is à la carte, but changes daily, and fresh foods in season are a	Lunch/dinner alc £12 Last dinner 9.30pm Credit cards [2] [3] Parking on premises Closed Mon, &

speciality. Cooking is careful and imaginative, dishes light and modern in style. Sunday lunch is particularly good value at under £6.

Sun dinner, & lunch Tue–Sat

REIGATE Surrey Map 4 TQ25

GH **Cranleigh Hotel**
41 West St
✆ (07372) 223417

This realistically priced private hotel is conveniently located on a main road just out of the town centre, and is within easy reach of both the M25 and Gatwick Airport. The building is beautifully maintained both inside and out, and has a large, attractive rear garden with a small patio and a heated swimming pool. Furnishings and décor are of a high standard in all the bedrooms and public areas. Six of the 10 bedrooms have private bathrooms, and all are equipped with telephones, CTV and hairdriers. There are two family rooms. Downstairs is a formal but comfortable and homely lounge, a dining room with good garden views and a small cosy residents' bar.

Price band B/C
Dinner, b&b £35–£47
Last dinner 9pm
Credit cards [1] [2] [3] [4] [5]
Limited parking on premises

RETFORD (EAST) Nottinghamshire Map 8 SK78

★★★ L **West Retford Hotel and Restaurant**
North Rd
✆ (0777) 706333
Tx 56143

The charm and elegance of the 18th century have been preserved at this large Georgian house. Stately public rooms, including a ballroom and several function or conference rooms, are in the main house, while 30 modern bedrooms are housed in two separate buildings in the grounds. All rooms have private bathrooms, telephones, CTV, radio, trouser-presses and hairdriers. Many of the rooms have accommodation for families, and there is also a luxuriously appointed suite. French cuisine is the basis of the stylish restaurant's à la carte menu. The table d'hôte lunch and dinner menus offer excellent value, with a choice of about five dishes for each course. Lunch features homely favourites such as roast pork or meat and potato pie, while the dinner menu might offer swordfish steak with a lobster sauce, or veal milanese. The chef will also do his best to provide, on request, any dish that is not on the menu, including vegetarian food. Dinner dances are held on Saturday evenings.

Price band C
Lunch td £6.95 or alc £7
Dinner td £9.25 or alc £10
Last dinner 10.30pm
Credit cards [1] [2] [3] [5]
Parking on premises

RHANDIRMWYN Dyfed Map 3 SN74

INN **Royal Oak**
✆ (05506) 201

Panoramic views are among the pleasures of a meal or a stay at this small, character-packed inn high in the Cambrian Mountains. Food here is enjoyable and well-prepared. Meals are served both in the attractive dining room and in the bars, which are kept cosy and cheerful by log fires in cold weather. The inn also has a separate pool room. Accommodation is in five bright, clean bedrooms, all attractively decorated, with duvets on the beds. Some rooms have private bathrooms and CTV, and one is suitable for families.

Price band A
Bar lunch 99p–£4.50
Dinner alc £8.95
Last dinner 11pm
Credit cards [1] [3]
Parking on premises

RICHMOND North Yorkshire Map 7 NZ10

FH **Whashton Springs** (3 miles N of town centre on Ravensworth Road) ✆ (0748) 2884	This delightful farm, though only three miles from the town centre, stands high in the hills of Herriot country, and you are welcome to begin your exploration of the peaceful countryside by roaming round its 600 acres. There are superb views from the unusual semi-circular bay windows of the old stone farmhouse. Inside, all is tranquillity and comfort, both in the house itself, which offers three charming bedrooms (one with four-poster bed and private facilities) and in the adjoining converted farm building, where all five attractive rooms have facilities en suite. The sitting room and dining room are comfortable and full of character. Meals are good, as you would expect, the set dinner menu including home-made soups, soufflés and sweets in addition to the main dishes with their home-grown vegetables. The whole family is involved in the running of the establishment, and you can be sure that you will be well-looked after.	Price band A/B Dinner, b&b £18.50–£25.50 Last dinner 7pm Parking on premises Closed Xmas & New Year

RIPPONDEN West Yorkshire Map 7 SE01

×× **Over the Bridge** Millfold ✆ Halifax (0422) 823722	Small but stylish, the well-operated little restaurant was created from 18th-century millworkers' cottages that stand beside the mill stream in the town centre. The cosy rooms include a first-floor reception lounge and a ground-floor dining room, where many original features have been retained in the effective modernisation. The charming surroundings are complemented by a relaxed, easy style of professional service, and French/international cuisine of a high standard of excellence is matched by a first-rate wine list.	Dinner td £15.50 Last dinner 9.30pm Credit cards [2] [3] Parking on premises Closed lunch, & Bank Hols

ROADE Northamptonshire Map 4 SP75

❀× **The Roadhouse** 16–8 High St ✆ (0604) 863372	Originally the village inn, the Roadhouse is now a cosy country restaurant, serving very good French country-style food at a realistic price. Fresh local produce, skilfully prepared, appears in such mouthwatering guises as chicken breasts stuffed with ginger in a light cream sauce or salmon and feta strudels in cider and raisin sauce, while desserts are equally tempting. Coffee and liqueurs, home-made petit four biscuits, a roaring log fire and the cheerful attention of young, friendly staff all encourage guests to linger pleasurably after their meal.	Dinner td fr £13 or alc £15 Last dinner 10pm Credit cards [1] [2] [3] Parking on premises Closed lst 2 wks Jan Closed lunch, & Sun

ROBERTSBRIDGE East Sussex Map 5 TQ72

×× **Trompe L'Oeil** 13 High St ✆ (0580) 880362	The smart little restaurant is decorated in pleasing, pastel shades and has a small cane-furnished bar for pre-dinner drinks. A range of fixed-price French menus (simplicite, gourmand and degustation) generally offers two choices for each course, and there is also a short à la carte selection. Cuisine is innovative, containing some surprisingly good combinations of	Lunch td £9.75 or alc £14 Dinner td £9.75 or alc Last dinner 10.30pm Credit cards [1]

	ingredients, such as the avocado, pink grapefruit and melon sorbet in hazlenut dressing of the assiette tendre, and the goose-liver served on edible flowers as foie gras frais aux fleurs.	[2] [3] [5] Parking on premises Closed 23–30 Dec & Bank Hols Closed lunch Oct-Apr, & Sun & Mon dinner

ROCKCLIFFE Dumfries and Galloway *Kirkcudbrightshire* Map 11 NX85

★★★ L **Baron's Craig** ✆ (055663) 225	This attractive baronial mansion, standing on high ground in a pretty little coastal village, offers good views of the Solway Firth and gentle shoreline walks in both directions. New and old are successfully blended in the lounges and bar, and modern bedrooms are as equally well-equipped as the original ones, though very much more compact. The dining room is rather regimental, but good honest food is served in a cheerful and well-organised way. An atmosphere of quiet tranquillity pervades the hotel, and you can really relax as you enjoy afternoon tea beside the open fire or idle in the well-tended gardens.	Price band C Bar lunch td fr £2 Lunch td fr £7 Dinner td fr £14.50 Last dinner 9pm Credit cards [1] [3] Parking on premises Closed mid Oct–Easter

ROGATE West Sussex Map 4 SU82

FH **Mizzards Farm** ✆ (073080) 656	This peacefully located 17th-century farmhouse, formerly the home of a famous pop star, now offers very good bed and breakfast accommodation. Three bedrooms, including one family room, all have private bathrooms and are equipped with amenities including CTV. Excellent farmhouse breakfasts are served in a most attractive dining room, which has a flagstone floor, a vaulted ceiling and an inglenook fireplace. No other meals are served. There is also a spacious, comfortable lounge. The farmhouse stands in 13 acres of gardens and farmland including a small lake, and there is also a covered, heated swimming pool. Owners Mr and Mrs Francis do not take children under six, or dogs.	Price band A/B Parking on premises Closed Xmas

ROMALDKIRK Co Durham Map 12 NY92

★★ B **Rose and Crown** (Village centre location) ✆ Teesdale (0833) 50213	This charming old coaching house is set at the centre of a delightful village, next to the ancient church of St Romald. It is attractively furnished throughout, all the comfortable bedrooms offering CTV and private facilities, while one of them has a four-poster bed. Very good food is served in both the dining room and the bars, where log fires burn in cold weather. The hotel makes an excellent base from which to tour beautiful Teesdale. Squash and clay pigeon shooting are available.	Price band B Bar lunch td £3.50–£4.25 or alc £5.50 Lunch td fr £3.50 or alc £6.50 Dinner td fr £12.75 Last dinner 9.30pm Credit cards [1] [2] [3] [5] Parking on premises

ROMILEY Greater Manchester Map 7 SJ99

× **Waterside**
166 Stockport Rd
✆ 061-430 4302

Set in a stone cottage at the side of the Lower Peak Canal, this bright, fresh and intimate little restaurant has been transformed over the last couple of years. Fresh flowers and candles enhance its relaxing atmosphere, and the delightful and interesting range of food on offer includes such dishes as chicken with prawns and duck with pineapple. All the food is freshly prepared, soups being particularly good, and you can make your choice from the three-course lunch or an à la carte menu. There is also a bistro in the basement.

Bistro lunch td £3.50
Dinner td £3.50 or alc £9.50
Last dinner 10pm
Credit cards [1] [2] [3]
Parking nearby
Closed 2 wks Feb, 2 wks Oct

ROSEDALE ABBEY North Yorkshire Map 8 SE79

★★ White Horse Farm
✆ Lastingham (07515) 239

In an idyllic setting overlooking the village, this hotel provides an ideal base for exploring the moors and dales, and the resident proprietors, with their friendly staff, will make every effort to ensure that guests enjoy their stay. Quaint bedrooms (all with en suite facilities and CTV) offer magnificent views of surrounding countryside, and there is an inviting residents' lounge with a well-stocked bookshelf. The residents' bar, however, tends to be neglected in favour of the character bar where the locals drink, and where a log fire crackles in colder weather. Dinner is the highlight of the day, offering both table d'hôte and à la carte menus. The four courses of the table d'hôte menu are, in fact, selections from the à la carte menu, and a good choice is offered for each course. You will find the home cooking and fresh vegetables that you would expect, but the food is by no means 'plain', for the range of starters includes mussels cooked in wine and prawn dishes, venison in red wine is a popular main course, and there is a mouthwatering array of such sweets as 'fruit crunch cream' and chocolate meringues. The wine list offers very good value, as does the extensive bar meal menu.

Price band B
Bar meal td £4.40–£10 or alc £6.50
Dinner td £14.50 or alc £18
Last dinner 9pm
Credit cards [2] [5]
Parking on premises
Closed 25 Dec

ROSS-ON-WYE Hereford and Worcester Map 3 SO62

GH **The Arches**
Walford Rd
✆ (0989) 63348

This attractive Georgian house has been tastefully modernised to provide comfortable accommodation, and its carefully tended garden is also appreciated by guests. Only one of the six bedrooms has en suite facilities, but all are well-maintained and very clean. A pleasant lounge overlooks the garden, and the small restaurant offers individually prepared meals such as lamb cutlets in Pernod or celery-stuffed ham with cheese sauce. The high standard of personal service is a token of the proprietors' twenty-year-long experience of catering for guests.

Price band A
Dinner, b&b £17.50–£20
Last dinner 7pm
Parking on premises
Closed Xmas & New Year

À la carte prices are based on an average for three courses without wine.

ROSTON Derbyshire Map 7 SK14

FH **Roston Hall** (6m SW of Ashbourne) ✆ Ellastone (033524) 287	This 90-acre arable farm, which also rears beef animals, is well-positioned as a base from which to tour the Peak District. The house, some parts of which date from the Elizabethan period, is mostly Georgian, and it was formerly the local manor. There are two enormous bedrooms which are ideal for family occupation. Both dining room and lounge, furnished with splendid antiques, are also very large. Ploughmans suppers are served 6–8pm. Children over 13 years old are welcome, but dogs are not allowed.	Price band A Parking on premises Closed Oct–Apr

ROTHERHAM South Yorkshire Map 8 SK49

★ **Elton Hotel** Main St, Bramley (Half a mile W of M18 junct 1—A631—turn R at traffic lights then L about a quarter mile—B6093) ✆ (0709) 545681	The hotel, a converted and adapted stone-built farmhouse near the centre of the village, offers a good-value four-course table d'hôte meal with a choice of four starters, soup, and five tempting main courses. A gourmet selection from the à la carte menu, though more expensive, covers a wide range of English and international cuisine and includes such dishes in the classic style as sole Florentine and tournedos Perigourdine. Appetising vegetarian dishes are also excellent value. There is a good appropriate wine list, staff are helpful, and the atmosphere is pleasant and relaxed. Overnight accommodation is at almost unbeatable rates, making a stay here an all-round bargain.	Price band B Bar lunch td 80p–£3.45 Lunch td fr £7.75 Dinner td £9.95 or alc £9–£12 Last dinner 9.30pm Credit cards [1] [2] [3] Parking on premises

ROWSLEY Derbyshire Map 8 SK26

★★★ BL **Peacock Hotel** ✆ Matlock (0629) 733518	Although the Peacock is now part of a large hotel group, it retains a charm and character of its own—due, partly, to the personal management style of Michael Gillson, who has run the hotel for many years. The beautifully preserved stone manor house dates from 1652. Furnishings and décor are tastefully in keeping with the beamed rooms and mullioned, leaded-light windows. The 14 bedrooms have recently been refurbished, each in its own individual style. All have good private facilities, CTV, radio and telephones. There are six more rooms, including family accommodation, in neighbouring Vernon House, and two self-catering properties are also available. A good choice of traditional English fare is offered from table d'hôte menus at both lunch and dinner. Bread is home-made from flour milled in the village, and eggs are free-range. Service is by professional, friendly and loyal staff, many of whom have been here a long time. The Peacock offers trout fishing on the Wye and the Derwent, and is within easy reach of Chatsworth, Hardwick Hall and the Peak District.	Price band C Bar lunch td fr £6 Lunch td fr £6 Dinner td fr £19 Last dinner 9pm Credit cards [1] [2] [3] [5] Parking on premises

RUCKHALL Hereford & Worcester Map 3 SO43

INN **Ancient Camp** ✆ Golden Valley (0981) 250449	An Iron Age camp provides a splendid, lofty setting for this increasingly popular inn overlooking the Wye valley. A private stretch of the river is available to	Price band B Snack lunch £6 Dinner alc £10

guests for coarse and game fishing. Excellent hospitality and a warm welcome are offered by the West family here: their attention to detail even extends to providing fresh milk, cream and lemon for tea and coffee in bedrooms. The three rooms are bright, clean and comfortable and all have private facilities. Meals are freshly prepared to order, using good-quality ingredients including fresh seasonal vegetables. The à la carte menu consists mainly of English dishes, and some quality wines are available, as well as traditional ales. Breakfasts are hearty and comprehensive, and everything is served in generous quantities.

Last dinner 10pm
Parking on premises

RUGBY Warwickshire Map 4 SP57

★★★ Grosvenor Hotel
9 Clifton Rd
✆ (0788) 535686

This former Victorian residence has been transformed with loving care to cater for the most discerning of clientele. A warm, sincere welcome prepares guests for the standard of traditional hospitality to be found here — not least in the luxurious restaurant, where a menu of light, modern-style dishes makes the most of fresh local ingredients and demonstrates the dedication and creativity of the chef. Stylish, individually designed bedrooms, all with en suite facilities, have a Victorian theme, but antique brass bedsteads and comfortable chesterfields exist side-by-side with such modern luxuries as the jacuzzi. Throughout the hotel, service is attentive, warm and cheerful.

Price band C
Bar lunch £1.95–£3.50
Lunch td fr £6.95 or alc £8.50
Dinner td £11.95 or alc £11.95
Last dinner 9.45pm
Credit cards [1] [2] [3] [5]
Parking on premises

RYE East Sussex Map 5 TQ92

FH **Cliff Farm**
Iden Lock
(2m NE of Rye on Military Rd)
✆ Iden (07978) 331

A six-acre smallholding with extensive views of Romney Marsh is the setting for this comfortable farmhouse. Free coarse fishing on the nearby River Rother is available to guests. Three prettily decorated, cosy bedrooms all have washbasins and share a shower room; there is no bathroom. Electric blankets, duvets and tea/coffee-making facilities are provided in rooms, and one of the rooms is suitable for families. CTV is available in the small lounge, which also has a wood-burning stove. Breakfast is served in a pretty, cottage-style dining room. No other meals are served, but nearby Rye has a good variety of eating places.

Price band A
Parking on premises
Closed Nov–Feb

★★ Broomhill Lodge
Rye Foreign
(2m NW of Rye on A268)
✆ (07978) 421

Amenities at this comfortable country house overlooking farmland near Rye include a sauna, a solarium sauna, and a full-size snooker table. Bedrooms all have private facilities and are fresh, clean and tastefully furnished. On the ground floor are an elegant lounge where a cheering coal fire burns in winter, a small bar and a restaurant, prettily decorated in pastel shades, where good home cooking is served.

Price band C
Bar lunch £1–£6.95
Last dinner 9.30pm
Credit cards [1] [3] [5]
Parking on premises

× **Flushing Inn**
Market St
✆ (0797) 223292

Rye Bay plaice is one of many enjoyable fish specialities at this cosy restaurant in a 15th-century inn near the church. Our Inspector commends the fresh, home-made food here — especially the soups, pâtés and fruit pies. Some fine wines are featured on the

Bar lunch td £6–£8
Lunch td fr £8 or alc £14
Dinner td fr £12

extensive wine list. Vegetarians can be catered for. The Mann family, proprietors here for over 20 years, provide careful, professional service and cultivate an informal, homely atmosphere. Polished tables and gleaming silverware make the beamed restaurant look well-cared for, and one entire wall is covered by a remarkable 16th-century wall painting. The small bar next to the dining room has open fires in winter. Set lunch menus start at around £8 and represent excellent value. Not surprisingly, the Flushing Inn is very popular with both visitors and local residents, so booking is always advisable.

Last dinner 9.15pm
Credit cards [1] [2] [3] [5]
No parking on premises
Closed 1st 2 wks Jan, 2nd & 3rd wk Jun
Closed Tue, & Mon dinner

× **Landgate Bistro**
5-6 Landgate
✆ (0797) 222829

Straightforward but well-executed British cooking is the mainstay of this unassuming bistro. Fresh local produce featured on the à la carte menu includes guinea fowl, rabbit, fish, wild duck and jugged hare. Vegetarian meals can be provided. Service is uncomplicated and cheerful, as is the décor: fresh white paintwork is complemented by black-and-white photographs, plants, and oiled tablecloths. Taped jazz music and candlelight in the evening add to a pleasantly relaxed atmosphere. There is a small bar for aperitifs. The restaurant has a well-established local following, so booking is advisable.

Dinner alc £10
Last dinner 9.30pm
Credit cards [1] [2] [3] [5]
Parking nearby
Closed 20–9 Dec, 1 wk Jun & 2 wks Aug
Closed lunch, & Sun & Mon

SAFFRON WALDEN Essex Map 5 TL53

★★ **Saffron Hotel**
10-8 High St
✆ (0799) 22676
Tx 81653

This 16th-century hotel near the town centre has been tastefully renovated to provide modern comforts, but retains much of its historic charm. Views of the pretty courtyard at its centre are a feature of the restaurant, where carefully prepared dishes may be chosen from an extensive menu. Bar snacks are also available. The hotel has 22 bedrooms, varying in size and character but mostly modernised to a high standard. About half the rooms have private facilities, and all have CTV and telephones. There is one four-poster room. Room prices include Continental breakfast.

Price band C
Bar lunch £1.50–£7.50 or alc £4
Lunch td £12.95 or alc £14
Dinner td £12.45 or alc £14
Last dinner 9.30pm
Credit cards [1] [3]
Limited parking on premises
Accommodation only 25–30 Dec

ST AGNES Cornwall Map 2 SW75

GH **Porthvean Hotel**
Churchtown
✆ (087255) 2581

This former hostelry in the centre of the village offers country-style bedrooms and relaxed good eating. Geoff and Frin Robinson have been proprietors here some 10 years, and offer a friendly welcome and homely accommodation. Five of the seven bedrooms have private shower rooms, and three are suitable for families. The small first-floor lounge has a television, and there is a well-stocked bar/lounge with a cheery log fire in winter. Appealing menus for breakfast, lunch and dinner are offered in Frin's Restaurant. Kedgeree, hog's pudding and smoked haddock enliven the hearty breakfast menu. The à la carte lunch and dinner menu is supplemented by dishes of the day,

Price band A/B
Dinner alc £8.50
Last dinner 9pm
Credit cards [1] [3]
Parking on premises
Closed Xmas & Jan

which are listed on a blackboard. A wide choice of hot and cold starters includes interesting items such as walnut pâté, or mussels in garlic butter, as well as some traditional favourites. Main courses are chosen from a selection of pizzas, pasta or rice dishes or traditional fare. Vegetarians are very well-catered for.

ST AUSTELL Cornwall Map 2 SX05

★★ ♣♣ HL
Boscundle Manor
Tregreham
(2m E of St Austell off A390)
✆ Par (072681) 3557

Proprietors Andrew and Mary Flint describe their 18th-century manor house as a 'restaurant with rooms which is run like a luxurious private house'. They have steadily improved and developed the property since they came here 10 years ago, and now run their business themselves, with Mary as chef and Andrew at front of house. Accommodation comprises nine bedrooms, two of which are in a cottage in the garden. All have private facilities (some have spa or jacuzzi baths), CTV and telephones, and are furnished with antiques ranging from simple stripped pine to handsome mahogany pieces. Amenities at Boscundle Manor include an exercise room with keep-fit equipment, a heated outdoor swimming pool and a croquet lawn. Beyond the garden are seven acres of secluded grounds featuring the ruins of a 17th-century tin mine, Wheal Eliza. The restaurant at Boscundle Manor (open to non-residents by prior arrangement except on Sundays) features fresh produce in season, much of it from Cornwall. The fixed-price three-course dinner menu usually offers a choice of several imaginative dishes for each course, and is supplemented by an extensive wine list. Vegetarian and other special diets can be catered for. Breakfast is served in the conservatory overlooking the delightful garden.

Price band C
Dinner td £16
Last dinner 9.30pm
Credit cards [1] [2] [3]
Parking on premises
Closed Nov-Feb
Closed lunch

★★★★ H **Carlyon Bay Hotel**
Sea Rd, Carlyon Bay
✆ (072681) 2304
Tx 42551

This large holiday hotel stands high on the cliffs, with splendid views of the Cornish Riviera. Its 250-acre grounds include an 18-hole golf course and even a helipad. The hotel offers a wealth of other leisure amenities including outdoor and indoor heated swimming pools, tennis courts, a children's play area and amusements, as well as a games room with two full-size snooker tables. All 74 spacious, comfortable bedrooms have private bathrooms, CTV, radio and telephones. Many have sea views, and family rooms are available. Children are well-catered for. A full restaurant service is offered, and room service is readily available. Entertainment includes dancing at least two nights a week throughout the year, and the hotel runs a special Christmas programme. Bargain breaks are offered at most times of the year, except during school summer holidays.

Price band C
Bar lunches £1–£4
Lunch td £7.76
Dinner td fr £11.50 or alc £13
Last dinner 9pm
Credit cards [1] [2] [3] [5]
Parking on premises

> À la carte prices are based on an average for three courses without wine.

ST CLEARS Dyfed Map 2 SN21

★★ B **Forge Restaurant and Motel** (E of St Clears on A40) ✆ (0994) 230300	Convenient for travellers on the A40, this small motel has 10 bedrooms, each with its own external front door and private bathroom. Rooms are well-appointed and equipped with CTV, telephones and tea/coffee-making equipment. Two of the rooms will accommodate families. Meals are served in a separate, large restaurant which specialises in grills. There is an outdoor heated swimming pool in the grounds, which guests are free to use during the summer. Vegetarian meals are available.	Price band B Lunch alc £7.50 Dinner alc £9 Last dinner 9.30pm Credit cards [1] [2] [3] Parking on premises Closed Xmas

ST IVES Cornwall Map 2 SW54

★★ **The Cornwallis** Headland Rd, Carbis Bay ✆ Penzance (0736) 795294 Tx 946240 CWEASY G quoting Easilink No 19022265	This friendly, holiday hotel overlooking Carbis Bay offers a good range of leisure activies and is ideal for families. Amenities include a heated outdoor swimming pool and a fitness centre with jacuzzi, sauna and solarium. The hotel is popular for its activity holidays, which include golf, bowls, bridge, birdwatching and painting, and a snooker tournament is held in the autumn. There is dancing or entertainment every evening in season. Food at the Cornwallis is likely to suit most tastes: the well-balanced five-course set dinner menu features mostly traditional fare, with an adequate choice, and represents good value. Local produce, including seafood, is a speciality. Public rooms include two lounges, a library (with pool table) and a bar, where lunch-time snacks are served. The 10 modern annexe bedrooms, all with private bathrooms, are all of a very high standard, while the 12 rooms in the main hotel (eight with private facilities) are smaller but have more character. There are several family rooms (cots and high chairs are available), and all rooms have CTV, radio/intercom and telephones. Dogs are not accepted.	Price band B Bar lunch £2.50 Dinner td £8.75 Last dinner 9pm Credit cards [1] [2] [3] [5] Parking on premises Closed Jan & Feb
GH **Dean Court Hotel** Trelyon Ave ✆ Penzance (0736) 796023	Views of the harbour and bay, as well as hearty, traditional home cooking, can be enjoyed in the dining room of this stone-built hotel which is run with dedication by Roger and Mary Dean. Mrs Dean is never happier than when she is cooking, and guests return year after year for her tempting roasts and mouthwatering fruit pies with clotted cream. Dean Court has 12 bedrooms, all with private facilities, CTV, radios and hairdriers, and with views of either woodland or the sea. Public rooms include a television lounge and a bar. No children or dogs are accepted.	Price band B Dinner, b&b £23–£31 Last dinner 6.30pm Parking on premises Closed Nov-Mar
GH **Old Vicarage Hotel** Parc-an-Creet ✆ Penzance (0736) 796124	Tucked away in secluded wooded grounds on the western edge of the town, this modernised 19th-century rectory retains its Victorian style. The dining room and bar have interesting period bric-à-brac, and there is a comfortable lounge with a television, as well as a library. The eight bedrooms include several large family rooms. Children of all ages are welcome, and children's tea is served at 5pm. Some rooms have private facilities and CTV. The hotel enjoys a good	Price band A Dinner £7.50 Last dinner 6.45pm Credit cards [1] [3] Parking on premises Closed Nov-Dec

	reputation for its food. Four-course dinners are imaginative and reasonably priced; a typical meal might be Stilton and walnut mousse, haddock Wellington, and pineapple with kirsch and clotted cream. Packed lunches are available.	Closed lunch, & Wed dinner

ST JUST Cornwall Map 2 SW33

GH **Boscean Country Hotel** ✆ Penzance (0736) 788748	Almost three acres of walled grounds, including a croquet lawn and putting green, surround this stylish Edwardian residence, which overlooks Cape Cornwall. Public rooms feature handsome oak panelling and are mostly furnished in keeping with the period of the house. All nine bedrooms, several with sea views, have private facilities and comfortable furnishings. There are 3 family rooms. Home-cooked fresh food, in generous quantities, is an important part of a stay here, and produce is sometimes home-grown. Vegetarian and other special diets can be catered for. Proprietors Joyce and Roy Lee pride themselves on the friendly, informal atmosphere of their hotel. They hold a residential licence, and there is a bar.	Price band A Dinner, b&b £19–£20 Last dinner 7pm Parking on premises Closed Nov–Feb Closed lunch

ST JUST-IN-ROSELAND Cornwall Map 2 SW83

GH **Rose-da-Mar Hotel** ✆ St Mawes (0326) 270450	Fine views over the River Fal are a feature of this attractive little hotel, which has a pretty garden. Five of the eight comfortable bedrooms have private facilities, and there is one family room, though children under 11 are not accepted. All meals (served to residents only) are freshly prepared in the hotel kitchen. The lounge is spacious and has CTV, and there is also a convivial little bar. Friendly service is provided by the resident proprietors.	Price band A/B Dinner, b&b £23.73–£28.14 Last dinner 7pm Parking on premises Closed Nov–Mar

ST MARY'S LOCH Borders *Selkirkshire* Map 11 NT22

INN **Tibbie Shiels** (A708 midway between Selkirk and Moffat) ✆ Cappercleuch (0750) 42231	Steeped in history, this authentic, enthusiastically run Scottish inn takes its name from the original innkeeper, who played hostess to such notable travellers as Scott, Stevenson and James Hogg. Accommodation is simple and homely, with a great deal of character, and most of the neat, attractively decorated bedrooms are on the ground floor. The cosy little bar offers real ale in first-class condition (the proprietor being an enthusiast!) and a wide range of reasonably priced, home-cooked dishes, both Scottish and international in flavour, is available in the dining room. Situated on the strip of land between St Mary's Loch and Loch of the Lowes, and passed by the Southern Grand Way, the inn is a favourite with both locals and tourists, particularly with fishermen and ramblers.	Price band A Bar lunch £3.50–£4 or alc fr £4.50 Dinner td fr £3.50 Last dinner 8.20pm–9.20pm Credit cards [1] [3] Parking on premises Closed Nov–Jan (residents) Bar closed 25 Dec

ST MAWES Cornwall Map 2 SW83

★★ **Rising Sun** ✆ (0326) 270233	The friendly new owners and their staff at this charming small hotel a few yards from the harbour have worked hard at redecoration and refurnishing, and public rooms are now very stylish — especially	Price band B Bar lunch 85p–£2.50 Lunch td £6.50

the restaurant, which is a delight. Food is good, too: the skills of the chefs are apparent everywhere, from the fresh rolls to the imaginative main courses, such as sea trout with capers and almonds or fillet steak with cream and peppercorns. First courses might be crab terrine, carrot and orange soup, or chicken liver mousse. Local fish features prominently, and vegetables are lightly cooked and delicious. Bar snacks are served at lunch-times. The hotel has 13 bedrooms, seven of them with private bathrooms. More rooms are available in a cottage opposite the hotel. All rooms have CTV.

(Sun)
Dinner td £11
Last dinner 9pm
Credit cards [1] [2] [3] [5]
Limited parking on premises

SALCOMBE Devon Map 3 SX73

★★★ H **Soar Mill Cove Hotel**
Soar Mill Cove, Marlborough
(3m W of Salcombe off A381)
✆ Kingsbridge (0548) 561566

This stylish hotel is skilfully designed on a single level, and with much use of local stone and slate, to blend into its magnificent surroundings — a stretch of National Trust coastline with a sandy bay. Most of the 14 bedrooms have patio doors opening onto a private sun terrace. All rooms are furnished and decorated to a high standard, and have private bathrooms and CTV. Two will accommodate families. The hotel's leisure facilities include a recently built indoor swimming pool, grass tennis courts, a putting green and a games room. Proprietors the Makepeace family are personally very much involved in running their hotel, including the all-important catering side of things (the hotel even runs its own cookery courses). Imaginatively prepared meals use the best of West Country produce in both traditional and modern dishes. Crabs and lobsters (a speciality) are caught in the bay.

Price band C
Bar lunch td fr £4 or alc £6
Lunch td fr £8.50 or alc £10
Dinner td fr £19 or alc £20
Last dinner 9pm
Credit cards [1] [3]
Parking on premises
Closed 29 Dec-19 Feb

★★★ HBL
Tides Reach
South Sands
✆ (054884 3466)

This secluded waterside hotel enjoys a lovely setting in a sandy cove, and offers guests comfort, friendly but efficient service, and a commendable range of sport and leisure facilities. These include a very attractive indoor swimming pool, squash courts, a gymnasium, a health spa, and a games room with a snooker table. Many of the 42 bedrooms overlook the estuary, where guests can swim, fish or sail. Bedrooms — especially the newer ones — are spacious and luxurious, with pretty décor, and amenities such as CTV and telephones. There are several family suites, but the hotel does not take children under eight. Comfortable public rooms include a cool, airy restaurant overlooking the water and the garden. Here service is professional and food good, with a strong emphasis on locally caught, fresh fish.

Price band C
Bar lunch td £1.15–£11.50
Dinner td £14.50 or alc £18
Last dinner 10pm
Credit cards [1] [2] [3] [5]
Parking on premises
Closed Dec–Feb

SAXELBY Leicestershire Map 8 SK62

FH **Manor House Farm**
✆ Melton Mowbray (0664) 812269

Set in a peaceful corner of the village, near the church, this lovely old farmhouse is a particular favourite of our Inspector's. Parts of the house date back as far as the 12th century, and much of the rest is 15th-century. Uneven floors, massive timbers and a lovely old staircase will enchant guests interested in historic

Price band A
Dinner, b&b £15.50
Last dinner 7pm
Parking on premises

buildings. There are three letting bedrooms including two family rooms. The proprietors are friendly and capable; Mrs Morris is a sound cook and dinner will usually be based on farm produce and home-grown vegetables. (Please order dinner by noon.) Roasts are very popular, and other traditional English dishes sometimes feature on the menu. Meals are likely to finish with Stilton cheese made at a dairy in the village. Manor House Farm has its own dairy herd, sheep and the usual farm pets, and arrangements can be made for pony-riding. An unusual attraction for railway enthusiasts is British Rail's test track for the Advanced Passenger Train, which is adjacent to the farmland. Trains still make occasional trips, and the Morrises will make enquiries on behalf of interested guests.

Closed Nov–Mar

SCARBOROUGH North Yorkshire Map 8 TA08

★★ 🏠 L **Wrea Head Country House Hotel**
Scalby
(3 miles NW of A171)
✆ (0723) 378211

This charming country house hotel is situated in wooded grounds and gardens, within easy reach of both Scarborough and the attractions of the North Yorkshire National Park. Public areas are full of character, and this is particularly true of the panelled hall lounge with its inglenook fireplace where a fire blazes in winter. All twenty bedrooms have private facilities and CTV. The fixed-price four-course dinner menu offers a good choice of dishes — smoked brown trout, roast duckling and lemon syllabub, for example — or there is a short à la carte menu. Pets are made welcome here, and there is stabling and grazing for horses.

Price band B
Bar lunch £4.50
Lunch alc £6.50
Dinner alc £10.75
Last dinner 9pm
Credit cards 1 2 3 5
Parking on premises

ISLES OF SCILLY
ST MARYS

★★ **Tregarthens**
Hugh Town
✆ Scillonia (0720) 22540

This popular hotel, set in small terraced gardens overlooking the harbour and coastline, has been extensively refurbished in recent years. In the tastefully decorated restaurant, which commands a view of the sea, guests may choose from a comprehensive fixed-price menu of interesting and well-prepared English and French dishes, including a range of excellent sweets. Vegetarian food is available. The lounge is comfortable, light and well-appointed, and the 33 bedrooms, many of which have private facilities, are being refurbished to a good standard. All bedrooms have CTV and telephones, and five are family rooms. Dogs are not accepted. The hotel, under the friendly and helpful direction of managers Mr and Mrs Chantry, has a particularly pleasing atmosphere.

Price band C (dinner inc)
Bar lunch td fr £1.50–£4.50
Lunch td £7
Dinner td fr £12
Last dinner 8pm
Credit cards 1 2 3 5
No parking on premises
Closed Nov-mid Mar

TRESCO

❀★★★ HB **Island Hotel**
✆ Scillonia (0720) 22883

It would be difficult to find a more peaceful island than Tresco, whose spectacular rocky coast is the setting for this relaxing hotel. Modernised to a good standard, it provides a comfortable lounge and bar and a light restaurant with huge windows overlooking the sea. The hotel is noted for its good food,

Price band C
Bar lunch £1.30–£5
Lunch alc £10
Dinner td £17
Last dinner

particularly seafood, which is presented on a fixed-price menu. The excellent Sunday evening cold buffet should not be missed. Managers John and Wendy Pyatt are charming hosts who, along with their courteous staff, offer fine hospitality. The hotel has attractive gardens and a heated open-air swimming pool, and guests can enjoy fishing, bowls and croquet. Most of the 32 bedrooms have a private bathroom and CTV, and all have telephones. Facilities for children are available; dogs are not accepted.

8.15pm
No parking on premises
Closed mid Oct-mid Mar

NEW GRIMSBY

★★ **New Inn**
✆ Scillonia (0720) 22844

Standing close to the harbour and a sandy beach, this old granite-built inn is recommended for its delightful informal atmosphere, friendly hospitality and cosy accommodation. It has 12 recently refurbished bedrooms, including three family rooms, 10 of which have private facilities. There is a small but comfortable residents' lounge and a larger public bar which is a popular rendezvous for locals, fishermen and tourists. The charming restaurant serves a choice of imaginative and nicely presented dishes from a fixed-price menu, and lobster can be enjoyed fresh from the sea if ordered in advance. Vegetarian meals are available. The hotel has its own heated outdoor swimming pool. Dogs are not allowed.

Price band C (inc dinner)
Bar lunch £3.75–£5.75
Dinner td fr £13.50
Last dinner 8.30pm
No parking on premises
Closed mid Oct-mid Nov
Open weekends only mid Nov-mid Mar

SCOTCH CORNER North Yorkshire Map 8 NZ20

INN **Vintage**
(150 yards W on A66 at AIM junct)
✆ Richmond (0748) 2961 or 4424

Though set on the A66 only a few yards from the A1, the Vintage Inn offers attractive views of the surrounding countryside, and you can be sure of both a warm welcome and attentive service throughout your stay. Small but cosy bedrooms have been carefully fitted to maximise space and ensure comfort; five of them have private facilities, and all have CTV and tea-making equipment. A rustic-style bar-lounge and sitting room have been tastefully furnished to create a relaxing atmosphere. The bar meal menu, available at both lunch and dinner, is extensive and offers exceptional value, while the restaurant's lunch-time table d'hôte and evening à la carte selections are equally competitively priced; the wine list, too, offers superb value.

Price band B
Bar lunch £1.95–£4.25
Lunch td fr £6.95 or alc £11.50
Dinner td fr £9.75 or alc £11.50
Last dinner 9.15pm
Credit cards 1 3
Parking on premises
Closed 25 Dec & 1 Jan

SEAHOUSES Northumberland Map 12 NU23

★★ H
Beach House
✆ Seahouses (0665) 720337

This friendly, family-run hotel stands on the sea-front, with views across to the Farne Islands. The proprietors offer a warm welcome to guests, whose happiness is considered at every turn. There are two very comfortable lounges, both overlooking the sea and providing an excellent atmosphere for relaxation, while the entrance hall doubles as reception and bar. The cosy, compact bedrooms all have en suite facilities, CTV, hairdriers and a host of little extras.

Price band B
Lunch td fr £4
Dinner td fr £11.75
Last dinner 8.0pm
Credit cards 1 3
Parking on

	Dinner offers sound, well-cooked dishes and is very good value.	premises Closed mid Nov-mid Mar
★★ **Olde Ship** (In Harbour) ☏ (0655) 720200	The Olde Ship stands in an elevated position overlooking the harbour, and its interior aptly carries through the maritime theme. Both the public bar and the coctail bar feature a wealth of marine bric-à-brac — and the former also boasts a fair number of old fishermen, who enjoys enthralling visitors with their tales. Bedrooms, most of which have private facilities, are small but cosy, equipped with tea/coffee-making utensils and CTV. There are two comfortable lounges, one of which adjoins the dining room where both lunch and dinner feature traditional Northumbrian fare.	Price band A/B Bar lunch £1.10–£2 Dinner td £7.50 Last dinner 8pm Parking on premises Closed Nov–Easter

SEATHWAITE Cumbria Map 7 SD29

Newfield Inn (Take the A595 west out of Broughton-in-Furness. Just before a sharp bend turn R down a narrow road signed Ulpha. It is situated about five miles on the R) ☏ Broughton-in-Furness (06576) 208	Nestling in this charming village is a delightful little restaurant consisting of two rooms, both with open fires. One, in lounge style, takes table reservations, while the second, slate-floored and less formal, is ideal for walkers and climbers. The excellent, value-for-money food includes such items as home-made soup, prawns, trout and cheese and onion flan; steaks are particularly good — large tender and full of flavour, served with salad and plenty of chips — and there is a tempting selection of puddings. The menu is supplemented by several daily 'specials' and accompanied by a short wine list.	Lunch/dinner alc £5 Last dinner 9pm Parking on premises

SEDGEFIELD Co Durham Map 8 NZ32

INN **Dun Cow** High St ☏ (0740) 20894	Bright with window boxes and hanging baskets, the charming old village inn on the main street has lost none of its character in the recent modernisation. Old bric-à-brac abounds in the two bar lounges, and the charming dining room with its chunky stone walls and polished floor displays a wealth of brass and pewter against its beams. Bedrooms are attractive, their warm red carpet an effective contrast to the roughcast walls and ceilings, and all have CTV and many thoughtful extras — a basket of fresh fruit, for example, and the hot chocolate and soup mixes provided in addition to the ususal tea and coffee. The bathrooms awaken memories of a bygone age, with their polished brass pipes and taps shining against expanses of wood. In the dining room, fresh food in traditional style is served, both as specialities from the chargrill and on the dinner menu, while an extensive range of bar foods offers very good value.	Price band B Bar lunch £1.30–£9.40 Lunch td fr £6.50 or alc £9 Dinner td fr £7.70 or alc £12.50 Last dinner 10pm Credit cards 1 2 3 5 Parking on premises

SEDLESCOMBE East Sussex Map 5 TQ71

×× **Holmes House** ☏ (042487) 450	Paintings by local artists help set the scene at this 15th-century cottage restaurant overlooking the village green. The small bar and beamed dining room are furnished with antiques, and the atmosphere is welcoming and unpretentious. Cooking is by the	Lunch td £9 or alc £14 Dinner alc £18 Last dinner 9pm Credit cards 1

proprietor, Frank Fleischer, who takes a personal interest in his customers' enjoyment. Set menus are reasonably priced and sometimes include welcome touches of luxury such as fresh lobster. Many more fish dishes appear on the à la carte menu, which also features some good old English favourities like steak and kidney pudding. Service is friendly and pleasant. A small outdoor swimming pool is available for customers' use.

[2] [3] [5]
No parking on premises
Closed Mon, & Sat lunch & Sun dinner

SELBORNE Hants Map 4 SU73

Bush House
The Street
✆ (042050) 339

Set at the foot of the zig-zag in Gilbert White's village, Bush House is a teashop with much to commend it — not least its relaxed atmosphere and tolerant attitude towards muddy walking shoes! It occupies several rooms, sharing one with a bric-à-brac shop, or you can eat in the flower-filled garden. In winter, a large log fire burns in the main room with its polished tables and willow pattern china. The menu always features steak, quiches and salads, together with a daily 'special', but the major attraction is the excellent Sunday lunch, costing £3.50 for a vast plate of roast beef or pork with four or five fresh vegetables; home-made starters and sweets each cost £1. In summer, afternoon tea on the vine-covered terrace is tempting, with such traditional favourites as egg-and-cress sandwiches and a range of home-made cakes.

Lunch alc fr £5.50
Last meal 5.15pm
Parking nearby

SETTLE North Yorkshire Map 7 SD86

★★★
Falcon Manor
Skipton Rd (On A65 on edge of town)
✆ (07292) 3814

This impressive building stands on the A65, in its own grounds and set against a background of craggy fells. Privately run, it offers guests good, honest hospitality, accommodation being provided in bedrooms furnished with all the home comforts. Guests can take their ease in pleasant lounges and bars, while well-cooked meals are served in the attractive, spacious restaurant. Vegetarian meals are available. The situation of the hotel makes it ideal for exploring and touring the lovely Yorkshire Dales.

Price band C
Bar lunch td 95p–£8 or alc £3.75
Lunch td fr £4.80 or alc £5.50
Dinner td £10.50 or alc £15
Last dinner 9.30pm
Credit cards [1] [2] [5]
Parking on premises

★★ B **Royal Oak**
Market Place
✆ (07292) 2561

The Royal Oak, originally built in 1684, stands in the centre of this bustling little market town. The charming family who own and run it ensure that guests are well-cared for, providing excellent menus in the lovely oak-panelled restaurant and an extensive range of bar meals in the comfortable bar-lounge. Bedrooms, too, are very comfortably furnished, and a great deal of attention has gone into their design. The beautiful Yorkshire Dales are within easy reach, so this makes an ideal base for touring.

Price band B
Bar lunch £1.05–£6.55
Lunch td fr £6
Dinner td fr £7.25 or alc £9
Last dinner 10pm
Parking on premises
Closed dinner 25 Dec

SHAFTESBURY Dorset Map 3 ST82

★★ L **Grove House Hotel**
Ludwell (2m W of Shaftesbury on A30)
✆ Donhead (074788) 365

Diane and Bill Baker have expended much time and energy on improvements since they took over this small hotel in 1985. Diane, a former college lecturer in home economics and catering, does the cooking with care and enthusiasm. Fresh local produce is used in all her meals, which are mainly Continental or traditional British in style. Bill spent many years working with the public as a detective sergeant in the Thames Valley Police Force, and is now a superb host. The hotel is friendly and comfortable; two lounges (one for non-smokers) are supplemented by a small, character bar, and there is an attractive dining room. The 11 bedrooms (including two family rooms) have modern furnishings and good facilities including bath or shower en suite. There is a good garden, and the hotel backs onto open fields. Be careful not to miss the entrance to the car park, which is through the arch. The hotel does not take children under five.

Price band B
Lunch (by arrangement)
Dinner td £10.50
Last dinner 8.30pm
Credit cards [1] [3]
Parking on premises
Closed last 3 wks Jan

SHAP Cumbria Map 12 NY51

GH **Brookfield**
✆ (09316) 397

You will be well-looked after in this cheerful house with its warm, friendly atmosphere. The comfortable, homely lounge, bright with fresh flowers and plants, is a pleasant place in which to relax in front of the television, and neat, clean bedrooms have attractive soft furnishings. A well-appointed restaurant with good linen, china and cutlery, serves imaginative home-cooked meals and is open to non-residents for dinner (by advance booking only).

Price band A
Dinner td £9.50
Last dinner 8.30pm
Parking on premises
Closed Jan

SHEARSBY Leicestershire Map 4 SP69

FH **Wheathill Farm**
Church Ln
✆ Peatling Magna (053758) 663

Peaceful Shearsby village, well off the A50 with its constant traffic, is the setting for this lovely old farmhouse. Parts of the house are believed to date back to Saxon times. Most is obviously more recent, but even so the bowed walls, sloping floors, beams and stone inglenook fireplace suggest several centuries of habitation. There are three bedrooms, one of which has a private shower and one a washbasin. Farmhouse food in abundance is provided by Mrs Timms. Home-produced milk, free-range eggs, beef and pork from the farm and vegetables from the garden are her raw materials. Roasts and pies are the general style, but she also enjoys preparing vegetarian dishes. Dinner should be ordered in the morning if required. Dogs are not accepted at the farm.

Price band A
Dinner, b&b £15–£15.50
Last dinner 6.30pm
Parking on premises
Closed Xmas

> The price band indicates the price of bed and breakfast for a single person or room. Price band A = £15 or less; price band B = £16–£30; price band C = £31–£50; price band D = more than £50.

SHEFFIELD South Yorkshire Map 8 SK38

★★★ B
Charnwood
10 Sharrow Ln
(1 mile from City Centre, junct London Road and Abbeydale Road)
✆ (0742) 589411

This delightful mansion, built about 1780, offers accommodation in 21 comfortable and very well-appointed bedrooms, all of which have private bathrooms and every modern amenity. The character of the original house has been maintained and is nowhere more in evidence than in the candle-lit Georgian restaurant, where excellent meals are served by a courteous staff. The table d'hôte and à la carte menus, both frequently changed, contain dishes in the light, modern style as well as traditional French cuisine, while the range of sweets spans both bread-and-butter pudding and vanilla bombe filled with orange sorbet.

Price band C
Lunch td fr £7.25 or alc £14
Dinner td fr £8.95 or alc £14
Last dinner 10pm
Credit cards [1] [2] [3] [5]
Parking on premises

SHEPTON MALLET Somerset Map 3 ST64

× **Blostin's**
29 Waterloo Rd
✆ (0749) 3648

The atmosphere is pleasant and relaxed at this popular little bistro-style restaurant on the edge of the town centre. Blackboard menus change daily and feature lots of fresh produce in season. Our Inspector thought the two set-price menus particularly good value, but there is an à la carte selection as well. Fresh fish is always available: sometimes Cornish squid, sometimes salmon or perhaps plaice. Various chicken dishes are among the range of main courses, and there are also dishes using pork, beef and veal. Vegetables are very good, and standards of cooking and presentation are generally high. Service is friendly and usually prompt.

Lunch td £6.95
Dinner td fr £9.95 or alc £13.95
Last dinner 9.30pm
Credit cards [1] [3] [5]
Closed Sun, Mon, & Sat lunch

INN **King's Arms**
Leg Sq
✆ (0749) 3781

Quietly situated, but conveniently close to the town centre, this 17th-century inn offers bed and breakfast accommodation in three comfortably furnished bedrooms equipped with washbasins and TV. There is a spacious lounge on the first floor, and the kitchen offers a good choice of fresh food, which is available either as bar snacks or in a small, pleasant dining area. Children under 10 are not accepted.

Price band A
Bar lunch fr £2.50
Last meal 9.30pm
Parking on premises
Closed Xmas
Closed bar food Sun evening

SHERBORNE Dorset Map 3 ST61

★★ B **Half Moon**
Half Moon St
✆ (0935) 812017

Our Inspector particularly recommends the Half Moon for its carvery, available at both lunch and dinner here in the heart of this pleasant old town. The dining room is attractive and service pleasant. Good snacks are also served, in the large lounge-bar, and vegetarians can be catered for. The hotel has 15 modern, fully fitted bedrooms, all with private bathrooms, CTV and telephones. Two of the rooms will accommodate families. Excellent-value weekend bargain breaks are available. The hotel does not take dogs (except guide dogs).

Price band B
Bar lunch 85p–£2.50
Lunch/dinner td fr £6.35 or alc £8.35
Last dinner 10pm
Credit cards [1] [2] [3] [5]
Parking on premises

SHIPSTON-ON-STOUR Warwickshire Map 4 SP24

×× **Old Mill**
✆ (0608) 61880

In a beautifully restored 17th-century water mill on the banks of the River Stour, two young couples work

Bar lunch £2.25–£7.50

together to provide fine food and friendly, informal service. Here, guests are assured of a warm welcome and can look forward to a country-style meal of a very high standard, where good presentation makes the most of fresh ingredients. One memorable feature of the menu is the 'Catch of the Day', featuring the freshest fish available, and the particularly well-prepared vegetables are also worthy of note. There are five extremely pleasant bedrooms, and the agreeable atmosphere of the Old Mill will certainly make a stay here an attractive proposition.

Lunch td fr £10.50 or alc £15
Dinner td £13 or alc £15.50
Last dinner 9.15pm
Credit cards [1] [2] [3] [5]
Limited parking on premises
Closed Sun dinner

INN **White Bear**
High St
✆ (0608) 61558

This fine, family-run inn has the warm, cheerful atmosphere that is so much a part of the great British tradition. Its small, cosy restaurant has rapidly gained a reputation for excellence with a menu of imaginative dishes, skilfully prepared. The range of home-made bar meals — accompanied by a good choice of real ales — is equally popular: soups, stews and casseroles are all tasty, wholesome and hearty creations. Quaint, individually decorated bedrooms are delightful, with charming floral fabrics and wallpapers.

Price band B
Bar lunch £1.60–£4.50
Dinner alc £10.50
Last dinner 9.30pm
Credit cards [1] [2] [3] [5]
Parking on premises
Closed Bank Hols

SHREWSBURY Shropshire Map 7 SJ41

★★★★
Albrighton Hall
Albrighton (3m N of Shrewsbury on A528)
✆ Bomere Heath (0939) 291000
Tx 35726

This historic hall in a fine country setting is now a very comfortable hotel. Bedrooms are splendidly furnished, all with en suite facilities, and there is one particularly sumptuous suite. Six of the rooms have four-poster beds. The restaurant offers well-cooked, attractively presented food, chosen from a very extensive menu. Our Inspector comments that 'portions are for trenchermen, not those brought up on nouvelle cuisine'. The sweet trolley 'will cause slimmers to despair'! Flambé dishes are prepared with a suitable flourish, and service, by a team of mostly Italian staff, is friendly and attentive.

Price band C
Lunch td £7 or alc £9
Dinner alc £12
Last dinner 10.30pm
Credit cards [1] [2] [3] [5]
Parking on premises

GH **Fieldside Hotel**
38 London Rd (1½ m SE of town centre on A5112)
✆ (0743) 53143

Good, comfortable accommodation suitable for tourists or business travellers can be found at this large mid-Victorian house. Five of the seven well-maintained bedrooms have shower rooms en suite. All rooms have washbasins and CTV, and there is one family room, though children under 11 are not accepted. Traditional English home cooking can be chosen from either table d'hôte or à la carte dinner menus. The pleasant, licensed dining room has an adjoining lounge area. Dogs are not accepted.

Price band B
Dinner td fr £6
Last dinner 8pm
Parking on premises

×× **Old Police House**
Castle Court
✆ (0743) 60668

Tucked away in a small courtyard in the town centre, this charming little restaurant occupies the site of the former County Gaol! The interior of the 19th-century building has been attractively restored to simulate its original period, and a wealth of Victorian furniture, pictures and bric-à-brac creates the atmosphere of that time. Fresh local produce is used to create a menu of

Lunch td fr £4.95 or alc £9.25
Dinner td fr £6.20
Last dinner 9.30pm

mainly English dishes which is equally evocative of the era, and a comprehensive wine list offers a good European selection. The popularity of this quaint establishment is growing rapidly, and its success is well-deserved.

Credit cards [1] [3]
Limited parking on premises
Closed 10–7 Jan
Closed Mon, & Sat lunch

SIMONSBATH Somerset Map 3 SS73

★★ HBL
Simonsbath House Hotel
Exford (064383) 259

A beautiful valley overlooking the River Barle is the setting for this well-appointed hotel in the heart of Exmoor. Dating from 1654, the house is thought to have been the first to be built on the moor. Each of the eight individually furnished bedrooms have a private bathroom and CTV, and two of the rooms have four-poster beds. Log fires cheer the public rooms in cooler weather, and the comfortable lounge is well-supplied with reading matter. Menus show considerable imagination, and well-prepared meals are served in the relaxed comfort of the restaurant. The hotel does not take dogs, or children under 10.

Price band B/C
Dinner alc £15
Last dinner 8.30pm
Credit cards [1] [2] [3] [5]
Parking on premises
Closed mid Dec–Jan

SIX MILE BOTTOM Cambridgeshire Map 5 TL55

★★★ B **Swynford Paddocks**
(063870) 234

Thoroughbred racehorses graze in well-manicured paddocks around this distinctive country house between Cambridge and Newmarket. Portraits of Lord Byron, his half-sister Augusta and the child of their alleged incestuous relationship hang in the hall, recalling the days when Swynford Paddocks, Augusta's home, was the focal point of a society scandal. Though the hotel now belongs to a chain, individuality is retained both in bedrooms and in public areas including the restaurant. Two four-poster rooms are among the 15 carefully converted bedrooms, all of which have private bathrooms and are well-equipped with guest facilities including CTV, telephones and many extras. General amenities at the hotel include a hard tennis court, a croquet lawn and a pitch-and-putt course. Booking is advisable for meals in the popular restaurant, whose à la carte and table d'hôte menus offer imaginative cooking based on quality fresh produce. Vegetarian meals can be provided

Price band C
Lunch td fr £7.95 or alc £18
Dinner alc £18
Last dinner 9.30pm
Credit cards [1] [2] [3] [5]
Parking on premises
Closed 1–2 Jan

SKEGNESS Lincolnshire Map 9 TF56

GH **Chatsworth Hotel**
North Parade
(0754) 4177

The Chatsworth — situated on the 'prom', so that guests can take advantage of all that Skegness has to offer—is an hotel in the true British seaside holiday tradition. The standards of hospitality, comfort and cooking are such that many people return here two or three times a year. Bedrooms are clean and bright, and guests can relax in the television lounge or the bar. Good fresh ingredients are used to provide the sort of satisfying meals that are really appreciated after a brisk walk along the seafront. Whatever the weather,

Prince band A
Bar lunch fr 70p
Lunch td £3.65 or alc £3.65
Dinner td fr £5 or alc £5
Last dinner 7.30pm
Credit cards [1] [3]

	a warm, sunny atmosphere is guaranteed at the Chatsworth!	Parking on premises Closed Dec–Mar (excluding Xmas) Open weekends Mar, Apr & Nov
GH **Crawford Hotel** South Parade ✆ (0754) 4215	Situated on the South Parade, overlooking the beach and Foreshore Gardens, this pleasant little hotel offers a good range of service, attracting both holidaymakers and businessmen. Well-equipped bedrooms (most of which have en suite facilities) are cheerful and warm, public rooms offer a choice of games room, lounge with bar or television lounge in which to take your ease. Meals of a high standard are served generously in the comfortable dining room. Should the Skegness air prove too 'bracing', you can relax in the hydro massage spa bath or take a dip in the fine, heated, indoor swimming pool.	Price band A/B Dinner, b&b £20.50–£24.50 Bar snacks available lunch & evening Last dinner 5pm Credit card [1] Parking on premises Closed Oct–Easter (except Xmas)

SKELMORLIE Strathclyde *Ayrshire* Map 10 NS16

★★★ BL **Manor Park** (2 miles S on A78) ✆ Wemyss Bay (0475) 520832	Commanding an imposing view over the Clyde Estuary, this lovely Victorian country house stands in its own magnificent gardens where peacocks roam freely. An abundance of pot plants brightens spacious public rooms which offer every modern convenience yet reflect the charms of a previous age, and in the quiet retreat of the cocktail bar you can take your choice of a fine range of malts. Bedrooms are fresh, bright and well-equipped, their beautifully polished furniture just one example of the high standard maintained throughout the hotel.	Price band C Bar lunch 85p–£4.50 Lunch alc £15 Dinner td £14.50 Last dinner 9.30pm Parking on premises Closed Jan–Feb

SKIPTON North Yorkshire Map 7 SD95

××× **Oats Restaurant Hotel** Chapel Hill ✆ (0756) 68118	This small, luxury hotel, which features a delightful restaurant, is located at the centre of the busy market town. Diners are welcomed into the lounge and bar, where comfortable furnishings are complemented by an attractive array of pictures and flowering plants. The restaurant is an equally pretty room and is both warm and inviting. Top-quality ingredients and nouvelle cuisine make for a fine standard of food, effectively presented, your meal being chosen from a menu which is changed regularly. Service is professional, though friendly, and a comprehensive wine list is available.	Lunch alc fr £9 Dinner alc fr £10 Last dinner 10pm Credit cards [1] [2] [3] [4] [5] Parking on premises Closed 25–6 Dec

SKYE
ISLE OF ARDVASAR Highland *Inverness-shire* Map 13 NG62

★★ **Ardvasar Hotel** ✆ (04714) 223	This white-painted former coaching inn is near Skye's southern end, conveniently close to Armadale Pier, from where an ageing ferry chugs across to the mainland in summer. The hotel offers fine views and a welcoming, informal atmosphere. It is run with enthusiasm by Bill and Greta Fowler, who continue to make improvements every year, aiming to retain the	Price band B Lunch £1–£6 & alc Dinner td £11–£14 & alc Last dinner 8.30pm

	hotel's character while introducing modern facilities. The 12 bedrooms (four with private bath) are bright and fresh. TV is available in rooms by request, and there is one family bedroom. The Ardvasar's four-course dinner is exceptional value for money, and vegetarians can be catered for. Locally caught lobster, crab, scallops and trout are all used to good purpose in Mr Fowler's cooking, while Mrs Fowler takes a personal interest in the welfare of every guest.	Credit card [3] Parking on premises Closed 25 Dec, 1–2 Jan

HARLOSH Map 13 NG24

❀ ★ H **Harlosh Hotel** ✆ Dunvegan (047022) 367	Any visitor to Skye should really experience a stay at this delightful hotel, an isolated white building superbly situated in the sheltered coastal bay of Loch Bracadale. Guests are offered an outstanding welcome, and accommodation is bright and modern, if rather modest. The cosy, wood-beamed dining room is the setting for an interesing, well-prepared dinner which makes good use of local seafood, and the evening can be rounded off by the traditional dram beside the roaring fire of the 'snug' bar. Vegetarian meals are available. Fishing, shooting, golf and pony-trecking can be arranged.	Bar lunch alc £2 Dinner td fr £8.50 or alc £9.50 Last dinner 9pm Parking on premises Closed Nov–Mar

ISLE ORNSAY Map 13 NG61

❀ ★★ ♣♣ HL **Kinloch Lodge** ✆ (04713) 214	At this lovely former shooting lodge you can be cosseted by the aristocracy! Lord and Lady McDonald (the latter a respected cookery book writer) welcome guests into charming surroundings and a most hospitable atmosphere. Bedrooms are modest but attractive, and public rooms are an interesting mélange of antiques, historical prints and more homely comforts. The greatest attraction, however, is the food, for the emphasis is on traditional Scottish fare prepared from first-class local produce. Though the price of dinner has recently increased sharply, the unpretentious home-cooked food is worthy of praise: home-cooked breads are good, kidneys in port and Scottish grain mustard are delicious, and lemon baked chicken is excellent. There are also mouthwatering desserts (such as apricot roulade with lemon cream), and a good wine list is available.	Price band C Dinner td £20 Last dinner 8pm Credit cards [1] [3] Parking on premises Closed 11–28 Dec & 6 Jan–29 Feb

---

SLAIDBURN Lancashire Map 7 SD75

GH **Parrock Head Farm** (Follow unclassified road N from Hark to Bounty Inn for about 2 miles) ✆ (02006) 614	Parrock Head Farm is set in beautiful countryside at the foot of Bowland Fells. The charmingly furnished house offers guests the use of two cosy lounges (one with an open fire and superb views), and a delightful dining room where excellent home-cooked food is served. All the bedrooms are warm, well-furnished and comfortable, with CTV. Privately owned and run, the farmhouse provides an exceptional standard of attentive service, and a stay here really is a special experience.	Price band B Bar lunch £3.50 Dinner alc £9 Last dinner 8.15pm Credit card [2] Parking on premises Closed Dec–Jan Closed lunch

SOLIHULL West Midlands Map 7 SP17

❀×× **Liaison French Cuisine** 761 Old Lode Ln ✆ 021-743 3993	Eating is leisurely and enjoyable at this small but stylish French restaurant tucked away in a row of shops on the outskirts of Solihull. Dinner is generally chosen from an à la carte menu, but on Tuesday evenings diners are offered a set menu based on the cuisine of a particular region of France. Miss Plunkett and Mrs Van der Tuin lavish great care and attention on the running of their restaurant. Presentation of food is most artistic; diners often comment on Patricia Plunkett's choice of an appropriately coloured platter to complement each dish. Vegetarian meals can be provided, and there is a knowledgeably chosen wine list.	Dinner td £15.95 or alc £22.50 Last dinner 10pm Credit cards 1 2 3 5 Closed Aug & 1 wk Xmas Closed lunch, & Sun & Mon

SOMERTON Somerset Map 3 ST42

★★ BL **Lynch House** Behind Berry ✆ (0458) 72316	A large and delightful garden surrounds this comfortable late Georgian country house. The hotel is personally run by its resident proprietors, who cultivate a very relaxing atmosphere and ensure that food is a priority. The menu choice is wide, and meals are carefully prepared and well-presented. The whole hotel is furnished to a high standard, including the six bedrooms, most of which have private bathrooms, CTV and telephones. Leisure amenities include an outdoor swimming pool and croquet. Children under 10 are not accepted.	Price band C Dinner td fr £13.50 Lunch td fr £10.50 Last dinner 9.30pm Credit cards 1 2 3 5 Parking on premises

SOUTHAMPTON Hampshire Map 4 SU41

Simon's Wine Bar Vernon Walk (off London Rd) ✆ (0703) 36372	The simple décor of this two-storey building is enlivened by old prints and an array of hats hung on the wall. The wine-bar is on the ground floor. Meals here range from traditional English to more imaginative international fare, with good home-made soups and pâtés to start. Main courses might be steak and kidney pie or Russian fish pie, and a choice of pasta dishes is available, as well as vegetarian food. Home-made sweets such as apple pie are offered to round off your meal. The wine list is good, and reasonably priced. A balcony overlooking the ground floor houses the restaurant, where more formal meals are served. The à la carte menu features mainly French-style cuisine, with chef's specialities, and is reasonably priced.	Lunch/dinner alc £8–£12 Last dinner 10.30pm Credit cards 1 2 3 5 Parking nearby Closed Sun lunch

SOUTHEND-ON-SEA Essex Map 5 TQ88

GH **West Park Private Hotel** 11 Park Rd, Westcliff-on-Sea ✆ (0702) 330729	This Victorian-style hotel is in a pleasant residential area. Comfortable and well-equipped bedrooms here include some refurbished annexe accommodation. Most of the 21 rooms have en suite facilities and are prettily decorated, with matching fabrics and wallpapers. There are three family rooms. The comfortable lounge is supplemented by a small residents' bar. Mr and Mrs Hollingshead, the proprietors, give their guests a warm welcome and are proud of their carefully prepared home-cooked food. Dinner should be ordered by 6.30pm.	Price band B Dinner, b&b £24–£26 Last dinner 7.30pm Credit cards 1 3 Parking on premises

SOUTHWOLD Suffolk Map 5 TM57

★★ The Crown
High St
✆ (0502) 722275
Tx 97223

Food and wine are the highlights here — the latter not surprisingly, since this former coaching inn houses the headquarters of Adnams brewery's wine department. Over 200 wines appear on the list in the restaurant. Prices start at around £4, and value for money is good all the way up the range. Menus — whether for bar meals or for table d'hôte lunch or dinner — change daily, and feature light, modern cooking, in generous portions, and with a choice of about four dishes for each course. Excellent raw materials include seafood from the local fishermen. On the table d'hôte menu, starters might be mussel soup or turbot mousse, and main courses escalope of veal in a lime sauce, pheasant with grapes or vegetable lasagne. Sweets could be as hearty as bread and butter pudding or as refreshing as rhubarb sorbet. The restaurant menu features a welcome wine idea: a glass of each of three different wines, selected to suit each course, is offered for an inclusive price. Accommodation at the Crown has recently been refurbished; most of the 12 bedrooms (including one family room) have private facilities, and all have CTV and telephones. Stripped, waxed furniture and fittings enhance the period character of the building.

Price band B
Bar meal alc £7.50
Lunch td £11
Dinner td £11
Last dinner 9.45pm
Credit cards 1 2 3
Parking on premises

SOUTH ZEAL Devon Map 3 SX69

GH **Poltimore**
✆ Okehampton (0837) 840209

Described by our Inspector as 'a real port in a storm', this family-run guesthouse on the edge of Dartmoor is a good base for walking (dogs are welcome), riding, fishing or touring the moor. Mr and Mrs Harbridge's charming thatched house has seven comfortable bedrooms, four of which have private facilities. The cosy, beamed lounge has an inglenook fireplace and there is a separate CTV lounge and a bar. Dinner is available to residents provided it is ordered by 10.30am. Food is all freshly prepared, using local produce. Children under 12 are not accepted.

Price band B
Dinner, b&b £19—£22.50
Last dinner 7pm
Parking on premises

SPRATTON Northamptonshire Map 4 SP86

★★★ Broomhill Hotel
Holdenby Road
✆ Northampton (0604) 845959

This impressive country house, set in tranquil parkland overlooking the rolling countryside of the Pytchley Hunt, provides the perfect combination of Victorian elegance and modern-day comforts. The building has been carefully refurbished and the spacious bedrooms are graced by beautiful antique furniture. Of particular note are the bathrooms, with large elegant suites of very high quality. Carefully prepared meals, using local produce and home-grown vegetables, are served in the dining room which commands superb views. Afterwards guests can relax in front of the log fire in the comfortable bar. For the athletically inclined there are tennis courts, a swimming pool, and riding from the hotel's own stables. The owners, Sue and Joe Kelly, offer a warm and friendly welcome.

Price band C
Bar lunch td £3.50–£7
Lunch td fr £7.50 or alc fr £12
Dinner td fr £10 or alc fr £12
Last dinner 10pm
Credit cards 1 2 3 5
Parking on premises

STAINES Surrey Map 4 TQ07

★★★ Thames Lodge Hotel
Thames St
✆ (0784) 64433

Formerly called the Pack Horse, this large Victorian hotel beside the river was completely refurbished several years ago. A new extension houses some 40 bedrooms, and existing rooms were made more spacious and comfortable. All 47 rooms are now equipped with private bathrooms, CTV, trouser-presses, hairdriers and telephones. Some have splendid views across the Thames. Public areas have also been given a face-lift. The large, popular bar has a fascinating collection of bygones, such as enamelled advertisements, and has a fine riverside terrace. At lunch-time there is a hot and cold buffet in the bar, while for more formal eating there is the 'Moorings' restaurant, which has been completely modernised and overlooks the river. À la carte and table d'hôte menus are available here, and occasionally special 'theme' evenings are held. Staff are helpful and friendly.

Price band C/D
Lunch/dinner £10–£15
Last dinner 10pm
Credit cards [1] [2] [3] [4] [5]
Parking on premises

STAMFORD Lincolnshire Map 4 TF00

★★★
Garden House
St Martins
✆ (0780) 63359
Tx 329230

A charming 18th-century house has been lovingly transformed by proprietors whose avowed aim was to create 'a small hotel with a touch of class'. While retaining the elegance and style of the original building, they have brought it into the 20th-century as regards comfort and convenience, and in its tranquil setting they provide the very best in hospitality and service. Bedrooms are tastefully furnished with antiques and pretty floral fabrics, and the candle-lit dining room provides an attractive background for the enjoyment of fine food and wine. Conservatory and bar, overlooking the acre of garden, delight the eye with hanging baskets and pot plants. Altogether, the Garden House offers an ideal atmosphere in which to relax and unwind.

Price band C
Bar lunch £2–£10
Lunch alc fr £6
Dinner alc fr £12
Last dinner 9.30pm
Credit cards [1] [3]
Parking on premises

STANFORD-ON-AVON Northamptonshire Map 4 SP57

Edgell Cottage
✆ Rugby (0788) 860589

This picture-postcard thatched cottage, standing in charming gardens, looks every inch the part of an English tea shop! Inside, the tiny room where teas are served maintains the mood with flower-sprigged wallpaper and tablecloths, fresh flowers and floral crockery, and the delicious selection of scones, cakes and snacks on offer is also in the best English tradition. Shelves and windowledges are laden with home-produced jam, marmalade and dried flower arrangements, all offered for sale. For visitors to nearby Stanford Hall, Edgell Cottage provides a delightful contrast of styles — as well as a particularly good morning coffee or afternoon tea.

Parking on premises
Closed Nov–Feb
Only open weekends and Bank Hols

> The price band indicates the price of bed and breakfast for a single person or room. Price band A = £15 or less; price band B = £16–£30; price band C = £31–£50; price band D = more than £50.

STIRLING Central *Stirlingshire* Map 11 NS79

Granada Lodge (M9 junct 9 with M80, 3 miles S of Town Centre) ✆ (0786) 815033	Granada Lodge is the first unit in Scotland to be designated a 'lodge' under the Association's new classification. Conveniently sited on the motorway service area at the junction of the M9/M30, it offers a very high standard of accommodation, with colour schemes attractively linked to soft furnishings and solid, fitted, wooden furniture. All the bedrooms are particularly well-equipped and have modern en suite bathrooms, but, as the only dining facility is that housed in the adjacent service area, the unit's main appeal would probably be as an overnight stop for the family or businessman making a long journey.	Price band B Lunch alc £4 Dinner alc £5.50 Last dinner 10pm Credit cards [1] [2] [3] [5] Parking on premises
×× **The Heritage** 16 Allan Park ✆ (0786) 73660	The Heritage, an attractively converted private house in the shadow of Stirling Castle, has been one of the best restaurants in the area for some years now. Unobtrusively expensive décor and furnishings provide a pleasant and comfortable setting, particularly in the lounge-bar, where there are a number of attractive pieces of antique furniture. Cuisine is international, though a French influence is detectable, and the reasonably-priced meals (accompanied by a fairly extensive wine list) are popular with tourists and businessmen alike. Vegetarian meals are available.	Lunch td £7.10 or alc £12 Dinner td £14.30 or alc £15 Last dinner 9.30pm Credit cards [1] [3] [5] Parking on premises Closed Xmas & New Year

STOKE-ON-TRENT Staffordshire Map 7 SJ84

GH **The White House** Stone Rd, Trent Vale ✆ (0782) 642460	Friendly, hospitable owners and staff make this licensed guesthouse a popular port of call, especially with business travellers. It is conviently located south-west of Stoke, close to the A34/A500 junction (but noise insulation is good) and only a mile from the M6. The 10 bedrooms range from comfortable, compact singles to new executive rooms, with private shower rooms, in the annexe. Some rooms have CTV, telephones and mini-bars, and there are two family rooms. The lounge and adjoining dining room are neat and well-furnished. Breakfasts are particularly good, and family-style home cooking is offered on the set dinner menu.	Price band B Dinner td £6 Last dinner 7pm Credit cards [1] [3] Parking on premises Closed Xmas and New Year

STONE Kent Map 5 TQ92

FH **Tighe Farmhouse** ✆ Appledore (023383) 251	There are marvellous views of Romney Marsh from this late 16th-century farmhouse, which is surrounded by well-kept gardens. The interior is charming and comfortable, and furnished with antiques. Exposed beams lend atmosphere and character to the cosy dining room, while the spacious lounge has an inglenook fireplace. There are three letting bedrooms, including one family room, though children under eight are not accepted. Substantial breakfasts are served, and the proprietors are very welcoming. Dogs are not accepted. Private fishing is available.	Price band A Parking on premises Closed Dec–Feb

STRACHUR Strathclyde *Argyllshire* Map 10 NN00

★★★
Creggans Inn
✆ (036986) 279

A charming 17th-century inn, which enjoys an ideal situation on the shores of Loch Fyne, has been tastefully modernised to offer good, up-to-date accommodation. Guests have a choice of two bars, and there are also two comfortable lounges — one, on the first floor, overlooking the loch, the other containing a colour television. If the day is fine, afternoon tea may be taken in the sun porch, and this is a delightful experience. Cottage-style bedrooms, though small, are bright and cheery, and good food is served in the attractive dining room. Fishing is available.

Price band C
Bar lunch alc £5
Lunch alc fr £7
Dinner alc fr £15
Last dinner 9.30pm
Credit cards [1] [2] [3] [5]
Parking on premises

STRATFORD-UPON-AVON Warwickshire Map 4 SP25

GH The Hollies
16 Evesham Place
✆ (0789) 66857

The ideal 'home from home' after a day's sightseeing in Stratford, The Hollies is run by a most hospitable mother-and-daughter team, Mrs Morgan and Mrs Burton. The six comfortable bedrooms have light, bright colour schemes with matching floral duvet covers and curtains. All have washbasins, one has a shower room en suite, and three have accommodation for families. Tea/coffee-making facilities are provided in each room. Good English breakfasts are served in the attractive dining room, but no other meals are available. Dogs are not accepted.

Price band A
Parking on premises

FH Monk's Barn
Shipston Rd
✆ (0789) 293714

After the hectic tourist dash from the Cotswolds to Stratford, Monk's Barn provides a friendly haven and the very best of English hospitality. This cosy farmhouse, standing just two miles south of the town, looks out over gently rolling Warwickshire countryside. The atmosphere is serene and peaceful, an ideal setting for rest and relaxation, and after a good night's sleep in a pleasant bedroom you can look forward to an egg-and-bacon breakfast in the finest country tradition.

Price band A
Parking on premises
Closed 25–6 Dec

GH Moonraker House
40 Alcester Rd
✆ (0789) 67115

Moonraker House is run by a friendly young couple who work hard to maintain its high standards of hospitality and comfort. Accommodation is available in one of two houses set just a short distance apart in a pleasant residential area, within easy walking distance of the town centre. The comfortable bedrooms (all of which have en suite facilities and CTV) have been made cheerful with attractive floral fabrics, and each house also has its own pleasant lounge and a dining room where good, substantial cooked breakfasts are served. All in all, a stay here represents good value for money.

Price band A
Parking on premises

GH Parkfield
3 Broadwalk
✆ (0789) 293313

The abundance of window boxes and hanging baskets that adorns this attractive Victorian house is an indication of the care and attention lavished upon it. Standing just five minutes' walk from the town centre, it provides high standards of comfort and hospitality; food is good (with such nice touches as fresh croissants for breakfast), and the lounge at the rear of the house, overlooking the patio and well-stocked garden, provides an oasis of tranquillity after the bustle of Stratford.

Price band A
Credit cards [1] [3]
Parking on premises
Closed 25–6 Dec

× **Rumours**
Charlecote Pheasant Hotel,
Charlecote
✆ (0789) 840200

Situated just outside Stratford-upon-Avon, Rumours specialises in a light, modern style of cooking. If you can't make up your mind what to eat, try the 'adventure' menu and sample small portions of seven of the more unusual dishes on offer. Vegetarian meals are available. Vegetables are excellent, the seven or eight served at each meal include such delights as fresh baby turnips and mangetout. The carefully cooked and beautifully presented food, based on the best of fresh local produce, is fast attracting a faithful following to this pretty little restaurant.

Dinner alc £16.50
Last dinner 10pm
Credit cards [1] [2] [3] [5]
Parking on premises
Closed lunch, & Sun

The Slug and Lettuce
38 Guild St
✆ (0789) 299700

During the tourist season it is advisable to book a table to be sure of sampling the excellent food at this lively and always-busy pub. The menu changes frequently, but tasty home-made soups are usually on offer, and other dishes might be deliciously light smoked trout pâté, garlicky baked chicken with avocado, or calf's liver with onions. The home-made sweets are thoroughly recommended. A good range of real ales is available. Smart, pine-panelled décor and cheerful young staff complete the enjoyment at this hostelry with a difference.

Lunch/dinner alc £9.50
Last dinner 10pm
Parking nearby

★★★★ HL
Welcombe Hotel
Warwick Rd
✆ (0789) 295252
Tx 31347

The driveway to this elegant prestigious hotel meanders through the 18-hole golf course, laid out in undulating parkland, which is at guests' disposal. The hotel is a large Jacobean-style mansion, with a more modern garden wing, offering superb hospitality. The 82 bedrooms, 10 of which can accommodate families, all have a private bathroom, CTV and telephone. These are comfortably furnished and decorated with coordinating colour schemes. Special facilities are available for children. The cocktail bar overlooks the first fairway, and in summer guests linger on the terrace watching the more energetic playing a game of golf. Fishing, croquet and snooker may also be enjoyed. The restaurant has a good reputation for its English and French cuisine and also caters for vegetarians. Both set and à la carte menus are offered.

Price band D
Bar lunch £3.50
Lunch td £12.50 or alc £20
Dinner td £18.50 or alc £20
Last dinner 9.30pm
Credit cards [1] [2] [3] [5]
Parking on premises
Closed 29–31 Dec & 1–3 Jan

STRETTON Leicestershire Map 8 SK91

★★ B **Ram Jam Inn**
(9 miles N of Stamford of W side of A1)
✆ (078081) 776

One of the best-known inns on the A1, the Ram Jam was revitalised during 1986 to create a luxurious establishment where the traveller can obtain refreshments throughout the day, snacks being served from 7am to 7pm and more sophisticated meals at lunch-time and in the evening. Service is quick and efficient, and the food of high quality — at breakfast, for example, you will be served with freshly-squeezed orange juice and fresh ground coffee. Satisfying hot sandwiches are featured among the snacks, and the main meal menus include such substantial puddings as treacle and nut tart or fruit pie with home-made custard. Accommodation in beautifully equipped bedrooms is reasonably priced, toilet facilities are excellently appointed and spotless, and staff are friendly and helpful.

Price band C
Snack meals fr £1.75
Lunch/dinner alc £7
Last dinner 11pm
Credit cards [1] [2] [3]

STURMINSTER NEWTON Dorset Map 3 ST71

❀×× **Plumber Manor**
(2m SW of Sturminster Newton on Hazelbury Bryan rd)
✆ (0258) 72507

Excellent cooking using top-quality raw materials is the hallmark of this fine restaurant in a handsome Jacobean country house. Plumber Manor is still run by members of the family that has owned it since the 17th-century, and the proprietor, Mr Brian Prideaux-Brune, is also the chef. Fresh food in season is the basis of his meals, and he cooks with skill and imagination. Our inspector particularly commends the vegetables and the mouthwatering sweets. The two fixed-price menus are very good value for money. A collection of interesting paintings is a notable feature of the two elegant dining rooms. Plumber Manor also has 12 very well-appointed bedrooms, including six tastefully furnished modern rooms in a converted stone barn in the grounds.

Dinner td fr £15
Last dinner 9.30pm
Credit cards [1] [3]
Parking on premises
Closed 1st 2 wks Feb
Closed lunch

STURTON BY STOW Lincolnshire Map 8 SK88

FH **Village Farm**
✆ Gainsborough (0427) 788309

The Village Farm provides a perfect base for touring the beautiful Lincolnshire Wolds and the historic city of Lincoln. An attractive 19th-century house at the village centre, it provides not only comfortably relaxing accommodation but also a taste of real country life, with pedigree cattle and Suffolk sheep on the farm itself and an aviary of lovebirds in the pretty little garden. Flowery chintz, Laura Ashley prints, samplers, patchwork, antiques and objects d'art (some of which are for sale to guests) make the whole house charming. Breakfasts are prepared from only the very best of fresh local produce, and the fruit-packed home-made preserves are a delight. Dinners are available by prior arrangement, and you may, if you are lucky, be given the chance to sample the proprietor's home-brewed wines and sloe gin!

Price band A
Dinner, b&b £16.50–£20
Last dinner 7pm
Parking on premises
Closed Nov–Mar

SUTTON Greater London

❀× **Partners 23**
23 Stonecot Hill
✆ 01-644 7743

Andy Thomason and Tim McEntire are the young proprietors of Partners 23, their first restaurant venture. Their enthusiasm and dedication shine through, both in the quality of the food and in the willing, friendly service. The best market produce available is used to create carefully prepared and imaginative dishes, often complemented by subtle, well-constructed sauces. Table d'hôte menus are sensibly priced according to the number of courses (two or three at lunch; four at dinner), and are partnered by an extremely well-chosen wine list including some modestly priced château-bottled wines. Not surprisingly, the restaurant has a strong local following as well as a clientele from further afield, so booking is recommended especially as the dining space is limited.

Lunch td fr £10.75
Dinner td fr £19.95
Last dinner 9.30pm
Credit cards [1] [2] [3] [5]
No parking on premises
Closed 25 Dec–3 Jan
Closed Sun & Mon, & Sat lunch

> À la carte prices are based on an average for three courses without wine.

SWINESHEAD Bedfordshire Map 4 TL06

FH **Manor Farmhouse**
✆ Bedford (0234) 708126

Leafy lanes in the heart of the countryside lead to this charming farmhouse, parts of which are as much as 600 years old. It stands on a three-acre smallholding, which includes traditional English gardens. There are only three bedrooms (including one family room), but they are all of a good size and prettily decorated, with coordinated soft furnishings and stripped pine furniture. The dining room, with its fresh white walls and exposed beams, has one large table where breakfast is served. No other meals are available. Antique furniture, comfortable armchairs and a wood-burning stove are features of the cosy lounge. Corners are filled with cheerful floral displays. The proprietors here are Mr and Mrs Marlow, charming hosts who can be justly proud of their lovely home, which is a quiet and relaxing retreat. They do not accept dogs, or children under 10.

Price band A
Parking on premises
Closed Xmas

TALLAND Cornwall Map 2 SX25

★★★ BL
Talland Bay Hotel
✆ Polperro (0503) 72667

An unspoilt bay on a lovely stretch of Cornish coastline between Looe and Polperro is the setting for this country house hotel. A modernised and extended manor house, parts of which date back to the 16th century, the Talland Bay has 19 bedrooms. All the double rooms have private bathrooms (many with bidets), and all bedrooms are equipped with CTV, radio, telephones, hairdriers and hot-water bottles. The hotel is furnished with taste and imagination: oak panelling, fireplaces and antiques in keeping with the house's character are complemented by many items of interest such as paintings and tapestries, and fresh flowers are used liberally. Both sitting rooms open on to the pool terrace, where morning coffee, lunches and Cornish cream teas are served. The oak-panelled restaurant enjoys a good reputation. Carefully planned four-course dinner menus often include local crab, lobster and oysters among a choice of English and French cuisine. A vegetarian dish is always available. Leisure facilities at the hotel include the swimming pool, a croquet lawn, a putting green, a solarium and a games room. Children under five are not accepted.

Price band B/C
Bar lunch £1–£6
Lunch td fr £1.50
Dinner td £11 or alc £15
Last dinner 9pm
Credit cards [1] [2] [3] [5]
Parking on premises
Closed Jan, b&b only Dec

TALSARNAU Gwynedd Map 6 SH63

★★ L
Maes-y-Neuadd
✆ Harlech (0766) 780200

The name of this hotel means 'mansion in the meadows', and it is set amid seven acres of landscaped lawns, orchards and paddock, with magnificient views of Snowdonia. The hotel is owned by a two-family partnership, and a friendly welcome and individual attention from the four proprietors is part of its attraction. The Horsfalls and the Slatters also pay close attention to their restaurant, which has recently been given a face-lift. Here, the set-price dinner menus are made up of a range of French, English and Welsh dishes using fresh ingredients soundly cooked. Presentation is creative, and some tasty vegetarian

Price band B
Lunch td fr £8.50
Dinner td fr £14.50
Last dinner 9pm
Credit cards [1] [3]
Parking on premises
Closed 3–31 Jan

dishes are usually on offer. Maes y Neuadd has 14 individually designed bedrooms, all with bathrooms en suite and all equipped with telephones, CTV and hairdriers. As well as modern comforts, the hotel also offers historic interest: parts of it date back to the 14th century, and the building's origins are preserved in features like oak beams and an inglenook fireplace. Children under seven are not accepted.

TAL-Y-LLYN Gwynedd Map 6 SH70

★ RED **Minffordd**
✆ Corris (065473) 665

This unassuming little hotel at the foot of Cader Idris owes much of its charm and character to its amiable proprietors, the Pickles family. Mr and Mrs Pickles cultivate a house-party atmosphere and look after the accommodation side of things, while their son Jonathan does the cooking. The menu is sensibly short, but changes daily, and the thoroughly enjoyable meals have a sound basis of fresh local raw materials. As well as the dining room, there are two sitting rooms and a sun lounge, plus seven bedrooms. Standards of housekeeping are high. The bedrooms are spotlessly clean, comfortably furnished and attractive. Radio, telephone and tea-making facilities are provided in each room, as well as a private bath or shower. There is one family room, but children under three are not accepted (and neither are dogs). The hotel has a garden and a paddock, but no television — which helps to encourage a sociable atmosphere. Lovely views complete the picture: Minffordd is an ideal base for a walking or touring holiday in this beautiful part of Wales.

Price band B
Dinner td £11.50
Last dinner 8.30pm
Credit cards [1] [3] [5]
Parking on premises
Closed Jan-Feb
Restricted service Mar, Nov-Dec (Open Fri & Sat only)
Closed lunch

TAUNTON Somerset Map 3 ST22

GH **Meryan House Hotel**
Bishop's Hull Rd (Outside Taunton, off A38)
✆ (0823) 87445

This pleasant little hotel is within easy reach of the amenities of Taunton, yet conveniently situated for drives to Exmoor, the Quantocks or the coast. The Georgian house stands in its own pretty gardens and has recently been refurbished by its present owners, Mr and Mrs Penney. The eight bedrooms all have private facilities, CTV, clock/radios and tea trays are provided with welcome little extras such as biscuits, sweets and fresh flowers. The whole hotel has a warm and homely atmosphere, and the public rooms are attractively decorated and furnished. Guests can relax in the lounge with an aperitif before a four-course dinner, which is cooked by Mrs Penney. Her set menu makes ample use of fresh local produce in season. Meryan House does not take dogs.

Price band B
Dinner, b&b £31.40–£35.40
Last dinner order 8pm
Parking on premises

TEIGNMOUTH Devon Map 3 SX97

★ B **Drakes Hotel**
33 Northumberland Place
✆ (06267) 2777

This small, unpretentious hotel is conveniently located in the town centre and is only about 25 yards from River Beach. Its six bedrooms include three with private facilities and one suitable for families. All the rooms have CTV and are warm and prettily decorated. A good choice of food (including

Price band A/B
Bar lunch £2.30–£5
Lunch td fr £4 or alc £10
Dinner td fr £5

vegetarian dishes) is available throughout the day in the Bistro Coffee Shop, while the cosy dining room offers an à la carte dinner menu. Main courses include duck breast en croûte with orange and wine sauce, or scallops Drake, while a typical first course might be seafood soup. Sweets are home-made and come in generous portions.

or alc £12
Last dinner 9.30pm
Credit cards [1] [3]
No parking on premises
Restaurant closed Oct/Nov 2 wks

★★ Ness House
Ness Drive, Shaldon
✆ (06267) 873480

There are fine views of the estauary or the open sea from many of the rooms of this comfortable Regency building. Our Inspector particularly commends the standard of the cooking here. Quality fresh ingredients are used to create inventive dishes like crevettes Othello (chilled egg pancake with prawns and fresh pineapple, served with a sauce Marie Rose) or mignon de veau aux fraises (fillets of pink veal with a sauce of fresh strawberries and rosemary). Service is prompt and friendly. At lunch-times, and for more informal evening eating, a good range of well-prepared bar snacks is offered. The hotel has bright, modern bedrooms and, on the ground floor, comfortable open-plan lounge and bar areas as well as an attractive dining room, all with fine seaside views. There is also a sun terrace, especially popular with families during summer.

Price band B
Bar lunch alc £7.50
Lunch alc £12
Dinner alc £16.50
Last dinner 10pm
Credit cards [1] [3]
Parking on premises
Closed Jan

TENBY Dyfed Map 2 SN10

★ HB **Harbour Heights**
11 The Croft
✆ (0834) 2132

This small, very comfortable hotel overlooks Tenby's North Beach and harbour. There are nine bedrooms, including four family rooms. All have private bathrooms and CTV, and are attractively furnished and decorated. Meals are chosen from a limited menu, but the food is of a high standard, and vegetarians can be catered for. Harbour Heights is owned and personally run by the Gower family. They do not accept dogs, or children under eight.

Price band B
Lunch td £3.50
Dinner td £9.50
Last dinner 8pm
Credit cards [1] [2] [3] [5]
No parking on premises

TETBURY Gloucestershire Map 3 ST89

× **Hubbits**
7 New Church St
✆ (0666) 53306

Barry and Fiona Howarth specialise in moderately priced, simple English home cooking at their unpretentious, friendly little restaurant in the centre of town. Everything is prepared to order, using carefully selected produce, and the results are pleasing. Vegetarian meals are available. There is a small bar, for aperitifs, at the rear of the restaurant, which has been converted from a terraced cottage of Cotswold stone.

Lunch alc £5
Dinner alc £10
Last dinner 10pm
Credit cards [1] [2] [3] [5]
Parking nearby
Closed Mon

> The price band indicates the price of bed and breakfast for a single person or room. Price band A = £15 or less; price band B = £16–£30; price band C = £31–£50; price band D = more than £50.

THAKEHAM West Sussex Map 4 TQ11

❀★★★ H
Abingworth Hall
Storrington Rd
✆ West Chiltington
(07983) 3636
Tx 827835

Gracious living and a relaxing atmosphere combine at this tastefully furnished country house on the Sussex Downs. Leisure activities available to guests here include tennis, croquet, pitch and putt, boules and fishing. The gardens include a natural lake. The 22 bedrooms have all the expected facilities — private bathrooms, CTV, telephones — and are elegantly and comfortably furnished, as are the lounge and cocktail bar. A soft, delicate colour scheme and well-appointed tables in the dining room are the background to superbly prepared meals. Cusine is mainly French, and both the à la carte and table d'hôte menus show imagination and flair. Service is by friendly and willing staff under the personal supervision of the proprietors, Mr and Mrs Bulman. Abingworth Hall does not accept children under 10, or dogs.

Price band C/D
Lunch td £11.50 or alc £25.00
Dinner td £18.50 or alc £25
Last dinner 9pm
Credit cards [1] [2] [3] [4] [5]
Parking on premises

THAME Oxfordshire Map 4 SP70

★★★ H
The Spread Eagle
Cornmarket
✆ (084421) 3661

Patrons of this hotel were once asked to take off their shoes and to write their names on the wall — and the very tall among them were awarded a free meal. This was when the Spread Eagle was owned by a colourful local character called John Fothergill, in the 1920s. The present proprietor, Mr Barrington, offers a less eccentric kind of hospitality, helped by his team of friendly staff. The hotel is well-furnished and decorated throughout, and all 26 bedrooms have private bathrooms, CTV and telephones. Mainly English dishes feature on the menu of the restaurant, where standards of cooking are high, Vegetarian food is available. Continental breakfast is included in room charges. The hotel does not accept dogs.

Price band C
Bar lunch £2
Lunch td fr £10.15 or alc £16.95
Dinner td fr £12.10 or alc £16.95
Last dinner 9.30pm
Credit cards [1] [2] [3] [5]
Parking on premises
Closed 28–30 Dec

THORNTON CLEVELEYS Lancashire Map 7 SD34

×× **Victorian House**
Trunnah Rd
✆ (0253) 860619

The Victorian House lives up to its name, the lounge and bar being veritable museums of Victoriana, filled with interesting items from that era, and a dining room in similar style providing a warm, comfortable setting for the enjoyment of English-style cooking. Attractively presented food, well-prepared from good fresh local produce, is deservedly popular and it is advisable to book in advance. There is ample parking, as the restaurant is set in its own grounds.

Bar lunches fr £2.75
Lunch td fr £6.50 or alc £15
Dinner td fr £13.50
Last dinner 9.30pm
Credit card [1]
Parking on premises
Closed Sun & Mon, Fri, Sat lunch

À la carte prices are based on an average for three courses without wine.

THREE COCKS Powys Map 3 SO13

GH **Old Gwernyfed Country Manor** Felindre (2m SE of Three Cocks) ✆ Glasbury (04974) 376	Secret rooms, a minstrels' gallery and a banqueting hall with a wealth of oak panelling make a stay at this fine Elizabethan manor house an experience to remember. Set in peaceful seclusion in the foothills of the Black Mountains, the house also offers plenty of modern comforts. All eight bedrooms have bathrooms en suite, and two are suitable for families. Good home cooking is the style of the meals here; the licensed dining room is open to non-residents by prior arrangement. The 12 acres of grounds include a croquet lawn.	Price band B Dinner td £12.50 Last dinner 8pm Parking on premises Closed Jan–Feb
❀ ★ L **Three Cocks Hotel** ✆ Glasbury (04974) 215	This fine old stone-built inn a few miles from the English border offers a friendly welcome and cooking of a high standard. Diners have a choice between a four-course fixed-price menu and an à la carte selection which changes monthly to take account of fresh foods in season. The cuisine shows a Belgian influence; preparation is skilful and imaginative, and presentation attractive. Fresh ingredients are used wherever possible, and vegetables are especially good. Lunch is served only by prior arrangement. The hotel has seven bedrooms, including one family room. Bargain breaks are available, and a special programme is offered at Christmas. Dogs are not accepted.	Price band B Bar lunch td £1.25–£3.50 Lunch/dinner td £15 Last dinner 9pm Credit cards 1 3 4 Parking on premises Closed Jan

THRESHFIELD North Yorkshire Map 7 SD96

GH **Greenways** Wharfeside Ave ✆ Grassington (0756) 752598	Standing close to the village in its own grounds, this family-owned and run guesthouse offers excellent value for money and is ideally positioned for touring the Dales. Its bedrooms are attractive and bright, a comfortable, homely lounge provides really comfortable seating in which you can relax and watch television, and the dining room looks out onto one the finest views of the river Wharfe. Great care is taken in the preparation and cooking of meals, and the menu changes daily.	Price band A Dinner, b&b £23 Last dinner 7.30pm Parking on premises Closed Nov–Mar

TISBURY Wiltshire Map 3 ST92

❀ × **Garden Room** 2–3 High St ✆ (0747) 870907	Bright, garden-style décor reflects the name of this delightful restaurant, which our Inspector describes as a little gem. It is owned and run by a two-man team: Paul Firmin cooks, while Jonathan Ford welcomes clients and looks after them. A sensibly priced table d'hôte menu is offered, and menus are changed frequently to make the most of meat, game, fish and vegetables in season, and vegetarian meals are available. The style of cooking is distinctly modern: dishes are imaginatively planned, carefully cooked, and presented attractively but without fussiness. A well-chosen wine list is offered, and service is attentive and friendly.	Lunch td fr £8.50 Dinner td fr £14.50 Last dinner 10pm Credit cards 1 2 3 Parking nearby Closed 1 wk Sep/Oct, 2 wks late Feb Closed Mon, & Sun dinner & Sat lunch

TONGUE Highland *Sutherland* Map 14 NC55

★★ **Ben Loyal**
☎ (048755) 216

You can enjoy a comfortable stay for a very modest price at this family-run tourist hotel. Bedrooms retain much of their original traditional style, but they are warm, well-equipped and brightly decorated, and they all have private bathrooms. Most of them command spectacular views across the Kyles of Tongue, as do the attractive lounge and dining room. The lounge bar is somewhat uncharacteristically modern and functional, but the area serving food is popular (children being allowed) and there is a homely little snug off reception; you may have to ask directions to the television lounge, as it is rather tucked away. The set-price dinner menu is limited in choice, but the choice is well-cooked and helpings are generous. Smart staff are friendly and attentive, and the proprietor's family are always on hand to ensure that everything is to your liking.

Price band B
Bar lunch td £1.80–£6.50
Dinner td fr £9.50
Last dinner 8pm
Credit cards [1] [3] [5]
Parking on premises
Restricted service 16 Oct–14 Apr

TOPSHAM Devon Map 3 SX98

★★ H
Ebford House
Exmouth Rd,
Ebford
☎ (039287) 7658

Conveniently situated for the M5 and Exeter, this detached Georgian house stands in its own grounds and has a pleasant outlook. There are ten comfortable bedrooms all with private bathrooms, CTV and telephones. General facilities include a sauna, a solarium and a gymnasium. Golf and riding are also available. Freshly prepared food, chosen from a well-planned menu, is served in the attractive restaurant, which also caters for vegetarians. Service is attentive and friendly, and the cooking is done by the proprietor, Mr Horton.

Price band B
Bar lunch £1–£7 or alc £7.50
Lunch td £8 or alc £8
Dinner td fr £12.75 or alc £16.50
Last dinner 9pm
Credit cards [1] [2] [3]
Parking on premises

TORQUAY Devon Map 3 SX96

★ H **Fairmont House Hotel**
Herbert Rd,
Chelston
☎ (0803) 605446

The secluded walled garden of this lovely Victorian house has as its centrepiece a beautiful 80-year-old magnolia tree. The hotel is set in a quiet residential area and has seven very prettily decorated bedrooms, including two ground-floor rooms that have been specially adapted and equipped for disabled guests, and which have direct access to the south-facing garden. Bedrooms are all cosy and have modern facilities. All have private bath or shower, and three are suitable for families. Public rooms include a nice new conservatory lounge. AA members continue to be impressed by the sound home cooking here, and by the warm, attentive hospitality of the proprietors, Noel and Maggie Tolkein.

Price band A
Bar lunch £2.50–£5.50
Dinner td £7
Last dinner 7.30pm
Credit cards [2] [3]
Parking on premises
Closed mid Nov–mid Feb

GH **Glenorleigh Hotel**
26 Cleveland Rd
☎ (0803) 22135

Hospitable proprietors Michael and Maureen Rhodes were worthy winners of an AA award for the best family hotel in Britain in 1984, and our members continue to praise the Glenorleigh. This well-established hotel is delightfully set in flower-filled gardens that lend it an air of seclusion rarely associated with a busy resort like Torquay. Guests

Price band A/B
Dinner, b&b £15–£20
Last dinner 6pm
Limited parking on premises

here can be sure of a warm welcome and comfortable accommodation. The hotel has 16 bedrooms, 14 of which have en suite facilities, and five are family rooms. Public rooms are elegant yet homely, and a good range of leisure facilities includes a heated outdoor pool, a sauna, a solarium and a games room. Bookings for July and August, and at Christmas, are accepted only for complete weeks. The hotel does not take dogs.

× **Old Vienna Restaurant**
6 Lisburne Square
(0803) 25861

Viennese hospitality, under the direction of the Austrian chef/proprietor Werner Rott, is the hallmark of this popular restaurant. Not surprisingly, the cooking shows a distinct Continental influence, and is carried out with flair and imagination. Be sure to leave some room for the rich and beautifully decorated sweets. Bright red-and-green décor is complemented by fresh flowers and lighted candles, and a small aperitif bar has recently been added. The atmosphere is pleasant and intimate, and service friendly and informal. Lunch is by reservations only.

Lunch/dinner alc £13
Last dinner 10pm
Credit cards [1] [2] [3]
No parking on premises
Closed 1 wk May & 1 wk Oct

★★★ H
Orestone House Hotel
Rockhouse Ln, Maidencombe
(0803) 38098

This charming family-run hotel manages to retain a country house atmosphere and an air of peaceful seclusion despite being in the heart of busy Torbay. Present owners, the hospitable Flude family, have continued a programme of upgrading and refurbishment over recent years, and the house now offers many modern comforts while retaining its charm and character. Leisure facilities include a heated outdoor swimming pool, a putting green and a games room, and there are sheltered, peaceful grounds and gardens in which to relax. Lounges and bedrooms alike are comfortably furnished and nicely decorated. Most of the 20 cosy bedrooms have sea views and all have private bath or shower, CTV, tea-makers and telephones. There are four family bedrooms. Food at Orestone House is of a high standard: good, fresh raw materials are used with flair, and service in the restaurant is friendly and efficient. Vegetarians can be catered for.

Price band B
Bar lunch alc £5
Sun lunch td fr £6
Dinner td fr £10.50 or alc £13.50
Last dinner 9pm
Credit cards [1] [2] [3] [5]
Parking on premises
Closed Jan–Feb

Table Restaurant
135 Babbacombe Rd
(0803) 34292

A recent change of ownership at this small restaurant (formerly the Green Mantle) has introduced a new young team offering good-quality well-presented food in a sophisticated atmosphere. Bright attractive dishes in the modern French style are served, such as light smooth terrines, steamed turbot in a delicate oriental sauce, médaillon of beef, and lemon sole paupiettes in a chive sauce, and these are complemented with fresh vegetables cooked al dente. Tempting rich sweets follow. Service is friendly.

Dinner td £13.50 or alc £14.50
Last dinner 10pm
No parking on premises
Closed lunch, & Mon

TORRINGTON, GREAT Devon Map 2 SS41

× **Rebecca's**
8 Potacre St
(0805) 22113

Meals and snacks are served from 9am to 10pm, six days a week, at this welcoming, cosy restaurant. A large choice of home-made food includes soups, pasta, fish and vegetarian dishes such as vegetable curry,

Bar lunch alc £7.50
Lunch alc £14
Dinner td fr

herb omelette or 'four vegetables with cheese'. There is a tempting à la carte menu (available at lunch and dinner), which changes according to seasonal produce available. It might include Lockets savoury (fresh pear slices with melted Stilton cheese), likky frizzle (a West Country dish of lamb, leeks and potatoes), pouting (similar to cod) fried in oatmeal, or Welsh pancakes. Vegetables are crisp and freshly cooked, and desserts are mouthwatering. The food is always well-prepared and attractively presented, and portions are generous. Service is pleasant and informal. Rebecca's arranges occasional speciality evenings such as theatre trips with dinner on the coach or, on one occasion, a 'teddy bears' picnic' tea.

£11.50 or alc £16
Last dinner 10pm
Credit cards [1] [2] [3] [5]
No parking on premises
Closed Sun

TOTNES Devon Map 3 SX86

GH **Old Forge**
Seymour Place,
Bridgetown
✆ (0803) 862174

Although offering only bed and breakfast accommodation, this charming and very friendly small guesthouse is well worth a visit. The building is a 600-year-old smithy, still operational, with proprietor Mr Allnut in the role of modern-day blacksmith, and it also incorporates the former village prison cell. Today, however, guests are made much more comfortable in the eight pretty bedrooms, (two are family rooms), all with CTV. They are also invited to enjoy the well-furnished lounge/breakfast room and the secluded small orchard and garden. Hospitality is good and there are special facilities for children, though dogs are not accepted.

Price band A/B
Parking on premises
Closed Xmas wk

TRECASTLE Powys Map 3 SN82

INN **Castle Hotel**
✆ Sennybridge
(087482) 354

This Georgian building in the village centre has been carefully renovated to provide modern facilities. The eight bedrooms are attractively decorated and comfortable, with extras including CTV, duvets and tea-making equipment. Three rooms have showers en suite, and there is one family room. The small residents' lounge on the first floor is supplemented by a lounge-bar and a more rustic public bar. Meals are served in both bars, and the well-prepared food represents good value.

Price band A
Bar meals alc £5
Dinner alc £9
Last dinner 9.30pm
Credit cards [1] [3]
Parking on premises

TROON Strathclyde *Ayrshire* Map 10 NS33

❀ × **Campbell's Kitchen**
3 South Beach
✆ (0292) 314421

The popular little town-centre restaurant has earned a sound local reputation for imaginative cooking based on good fresh produce. A strong French influence is reflected in such dishes as boeuf campbelloise — tender chopped fillets of beef in a richly flavoured sauce — and there are some particularly delectable sweets. Considerable care is taken over the presentation of food, service is both efficient and friendly, and subdued lighting makes for a relaxed, intimate atmospere.

Lunch td fr £2.95 or alc £12
Dinner td fr £8.25 or alc £16.50
Last dinner 9.30pm
Credit cards [1] [2] [3]
Closed 25–6 Dec & 1st 2 wks Jan
Closed Mon, & Sun dinner

★★★
Piersland House
Craigend Rd
✆ (0292) 314747

This impressive Tudor-style house, which is of considerable architectural interest, stands opposite the Royal Troon Golf Course in four acres of grounds. Its charming public rooms have extensive panelling and wood carvings, while open fires provide a focal point for friendly chat and a relaxing drink. Bedrooms have been tastefully refurbished, and four superior, particularly well-appointed rooms have been created. Though some of the other rooms are rather small, all are warm, comfortable and well-equipped. The elegant, panelled restaurant offers an interesting range of international dishes.

Price band C
Bar lunches td £2.20–£11
Lunch alc £19
Dinner td fr £14.50 or alc £19
Last dinner 9.30pm
Credit cards [1] [2] [3] [5]
Parking on premises

TROUTBECK (Nr Penrith) Cumbria Map 11 NY32

FH Lane Head
(On the A66 9 miles from Penrith and 8 miles from Keswick)
✆ Threlkeld (059683) 220

Oak beams and shining horse brasses set the scene in this charming Lakeland farmhouse. The excellent meals served in the old world dining room — a hearty breakfast and five-course dinner — make good use of local produce and are traditionally English in style. Both the snug little television lounge and the comfortable sitting room are very pleasant places in which to relax, and bedrooms are cosy and individual in style, one featuring a four-poster bed and one conveniently situated on the ground floor. Unfailingly friendly service ensures that your holiday is a pleasant one.

Price band A/B
Dinner, b&b £19–£24
Last dinner 6.30pm
Parking on premises
Closed Nov

TUNBRIDGE WELLS Kent Map 5 TQ53

× **Cheevers**
56 High St
✆ (0892) 545524

A well-balanced fixed-price menu offers excellent eating at this simple but charming French-style restaurant. Tempting dishes on our Inspector's visit included crab mousse wrapped in spinach, followed by médaillons of venison sautéed with Seville oranges. Wines are reasonably priced. Cheevers is run by enthusiastic young owners, and represents very good value for money.

Lunch alc £11
Dinner td £13.95
Last dinner 10.30pm
Credit cards [1] [3]
Parking nearby
Closed 1 wk Xmas, Easter, & Sep
Closed Sun & Mon

TWEEDSMUIR Borders *Lanarkshire* Map 11 NT12

GH Menzion Farmhouse
✆ (08997) 247

Menzion (pronounced Minyon) Farmhouse has been converted from its earlier use to become a superior style country guesthouse. The atmosphere is friendly and relaxed, and you will be introduced to your fellow guests in the attractive lounge. Since there is no television, you can enjoy relaxing in front of a log fire and listening to music as you browse through periodicals and books. Bedrooms, of which two are particularly spacious, are typical of the character of the house; extras like tea and coffee-making equipment and plenty of reading material are provided. Memorable hearty breakfasts and five-course set dinners are served in an elegant period dining room. The house's setting, in its own grounds about a mile

Price band A
Dinner, b&b £20–£22
Last dinner 7pm
Parking on premises

from the village, and surrounded by hills and trees, makes it an ideal spot for a peaceful holiday, but is within easy reach of Peebles and Moffat, while fishermen will find its proximity to the River Tweed and several reservoirs an attraction.

ULLINGSWICK Hereford & Worcester Map 3 SO54

GH The Steppes Country House Hotel
✆ Hereford (0432) 820424

This gleaming white stone house in a tranquil Herefordshire hamlet is run by charming, attentive hosts Henry and Tricia Howland, whose love of cooking and entertaining has gained them a good reputation. Their delightful little licensed hotel has been skilfully brought up to date with all the expected modern comforts, but it has lost none of the 17th-century character shown in ancient timbers, wattle-and-daub walls and stone fireplaces. The three bedrooms have CTV and showers en suite. There is one family room, but children under 10 are not accepted. Home-baked bread, home-grown vegetables and other local produce feature at dinner. There is a set menu, but dishes from a wide à la carte selection can be prepared by prior arrangement. Breakfasts are highly spoken of by many visitors; again, local produce figures prominently on the menu.

Price band A/B
Dinner, b&b £26–32
Last dinner 7pm
Parking on premises
Closed 2 wks before Xmas

UPHOLLAND Lancashire Map 7 SD50

★★ Holland Hall
6 Lafford Ln
✆ (0695) 624426

Well-furnished and comfortable, Holland Hall enjoys a quiet position at the end of a lane near the golf course. The well-appointed bedrooms are provided with a wealth of thoughtful extras, as well as en suite facilities and CTV. But pride of place must go to the excellent French-style restaurant with its high standard of cuisine. Service is both professional and friendly, and the hotel offers all-round value for money. Vegetarians can be catered for and music and dancing is available at weekends.

Price band C
Bar lunch £2–£5
Lunch td fr £5
Dinner td fr £11.50 or alc £15
Last dinner 10pm
Credit cards 1 2 3 4 5
Parking on premises
Closed 25 Dec–2 Jan

UPPINGHAM Leicestershire Map 4 SP89

★ Garden House
16 High St West
✆ (0572) 822352

This pleasant little hotel, which takes its name from its attractive walled garden, provides a haven of hospitality where cheerful, enthusiastic hosts make guests feel welcome from the moment they enter the elegant hallway. Most of the bedrooms have en suite facilities and all have CTV. A good deal of care goes into seeing that the highest standards of comfort are maintained, and the charming pink restaurant with its fresh flowers is tribute to this. Meals are excellent, and every need is catered for.

Price band B
Bar lunch alc £3.50
Lunch alc £6.50
Dinner alc £9.75
Last dinner 9pm
Credit cards 1 2 3
No parking on premises

❀ ★ HB
The Lake Isle
High St East
✆ (0572) 822951

David and Claire Whitfield have created an oasis of good eating, comfortable rooms and a very warm, friendly atmosphere here in the heart of this old town. Former Uppingham schoolboys may remember the premises as 'Sweeney Todd's', the hairdressers. The

Price band B
Lunch td fr £8.50
Dinner td £13 or alc £16

room where the barber's chair once stood is now a cosy bar. The restaurant itself has delightful rustic décor and furnishings. Here the Whitfields offer a three or five-course set menu with a limited choice of French-style dishes for each course. On our Inspector's visit, the menu listed artichoke and leek soup or prawn bisque, followed by a fish course or terrine of duck, and then a choice of three main courses including chicken with a walnut and orange sauce. A simpler menu is available at lunch-times. David Whitfield takes great pride in his two extensive wine lists, which include a good selection of half-bottles, and are very modestly priced. There are eight bedrooms, all prettily decorated and equipped with many comforts including en suite facilities, CTV, clock/radio, trouser-press, telephone socket and fresh fruit. Continental breakfast is served in rooms, and English breakfast in the restaurant.

Last dinner 10pm
Credit cards 1 2 3 5
Limited parking on premises

USK Gwent Map 3 SO30

★★ Three Salmons
Bridge St
(02913) 2133

The Three Salmons Hotel has offered a convivial welcome at the heart of this busy market town since the days when it was a coaching inn, and local farmers and businessmen, as well as visitors to the area, still flock to it today. The oak-panelled restaurant, with its original 18th-century cartoons, forms a fitting background for the enjoyment of fine food, while reasonably priced snacks are offered in the beam-and-plaster bar. All bedrooms have en suite facilities, CTV and telephones.

Price band B
Bar lunch alc £3.95
Lunch/dinner alc £13
Last dinner 9.30pm
Credit cards 1 2 3 4 5
Parking on premises
Closed 24–6 Dec

VOWCHURCH Hereford & Worcester Map 3 SO33

GH **The Croft**
Peterchurch
(09816) 226

Amy Spencer has gained many awards for her previous ventures, and her hospitality and good cooking are highlights of a stay at this fine 18th-century house in the Golden Valley. The grounds are a further attraction; her husband, Graham, is steadily restoring the original Edwardian garden layout, including the grass tennis court. Three bedrooms in the main house all have private bathrooms and CTV, and are fitted out to a high standard. (Self-catering accommodation is available in the adjoining cottages.) Mrs Spencer personally prepares all the food. Local produce features prominently in her soups, pâtés and mouthwatering sweets, which are served with fresh Jersey cream. Chicken in vermouth and dill sauce was a main course especially enjoyed by our Inspector. Dinner should be ordered by 6pm. The Croft does not take dogs, or children under 10.

Price band A/B
Dinner, b&b £22–£25
Last dinner 8pm
Parking on premises
B&b only at Xmas

WARE Hertfordshire Map 5 TL31

× **Ben's Brasserie**
14 High St
(0920) 68383

Good-value food is served in an amiable atmosphere at this simply furnished restaurant and wine-bar. Quality raw materials are used in the preparation of

Lunch alc £8.95
Dinner alc £11
Last dinner

the honest, no-nonsense food, and the blackboard menu changes daily. The à la carte menu offers a wider choice of dishes, including traditional English cooking as well as more unusual items, and fish is a speciality. Friendly, helpful service has contributed to the popular following enjoyed by this pleasant little brasserie.

9.30pm
Credit cards [1] [3]
Parking nearby
Closed 25–8 Dec
Closed Sun

WAREHAM Dorset Map 3 SY98

★★ L
Kemps Country House Hotel
East Stoke
(W of Wareham on A352)
✆ Bindon Abbey
(0929) 462563

Michael and Valerie Kemp steadily improved this small hotel just outside Wareham since they bought it in 1980. It stands in 1½ acres of grounds, which include the separate Coach House, now converted into two self-contained suites. The main hotel has five bedrooms, all with private facilities and CTV. Public rooms include two pleasant lounges and a Victorian panelled bar. The charming, busy restaurant, rebuilt several years ago, is the highlight of a stay at Kemps. It offers food with a French influence, chosen from either the table d'hôte or the à la carte menu. The four-course set dinner menu, which is changed daily, might start with home-made duck and orange terrine, crab and courgette thermidor or pancakes florentine, followed by a home-made soup and then grilled local trout, coq au vin or a roast. Sweets, chosen from the trolley, are followed by coffee with petits fours. A reasonably priced four-course lunch, including a choice of roasts, is served on Sundays. There is also a good choice of lighter lunches and snacks. Children are welcome at the hotel, but dogs are not accepted.

Price band C
Bar lunch td £3–£5
Lunch td fr £6 or alc £15
Dinner td fr £12 or alc £15
Last dinner 9.30pm
Credit cards [1] [2] [3] [5]
Parking on premises
Closed 11 Dec–9 Jan

★★★ BL
Priory Hotel
Church Green
✆ (09295) 2772/51666
Tx 41143
PRIORY G

It is especially for its food that our Inspector has chosen to include this lovely 16th-century priory. Dinner is served in the Abbot's Cellar, a room full of character, with a flagstone floor and stone walls. The set-price menu is very good value for four courses plus coffee with petits fours, and the quality of both food and service is excellent. Lunches are available in the Greenwood Room, which overlooks the gardens and river. A good choice is offered, ranging from salads and sandwiches to a full three-course meal, and again reasonably priced. Vegetarians can be catered for. The hotel also serves morning coffee, which comes with home-made shortbread. The Priory has 15 bedrooms, most with private facilities and all with CTV and telephones. Like the public rooms, they are very tastefully decorated, and the furnishings include some fine antiques. Equally delightful are the four acres of lovely gardens running down to the River Frome. The hotel does not accept dogs.

Price band C
Lunch td £8.75–£10.95
Dinner td £15–£17.50
Last dinner 10pm
Credit cards [1] [2] [3] [5]
Parking on premises

FH **Redcliffe Farm**
(1m SE of Wareham on unclassifield rd)
✆ (09295) 2225

A riverside footpath leads to Wareham from the Barnes family's 250-acre dairy farm. Here guests can stay in the heart of the country, with magnificent views, and still be within easy reach of Dorset's coastal resorts: Swanage, Poole and Bournemouth are all within 12 miles. Mrs Barnes lets five bedrooms, and provides hearty farmhouse breakfasts. No other meals

Prices on request
Parking on premises

are served. The bedrooms all have washbasins but share a bathroom. On the ground floor is a spacious, cosily furnished lounge which has a sun lounge adjacent. Dogs are not accepted.

WARREN STREET Kent Map 5 TQ95

INN **Harrow**
✆ Maidstone (0622) 858727

Pilgrims travelling to Canterbury on the nearby Pilgrims' Way once stopped to rest at this old inn high on the North Downs. Today, good food is available here, and there are seven bedrooms, among them one family room and four rooms with private facilities. Most of the rooms offer fine views of the surrounding countryside. There is a comfortable residents' lounge, and meals are served in both the restaurant and the bar, where a range of draught beers is available.

Price band B/C
Bar lunch td £2–£10
Lunch td fr £5.95 (Sun only)
Dinner td £8.50 or alc £12
Last dinner 9.45pm
Credit cards [1] [3]
Parking on premises
Closed Xmas & New Year

WARWICK Warwickshire Map 4 SP26

GH **Old Rectory**
Stratford Rd, Sherborne
(Off A46 2 miles SW of Warwick)
✆ Barford (0926) 624562

The Old Rectory offers accommodation in surroundings which are reminiscent of bygone days, for flagstone floors, inglenook fireplaces and low beams have all been lovingly restored. An antique-furnished dining room provides the perfect setting for guests to enjoy dinner by candlelight; more prosaically lit, it sees them enjoying a traditional English breakfast round the oak table. Elegance and style are continued into the bedrooms with their antique brass beds and floral décor, while the lounge is a charming blend of chintz, velour and stripped pine. In summer the attractive walled garden is popular. Dinner should be ordered by 3pm.

Price band A/B
Dinner, b&b £16–£24
Last dinner 7pm
Parking on premises
Closed 23 Dec–1 Jan

❀ ×× **Randolph's**
Coten End
✆ (0926) 491292

Until 1980, this cosy, low-beamed restaurant on the edge of the town was a row of tiny, timbered cottages. Today, you can relax in its informal atmosphere and enjoy food prepared with flair and a meticulous attention to detail. The short menu features predominantly French dishes, cooked in an imaginative, modern style. Sauces are light, complementing the very best of fresh ingredients and herbs from the garden. Vegetarian dishes are available. Children under nine are not accepted.

Dinner alc £20.10
Last dinner 9.30pm
Credit cards [1] [2] [3]
Parking nearby
Closed 25–30 Dec & 13–25 Jul
Closed lunch & Sun

WASDALE HEAD Cumbria Map 11 NY10

★★ **Wasdale Head Inn**
✆ Wasdale (09406) 229

Set at the head of Wasdale Valley and overlooked by Scafell and Great Gable, Wasdale Head is surrounded by breathtaking scenery. Its position makes it an ideal base for a walking or climbing holiday — and at the end of the day you can return to a hearty five-course dinner in the impressive oak-panelled dining room.

Price band B
Bar lunch £2.65–£8.55
Dinner td £11
Last dinner 7.30pm

Should you wish to eat more informally, the public bar serves good bar meals. After eating, you can relax in the warmth and comfort of the recently refurnished lounge, or there is a fascinating cocktail bar which contains many interesting antiques. The bedrooms are unusual, with fine furniture and panelled walls complemented by attractively coordinated soft furnishings.

Credit cards [1] [3]
Parking on premises
Closed mid Nov-mid Mar
Bar open weekends only in winter

WATERHOUSES Staffordshire Map 7 SK05

GH **Croft House Farm**
Waterfall
(1m NW of Waterhouse on unclassifield rd)
✆ (05386) 553

Former motor mechanic Stefan Lewy and his schoolteacher wife Barbara launched themselves into a new career when they decided, in 1985, to convert their 17th-century stone farmhouse into this cosy, welcoming guesthouse. Six comfortable modern bedrooms are now available here, and meals are served both to guests and non-residents. Children are welcome: there are two family rooms, and cots and high chairs are available. Bedrooms all have washbasins and CTV, and there are two lounges, one of which has a small bar where Stefan is adapting most successfully to his new role as host and barman. The kitchen is Barbara's domain: wholesome, traditional home cooking is her speciality, served (in generous portions) in the pleasantly furnished dining room. Value for money at Croft House Farm is excellent, and there are special reductions for senior citizens.

Price band A
Dinner, b&b £15–£16.50
Last dinner 9pm
Parking on premises

❀×× **Olde Beams**
Leek Rd
✆ (05386) 254

Situated in an area where quarrying and cement production are the key industries, Waterhouses might seem an unlikely location for what is one of the best restaurants in the provinces. Built in 1746, this lovely old stone cottage has steadily been improved over recent years by owners Nigel and Ann Wallis, yet still retains its original character, with oak beams and an open fire. The French country-style cuisine, presided over by Nigel Wallis who trained at the Savoy and is a member of the Master Chefs' Institute, is of a very high standard. Excellent use is made of the best fresh seasonal ingredients and both à la carte and table d'hôte menus represent very good value for money. All in all, this is a first-class restaurant whose reputation is justifiably growing.

Lunch td fr £9.85 or alc £18.50
Dinner alc £18.50
Last dinner 10pm
Credit cards [1] [2] [3] [5]
Parking on premises
Closed 1st 2 wks Jan & 1st wk Oct
Closed Sun & Mon

WATERMILLOCK Cumbria Map 12 NY42

★ RED ♣♣
Old Church Hotel
✆ Pooley Bridge (08536) 204

This is a really special hotel, and its prices are quite reasonable, considering the luxury that guests are offered. Its setting, in its own grounds on the shores of Lake Ullswater, is spectacular and the atmosphere is pleasant and friendly,.special touches such as the servicing of bedrooms in the evening giving the impression that nothing is too much trouble for the staff. The house is comfortable, with a log fire often burning in the carved wooden fireplace in the hall and

Price band C (inc dinner)
Dinner td £15
Last dinner 8pm
Parking on premises
Closed Dec–Easter
Restricted

fresh flowers everywhere. The charming main lounge has been refurbished this year, and there are also a television lounge and a cocktail bar. Bedrooms, some of which have magnificent views, are very attractive, and the dining room with its polished oak tables provides a pleasant setting in which to enjoy a really good home-cooked five-course dinner, chosen from a limited menu but of first-class quality and generously served.

service Nov & Mar

WATH (IN NIDDERDALE) North Yorkshire Map 87 SE16

Sportsman's Arms
(2 miles N)
✆ Harrogate (0423) 711306

This 17th-century inn with bedrooms, set in the midst of delightful scenery, features a restaurant of quality and style. The menu of traditional English cuisine is expertly designed to reflect the countryside, with game in season and a predominance of top-quality fresh produce, while the excellence of the food is complemented by a high standard of service and attractive presentation. There is also an exceptionally good wine list of around 133 wines from most of the world's producers. Surroundings are particularly pleasant, smart décor and furnishings providing just the right element of sophistication for an elegant meal.

Price band B
Bar lunch 95p–£5.95
Lunch td £6.80 (Sun only)
Dinner td £7.50–£12.80 or alc £16
Last dinner 9pm
Credit cards [1] [2] [3] [5]
Parking on premises
Closed Sun dinner (except residents)

WATTON Norfolk Map 5 TF90

★★ H
Clarence House
78 High St
✆ (0953) 884252

Lovers of Victoriana will be enchanted by this small hotel, dating from the 19th century and attractively furnished in the style of the period, though with the addition of modern comforts. The six bedrooms all have private bath or shower and CTV, and a warm welcome is assured by owners Edward and Stella Bullen. Edward Bullen is in charge of the cooking, which is mostly in the grand British style. A typical menu might include vegetable soup, Cromer crab or Norfolk mussels followed by beef Wellington, fillet of pork with sage and onion, or guinea fowl in red sauce. Flavours of Victorian India are sometimes evident in mulligatawny soup, and lamb or chicken with turmeric or cardamon. The set-price dinner is available to non-residents but lunch is served to residents only. Children over 12 years of age are welcome; dogs are not accepted.

Price band B
Lunch td £9.50
Dinner td £12.50
Last dinner 8.30pm
Credit cards [1] [2] [3] [5]
Parking on premises

WELLINGBOROUGH Northamptonshire Map 4 SP86

GH **Oak House Private Hotel**
9 Broad Green
✆ (0933) 71133

This private hotel was formed by the conversion of a row of three cottages standing opposite the original village green. Bedrooms (all but one of which have en suite facilities) provide excellent accommodation for the business traveller, being compact but thoughtfully furnished and well-equipped with CTV, clock/radios and tea-making equipment. There are two small, cosy lounges (one with colour television), and meals are served in a light, split-level dining room. Standards of service are professional throughout, and there is a genuine desire to please guests.

Price band A/B
Dinner, b&b £21.50–£27.50
Last dinner 6.15pm
Credit cards [1] [3]
Parking on premises
Closed Xmas

WELLS Somerset Map 3 ST54

GH The Coach House
Stoberry Park
✆ (0749) 76535

Although it is within easy walking distance of the centre of Wells, this beautifully converted coach house enjoys a peaceful setting in six acres of parkland. There are magnificent views of Wells Cathedral and, in the distance, Glastonbury Tor. Mr and Mrs Poynter are welcoming hosts and make sure their guests are comfortable here. The three bedrooms all have private bathrooms and attractive furnishings, and there is a large, homely lounge and dining area. Dinner is available if ordered by 8.30am.

Price band A/B
Dinner, b&b £20.50 £24
Last dinner 7pm
Parking on premises
Closed 24–31 Dec

WEMBLEY Greater London

×× **Moghul Brasserie**
525 High Rd
✆ 01-903 6967

The nomadic way of life of the Moghuls of Northern India gave rise to their typical style of cooking, which involves using open fires and makeshift earthenware ovens. Their ideas were gradually introduced into other parts of India and have become part of Indian cookery as it is known in Britain. Mughlai specialities at this stylish modern restaurant include a large selection of kebabs, as well as tandoori dishes. Prices are sensible, and one of the dishes on offer allows customers to sample half-a-dozen traditional Mughlai foods. A buffet lunch is available on Sundays at £7.50. Vegetarians are well-catered for. Competent service is by helpful, friendly young waiters.

Lunch td fr £8 or alc £12
Dinner td fr £8 or alc £12
Last dinner 11.15pm
Credit cards [1] [2] [3] [5]
Parking on premises
Closed 25–6 Dec

WEST BEXINGTON Dorset Map 3 SY58

★★ **Manor Hotel**
Beach Rd
✆ Burton Bradstock (0308) 897616

The sea is only a few hundred yards from this peacefully situated stone manor house, and most bedrooms have sea views. Comfort and character in abundance make Mr and Mrs Childs' little hotel well worth seeking out. Good table d'hôte lunch and dinner menus in the most attractive dining room are supplemented by bar meals, as well as afternoon tea, and there is children's high tea for residents. Meals are based on fresh local produce, and vegetarian food is available. All 10 bedrooms (including one family room) have private facilities, CTV and radio, and are prettily decorated. Downstairs there is a fine lounge and a bar which leads out into the garden. Service is always friendly and efficient. Dogs are not accepted.

Price band B
Bar lunch £1.60–£5.50
Lunch td fr £9.65
Dinner td fr £11.95
Last dinner 10pm
Credit cards [1] [2] [3]
Parking on premises

WEST BROMWICH West Midlands Map 7 SP09

Darby's
Wood Lane
✆ 021-553 4007

This pub was the flagship of Darbys Brewery before it became part of the Bass, Mitchell and Butler group. One of Darby's senior executives was born here before it was modernised in about 1930 when, it is claimed, the glow from nearby foundries and furnaces was 'so bright that lights were not needed at night to read newspapers'! Recently the building's interior was refurbished in 1930s style with pink and grey décor, and at the same time a fish restaurant was incorporated. Here, tasty filling meals of both the common and more unusual varieties of fish can be enjoyed, including swordfish and dogfish when in

Last dinner 10pm
Credit cards [1] [2] [3]
Parking on premises

season. For non-fish-eaters there are steaks and pizzas, while a bar snack may be taken in to the lounge or even a chip butty in the bar.

WEST CHILTINGTON West Sussex Map 4, TQ01

FH **New House**
✆ (07983) 2215

Mr and Mrs Steele offer excellent bed and breakfast accommodation at their 15th-century listed farmhouse, which is set in beautifully kept grounds in this peaceful and delightful village. Oak-beamed rooms and an inglenook fireplace add to the atmosphere, and an open log fire warms the lounge and dining room in winter. Good traditional English breakfasts are served and, although no other meals are provided, food is available at two inns within easy reach. CTV is provided in all four bedrooms, which are of good size and furnished in keeping with the house. Two of the rooms have private facilities, and two are family rooms. Children under 10 are not accepted, and neither are dogs.

Price band A
Parking on premises
Closed Jan–Nov

WESTERHAM Kent Map 5 TQ45

★★★ B
King's Arms
Market Square
✆ (0959) 62990

Proprietors Mr and Mrs Boatwright take great pride in their 18th-century hotel, which has been tastefully renovated to give spacious and comfortable accommodation. There is a cosy bar/lounge, and a charming restaurant where a reasonably priced set menu is usually offered in addition to the à la carte menu. Standards of cooking are generally high. Telephones, CTV and tiled private bathrooms are standard in all 13 bedrooms, which include two family rooms.

Price band C
Bar lunch td £2–£8
Lunch/dinner td fr £11 or alc fr £15
Last dinner 10pm
Credit cards [1] [2] [3] [5]
Parking on premises

WEST LAYTON North Yorkshire Map 12 NZ10

GH **West Layton Manor Hotel**
(¼ mile off A66—signed—N of Scotch Corner)
✆ Darlington (0325) 718633

Spacious elegance and the luxuries of country life in bygone days are the keynotes of this gabled Victorian manor house, which stands in its own wooded grounds near Richmond. The high-ceilinged entrance hall has an inviting log fire, the warmth of which is outdone only by that of the welcome extended to guests. No detail is forgotten in the elegant sitting room, while the large, comfortable bedrooms all have private bathrooms, CTV, tea/coffee-making facilities and a wealth of extras. Meals are excellent, freshly cooked to Cordon Bleu standards and based on first-class local produce wherever possible.

Price band B/C
Dinner, b&b £30–£37
Last dinner 8pm
Credit cards [1] [3]
Parking on premises
Closed 23 Dec–3 Jan

WEST LINTON Borders *Peeblesshire* Map 11 NT15

GH **Medwyn House**
Medwyn Rd
✆ (0968) 60542

Medwyn House is set in 30 acres of beautiful grounds, the splendour of which is matched only by the quality of its interior — in particular, the baronial, wood-panelled hall and the elegant drawing room. Bedrooms are comfortable and thoughtfully equipped, with spacious en suite bathrooms. The house in unlicensed, but a complimentary sherry is served before dinner

Price band B
Dinner td £11
Last dinner 7.30pm
Parking on premises

and guests are encouraged to bring in their own wine. The three-course meals usually feature home-made soups, roasts and a choice of sweets, with extras such as trout with cream sauce added on occasion.

WESTON-SUPER-MARE Avon Map 3 ST36

★★★ L **Royal Pier Hotel**
Birnbeck Rd
✆ (0934) 26644

From its elevated position near the Old Pier, this recently refurbished hotel offers unrivalled views of Weston Bay and the Bristol Channel from most of its rooms. As well as a comfortable lounge, the hotel has two bars. A good range of reasonably priced snacks and hot meals is available in the Prince Consort Bar, and there is a more formal cocktail bar, Kennedy's, for pre-dinner drinks. A choice between a five-course set dinner and an à la carte menu is offered in the spacious, well-appointed restaurant overlooking the sea. Lunch is also available here, and vegetarian food can be provided. Most of the 40 bedrooms have private bathrooms, and all have CTV, radios and telephones. There are four family rooms. Leisure amenities include table tennis and pool tables, and there is live music twice weekly as well as a special programme at Christmas. Dogs are not accepted.

Price band B
Bar lunch 65p–£5.20
Lunch td fr £5.95 or alc £12
Dinner td fr £10.50 or alc £12
Last dinner 9.15pm
Credit cards 1 2 3 5
Parking on premises

WEST RUNTON Norfolk Map 9 TG14

×× **Mirabelle**
Station Rd
✆ (026375) 396

The inexpensive table d'hôte meals served by this simple, comfortable little restaurant are a major factor in its popularity. Service is friendly, a good choice is offered in each of the three courses, and helpings are generous. At lunch the cost varies according to the main course selected, while at dinner time a wide range of alternatives feature on each of the two set-price menus. Seafood is a speciality, and the inclusion of such dishes as Wiener Schnitsel is an indication of the chef's background. The splendid wine list includes a wide range of some quite classic wines. Vegetarian meals are available.

Lunch td fr £7 or alc £16
Dinner td fr £10.50 or alc £16
Last dinner 9.15pm
Credit cards 1 2 3 5
Parking on premises
Closed 1st 2 wks Nov
Closed Mon, & Sun dinner Nov–May

WETHERAL Cumbria Map 12 NY45

× **Fantails**
The Green
✆ (0228) 60239

Situated in the middle of the peaceful village, on the first floor of a building that dates back to the 17th century, this tastefully modernised restaurant retains much of its original character. Oak beams, leaded windows and open fires provide a charming background for candlelit dinners. The atmosphere is helpful and service friendly, the proprietor joining you in the cosy cocktail bar to explain the menu and take your order. A short but interesting à la carte menu changes regularly to take advantage of seasonal items, and the freshly prepared food is of a very high standard, featuring such dishes as mussels and scallops in an orange and cream sauce, or pork escalopes cooked with tomatoes, mushrooms, cream and whisky.

Light lunch alc £5
Lunch alc £10
Dinner alc £13.50
Last dinner 9.30pm
Credit cards 1 2 3 5
Parking on premises
Closed 26 Dec, 1 Jan & Feb
Closed Sun & Mon

WHAPLODE Lincolnshire Map 8 TF32

FH **Guy Wells**
✆ Holbeach (0406) 22239

An English country garden in the depths of Fenland is the ideal setting for this splendid Queen Anne farmhouse, in whose elegant surroundings guests can enjoy genuine hospitality. The three bedrooms are prettily furnished, one boasting an interesting half tester bed, and all have homely personal touches. A happy, family atmosphere prevails in the lounge as guests drink tea in front of the fire while discussing dinner with their hostess, and the subsequent meal, served in the cosy, oak-beamed dining room, will be a pleasurable experience. Warm, personal attention — which can include a guided tour of the farm, if desired — is the hallmark of this establishment.

Price band A
Dinner, b&b £16.50–£18.50
Dinner alc £6.50
Last dinner 7pm
Parking on premises
Closed Oct–Mar

WHITEBRIDGE Highland *Inverness-shire* Map 14 NH41

★★ RED
Knockie Lodge
(8 miles NE of Fort Augustus off B862 E Loch Ness side road)
✆ Gorthleck (04563) 276

Knockie Lodge stands in splendid seclusion, well off the east Loch Ness side road, and it offers an ideal environment not only to those seeking a quiet holiday but also to those who want to fish or shoot. The house, a former hunting lodge, has been transformed to provide first-class accommodation, its focal point being the fine drawing room, with its log fire, antique furniture, paintings, and a wealth of reading material that gives it a relaxed, library-like atmosphere. It is here that the proprietors mingle with their guests before and after dinner, in house party-style. Guests help themselves at the bar on the 'trust' principle, and, while they drink, can enjoy delightful views of surrounding lochs and mountains from the small patio sun lounge that leads off the drawing room. Bedrooms vary in size but are all tastefully appointed, reflecting the country house-style. Dinner is a set four-course meal, usually featuring Scottish meat and game.

Price band B
Bar lunch td £3–£8
Dinner alc £15
Last dinner 8.30pm
Credit cards [1] [2] [3]
Parking on premises
Closed 23 Oct–Apr

WHITEBROOK Gwent Map 3 SO50

❀ ★★ H **Crown at Whitebrook**
(Adjacent to hamlet of Whitebrook)
✆ Monmouth (0600) 860254
Tx 498280

This one-time inn, now converted to a restaurant with some rooms to let, stands in a quiet valley overlooking the river and a spread of peaceful countryside. Its cuisine has established such a reputation for excellence that you will need to reserve a table in advance, but the standard of the meal you are served makes this effort — and that involved in negotiating meandering country lanes — well-worthwhile.

Price band C/D
Bar lunch td fr £4.85
Lunch td fr £9.25
Dinner td fr £2.75 or alc £18.50
Last dinner 10pm
Credit cards [1] [2] [3] [5]
Parking on premises & nearby
Closed 25–6 Dec

WHITEHAVEN Cumbria Map 11 NX91

× **Bruno's**
9–10 Church St
✆ (0946) 65270

This surprisingly good little restaurant, standing above a basement wine-bar where pizzas and pasta are served, has the intimate yet friendly atmosphere that is typically Italian. À la carte menus offer a wide range of interesting dishes both at lunch-time and in the evenings, and all the food is very well-prepared. A typical meal might be fungi ripieni (mushrooms filled with pâté, topped with Parmesan then baked in a rich garlic, onion and cream sauce), followed by involtini di maiale (pork stuffed with spinach, cheese and ham) and a home-made sweet from the tempting selection. Vegetarian dishes are available, and the restaurant is fully licensed. Should you wish to sample one of 'Bruno's Special Dishes', you must place your order 24 hours in advance.

Bar lunch fr £1.40
Lunch alc £4–£5
Dinner alc £10
Last dinner 10.30pm
Credit cards 1 3
Parking nearby
Closed Sun lunch

WHITLAND Dyfed Map 2 SN21

★ HB **Waungron Farm Hotel**
Waungron Isaf
(1m SW of Whitland off B4328)
✆ (0994) 240682

The Daniels family are attentive and caring hosts at their delightful, secluded farm hotel. The 14 comfortably furnished bedrooms each have external access and are equipped with CTV and private bath or shower rooms. Three are family rooms, and there is also a bridal suite with a four-poster bed and an executive suite with a jacuzzi bath. Food of a very high standard, with a wide choice of dishes, is served in the beamed restaurant, which is an attractive converted barn.

Price band B
Bar lunch fr £1.75
Dinner td fr £9
Last dinner 9pm
Credit cards 1 3
Parking on premises
Closed Xmas week

WHITLEY BAY Tyne and Wear Map 12 NZ37

GH **White Surf**
8 South Parade
✆ 091-253 0103

This small, friendly guesthouse, set in the middle of a terrace close to the town centre and the sea, offers bright, comfortable accommodation in rooms displaying a strong Scandinavian influence, with pine much in evidence. Light décor and furnishings create a feeling of spaciousness in the compact bedrooms, while the sitting room with its colour television, is roomy and relaxing. The home-made dinners served in the white dining room represent very good value for money, offering such main course options as mixed grill, a variety of salads, local fish or sweet and sour prawns, all accompanied by fresh vegetables and followed by a traditional range of puddings. Breakfasts, too, are substantial and offer a choice.

Price band A
Dinner, b&b £13–£14
Last dinner 8pm
Parking on premises

GH **York House Hotel**
30 Park Parade
✆ 091-252 8313

Set in a quiet residential area, York House is within walking distance of both the town centre and the sea. A friendly proprietress welcomes guests warmly and ensures that they are comfortable throughout their stay. Bedrooms, though small, are well-appointed, having CTV and tea-making facilities, and en suite facilities in most. And there is a comfortable lounge. The home-made dinners are particularly noteworthy, offering exceptionally good value for money.

Price band A
Dinner, b&b £18.50
Last dinner 7.30pm
Credit cards 1 3
Parking on premises

WHITNEY-ON-WYE Hereford & Worcester Map 3 SO24

INN **Rhydspence**
(2m W of Whitney on A438)
✆ Clifford (04973) 262

This timber-framed 16th-century inn is one of many that can claim to the 'first and last' in England on roads crossing into Wales. At one time it was much frequented by Welsh drovers, and it is mentioned several times in Kilvert's Diary. Travellers are still greeted by a log fire that burns for most of the year in the bar. A large menu of bar meals is supplemented by a blackboard list of 'specials'. Food ranges from modest snacks to full meals, which are served in a comfortable little dining room. Good use is made of game and fish. Fresh, wholesome food is also a feature of breakfasts here, which are served in a pleasant room recently refurnished with stripped, waxed settles. All of the five bedrooms have private facilities, and CTV, and further improvements are currently being made.

Price band B
Bar lunch alc £3
Lunch/dinner £8
Last dinner 10pm
Credit cards [1] [2] [3]
Parking on premises

WIDDINGTON Essex Map 5 TL53

FH **Thistley Hall**
✆ Saffron Walden (0799) 40388

Flower-filled gardens amid a rural landscape surround this beautiful and historic farmhouse. There is a warm and cheerful welcome here from Mrs Vernon, who lets three prettily decorated bedrooms and provides hearty breakfasts. The house is full of character: bedrooms have exposed beams and the large lounge/dining room is furnished with antiques. One of the bedrooms is suitable for familes, but children under five are not accepted (and neither are dogs). Weekly terms only are available from Jan to May.

Price band A
Parking on premises
Restricted accommodation Sep

WIDEGATES Cornwall Map 2 SX25

GH **Coombe Farm**
✆ Looe (05034) 223

Children (though not under-fives) are welcome at this eight-bedroom guesthouse owned by Alexander and Sally Low. Family leisure amenities include a heated outdoor swimming pool, a croquet lawn and a stone barn that has been converted into a games room where guests can play table tennis or snooker. The house stands in 10 acres of grounds with woods, streams and ponds, and there is a variety of domestic animals. The Lows are hospitable and welcoming hosts, and the warm atmosphere of their home is highlighted by log fires in the comfortable lounge in winter. Fresh local produce is the basis of the set dinner, which is available to residents only. All the bedrooms have washbasins, and four are family rooms.

Price band A/B
Dinner, b&b £18–£24
Last dinner 7.30pm
Parking on premises
Closed Nov–Feb

WIGHT, ISLE OF
FRESHWATER Map 4 SZ38

★★★
Albion Hotel
Freshwater Bay
✆ (0983) 753631

This pleasant holiday hotel stands right at the water's edge, in the delightful, unspoilt bay that nestles between Tennyson Down and Afton Down at the western end of the island. Most of the 43 bedrooms are of good size and have sea views, and many also have balconies. Almost half the rooms will accommodate families. CTV and telephones are

Price band B
Bar lunch td fr £2.50
Lunch td £6
Dinner td fr £10.50
Last dinner

provided in all rooms, and most have bathrooms en suite. The Albion has excellent lounge facilities and a comfortable cocktail bar with a relaxing, friendly atmosphere. The restaurant, bright and spacious, offers reasonably priced table d'hôte menus at lunch and dinner. There is a well-balanced wine list of mostly popular wines at moderate prices. Staff are helpful and willing.

8.30pm
Credit cards [1] [2] [3]
Parking on premises
Closed Nov–Mar

NEWPORT Map 4 SZ48

× **Lugley's**
42 Lugley St
✆ (0983) 521062

Good, fresh ingredients go into the French-influenced dishes produced by proprietress Angela Hewitt at this small restaurant. Some of her own specialities add interest and variety to the menu, and she cooks competently and with flair. There are some unusual sweets, and a list of mostly popular, inexpensive wines complements the menu. The atmosphere here is casual and informal, and service is by pleasant young waitresses. Children under 12 are not admitted.

Lunch td fr £7.95
Dinner alc £11.65
Last dinner 9.30pm
No parking on premises
Closed 2 wks Feb & 2 wks Oct
Closed Sun

SANDOWN Map 4 SZ58

GH **St Catherine's Hotel**
1 Winchester Park Rd
✆ (0983) 402392

This small private hotel is one of the best of its kind on the island. It is in a residential area, but within easy reach of the beach. Bedrooms and public rooms alike are comfortably furnished and tastefully decorated. All 18 bedrooms have private facilities and CTV. There are three family rooms. Proprietors Mr and Mrs Hitchcock offer their guests a warm welcome, and personally supervise the running of their hotel. Cooking here is of a high standard: plain English food, using good fresh materials, is the basis of the dinner menu, and the hotel holds a residential licence.

Price band A/B
Dinner td fr £5
Last dinner 7pm
Credit cards [1] [3]
Limited parking on premises
Closed Xmas & New Year

SEAVIEW Map 4 SZ69

❀ ★★ **Seaview Hotel & Restaurant**
High St
✆ (0983) 612711

Traditional hospitality is still to be found at this delightful Edwardian-style hotel in an old fishing village between Ryde and Bembridge. Proprietors Nicola and Nicholas Hayward maintain exceptionally high standards of accommodation, food and service. The 14 bedrooms have been thoughtfully furnished and decorated, in keeping with the style of the house, and are provided with many extras such as sewing kits, toiletries and mineral water. Most have private bathrooms and all have CTV. Public rooms include a peaceful first-floor drawing room and two bars. The cocktail bar has a patio overlooking the sea, and the Pump Bar has a welcoming open fire in winter and serves local real ale. Bar snacks range from sandwiches to fresh whole lobster, or crab cooked with cheese and spices and browned under the grill. Cuisine at the Seaview is of a very high standard. The elegant restaurant, with its collection of antique clocks, offers mainly French-style food, chosen from à la carte or reasonably priced table d'hôte menus.

Price band B
Bar lunch fr £2
Lunch td fr £6.95 or alc £10
Dinner td fr £7.50 or alc £11
Last dinner 9.30pm
Credit cards [1] [2] [3]
Parking on premises
Restaurant closed Sun dinner

SHANKLIN Map 4 SZ58

★★ **Luccombe Hall**
Luccombe Rd
✆ (0983) 862719
Tx 869441

This family-run hotel, catering for families, stands away from the sea front on a cliff top. It offers excellent leisure facilities, with indoor and outdoor heated swimming pools, tennis and squash courts, sauna and solarium. Bedrooms are spacious, modestly furnished but equipped with many modern amenities, and the public rooms have been upgraded to provide a high standard of comfort. Food is basically English in style, well-prepared and offering a reasonable degree of choice.

Price band B
Bar lunch fr £2.50
Lunch td fr £6
Dinner td fr £11.25
Last dinner 8pm
Credit cards [1] [3]
Parking on premises
Closed Jan

❀ × **Smalls Brasserie**
34 High St
✆ (0983) 865195

As the name suggests, this restaurant is not spacious, but it is comfortable, with a pleasant atmosphere, and lacks neither quality nor style. Cuisine in the light, modern style makes use of first-rate ingredients, guests enjoying such dishes as rabbit and apricot pâté en brioche with Cumberland sauce, or noisette of lamb in fragrant basil, tomato and wine sauce. The menu is short, and the charge varies with the number of courses taken.

Dinner td fr £11.45
Last dinner 10pm
Credit cards [1] [2] [3]
No parking on premises
Closed 1–30 Jan
Closed lunch

VENTNOR Map 4 SZ57

★★ HBL
Bonchurch Manor
Bonchurch
(1m E of Ventnor)
✆ (0983) 852868

This imposing Victorian country house is splendidly sited overlooking the sea and sheltered by St Boniface Down to the north. Proprietors Jean and Alan Smith encourage an informal, relaxing atmosphere. The large lounge has plenty of comfortable armchairs and two open fires, and a good selection of books and games is provided. There is also a grand piano. All 12 bedrooms, most of which have sea views, have private facilities, telephones, hairdriers, radios and CTV. There are four family rooms, though the hotel does not take children under seven. Breakfast, dinner and Sunday lunch are served in the bright, cosy restaurant. The five-course table d'hôte dinner menu offers a good choice for each course. Local seafood or home-made soup might appear on the list of starters, while main courses include roasts, fish and poultry dishes, often served with interesting sauces. Home-made desserts are chosen from the trolley. Amenities at Bonchurch Manor include a heated indoor pool, and the hotel stands in its own neatly kept grounds.

Price band B
Dinner td fr £10.95 or alc £14
Last dinner 9pm
Credit card [3]
Parking on premises
Closed Jan
Closed lunch (except Sun)

Four Seasons
15 High St
✆ (0983) 852169

A friendly atmosphere prevails at this simple wine-bar in Ventor's main shopping area. Wine is the theme of the numerous posters and photographs on the walls, and the furnishings are of plain pine. A short menu is supplemented by daily specials; the cooking is basically English in style, and of a high standard. Popular, inexpensive wines form the basis of a limited list. There is live music here on Saturday evenings.

Lunch/dinner alc £7
Last dinner 11pm
Credit cards [1] [2] [3] [4] [5]
Parking nearby
Closed Mon–Fri dinner in winter

★★ B
Highfield Hotel
Leeson Rd,
Bonchurch
(1½m NE of
Ventnor on A3055)
✆ (0983) 852800

Dennis and Thelma Flaherty are welcoming hosts at their charming Victorian country house, which stands in an attractive garden and overlooks the sea. Décor and furnishings are tasteful and attractive throughout, and the comfortable public rooms include a sun lounge and a bar. The 12 large bedrooms all have bathrooms en suite, and other standard facilities include CTV and telephones. Meals feature sound, honest cooking by Mrs Flaherty, including vegetarian meals.

Price band B
Bar lunch td £1–£4
Lunch td fr £4 or alc £6
Dinner td fr £8 or alc £10
Last dinner 7.30pm
Credit cards [1] [3] [4] [5]
Parking on premises
Closed Nov–Mar

GH **Under Rock Hotel**
Shore Rd,
Bonchurch
✆ (0983) 852714

A former winner of the AA's 'Guesthouse of the Year' award, this secluded 18th-century house has remained a delightful place to stay. It is surrounded by beautiful gardens and woodland with sub-tropical trees and shrubs, and the house itself is tastefuly furnished and decorated. Seven bedrooms are available, all with washbasins and CTV. The hospitable proprietors are Mr and Mrs Kellway, who personally ensure their guests' comfort. Food is a highlight here: bread and preserves are home-made, and breakfasts are exceptionally good. The hotel has a residential licence. Dogs are not accepted, and neither are children under 10.

Price band B
Dinner, b&b £21
Last dinner 6.30pm
Parking on premises
Closed Nov–Feb

WILLERSEY Gloucestershire Map 4 SP13

GH **Old Rectory**
Church St
✆ Broadway (0386) 853729

This fine 17th-century house stands in a quiet village only five minutes' drive from Broadway, and is an ideal bed and breakfast base for touring the Cotswolds. The house, and the wall that encloses its lovely garden, are built of Cotswold stone, and each of the six bedrooms is named after a well-known Cotswold town or village. All the rooms are individually furnished and have private facilities and a host of thoughtful extras ranging from CTV, radio, telephones, trouser-presses and hairdriers to toiletries and good-quality towels. There are two family bedrooms, but children under 10 are not accepted. Public rooms retain their original fireplaces and oak beams, and are comfortable and elegant. Breakfast is served in a most attractive dining room overlooking the garden. The Old Rectory does not accept dogs.

Price band B/C
Credit cards [1] [3]
Parking on premises
Closed Xmas week

WILLITON Somerset Map 3 ST04

GH **Curdon Mill**
Lower Vellow
✆ Stogumber (0984) 56522

Situated amid peaceful farmland at the foot of the Quantock Hills, this former mill offers excellent accommodation in six bedrooms, all of which have private facilities and CTV. The building has been restored with care to retain original features such as the water wheel, which can be seen working. The lounge and dining room are both on the first floor, the latter offering a view of the pretty stream and

Price band A/B
Dinner, b&b £19.50–£21.50
Last dinner 8.30pm
Parking on premises

waterfall. Here guests can enjoy delightful and imaginative home-cooked meals, made with local produce, and the dining room is also open to non-residents by prior arrangement. The warm hospitality of the proprietor, Daphne Criddle, will long be remembered by visitors to Curdon Mill.

WILMCOTE Warwickshire Map 4 SP15

★★ Swan House Hotel
The Green
Stratford-upon-Avon (0789) 67030

This delightful village contains the house of Mary Arden, Shakespeare's mother, and provides a welcome retreat from the noise and bustle of Stratford. The 18th-century Swan House provides visitors with accommodation of traditional charm enhanced by modern comfort, and guarantees a warm welcome, a friendly atmosphere and attentive service. The bar, with its roaring log fire and selection of real ales, is predictably popular, and food of a consistently high standard is served both here and in the restaurant. Bedrooms with bright, warm bathrooms are cosy and attractively furnished, fresh flowers adding the finishing touch.

Price band B
Bar lunch td £1–£5.50
Lunch td £6.25 (Sun only)
Dinner alc £11
Last dinner 9.30pm
Credit cards [1] [2] [3]
Parking on premises
Closed 24–8 Dec

WINCHELSEA East Sussex Map 5 TQ91

× Manna Plat
Mill Rd
Rye (0797) 226317

This delightful slate-hung house, which boasts 13th-century vaulted cellars once used by smugglers, is tucked away among the historic lanes of Winchelsea. It is now a small, informal restaurant run by its owners Tina Duggan and Stewart Palmer. Fresh local ingredients are used liberally in the fixed-price lunch and dinner menus, which represent excellent value. Home-made soups are good, and our Inspector enjoyed chicken in cream and mushroom sauce followed by treacle tart. An à la carte menu is also offered. The restaurant has a pleasant atmosphere, and the small bar and dining room are enhanced by local artists' work on the walls.

Lunch alc £5.50
Dinner alc £9.50
Last dinner 9pm
Credit card [1]
Parking on premises
Closed Mon (except Bank Hols)
Closed Sat lunch & Sun dinner

WINDERMERE Cumbria Map 7 SD49

★ H Cedar Manor
Ambleside Rd
(09662) 3192

A magnificent old Indian cedar tree standing in the garden gave its name to this traditional Lakeland house which has attractive Gothic-style windows. The public rooms are furnished with taste and the six bedrooms, five of which have en suite bathroom or shower and all with CTV, are individually styled. One of the bedrooms has a four-poster bed, two are family rooms and there are special facilities for children. The hotel offers a particularly good home-cooked five-course dinner, a typical menu might include an unusual soup such as chestnut and mushroom, followed by sorbet in sparkling wine, then hake in smoked salmon and prawn sauce or roast duckling with cherries. A deliciously tempting sweet and cheese round off the meal. The hospitality of the owners, Mr and Mrs Hadley, is excellent.

Price band B
Dinner td £10.50
Last dinner 8.30pm
Credit cards [1] [3]
Parking on premises
Closed 1st 2 wks Jan
Closed lunch

★★ HBL
Linthwaite
Bowness
(Leave Bowness on A5074 for Kendal, turn L on B5284 for Crook. Hotel drive 300 yds on R)
✆ (09662) 3688

A charming country house set in idyllic countryside, Linthwaite Hotel not only has 14 acres of beautiful grounds, it even has its own fishing tarn, putting green and golf practice area. Lounges are relaxing, with blazing fires, bedrooms are spacious and well appointed, and the excellent five-course table d'hôte dinner served each day includes many English favourites and a few interesting specialities. Caring personal service ensures both a warm welcome and a pleasant and comfortable stay.

Price band C (inc dinner)
Dinner td £12
Last dinner 8pm
Parking on premises
Closed Dec

❀ × **Porthole Eating-House**
3 Ash St
✆ (09662) 2793

This cosy welcoming 17th-century cottage, located in a narrow side street, has been a restaurant since the late 1950s and was taken over by the current owners, Judy and Gianni Berton, in 1972. The menu features an interesting mix of Italian, English and French dishes, all very well-cooked. Try penne alla zingara (pasta with a sauce of chicken, garlic, anchovies, herbs, white wine vinegar, tomatoes and white wine), followed by baked Scottish salmon with dill, Chablis, Campari and lemon juice served with a two-pepper sauce. A appropriate wine is recommended beside each dish on the menu, and indeed the restaurant boasts a most impressive wine list.

Dinner alc £15
Last dinner 11pm
Credit cards [1] [2] [3] [5]
No parking on premises
Closed mid Dec–mid Feb
Closed lunch & Tue

× **Rogers**
4 High St
✆ (09662) 4954

Rogers is not a cheap restaurant, but it offers value for money in the quality of food and service it provides, together with a pleasant ambience. Though small, it is tastefully decorated, comfortably furnished and equipped with quality linen napery. Guests are greeted warmly on their first visit, and tend to be treated like friends of the family on subsequent occasions! The limited menu of French and English dishes, which is changed daily, includes such interesting choices as cream of parsnip soup, mousseline of scallops with prawn sauce, sauté of monkfish in herb cream sauce and a delicious almond and apricot pudding — all freshly made and of a very high standard. Lunch is by prior arrangement only.

Lunch alc £8
Dinner td £10.50 or alc £13
Last dinner 9.45pm
Credit cards [1] [2] [3] [5]
Closed Sun

Victoria Cottage
21 Victoria St
✆ (09662) 5234

Charmingly decorated in a smokey-pink colour scheme, the delightful teashop/restaurant has a peaceful, relaxing atmosphere. Home-made food is its speciality, so customers for morning coffee and afternoon tea are tempted by wickedly rich truffle cake, date and walnut loaf or freshly-baked scones. The interesting range of savouries offered at lunch-time includes Cumbrian rarebit, vol-au-vents filled with chicken in a white wine and thyme sauce, baked fish and vegetable pie with jacket potatoes. Dinner dishes are rather more elaborate — for example, broccoli soup, pork fillet with an apricot cream sauce and vegetable crumble. Should you wish to take home a reminder of your visit to Victoria Cottage, there is an interesting range of marmalades on sale.

Lunch/dinner alc £6
Last meal 5.30pm (Sun–Wed), 9.15pm (Fri–Sat)
Parking nearby
Restricted service Jan–Feb
Closed Thu

À la carte prices are based on an average for three courses without wine.

WINSTER Cumbria Map 7 SD49

★★ 🏰 BL
Birket Houses
(From Bowness take A5047 towards Lythe valley. At Winster turn R at Brown Horse Inn. Follow lane for ½ mile. Turn R at Bryan Houses, and follow signs for Birket Houses)
✆ Windermere (09662) 3438

This Edwardian country house, maintained to the highest standard, is set in 20 acres of grounds in the beautiful Winster Valley. The interior is magnificent, the ground floor featuring elaborately carved oak panelling. The relaxing main lounge in the Great Hall has a roaring log fire and a grand piano, while another elegant sitting room offers colour television. All bedrooms have four-poster beds, lovely views and a level of luxury and comfort rarely found, each one being individually decorated and furnished. The food, from the incredibly hearty breakfast to the excellent six-course dinner, is of a very high standard.

Price band C (inc dinner)
Last dinner 8pm
Parking on premises

WINTERBOURNE ABBAS Dorset Map 3 SY69

★★ L **Whitefriars Hotel**
✆ Martinstown (030588) 206

This former farmhouse was given a face-lift at the turn of the century, and many of its late Victorian embellishments remain. The eight bedrooms, all with private facilities and CTV, are individually styled and comfortably appointed. Public rooms include a lounge where log fires burn in winter, and a cocktail bar. Proprietors George and Pamela Holford-Rainbow make good food a priority, and the stylish restaurant is the focal point of their hotel. Mrs Holford-Rainbow produces varied and interesting dishes at both lunch and dinner. Vegetarian and other special diets can be catered for by prior arrangement. The restaurant is open to non-residents, but booking is advisable. Whitefriars does not accept children under 12.

Price band B
Bar lunch fr £1.50
Lunch alc £7
Dinner td £9
Last dinner 9.30pm
Credit cards [1] [3]
Parking on premises

WISBECH Cambridgeshire Map 5 TF40

★★ L **Rose & Crown Hotel**
Market Place
✆ (0945) 583187
Tx 32817

This market-town coaching inn underwent quite a transformation when it was taken over by David Owen and John Martin, two Londoners who sold their successful Covent Garden restaurant to move here. They brought with them their talented young chef, Christopher Lennox-Bland, and it is especially for the food that our Inspector has chosen the hotel. Whether you opt for à la carte or table d'hôte, the cooking shows flair and imagination, and the restaurant is now a place where any meal is a special occasion. The very best produce the area can offer is put to good use, and our Inspector specially mentions the poultry, game, beef and unusual fish dishes. The à la carte menu might feature fresh Norfolk duck with plums, for example, or roast salmon with red and yellow pimentos. Vegetables are outstanding: crisply fresh, and to be remembered with delight, whether used as a garnish or in the selection (usually six or seven) served with a main course. Sometimes vegetables are used imaginatively in first courses, such as celeriac mousse on a bed of leeks cooked in lemon vinegar. Accommodation at the Rose and Crown has also seen

Price band B
Bar lunch td £2.50–£5.50
Lunch alc £16.50
Dinner td fr £12 or alc £16.50
Last dinner 10pm
Credit cards [1] [2] [3] [5]
Limited parking on premises

striking changes, particularly in the modern, light décor and furnishings of the public rooms on the ground floor and first floor. The hotel has 20 bedrooms, all with CTV and telephones, and most with private bathrooms. There are two four-poster rooms and two family rooms.

WITHERSLACK Cumbria Map 7 SD48

★ RED
Old Vicarage Country House
(044852) 381

Formerly a vicarage, this lovely Georgian House standing in its own extensive grounds, has been converted by its four owners, Roger and Jill Burrington-Brown and Stanley and Irene Reeve, into a most comfortable and friendly hotel, warmly recommended by our members and inspectors. There are two lounges — one with a small wine-bar and French windows opening onto the garden on the south side of the house — and seven charming bedrooms, all with en suite bathroom or shower, CTV and telephone, plus many useful and welcome extras. Surprisingly, all four owners take a turn in the kitchen, and each has his or her own speciality. Their combined efforts produce a superb five-course dinner, but there is no choice until the dessert stage when a hot or cold pudding is offered. However, guests are encouraged to have both, and to reach the final course of cheese a hearty appetite is a necessity! Breakfast is equally substantial, featuring home-made bread and preserves, porridge with whisky, local Cumberland sausage and black pudding. An area of the dining room is reserved for non-smokers. Children over 10 years old are welcome.

Price band C
Dinner td £16.50
Last dinner 6pm
Credit cards [1] [2] [3] [5]
Parking on premises
Closed Xmas week
Closed lunch

WIVELISCOMBE Somerset Map 3 ST02

★ RED
Langley House
Langley Marsh
(1m N of Wiveliscombe on unclassified rd)
(0984) 23318
Tx 46648

Three acres of lovely gardens surround this comfortable hotel, which has maintained the high standards that earned it our red star under its former owners. Hospitality is excellent; bedrooms have homely touches such as plants, books and toiletries as well as CTV and radio. Seven of the nine rooms have private facilities, and there is one family room (though children under seven are not accepted). There are two sitting rooms, again welcoming and well-cared for, with fresh flowers and polished silver and crystal. The kitchen is the province of Peter Wilson, the proprietor. The set four-course dinner menu is short but well-balanced, and his style of cooking is basically simple, but with imaginative use of the best fresh ingredients. Leisure amenities at the hotel include croquet and tennis. Langley House does not accept dogs.

Price band C
Lunch td fr £10.50
Dinner td fr £15.50
Last dinner 9pm
Credit cards [1] [2]
Parking on premises

The price band indicates the price of bed and breakfast for a single person or room. Price band A = £15 or less; price band B = £16–£30; price band C = £31–£50; price band D = more than £50.

WOOBURN COMMON Buckinghamshire Map 4 SU98

★★ B
Chequers Inn
Kiln Ln
(1m W of Wooburn Common on unclassified rd)
☎ Bourne End (06285) 29575
Tx 849832

Although it is only minutes away from towns like Slough, High Wycombe and Marlow, and within an easy drive of the M4 and M40 motorways, the Chequers is situated along a quiet by-road and has open views over rolling Chiltern countryside. The inn has been sympathetically renovated and extented to combine old and new. The 17 bedrooms (including one family room) are cosy and comfortable, with cottage-style décor and furniture, but all have modern bathrooms en suite and are equipped with present-day facilities like CTV and telephones. Bare brick walls, exposed timbers and an open fire give the bar a charming, old-world atmosphere. Our Inspector particularly recommends the bar meals, which are listed on a blackboard along with popular cocktails and wines. Children's meals are available. For more formal eating, there is a restaurant where both á la carte and table d'hôte menus are offered. The Chequers Inn does not accept dogs.

Price band C/D
Bar lunch £1.75–£6
Lunch td £9.75 or alc £13
Dinner alc £15
Last dinner 10pm
Credit cards [1] [3] [5]
Parking on premises

WOODFORD Greater Manchester Map 7 SJ88

× **Three Gates**
547 Chester Rd
(Situated on A5102 ½ mile SW of its roundabout junction with the A5149. Approx 1 mile S of Bramhall village centre)
☎ 061-440 8715

Although within easy reach of Manchester's southern suburbs, this small, friendly restaurant stands in rural surroundings, next to a country church. Under the personal supervision of the owners, it offers a good selection of dishes, all freshly prepared each day. Main dishes range from the traditional steak to a puff pastry case filled with smoked haddock, salmon and prawns poached in cream, while starters are imaginative, and you can complete your meal with either a choice from the sweet trolley or cheese and biscuits. The good English Sunday lunch is particularly fine value, and the daily 'specials' displayed on a blackboard during the week are also competitively priced.

Lunch/dinner alc fr £10
Last dinner 10pm
Credit cards [1] [2] [3] [5]
Parking on premises
Closed Mon, & Sat lunch & Sun dinner

WOODLANDS Hampshire Map 4 SU31

★★
Woodlands Lodge
Bartley Rd
☎ Ashurst (042129) 2257

Improvements continue at this quiet, well-managed hotel which has been converted from a Forest Lodge built in 1826. All 11 bedrooms (including two family rooms) have private bathrooms, CTV and radio, and each of the rooms is individually decorated and furnished with antiques. The lounge-bar and the dining room have recently been refurbished, and both dinner and bar lunches are now available in tasteful and pleasant surroundings. Cooking is reliable, with good use of local fresh produce, and meals here are good value for money. The hotel stands in four acres of secluded gardens and paddocks, but is within easy reach of the recreational amenities of Southampton. To the south and west, the many square miles of the New Forest invite exploration. Woodlands Lodge does not accept dogs, or children under five.

Price band B
Bar lunch £1.50–£6
Dinner td £9–£11
Last dinner 8pm
Credit cards [1] [3]
Parking on premises

WOOLER Northumberland Map 12 NT92

★ **Ryecroft Hotel**
Ryecroft Way
✆ (0668) 81459

Situated in the peaceful, unspoilt village of Wooler, this charming and friendly hotel is an ideal spot for either a relaxing weekend break or holiday. There is a comfortable hall/lounge, and you can enjoy a pre-dinner drink in the lounge-bar. Bedrooms, though simple, are very neat and impeccably clean, while the dining room provides an opportunity to sample both good English home cooking and international specialities.

Price band B
Lunch td £6
Dinner td £12
Last dinner 8pm
Credit cards [1] [3]
Parking on premises
Closed 6–18 Nov & 24–30 Dec

WOOLHOPE Hereford and Worcester Map 3 SO63

INN **Butchers Arms**
✆ Fownhope (04327) 281

This quaint, 14th-century, black-and-white half-timbered building is a foreign visitor's dream of an English country inn, and it occupies an idyllic rural position in a quiet country lane, surrounded by meadows and wooded hills. In summer, you can relax on a patio flanked by a trickling stream, and in winter there are open fires to warm the public rooms in traditional style. Bedrooms are prettily decorated and well-equipped, a little basket of fruit adding a welcoming touch. Bar snacks (available both at lunch-time and in the evening) include temptations like mushroom biriani and prawn pot with garlic mayonnaise. Dinner is also served in the dining room from Wednesday to Saturday, and here you can sample such unusual dishes as spinach and goats' cheese strudels or woodpigeon with red wine and juniper berries, chosen from a varied menu that is changed monthly. As the proprietor feels that an inn is not the ideal holiday environment for children, only those over the age of 14 are accepted.

Price band B
Bar meal alc £5.35
Dinner alc £10
Last dinner 9pm
Parking on premises

WORFIELD Shropshire Map 7 SJ40

★★ ♣♣ B **Old Vicarage Hotel**
✆ (07464) 498
Tx 35438

Proprietor Peter Iles became a hotelier in 1982 when, as he puts it, the furniture industry gave him up. Instead of selling his lovely Edwardian vicarage home, he and his wife Christine set about turning it into a hotel. Their carefully chosen period furnishings, with décor in keeping, enhance the character of the house, and a sympathetic conversion has provided 10 bedrooms of great charm and individuality, all with en suite facilities. Telephones, CTV and clock/radios are standard in all the rooms. Public rooms include a bar and an attractive dining room, where traditional cuisine, using fresh local produce, is complemented by a good choice of fine wines. Vegetarians can be catered for. The Old Vicarage stands in two acres of mature grounds which include a croquet lawn.

Price band C
Bar lunch £1–£3
Lunch td fr £6.95 or alc £11.95
Dinner td fr £12.50 or alc £17.50
Last dinner 9pm
Credit cards [1] [2] [3] [5]
Parking on premises

WORTHING West Sussex Map 4 TQ10

★★★ L
Beach Hotel
Marine Parade
✆ (0903) 34001

The atmosphere is friendly and the staff are helpful and willing at this well-run traditional resort hotel on the seafront. Many of the 91 bedrooms have sea views, and some have private balconies. The rooms

Price band C
Bar lunch £1.50–£4
Lunch td fr

	are airy, spacious and well-appointed: private bath or shower, double glazing, telephone, CTV and radio are standard. All bedrooms can be reached by lift. Lounge facilities are very good, and the restaurant is smart and pleasant, and overlooks the sea. English and French-style food form the basis of the table d'hôte menus. The hotel does not accept children under eight, or dogs.	£8.50 or alc £12 Dinner td £12 or alc £15 Last dinner 8.45pm Credit cards [1] [2] [3] [4] [5] Parking on premises

WRIGHTINGTON Lancashire Map 7 SD51

❀×× **High Moor** Highmoor Ln (From M6 junct 27 follow Parbold signs. Pass Wrightington Hospital then turn R into Robin Hood Lane. Then L into High Moor Lane) ✆ Appleby Bridge (02575) 2364	The High Moor, one of Lancashire's best restaurants, stands in a picturesque location in open countryside, with good views towards Parbold Hill. Originally a 17th-century coaching house, it retains its low-beamed ceilings but has been made warm and comfortable. It has a reputation for providing fine, well-prepared food, using top-quality fresh produce from local markets, and you can enjoy such specialities as quail soup with ham and cabbage, fillet of beef with mushroom sauce, or Anglesey scallop with curry and mangos. Service, under a charming Italian head waiter, is excellent and there is a very good wine list.	Lunch/dinner alc £16 Last dinner 9.45pm Credit cards [1] [2] [3] [5] Parking on premises Closed Mon, & Sat lunch & Sun dinner

YATTENDON Berkshire Map 4 SU57

❀★★ HB **Royal Oak** ✆ Hermitage (0635) 201325	This welcoming and hospitable roadside inn, dating back to the 16th century, has a bar renowned for its snacks and therefore much frequented by a local clientele. The restaurant is more formal and boasts well-prepared, imaginative English and French cuisine. Tastefully decorated, well-equipped bedrooms provide comfortable accommodation, while the relaxing atmosphere of the cosy lounge is enhanced by a roaring log fire on colder days. Cheerful, helpful service also plays its part in creating the charm and appeal of this hotel.	Price band C Lunch/dinner alc £15 Last dinner 9.45pm Credit cards [1] [2] [3] Parking on premises Closed 2 wks Jan–Feb

YORK North Yorkshire Map 8 SE65

× **Tony's** 39 Tanner Row, off Rougier St ✆ (0904) 59622	Tony's, a charming little Greek restaurant with a cosy aperitif bar, is notable for its warm, friendly atmosphere and for the dedicated service provided by members of the patron's family. The food served is wholesome, tasty and authentic, with a Cypriot bias. Favourites like moussaka appear side by side with more adventurous choices such as koupepia — a mixture of rice, beef, herbs and spices, rolled inside vine leaves and served with a tomato sauce. The menu also features fresh cod and plaice, marinated in a spicy, herb-flavoured sauce, while the choice of sweets includes Greek yogurt with honey and a syrup-soaked gâteau formed from thin layers of pastry.	Dinner td fr £8.50 or alc £8.15 Last dinner 10.30pm Credit cards [1] [2] No parking on premises Closed 1–25 Jan Closed lunch, & Sun

Key to Atlas

The National Grid

The National Grid provides one system of reference for the whole country correct for a scale map. The major squares are 62½ miles across and each sub-divided 6¼ miles across. In the National Grid system the letters of major squares are always given first followed by numbers into which the major squares are sub-divided (in the margins of each map page) eg: **SP50** this is the reference for **Oxford** which lies within major square **SP** and is **5** sub divisions east (or from left to right) and **0** sub-divisions north (reading from zero upwards). Where a major or sub-division line cuts through a town, the letter or number given are based on the square containing the larger part of the town eg:**Manchester SJ89**

For a fuller explanation see the Ordnance Survey maps.

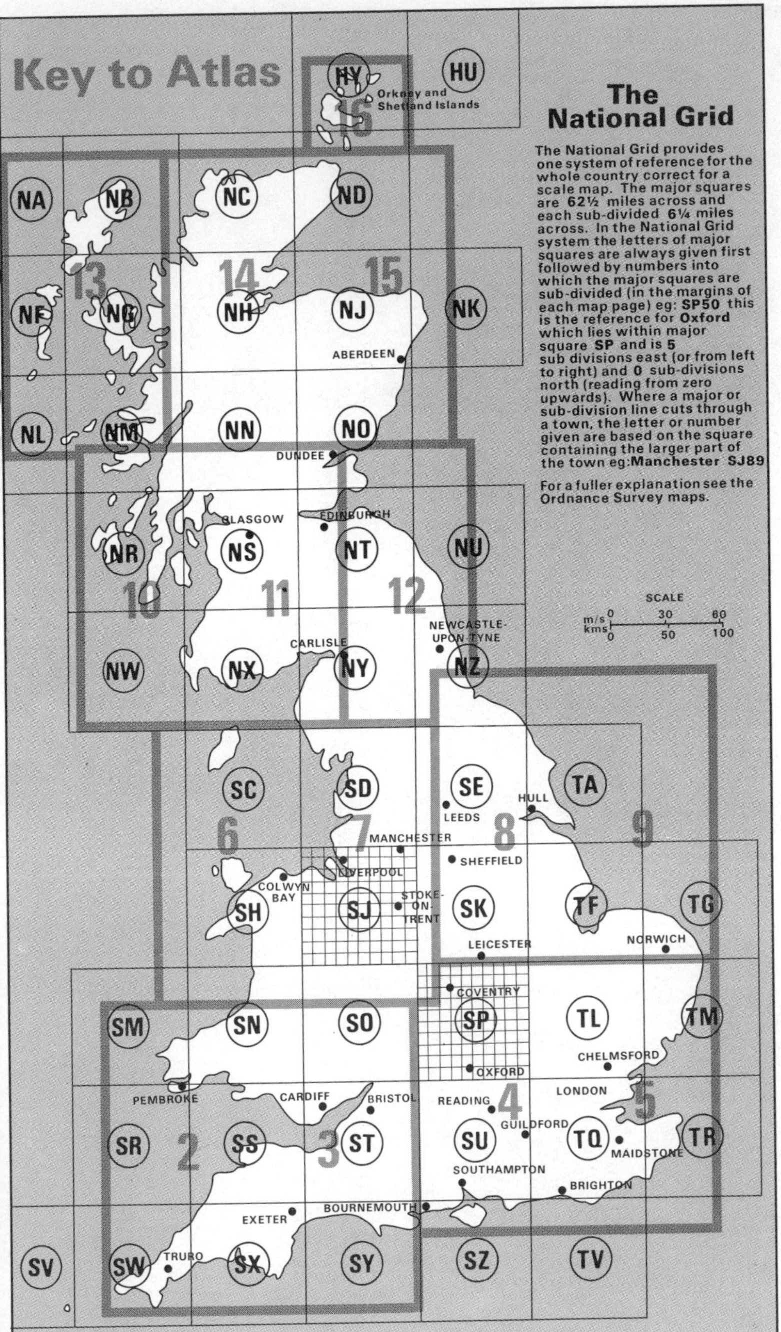

See page 16 for Channel Islands

Maps produced by

The AA Cartographic Department (Publications Division), Fanum House, Basingstoke,Hampshire RG21 2EA

This atlas is for location purposes only: see member's Handbook for current road and AA road services information.

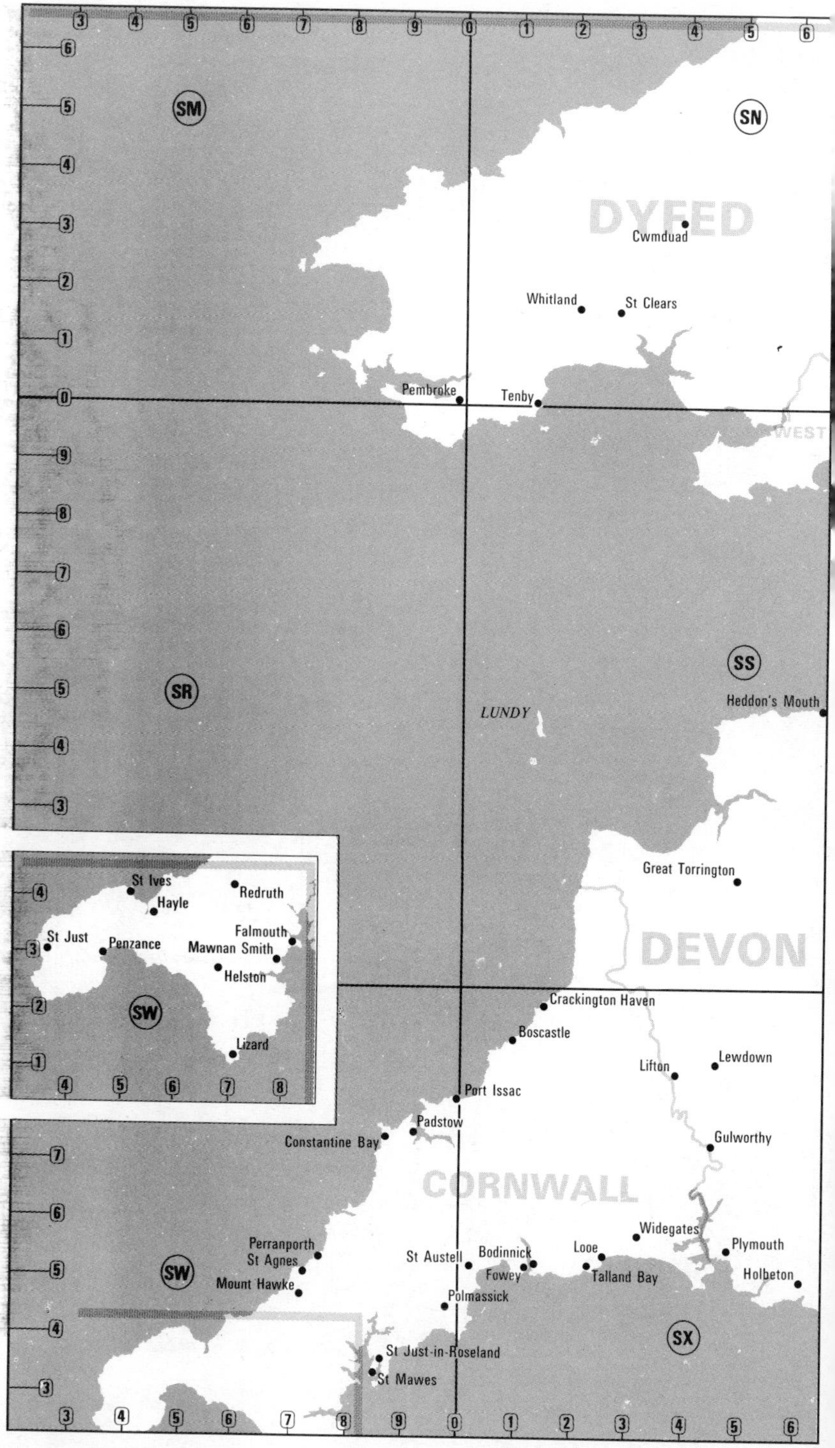
SM
SN
DYFED
Cwmduad
Whitland
St Clears
Pembroke
Tenby
WEST
SR
SS
LUNDY
Heddon's Mouth
Great Torrington
DEVON
St Ives
Hayle
Redruth
St Just
Penzance
Falmouth
Mawnan Smith
Helston
SW
Lizard
Crackington Haven
Boscastle
Lifton
Lewdown
Port Issac
Padstow
Constantine Bay
Gulworthy
CORNWALL
Widegates
Perranporth
St Agnes
Mount Hawke
St Austell
Bodinnick
Fowey
Looe
Talland Bay
Plymouth
Holbeton
Polmassick
SX
St Just-in-Roseland
St Mawes

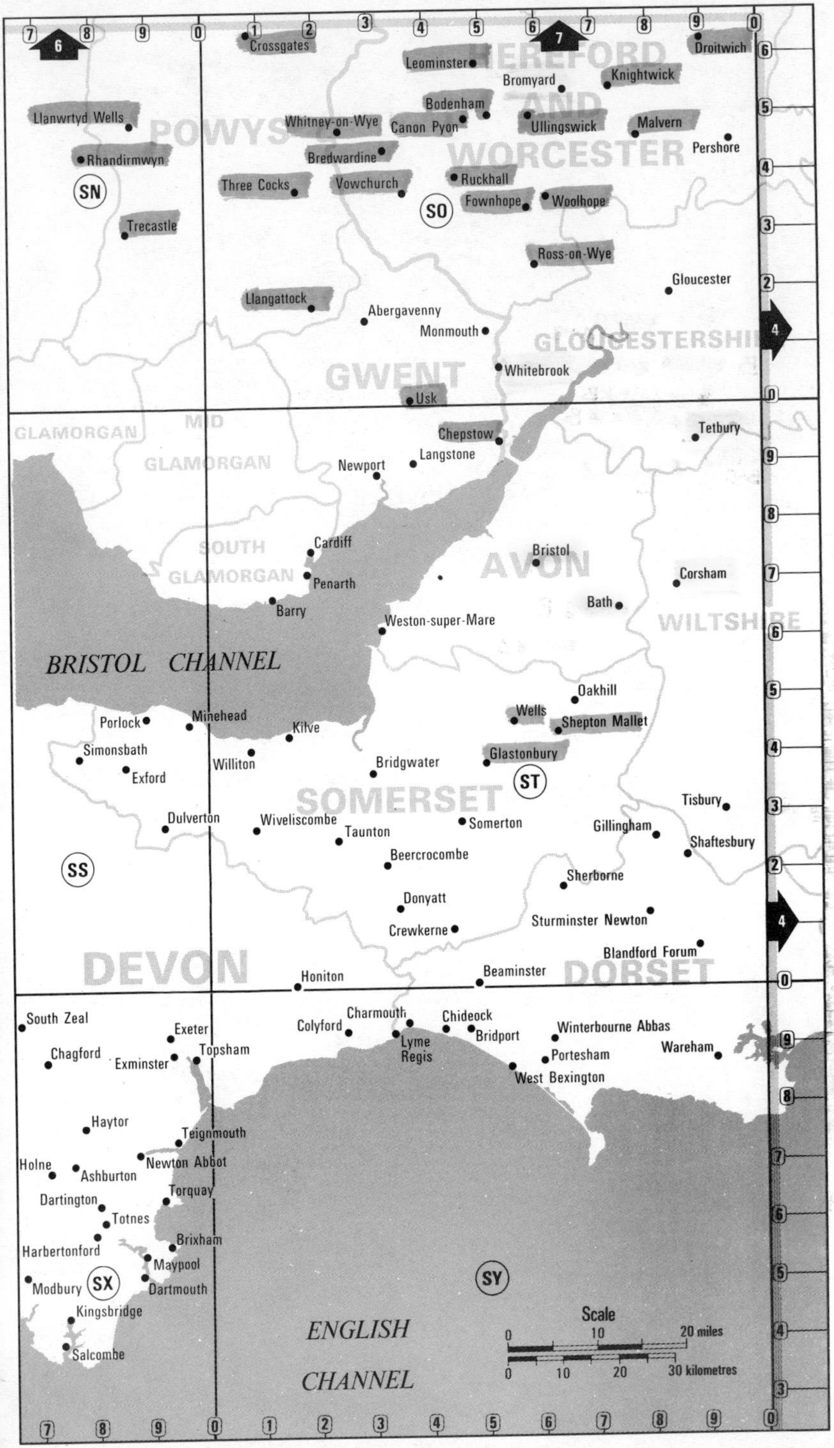

6
7
4
4
Crossgates
Droitwich
Leominster
HEREFORD AND WORCESTER
Bromyard
Knightwick
Llanwrtyd Wells
POWYS
Bodenham
Whitney-on-Wye
Canon Pyon
Ullingswick
Malvern
Pershore
Rhandirmwyn
Bredwardine
SN
Three Cocks
Vowchurch
Ruckhall
Fownhope
Woolhope
SO
Trecastle
Ross-on-Wye
Gloucester
Llangattock
Abergavenny
Monmouth
GLOUCESTERSHIRE
Whitebrook
GWENT
Usk
GLAMORGAN
MID GLAMORGAN
Chepstow
Tetbury
Langstone
Newport
SOUTH GLAMORGAN
Cardiff
Bristol
AVON
Corsham
Penarth
Bath
Barry
Weston-super-Mare
WILTSHIRE
BRISTOL CHANNEL
Oakhill
Wells
Shepton Mallet
Porlock
Minehead
Kilve
Simonsbath
Williton
Bridgwater
Glastonbury
Exford
SOMERSET
ST
Tisbury
Dulverton
Wiveliscombe
Taunton
Somerton
Gillingham
Shaftesbury
Beercrocombe
SS
Sherborne
Donyatt
Sturminster Newton
Crewkerne
Blandford Forum
DEVON
Honiton
Beaminster
DORSET
South Zeal
Charmouth
Chideock
Colyford
Bridport
Winterbourne Abbas
Exeter
Lyme Regis
Wareham
Chagford
Topsham
Portesham
Exminster
West Bexington
Haytor
Teignmouth
Newton Abbot
Holne
Ashburton
Torquay
Dartington
Totnes
Brixham
Harbertonford
Maypool
SX
Modbury
Dartmouth
SY
Kingsbridge
Scale
0
10
20 miles
ENGLISH CHANNEL
Salcombe
0
10
20
30 kilometres

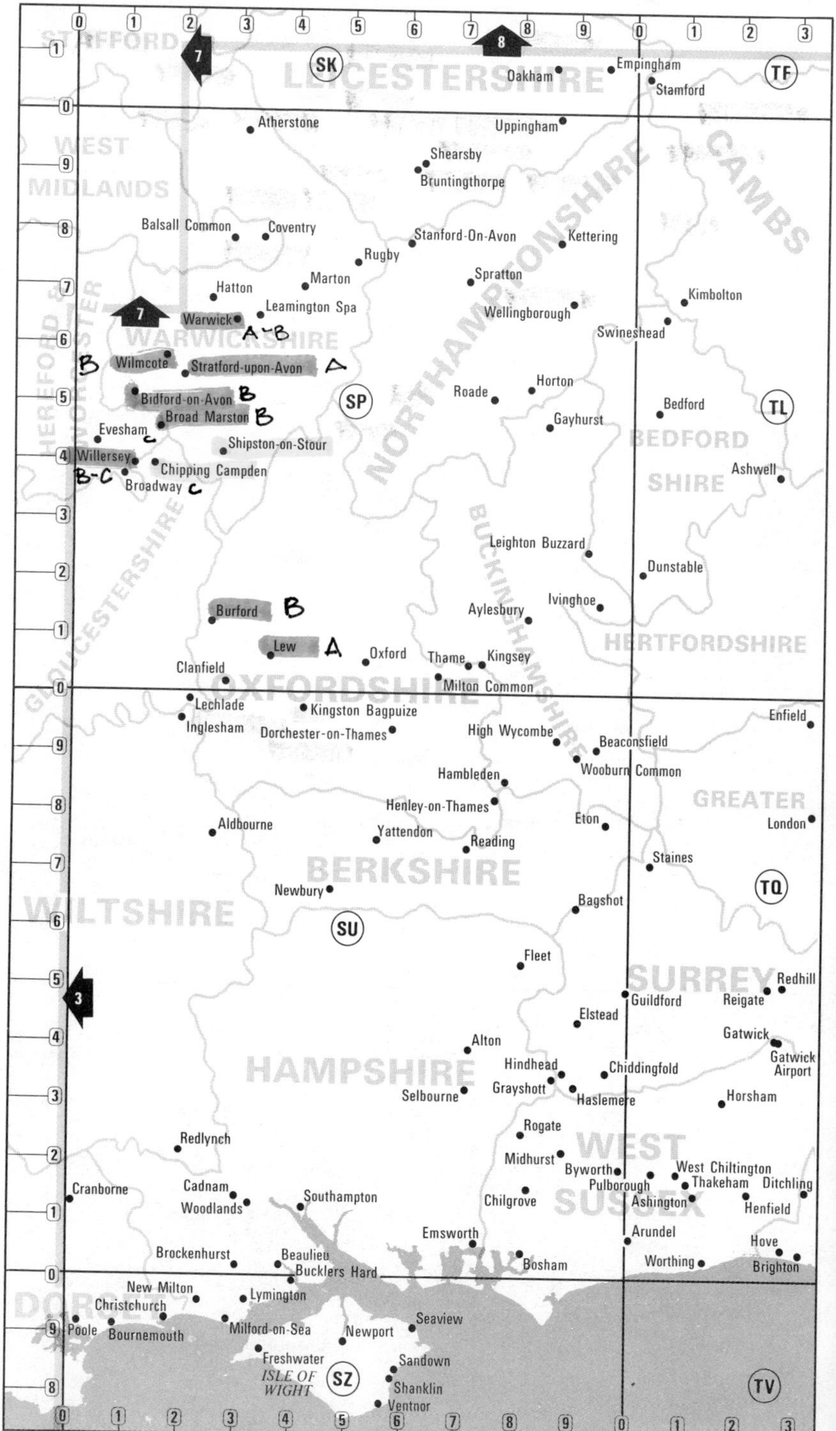

SK
TF
SP
TL
SU
TQ
SZ
TV
STAFFORD
LEICESTERSHIRE
WEST MIDLANDS
CAMBS
NORTHAMPTONSHIRE
WARWICKSHIRE
HEREFORD & WORCESTER
BEDFORD SHIRE
BUCKINGHAMSHIRE
GLOUCESTERSHIRE
HERTFORDSHIRE
OXFORDSHIRE
GREATER LONDON
BERKSHIRE
WILTSHIRE
SURREY
HAMPSHIRE
WEST SUSSEX
DORSET
ISLE OF WIGHT
Oakham
Empingham
Stamford
Atherstone
Uppingham
Shearsby
Bruntingthorpe
Balsall Common
Coventry
Stanford-On-Avon
Kettering
Rugby
Spratton
Kimbolton
Hatton
Marton
Leamington Spa
Wellingborough
Warwick
Swineshead
Wilmcote
Stratford-upon-Avon
Roade
Horton
Bidford-on-Avon
Bedford
Broad Marston
Gayhurst
Evesham
Shipston-on-Stour
Willersey
Chipping Campden
Ashwell
Broadway
Leighton Buzzard
Dunstable
Ivinghoe
Burford
Aylesbury
Lew
Oxford
Thame
Kingsey
Clanfield
Milton Common
Lechlade
Kingston Bagpuize
Enfield
Inglesham
Dorchester-on-Thames
High Wycombe
Beaconsfield
Wooburn Common
Hambleden
Henley-on-Thames
Eton
Aldbourne
Yattendon
Reading
London
Staines
Newbury
Bagshot
Fleet
Redhill
Guildford
Reigate
Elstead
Alton
Gatwick
Gatwick Airport
Hindhead
Chiddingfold
Grayshott
Selbourne
Haslemere
Horsham
Rogate
Redlynch
Midhurst
Byworth
West Chiltington
Pulborough
Thakeham
Ditchling
Cranborne
Cadnam
Woodlands
Southampton
Chilgrove
Ashington
Henfield
Emsworth
Arundel
Hove
Brockenhurst
Beaulieu
Bucklers Hard
Bosham
Worthing
Brighton
New Milton
Christchurch
Lymington
Poole
Bournemouth
Milford-on-Sea
Newport
Seaview
Freshwater
Sandown
Shanklin
Ventnor

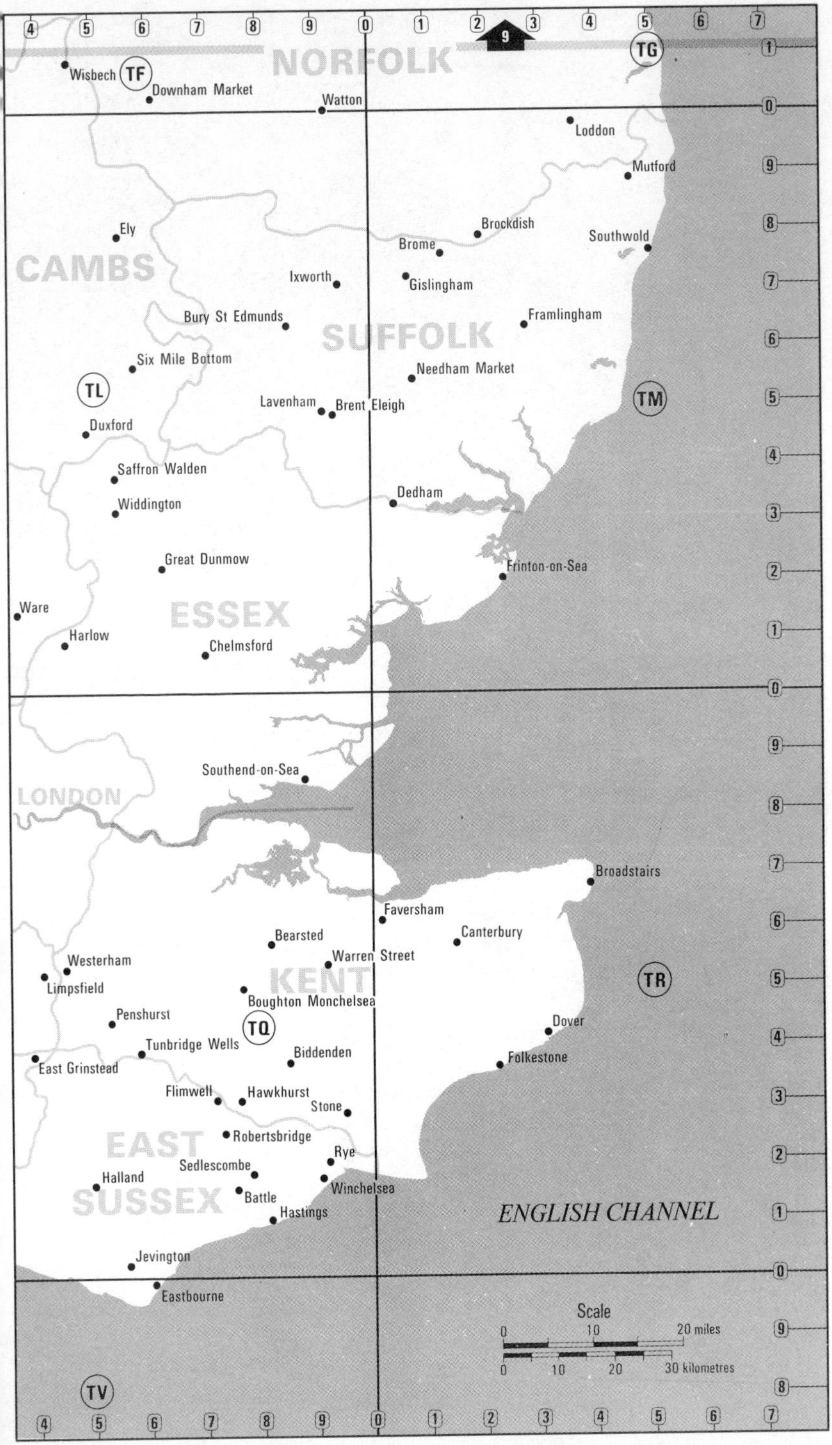
NORFOLK
TF
TG
Wisbech
Downham Market
Watton
Loddon
Mutford
Ely
Brockdish
Southwold
Brome
CAMBS
Ixworth
Gislingham
Bury St Edmunds
Framlingham
SUFFOLK
Six Mile Bottom
Needham Market
TL
TM
Lavenham
Brent Eleigh
Duxford
Saffron Walden
Dedham
Widdington
Great Dunmow
Frinton-on-Sea
Ware
ESSEX
Harlow
Chelmsford
Southend-on-Sea
LONDON
Broadstairs
Faversham
Bearsted
Canterbury
Westerham
Warren Street
Limpsfield
KENT
TR
Boughton Monchelsea
Penshurst
TQ
Dover
Tunbridge Wells
Biddenden
East Grinstead
Folkestone
Flimwell
Hawkhurst
Stone
EAST
Robertsbridge
Rye
Sedlescombe
Halland
Winchelsea
SUSSEX
Battle
Hastings
ENGLISH CHANNEL
Jevington
Eastbourne
Scale
0
10
20 miles
0
10
20
30 kilometres
TV

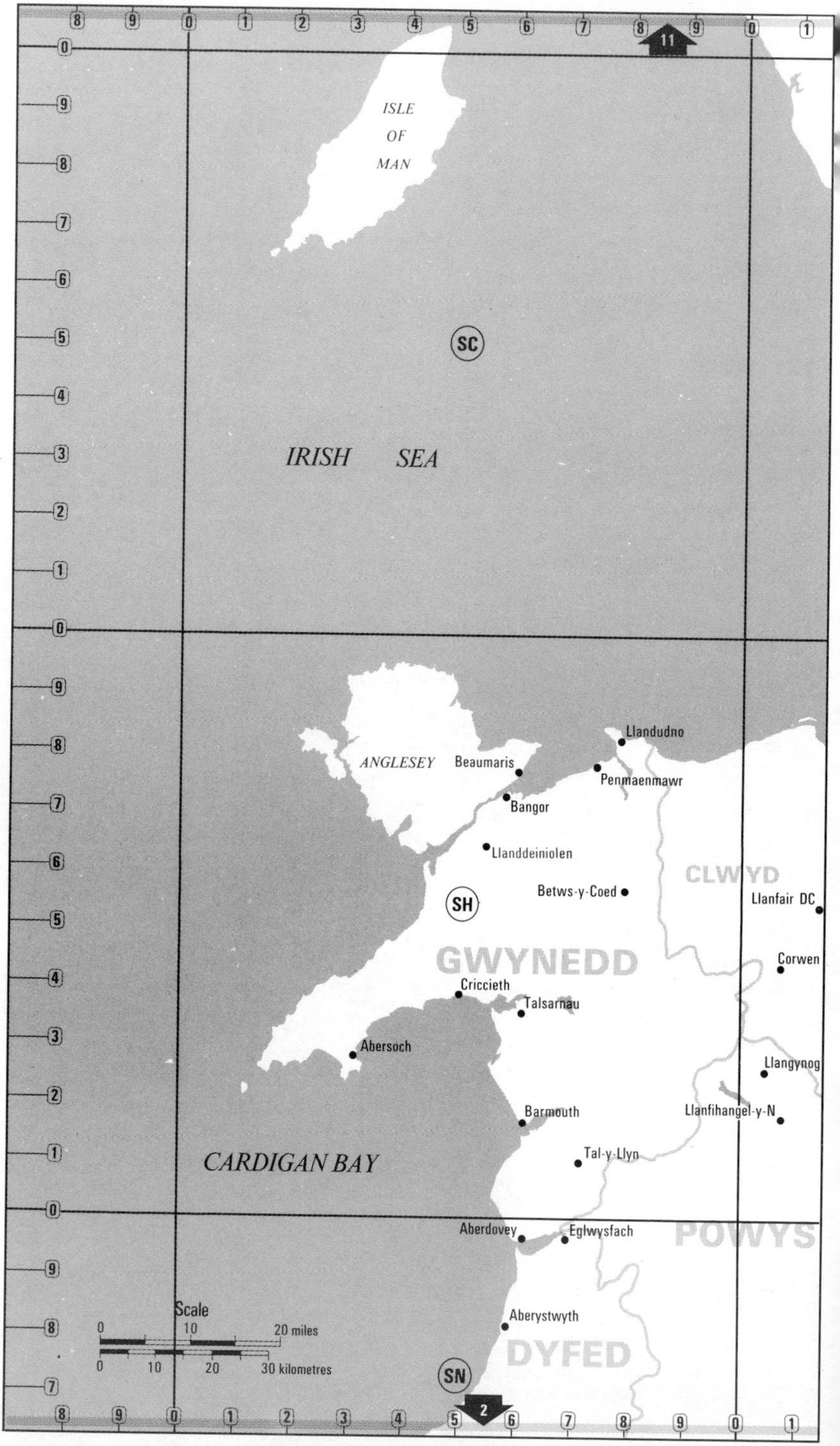
ISLE OF MAN
SC
IRISH SEA
11
ANGLESEY
Beaumaris
Llandudno
Penmaenmawr
Bangor
Llanddeiniolen
CLWYD
Betws-y-Coed
Llanfair DC
SH
GWYNEDD
Corwen
Criccieth
Talsarnau
Abersoch
Llangynog
Barmouth
Llanfihangel-y-N
Tal-y-Llyn
CARDIGAN BAY
Aberdovey
Eglwysfach
POWYS
Aberystwyth
DYFED
Scale
0 10 20 miles
0 10 20 30 kilometres
SN
2

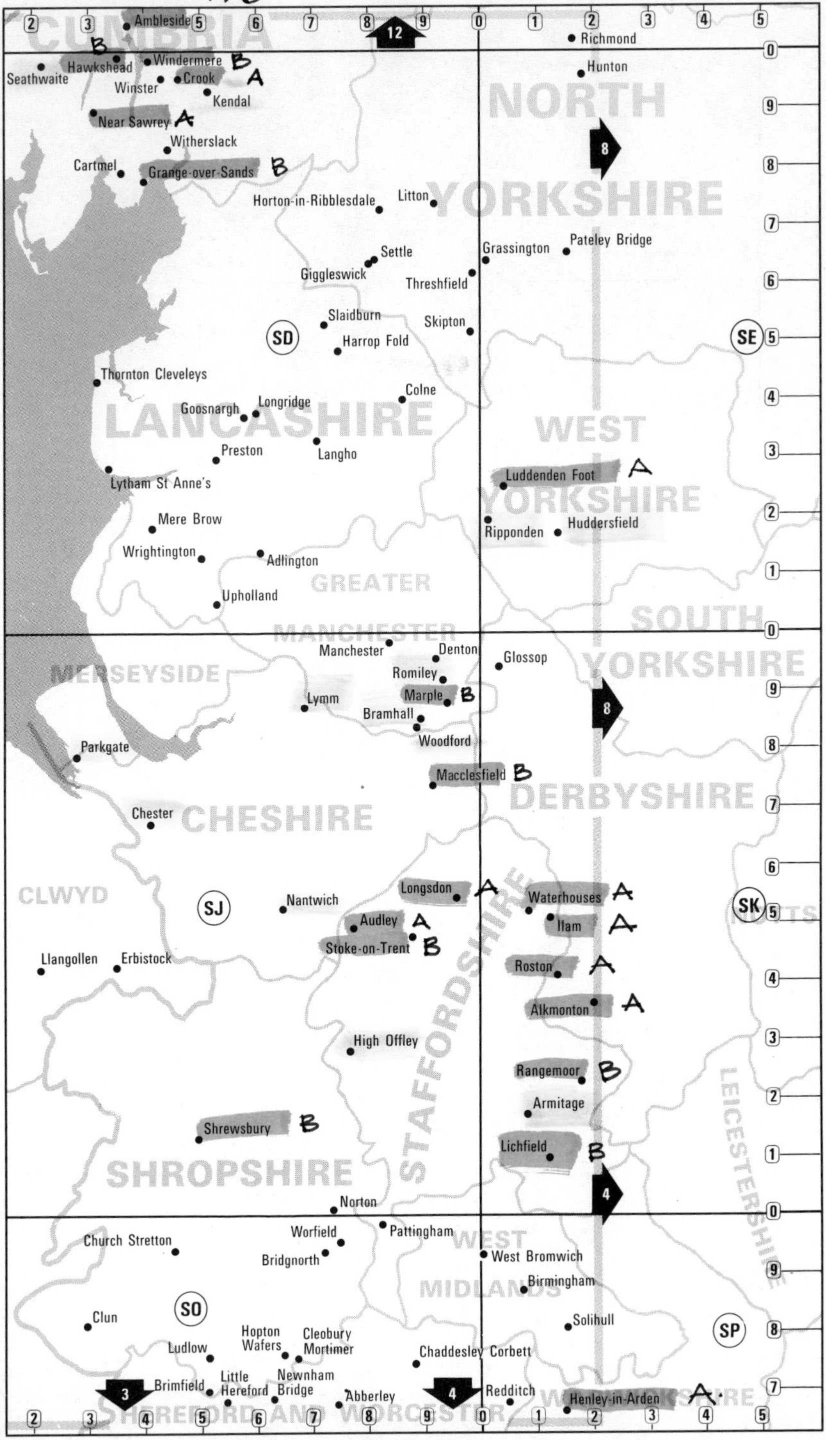
CUMBRIA
NORTH
YORKSHIRE
LANCASHIRE
WEST
YORKSHIRE
GREATER
MANCHESTER
SOUTH
YORKSHIRE
MERSEYSIDE
CHESHIRE
DERBYSHIRE
CLWYD
STAFFORDSHIRE
SHROPSHIRE
LEICESTERSHIRE
NOTTS
WEST
MIDLANDS
HEREFORD AND WORCESTER
WARWICKSHIRE
SD
SE
SJ
SK
SO
SP
12
8
8
4
3
4
Ambleside
Richmond
Hawkshead
Windermere
Seathwaite
Winster
Crook
Kendal
Hunton
Near Sawrey
Witherslack
Cartmel
Grange-over-Sands
Horton-in-Ribblesdale
Litton
Settle
Giggleswick
Threshfield
Grassington
Pateley Bridge
Slaidburn
Skipton
Harrop Fold
Thornton Cleveleys
Colne
Goosnargh
Longridge
Preston
Langho
Lytham St Anne's
Luddenden Foot
Ripponden
Huddersfield
Mere Brow
Wrightington
Adlington
Upholland
Manchester
Denton
Glossop
Romiley
Marple
Lymm
Bramhall
Woodford
Parkgate
Macclesfield
Chester
Longsdon
Waterhouses
Nantwich
Audley
Ilam
Stoke-on-Trent
Llangollen
Erbistock
Roston
Alkmonton
High Offley
Rangemoor
Armitage
Shrewsbury
Lichfield
Norton
Worfield
Pattingham
Church Stretton
Bridgnorth
West Bromwich
Birmingham
Clun
Solihull
Hopton Wafers
Cleobury Mortimer
Ludlow
Chaddesley Corbett
Brimfield
Little Hereford
Newnham Bridge
Abberley
Redditch
Henley-in-Arden

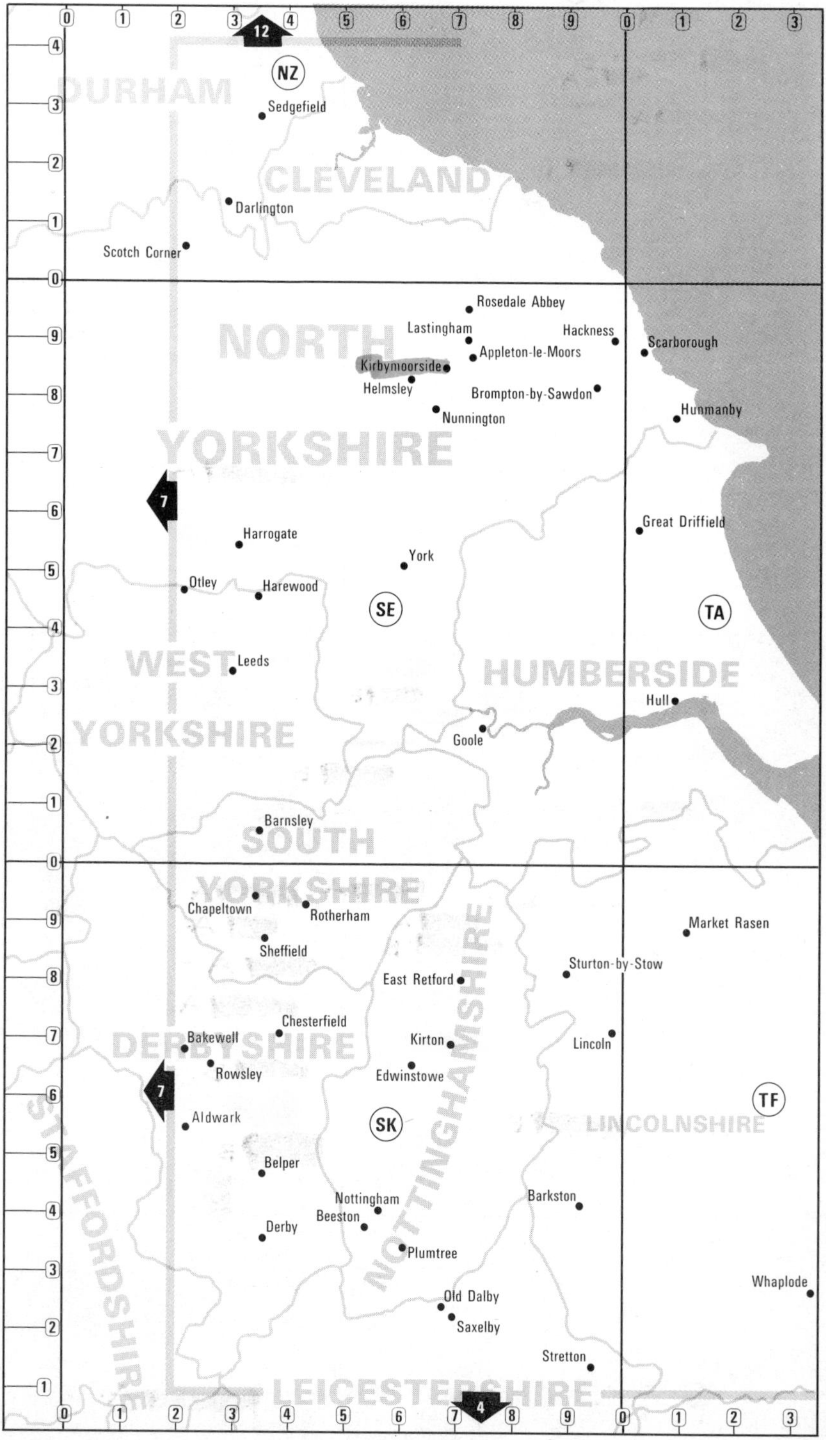

12
NZ
DURHAM
Sedgefield
CLEVELAND
Darlington
Scotch Corner
Rosedale Abbey
NORTH
Lastingham
Hackness
Scarborough
Appleton-le-Moors
Kirbymoorside
Helmsley
Brompton-by-Sawdon
Nunnington
Hunmanby
YORKSHIRE
7
Great Driffield
Harrogate
York
Otley
Harewood
SE
TA
WEST
Leeds
HUMBERSIDE
Hull
YORKSHIRE
Goole
Barnsley
SOUTH
YORKSHIRE
Chapeltown
Rotherham
Market Rasen
Sheffield
Sturton-by-Stow
East Retford
NOTTINGHAMSHIRE
Chesterfield
Bakewell
DERBYSHIRE
Kirton
Lincoln
Rowsley
Edwinstowe
7
TF
Aldwark
SK
LINCOLNSHIRE
STAFFORDSHIRE
Belper
Nottingham
Barkston
Beeston
Derby
Plumtree
Whaplode
Old Dalby
Saxelby
Stretton
LEICESTERSHIRE
4

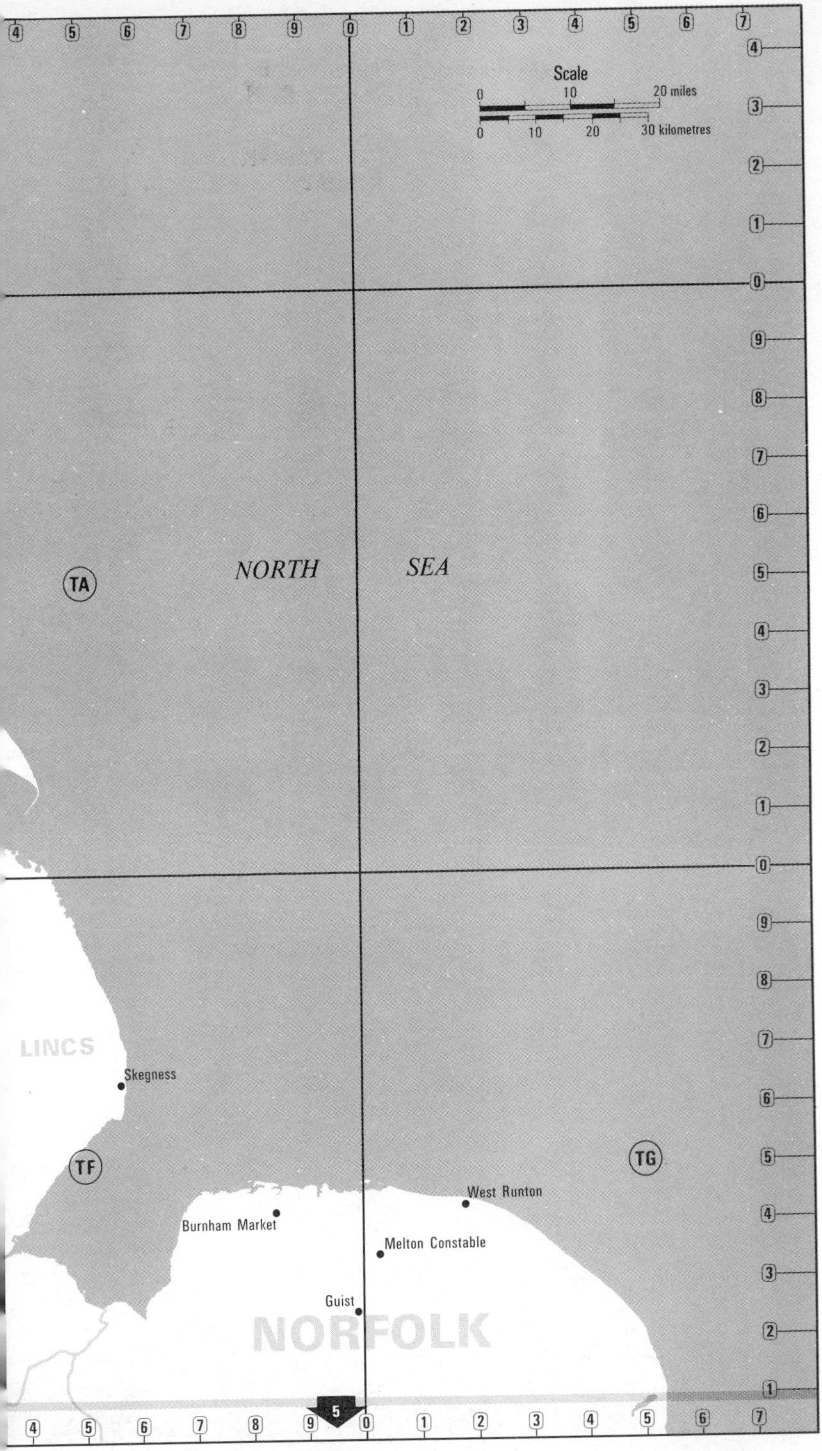
Scale
0 10 20 miles
0 10 20 30 kilometres
TA
NORTH SEA
TF
TG
LINCS
Skegness
Burnham Market
West Runton
Melton Constable
Guist
NORFOLK
5

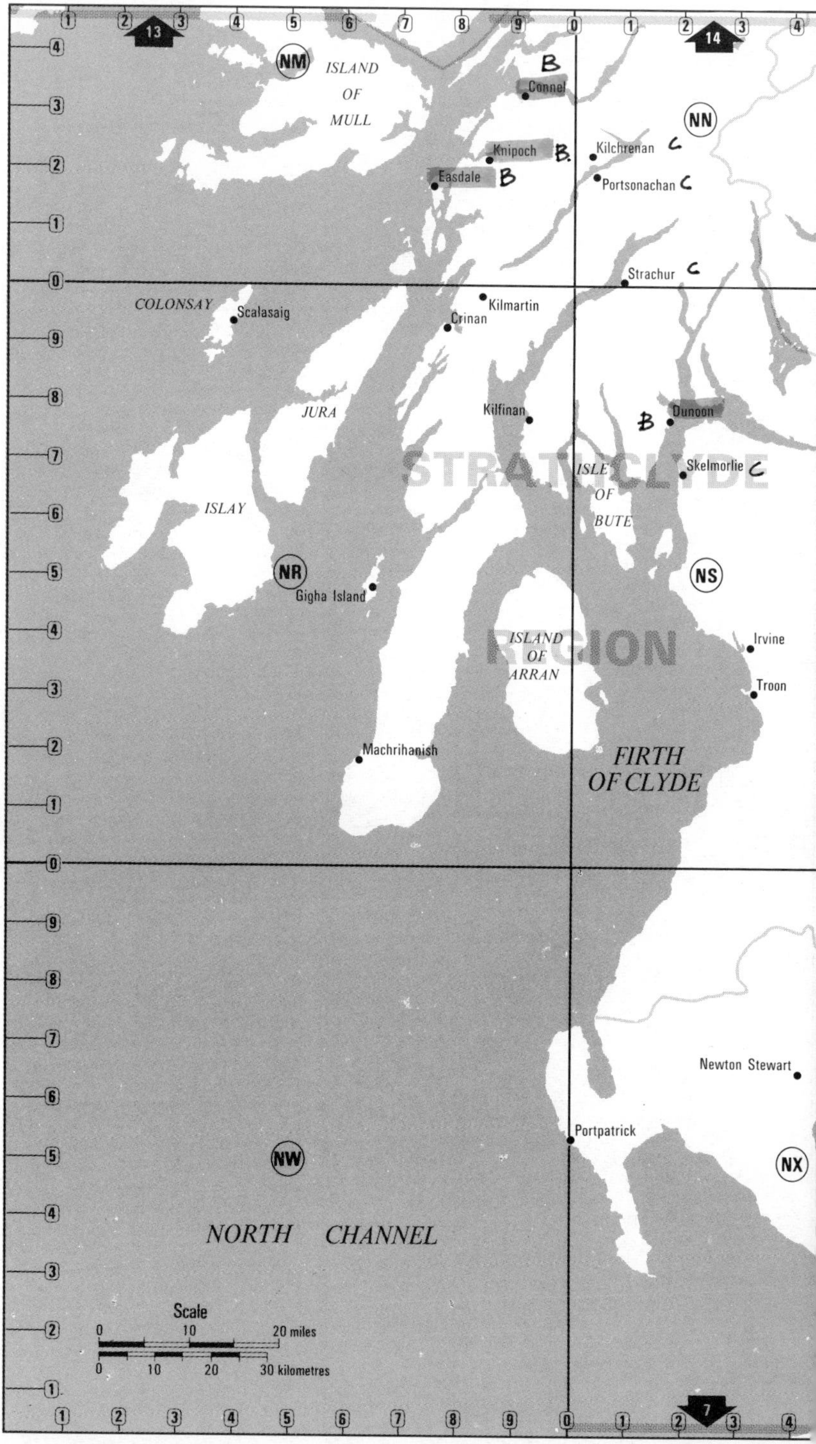
13
14
NM
ISLAND OF MULL
B
Connel
Knipoch B.
Easdale B
Kilchrenan C
Portsonachan C
NN
Strachur C
COLONSAY
Scalasaig
Kilmartin
Crinan
JURA
Kilfinan
B
Dunoon
STRATHCLYDE
ISLE OF BUTE
Skelmorlie C
ISLAY
NR
NS
Gigha Island
ISLAND OF ARRAN
REGION
Irvine
Troon
Machrihanish
FIRTH OF CLYDE
Newton Stewart
Portpatrick
NW
NX
NORTH CHANNEL
Scale
0 10 20 miles
0 10 20 30 kilometres
7

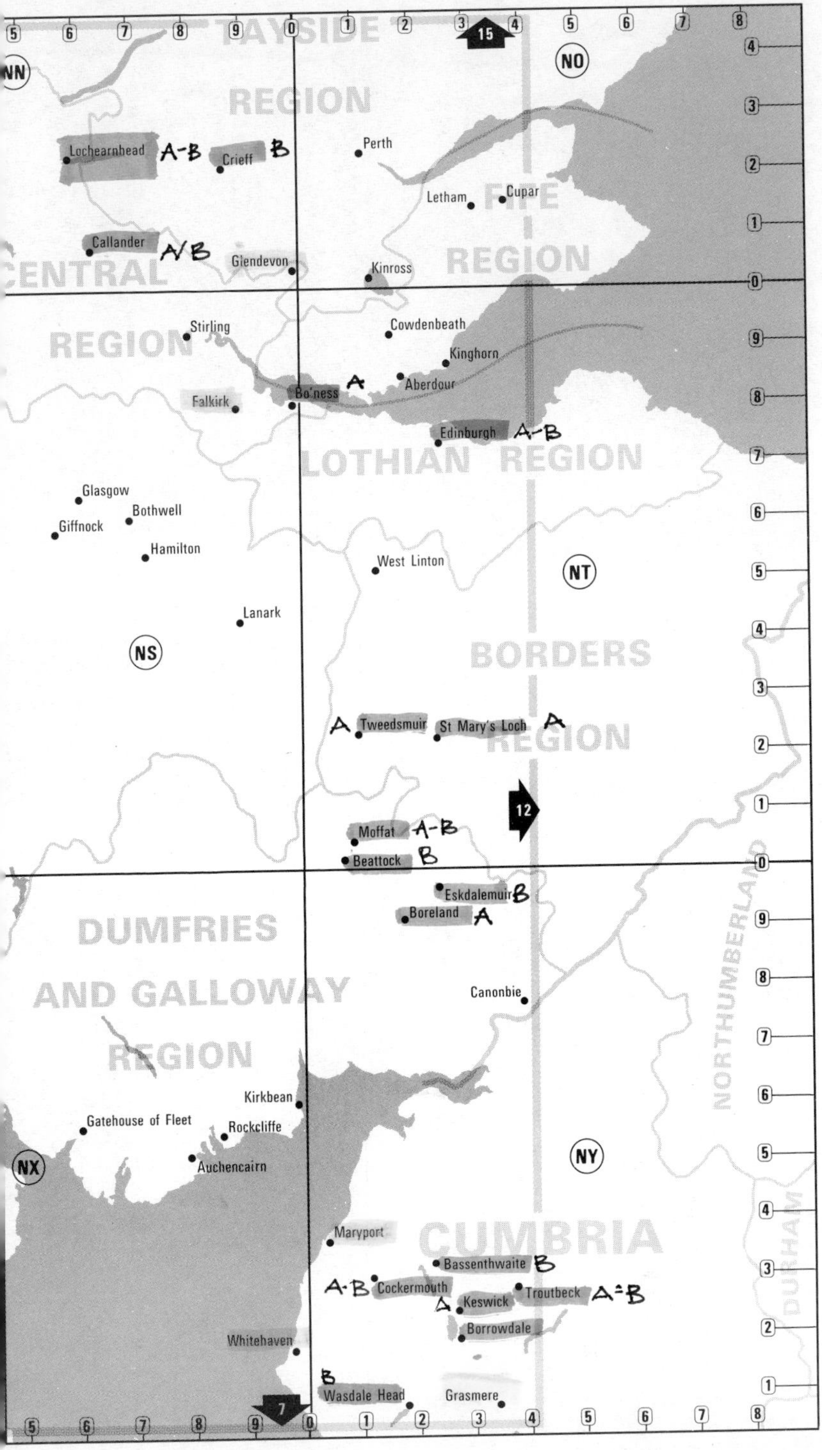
TAYSIDE REGION
FIFE REGION
CENTRAL REGION
LOTHIAN REGION
BORDERS REGION
DUMFRIES AND GALLOWAY REGION
CUMBRIA
NORTHUMBERLAND
DURHAM
NN
NO
NT
NS
NX
NY
15
12
7
Lochearnhead A-B
Crieff B
Perth
Letham
Cupar
Callander A/B
Glendevon
Kinross
Stirling
Cowdenbeath
Kinghorn
Aberdour
Bo'ness A
Falkirk
Edinburgh A-B
Glasgow
Bothwell
Giffnock
Hamilton
West Linton
Lanark
A Tweedsmuir
St Mary's Loch A
Moffat A-B
Beattock B
Eskdalemuir B
Boreland A
Canonbie
Kirkbean
Gatehouse of Fleet
Rockcliffe
Auchencairn
Maryport
Bassenthwaite B
A-B Cockermouth
Troutbeck A-B
A Keswick
Borrowdale
Whitehaven
B Wasdale Head
Grasmere

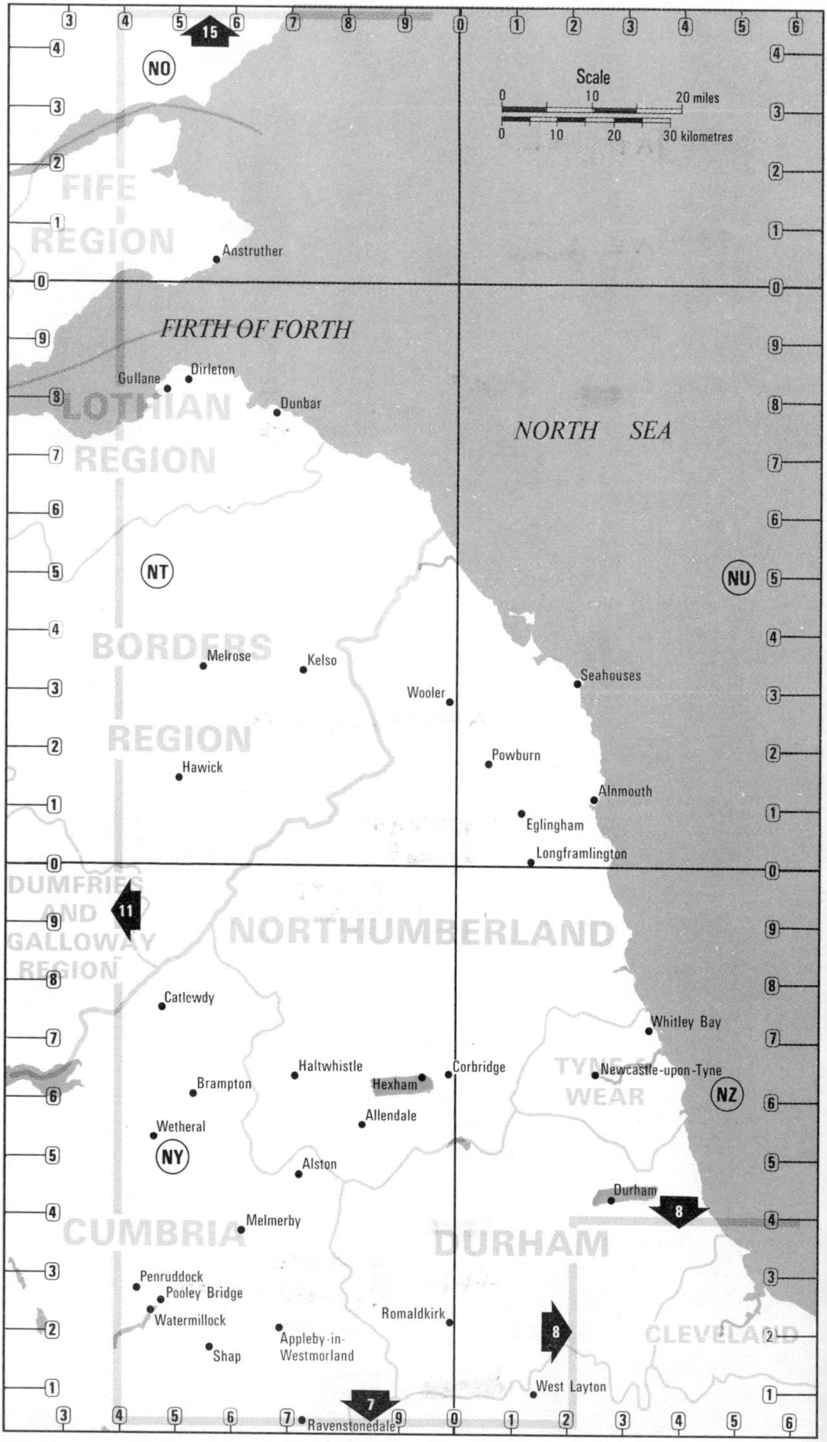
15
NO
Scale
0
10
20 miles
0
10
20
30 kilometres
FIFE
REGION
Anstruther
FIRTH OF FORTH
Gullane
Dirleton
Dunbar
LOTHIAN
REGION
NORTH SEA
NT
NU
BORDERS
REGION
Melrose
Kelso
Wooler
Seahouses
Powburn
Hawick
Alnmouth
Eglingham
Longframlington
DUMFRIES
AND
GALLOWAY
REGION
11
NORTHUMBERLAND
Catlowdy
Whitley Bay
Haltwhistle
Hexham
Corbridge
Newcastle-upon-Tyne
TYNE &
WEAR
NZ
Brampton
Wetheral
NY
Allendale
Alston
Durham
8
Melmerby
CUMBRIA
DURHAM
Penruddock
Pooley Bridge
Watermillock
Romaldkirk
Shap
Appleby-in-
Westmorland
CLEVELAND
West Layton
7
Ravenstonedale

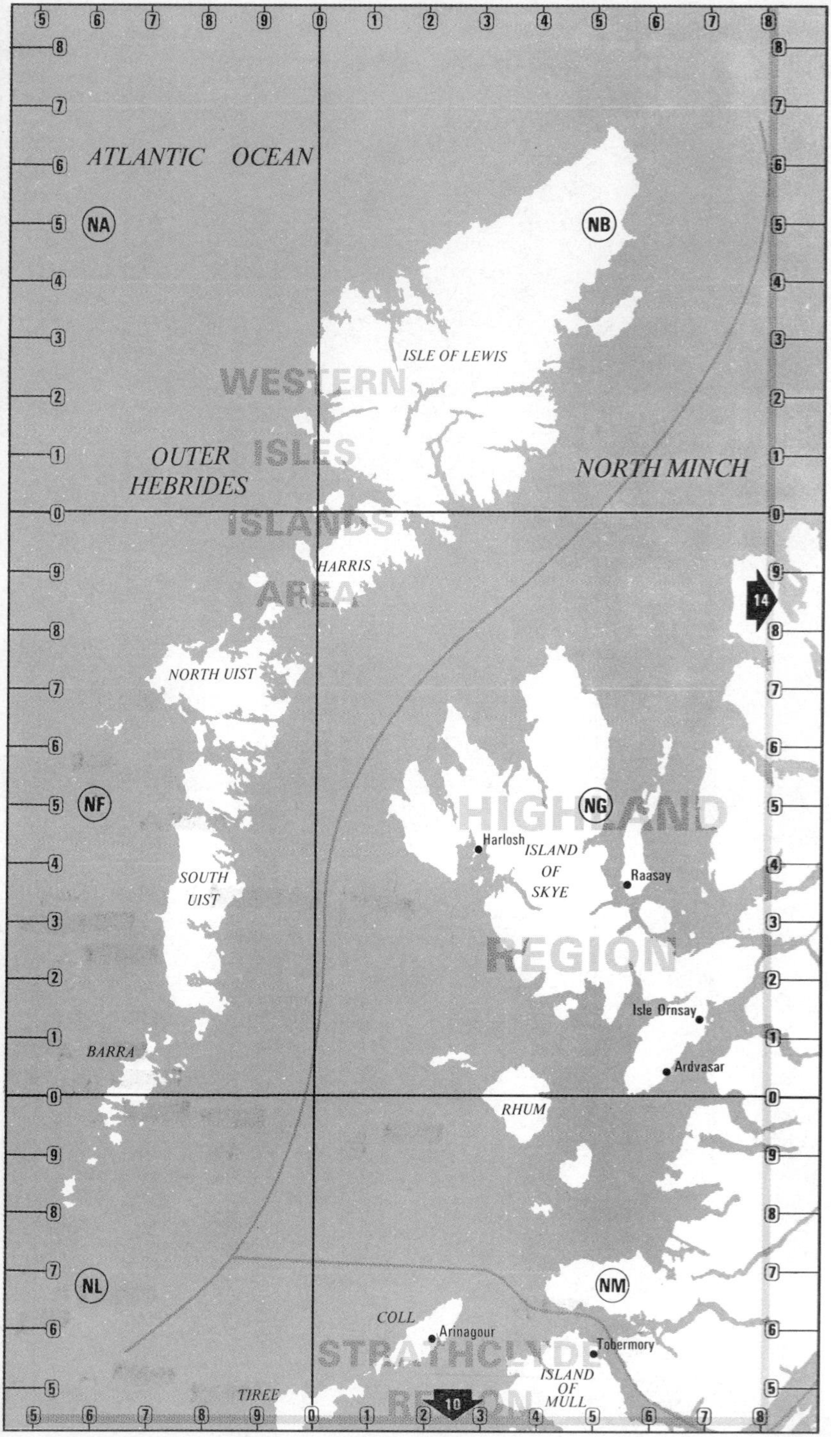
ATLANTIC OCEAN
NA
NB
ISLE OF LEWIS
WESTERN ISLES ISLANDS AREA
OUTER HEBRIDES
NORTH MINCH
HARRIS
14
NORTH UIST
NF
NG
HIGHLAND REGION
Harlosh
ISLAND OF SKYE
Raasay
SOUTH UIST
Isle Ornsay
Ardvasar
BARRA
RHUM
NL
NM
COLL
Arinagour
Tobermory
STRATHCLYDE REGION
ISLAND OF MULL
TIREE
10

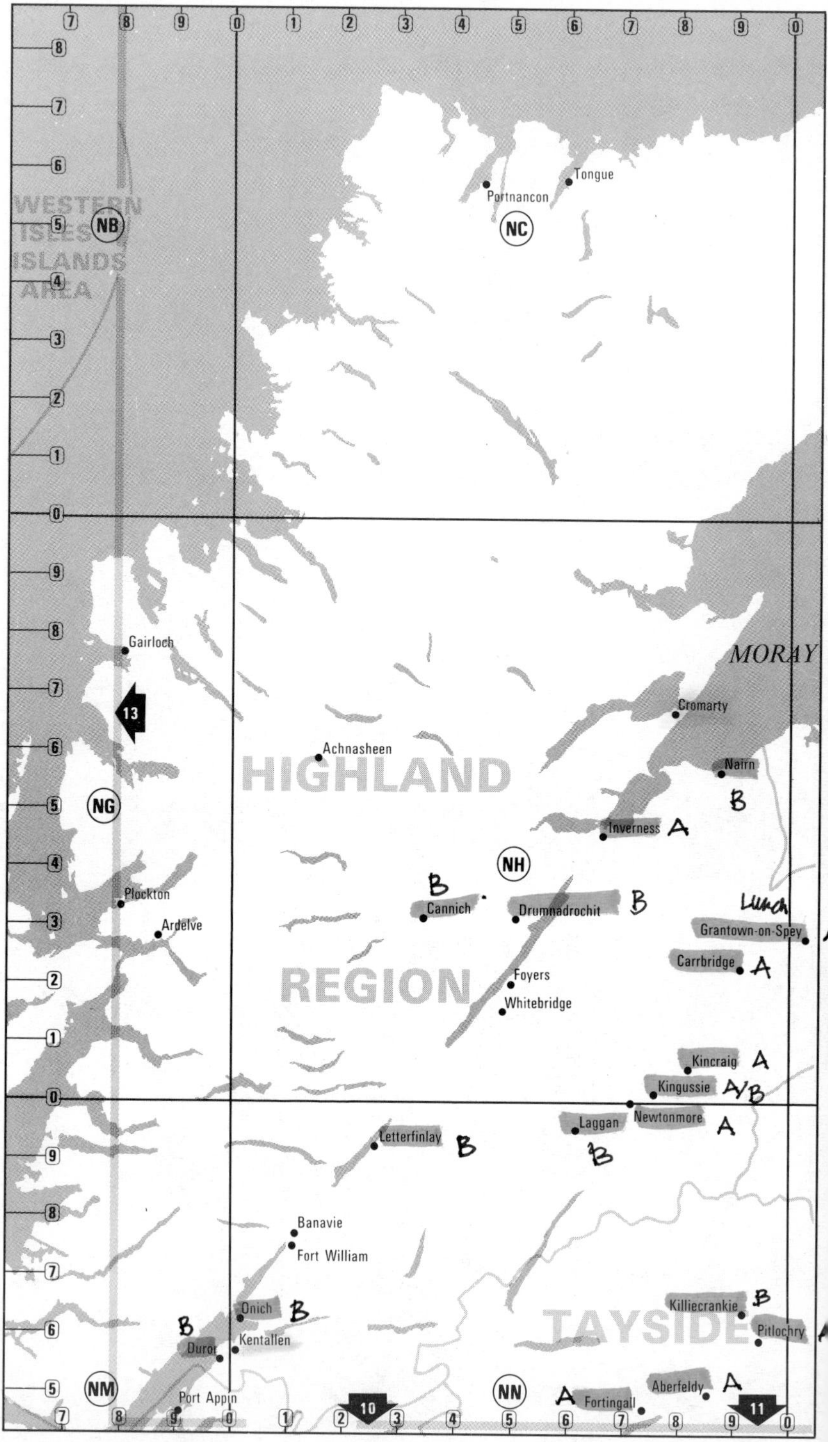
WESTERN ISLES ISLANDS AREA
NB
NC
Tongue
Portnancon
Gairloch
13
NG
Plockton
Ardelve
Achnasheen
HIGHLAND
REGION
MORAY
Cromarty
Nairn
B
Inverness A
NH
B
Cannich
Drumnadrochit B
Lunch
Grantown-on-Spey
Carrbridge A
Foyers
Whitebridge
Kincraig A
Kingussie A/B
Newtonmore A
Laggan
B
Letterfinlay B
Banavie
Fort William
Onich B
B
Duror
Kentallen
NM
Port Appin
10
NN
A Fortingall
Aberfeldy A
Killiecrankie B
TAYSIDE
Pitlochry
11

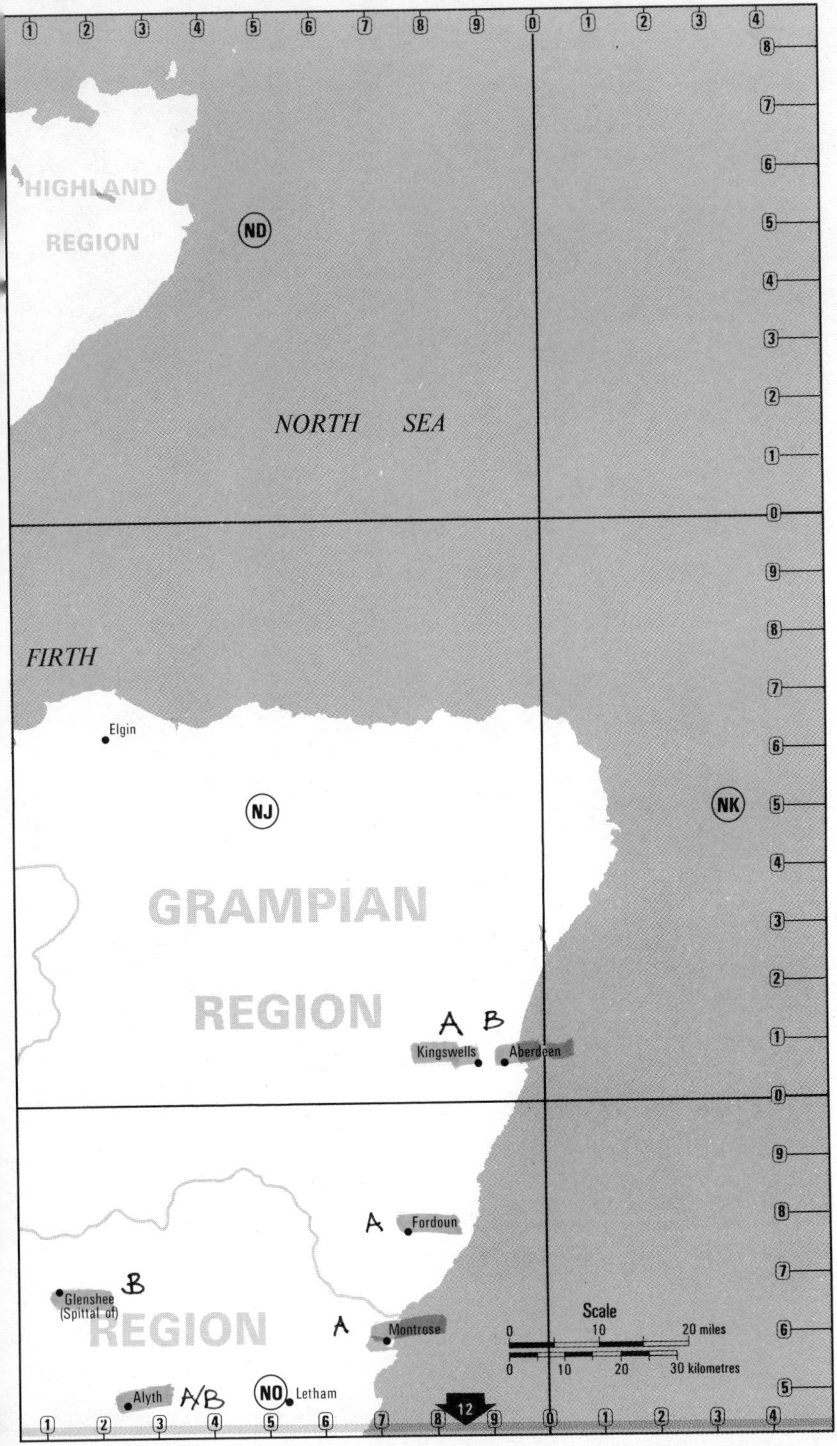
HIGHLAND
REGION
ND
NORTH SEA
FIRTH
Elgin
NJ
NK
GRAMPIAN
REGION
A B
Kingswells
Aberdeen
A
Fordoun
B
Glenshee
(Spittal of)
REGION
A
Montrose
Scale
0
10
20 miles
0
10
20
30 kilometres
Alyth
A/B
NO
Letham
12

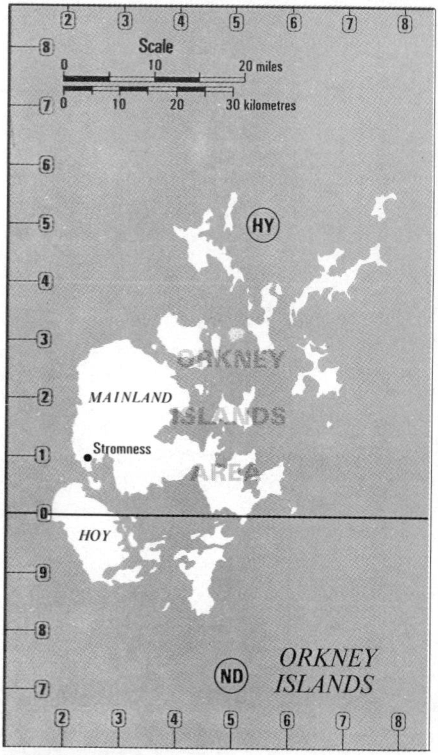
Scale
0 10 20 miles
0 10 20 30 kilometres
HY
ORKNEY ISLANDS AREA
MAINLAND
Stromness
HOY
ND
ORKNEY ISLANDS

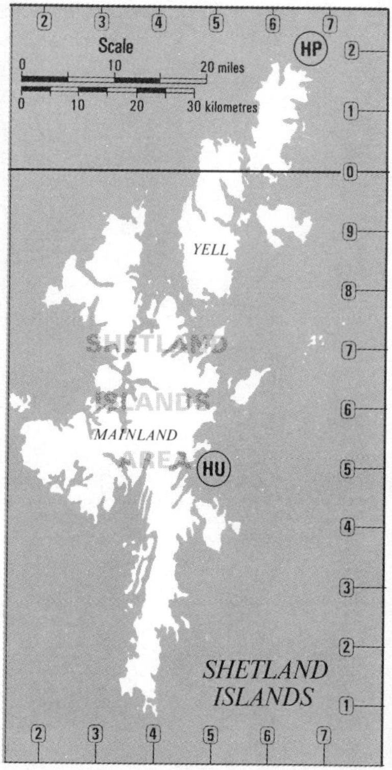
Scale
0 10 20 miles
0 10 20 30 kilometres
HP
YELL
SHETLAND ISLANDS AREA
MAINLAND
HU
SHETLAND ISLANDS

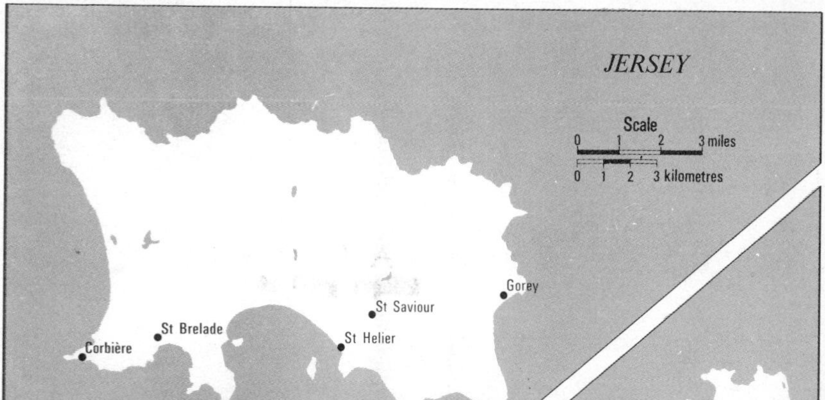
JERSEY
Scale
0 1 2 3 miles
0 1 2 3 kilometres
Gorey
St Saviour
St Brelade
St Helier
Corbière

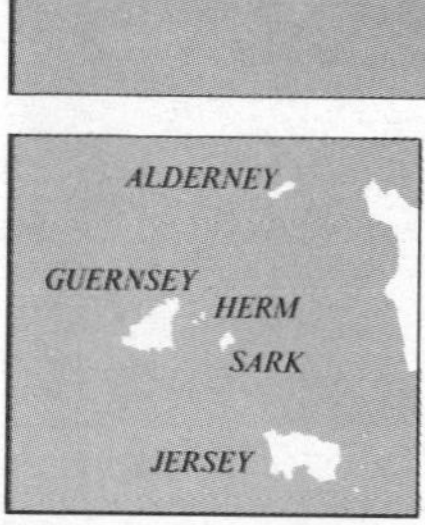
ALDERNEY
GUERNSEY
HERM
SARK
JERSEY

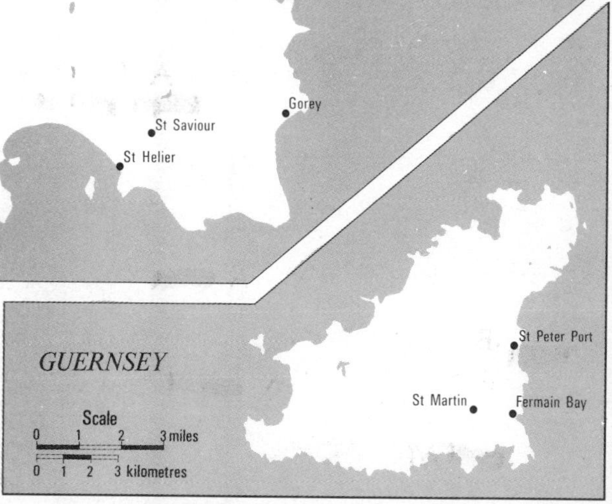
GUERNSEY
Scale
0 1 2 3 miles
0 1 2 3 kilometres
St Peter Port
St Martin
Fermain Bay